T0311896

Assessing the Impact of Foreign Aid
Value for Money and Aid for Trade

Assessing the Impact of Foreign Aid
Value for Money and Aid for Trade

Edited by

Viktor Jakupec

Max Kelly

AMSTERDAM • BOSTON • HEIDELBERG • LONDON
NEW YORK • OXFORD • PARIS • SAN DIEGO
SAN FRANCISCO • SINGAPORE • SYDNEY • TOKYO

Academic Press is an Imprint of Elsevier

Academic Press is an imprint of Elsevier
125 London Wall, EC2Y 5AS, UK
525 B Street, Suite 1800, San Diego, CA 92101-4495, USA
225 Wyman Street, Waltham, MA 02451, USA
The Boulevard, Langford Lane, Kidlington, Oxford OX5 1GB, UK

Notices
Knowledge and best practice in this field are constantly changing. As new research and experience broaden our understanding, changes in research methods, professional practices, or medical treatment may become necessary.

Practitioners and researchers must always rely on their own experience and knowledge in evaluating and using any information, methods, compounds, or experiments described herein. In using such information or methods they should be mindful of their own safety and the safety of others, including parties for whom they have a professional responsibility.

To the fullest extent of the law, neither the Publisher nor the authors, contributors, or editors, assume any liability for any injury and/or damage to persons or property as a matter of products liability, negligence or otherwise, or from any use or operation of any methods, products, instructions, or ideas contained in the material herein.

British Library Cataloguing-in-Publication Data
A catalogue record for this book is available from the British Library

Library of Congress Cataloging-in-Publication Data
A catalog record for this book is available from the Library of Congress

ISBN: 978-0-12-803660-0

For information on all Academic Press publications
visit our website at http://store.elsevier.com/

Working together
to grow libraries in
developing countries

www.elsevier.com • www.bookaid.org

Publisher: Nikki Levy
Acquisition Editor: J. Scott Bentley
Editorial Project Manager: Susan Ikeda
Production Project Manager: Julie-Ann Stansfield
Designer: Mark Rogers

Typeset by Thomson Digital
Printed in the United States of America

Contents

CHAPTER 11 **Inside the Black Box: Modeling the Inner Workings of Social Development Programs**.......................................**149**

Sebastian Lemire and Gordon Freer

CHAPTER 12 **Impact Assessment and Official Development Assistance: Ethnographic Research of the World Bank's Community-Based Rural Development Projects in Ghana**.......................**169**

Kwadwo Adusei-Asante and Peter Hancock

List of Contributors

Kwadwo Adusei-Asante
School of Psychology and Social Science, Edith Cowan University, Western Australia, Australia

Yasamin Alttahir
Save the Children Australia, Australia

Veronica Bell
Save the Children Australia, Australia

Steve Bertram
Independent Consultant, UK

Alwyn Chilver
Growth, Private Sector & Livelihoods, GRM International, Canberra, Australia

Marc M. Cohen

Gordon Freer
Department of International Relations, University of the Witwatersrand and Insight Strategies, South Africa

Peter Hancock
School of Psychology and Social Science, Edith Cowan University, Western Australia, Australia

Viktor Jakupec
School of Education, Faculty of Arts and Education, Deakin University, Warrnambool, Australia

Max Kelly
School of Humanities and Social Sciences, Faculty of Arts and Education, Deakin University, Warrnambool, Australia

Sebastian Lemire
University of California, Los Angeles, California, USA

Donna Loveridge

William Loxley
Comparative Research Analyst, Philippines

Jonathan J. Makuwira
School of Economics, Development and Tourism, Nelson Mandela Metropolitan University, Port Elizabeth, South Africa

John McKay
Analysis International & Honorary Professor in Development Studies, Deakin University, Geelong, Australia

Simon Milligan
Independent Consultant, UK

Mateusz Pucilowski
Impact Evaluation, Social Impact, Inc., Arlington, Virginia, USA

Amerita Ravuvu
School of Physical, Environmental and Mathematical Sciences, University of New South Wales, Canberra, Australia

Alec Thornton
School of Physical, Environmental and Mathematical Sciences, University of New South Wales, Canberra, Australia

Author Biographies

KWADWO ADUSEI-ASANTE

Kwadwo Adusei-Asante is a lecturer and research scholar in the School of Psychology and Social Science at Edith Cowan University. He holds a PhD from Edith Cowan University. He has over a decade of international experience in policy research and program impact assessment in the public, private, and not-for-profit sectors, spanning three countries: Australia, Ghana, and The Netherlands. He has worked with several organizations in Western Australia in senior policy advice positions, including the Public Sector Commission. Recent publications include journal articles (forthcoming) Community-based programs in non-existent communities. *African Studies Quarterly*, 15(2), 2013; When empowerment disempowers: the case of Ghanaian Traditional Chiefs and local government officials. *Ghana Journal of Development Studies*, 9(2), 43–62 (with Hancock); and (2012) The State of Ghana's local government. The case of Assembly Members. *Inkanyiso: Journal of Humanities and Social Sciences*, 4(2), 94–103. He has also written an extensive collection of Impact Assessment research reports including most recently: "Planning public sector employees' perceptions census: conceptual issues, proposed models, strategic implementation plans and implications." PSC, Perth. WA. "Managing family employment conflict of interest in the public sector recruitment." Public sector Commission, Perth, WA. "The impact of 'unequal marks technique' on students' group work and presentation outputs" (O'malley and Gardiner), 2013 "DFAT asylum seekers' Status Resolution Support Services Program: implementation implications for faith-based community service organizations."

YASAMIN ALTTAHIR

Yasamin Alttahir has over 5 years' field experience managing projects in Africa, the Middle East, and South East Asia. She has worked with grassroots NGOs in Senegal, Guinea-Bissau, Sierra Leon, and Cote D'Ivoire on UNICEF sponsored initiatives including maternal and early childhood health, livelihoods, and capacity building among women affected by ongoing conflict, as well as advising on financial and reporting procedures for major donor organizations. She also worked with refugee programs in Iraq, Jordan, and Iran where she was based from 2007 to 2008.

VERONICA BELL

Veronica Bell is an experienced international development professional with extensive multisectoral experience in East and Southern Africa, Asia, the Pacific, Central America, Mexico, and Haiti in both emergency and development contexts. Her areas of expertise include program design, monitoring, and evaluation, and impact measurement. She is responsible for strengthening Save the Children Australia's organizational capacity to deliver high-quality programs that achieve change through capacity building and supporting the implementation of systems, policy, and practice to improve program performance and accountability, and generate information to enable evidence-based programs with increased reach and impact. She is a member of the Australian Council for International Development (ACFID) Development Practice Committee (DPC).

STEVE BERTRAM

Steve Bertram is a governance and natural resources consultant, based in Edinburgh, UK. He has managed projects and provided consultancy services for 20 years in sub-Saharan Africa, South Asia, and South-East Asia. For the last 9 years, he has worked as a freelance consultant, specializing in reviews, evaluations, and strategy development, including multidonor programming. Prior to that, his long-term posts have included management of the ODA/DFID-financed Capacity Building for Decentralized Development programme in Nigeria, management of the training and extension component of a DANIDA-financed forestry programme in Nepal, and lecturing at the Department of Forestry and Natural Resources of Edinburgh University in Scotland. He holds both an MSc in Resource Management and an MBA.

ALWYN CHILVER

Alwyn Chilver is GRM International's Director of Growth, Private Sector and Livelihoods, based in Canberra, Australia. He has worked as a technical adviser to AusAID (now DFAT) and DFID. During his 7-year tenure at AusAID, he was Principal Advisor for Rural Development, where he helped promote and establish a suite of innovative market development and private sector development programs in the Asia-Pacific region. Before joining AusAID, he was a Socio-Economic Adviser on a DFID-financed livestock services reform programme in Indonesia, and a Sustainable Livelihoods Adviser to a rural poverty reduction programme for ethnic minorities in Vietnam. He also managed a portfolio of natural resource management projects for DFID in Uganda. He holds a PhD on developing country innovation systems and a Masters in Agricultural Economics.

MARC M. COHEN

Marc M. Cohen is an International Development Practitioner with over 20 years of experience in Multilateral Development Agencies. Currently Manager, Quality Assurance and Results, at the African Development Bank (AfDB), his responsibilities include establishing tools, processes, and mechanisms for planning, tracking, and reporting operational results. Between 1998 and 2009, he worked for the Asian Development Bank (AsDB), successively as Senior Education Specialist, Principal Results Management Specialist, and Head for assistance in fragile and conflict-affected situations. With the Results Management Unit of the AsDB, he led the design of the first corporate results measurement framework and launched the series of development effectiveness reports. Between 1992 and 1998, he was Education Sector Analyst/ Social Development Expert with the United Nations Educational, Scientific and Cultural Organization (UNESCO), conducting education sector work and coordinating some of the first inter-agency Human Development Initiatives (HDI) financed by the United Nations Development Programme (UNDP).

He has operational experience in some 30 countries in transition and/or reconstruction in Asia, Africa, and Eastern Europe. His main areas of expertise include integrated poverty reduction approaches; education and human development; formulation of country partnership strategies; management of operational portfolios; quality assurance systems; monitoring and evaluation of development interventions; aid effectiveness and harmonization; organizational performance assessments, and results-based management.

He graduated from the University of Oxford (MSc Development Economics), the Institut d'Etudes Politiques de Paris (D.E.A. Economie Internationale), Paris-IX Dauphine University (D.E.S.S. Affaires Internationales, Maîtrise de Gestion), and Paris-I Sorbonne University (Maîtrise de Science Politique).

GORDON FREER

Gordon Freer used to lecture full time at the University of the Witwatersrand, Johannesburg before he was lured away, 15 years ago, to practice instead of preach. He continues to hold a part time lecturing post in International Relations at the university where he continues to postulate on his ideals. These ideals are tested to the extreme and tempered by reality in his socioeconomic development work for Insight Strategies. A large portion of this time is spent on monitoring and evaluation and research including private sector development, value chain, and local economic development. He is an established author on South African foreign policy, and has written numerous media articles and conference papers. He has also contributed to the authoring and publishing of *Making Markets Work for the Poor: An Objective and an Approach for Governments and Development Agencies* and *Habits of Highly Effective Countries.*

PETER HANCOCK

Peter Hancock is a Senior Lecturer in the School of Psychology and Social Science at Edith Cowan University. He holds a PhD from Edith Cowan University and has 20 years of experience researching and teaching international and community development studies at Deakin University, Curtin University, and Edith Cowan University. He has worked on large international grants for AusAID, DFAT-Australia, and for various other stakeholders in Australia and the Netherlands and Indonesia. He is currently the Principal Investigator on a DFAT funded grant that examines social capital among women in rural Sri Lanka that he has published widely. Selected recent publications include: Hancock et al. (2014). Women's Economic Empowerment and Formal Income: Sri Lankan Export Processing Zones (EPZs) and Their Impact on Gender Perceptions of Empowerment. *Norsk Geografisk Tidsskrift – Norwegian Journal of Geography*; Adusei-Asante and Hancock (2013). When Empowerment Disempowers: The Case of Ghana's Community-Based Rural Development Projects. *Ghana Journal of Development Studies*, 13 (9); Hancock and Edirisinghe (2012). Inclusion and Empowerment of Export Processing Zone Workers in Sri Lanka: Stakeholder Perceptions and Perspectives. *Journal of Labour and Management in Development*, 13 (2); Hancock, Middleton, and Moore (2012). Gender, Globalisation and Empowerment: A Study of Women who Work in Sri Lanka's Export Processing Zones. *Work, Organisation, Labour and Globalisation*, 6 (1).

VIKTOR JAKUPEC

Viktor Jakupec is Honorary Professor of Education at Deakin University. He also holds a professorship at Potsdam University, Germany. He held academic positions at University of Technology, Sydney, University of South Australia, Queensland University of Technology, and Deakin University. His research over the last 3 years has focused on Impact Assessment within a context of Official Development Assistance and Political Economy Analysis for Official Development Assistance projects and programmes.

He worked as an international consultant for World Bank, Asian Development Bank, International Financial Corporation, Millennium Challenge Corporation, and AusAID funded projects in Bangladesh, PR China, Georgia, Jordan, Kyrgyz Republic, Maldives, Sri Lanka, and Vietnam. He has produced a range of ODA project design and project implementation reports, and strategic plans. He has advised on implementation of IA and has undertaken IA and other associated evaluations within the education and social sectors in developing countries.

He is: Member, Leibniz-Sozietät der Wissenschaften zu Berlin (Academy of Sciences); Member, International Society for Development and Sustainability; Member, Arbeitskreis für Internationale PolitischeÖkonomie.

MAX KELLY

Max Kelly is a Senior Lecturer in International and Community Development Studies at Deakin University, Australia. Her main research areas are development policy and practice, with particular emphasis on social development, livelihoods, food security, agriculture, community participation and community engagement. She previously worked at RMIT University, Melbourne. Her recent research focuses on Impact Assessment in development policy and practice, Political Economy Analysis of ODA, civil society in postconflict settings, and farmer groups, Organizational and social networks in postconflict settings. She has consulted and volunteered with a wide range of organizations, including international NGOs, multilateral organizations, and government departments. She has experience in Malawi, Uganda, Timor Leste, Bangladesh, Pakistan, Papua New Guinea, Solomon Islands, and Vanuatu.

SEBASTIAN LEMIRE

Sebastian Lemire is a doctoral candidate in the Social Research Methods division at the University of California, Los Angeles. He also serves as a Managing Editor for the *American Educational Research Journal – Social and Institutional Analysis*. As a former evaluation consultant, he has gained first-hand experience with the process of crafting and carrying out a broad range of evaluations. His area of interest revolves around causal modeling and explanation, research quality appraisal, research synthesis, and evaluation capacity building. He has published on these topics in the *American Journal of Evaluation, Evaluation*, and the *Canadian Journal of Program Evaluation*.

DONNA LOVERIDGE

Donna Loveridge holds a PhD in programme evaluation and a masters degree in international development from the University of Melbourne. She has extensive experience as a consultant for international development organizations and programs, focusing on strategic planning, monitoring, and evaluation. She works with public and private NGOs in Africa, Asia, and the Pacific and across a range of sectors. Her publications include *Theories of change: monitoring and evaluation capacity development in the government of Tanzania*, The University of Melbourne.

WILLIAM LOXLEY

As a Social Science Research Scientist with a PhD from the University of Chicago (1979), the author has over 30 years' experience conducting research and evaluation worldwide. Selected expertise and experience include research and evaluation in sociology and economics of education; project design, management, implementation, and evaluation at all levels including projects such as setting up the Maldives College of Higher Education; reorganizing the Open University, and introducing computers to secondary schools in Sri Lanka; and providing 2,000 five-room Pakistani Primary Girls schools along with science education labs and equipment in secondary schools throughout the country. Evaluation experience includes examining secondary school academic and vocational effects on school outcomes in Colombia and Tanzania for the World Bank; assessing primary school effects in Bangladesh, Bhutan, Nepal, and Pakistan in South Asia for the Asian Development Bank, as well as comparing educational outcomes in 29 additional countries around the world; and assessing ICT readiness throughout Asia and the Pacific. Teaching research methods at the Universities of Can-Tho, and Ho Chi Min Cities in Vietnam under the Fulbright Program; UGM and IKIP universities in Indonesia with the Ford Foundation; Chicago inner-city teaching as a certified public school teacher; and training classroom teachers with the Peace Corps in Mindanao, the Philippines. Research and evaluation skills include all aspects of project design, management, policy and evaluation; comparative survey research, and quantitative analysis employed in technical assistance. Recent books include *Smart World Dumb World: Developing Knowledge Rich Economies; and Economies of Knowledge in a Smart World; both available as e-reading on I-books Store or free download on Google+.*

JONATHAN J. MAKUWIRA

Jonathan J. Makuwira is an Associate Professor in Development Studies at Nelson Mandela Metropolitan University (NMMU), South Africa. Prior to joining NMMU, he was a Senior Lecturer in International Development at The Royal Melbourne Institute of Technology (RMIT) University, Melbourne, Australia where he taught courses in International Project Planning and Design; International Project Management, Monitoring and Evaluation; International NGOs, Civil Society and Development; Aid, Adjustment and Development; and Contemporary Africa. His academic career has seen him teach Peace Studies at the University of New England, and Comparative Indigenous Studies at Central Queensland University, both Australia. He has worked for the Ministry of Education in Malawi as a Primary, Secondary and Teacher Educator before joining Malawi Institute of Education. In 1998, he joined The Council for NGOs in Malawi (CONGOMA), as a Research Officer before going for his doctoral studies in Australia. He is a Visiting Scholar at LUANAR, Department of Extension and Rural Sociology.

SIMON MILLIGAN

Simon Milligan is a freelance design, review, and evaluation specialist who has undertaken assignments for AusAID/DFAT, DFID, IFAD, SDC, and the EC in sub-Saharan Africa, South Asia, and South-East Asia. He has worked as a Community Development Specialist on an EC-financed rehabilitation and reintegration programme in post-war Liberia and a State Programme Manager of a DFID-financed governance programme in Nigeria. His most assignments have focused on measures to promote access to markets and services. He is currently based in South-East Asia, where he is involved with performance oversight and monitoring of a large donor-financed programme managed by GRM International. He holds a PhD in livelihoods and conflict dynamics in West Africa. He has published several papers in peer-reviewed journals.

MATEUSZ PUCILOWSKI

Mateusz Pucilowski is an evaluation methodologist working to improve development effectiveness through the design, implementation, and utilization of policy-relevant research. He specializes in integrating qualitative and quantitative methodologies and has field experience conducting impact evaluations, performance evaluations, multicountry thematic assessments, and cost-effectiveness studies. He has worked on 20+ evaluations for clients including USAID, MCC, DOS, IDB, foundations, and NGOs. In addition to applied evaluation work, he has built evaluation capacity of hundreds of donor and project staff through dozens of trainings worldwide. He has worked in 16 countries and holds a Master's Degree in International Development from the American University in Washington, DC.

AMERITA RAVUVU

Amerita Ravuvu is a PhD candidate in Geography at The University of New South Wales, Australia. Her research areas are in climate change financing, development aid effectiveness, and grassroots development for sustainable livelihoods and pro-poor growth in Melanesia and the wider South Pacific region. She has been the recipient of the Best Undergraduate Paper Award in Political Geography from the Association of American Geographers in 2009 for her paper titled *Fiji's Weak and Divided State: The Rhetoric of Ethnic Polarization in the Political Process.* She also contributed to a UNDP publication, *Financial Capability, Financial Competence and Wellbeing in Rural Fijian Households,* where she was involved in the finalization of the survey instrument and data collection. She has worked with a number of institutions in Fiji including the Fiji Islands Trade & Investment Bureau, the Attorney General's Office, Future Forest Fiji Limited, the Pacific Islands Forum Secretariat, and the University of the South Pacific.

ALEC THORNTON

Alec Thornton is a Senior Lecturer in Geography at The University of New South Wales, Australia. His main research areas include community-based development, urban agriculture, and local food networks for food security and social justice in Sub-Saharan Africa and the South Pacific. He has published numerous peer-reviewed journal articles on these issues. His recent books are *Beyond the Metropolis: Urban Agriculture in South Africa* (2012, Edwin Mellen Press) and *Disaster Relief in the Asia Pacific* (2014, co-edited with Sakai et al., Routledge). He has contributed chapters to edited books,

Dimensions of the Global Food Crisis (2011, Campbell et al. (Eds), Earthscan Routledge), *Religion, Religious Organisations and Development: Scrutinising religious perceptions and organisations* (2013, Rakodi, ed., Routledge), and *Disaster Relief in the Asia Pacific* (2014, Sakai et al. (Eds.), Routledge). He is on the editorial boards of the peer-reviewed journals, *Applied Geography* and *Urban Forum*. Since 2010, he is vice president of the African Studies Association of Australasia and the Pacific.

Preface

The demand to demonstrate the impact of foreign aid funding has grown exponentially in the last decade. This results from both increasing disbursements of Official Development Assistance (ODA), as well as tightening fiscal environments in most OECD countries, resulting at least in part from the Global Financial Crisis. There is considerable agreement that assessing the impact of investment in social sector development programming of foreign aid is both essential and highly problematic. Significant literature exists on methodological disagreements on how best to measure impact, as well as a wide range of technical manuals and "toolkits." Most evaluation does not focus on impact. When it does, there are often significant methodological issues. Much of the literature on impact assessment of foreign aid is either atheoretical, or loosely based on thinking embedded either in evaluation, or risk mitigation.

The aim of this volume is to provide a critical analysis of social sector impact assessment of foreign aid, within a theoretical framework of development theory and practice, with particular reference to the dominance of the neoliberal paradigm in international aid. This book provides a contemporary discourse and critical analyses of existing practical and theoretical approaches to Impact Assessment for ODA. It juxtaposes perceptions and problematics of existing *a priori* assumptions governing impact assessment for ODA with newly emerging paradigm shifts including the rise and rise of neoliberalism, the fallout from the Global Financial Crisis, and post European Monitory Crises. Within this context, the book provides insights into emerging policies and practices, theoretical and practical frameworks, and IA design and implementations activities.

The core argument in the book is that *Aid for Trade* and *Value for Money* paradigms are the main promoters driving the global ODA in our "post GFC," post EMC agenda. Thus, multi and bilateral aid agencies are required by their political masters to meet these new agenda goals as efficiently and effectively as possible at minimum of cost, with best possible benefits for the target audiences such as recipient countries' citizens, businesses, the workforce, and other stakeholders. Additionally, new donors and nontraditional aid partners in the private sector provide further challenges and opportunities for Impact Assessment.

This book consists of a range of diverse views, contexts, experiences, and analysis. There is no intent for the chapters to be read sequentially. However, they all contribute to the core theme. The first two chapters provide a detailed analysis and critique of the current state of thinking on aid flows within international development, and the demand for both effectiveness and efficiency (Chapter 1); the increasing demand for, evolution of, and context for impact assessment in foreign aid (Chapter 2). Chapter 3 engages in an in-depth analysis of global economic paradigms, and the dominance of the neoliberal agenda as the driving force in aid allocations, and quality or results measurement. Chapter 4 extends this debate with an analysis of Aid for Trade, a classification of ODA which now accounts for up to one third of ODA flows, and is unashamedly a trade-focused construct.

The following two chapters move into a more applied discussion about aid effectiveness and aid impact with; an applied view of the theory and practice of impact assessment from three highly experienced practitioners (Chapter 5); and the application of neoliberal and neostructural reforms in the Pacific (Chapter 6).

Following on from these chapters, which provide a clear context and discourse from which the remainder of the contributions follow, the next five contributions delve more deeply into specific debates around specific applications of impact assessment, through Regulatory Impact Assessment (Chapter 7), an analysis of the potential overall impact of development agencies (Chapter 8), and the role of knowledge (Chapter 9) co-ordination (Chapter 10), innovative approaches to existing information (Chapter 11), and an application on qualitative methodology within the contemporary development context (Chapter 12).

Some opportunities, and issues with the Impact Assessment Agenda area were raised through an analysis of the link between monitoring and impact assessment (Chapter 13). Chapter 14 explores some of the challenges and opportunities of understanding and measuring impact through an analysis of two diverse, but informative case studies from Save the Children, Australia. Chapter 15 takes a wider look at issues facing Non Government Development Organizations in assessing the impact of their work. The contributions to this volume provide a unique range of vantage points from which Aid for Trade, Value for Money impact assessment in foreign aid paradigms. The contributions explore bilateral, multilateral, and Non-Government Organizational perspectives. The final chapter (Chapter 16) identifies and explores the areas of commonality between the diverse contributions, both in terms of theoretical and practical applications.

Viktor Jakupec and Max Kelly
Deakin University, Warrnambool, Australia

OFFICIAL DEVELOPMENT ASSISTANCE AND IMPACT ASSESSMENT – THEORETICAL AND PRACTICAL FRAMEWORKS

Viktor Jakupec* and Max Kelly[†]

*School of Education, Faculty of Arts and Education, Deakin University, Warrnambool, Australia
†School of Humanities and Social Sciences, Faculty of Arts and Education, Deakin University, Warrnambool, Australia

CHAPTER OUTLINE

INTRODUCTION

Official Development Assistance (ODA) remains the most prominent development instrument for allocation of foreign aid with the aim of promoting prosperity in developing countries. This includes economic, political, and social development, and most significantly poverty alleviation. However, it needs to be noted that the positive impact of ODA on recipient countries economic, social, political, and other forms of development is not a foregone conclusion. As such it is subject to diverse interpretations, value claims, perceptions, and a range of indicators. Thus, ODA has it proponents and opponents. As such the need for an assessment of the impact of ODA, be it positive or negative, remains a subject of discourse amongst academics, practitioners, aid agencies, politicians, governments, and other stakeholders.

The purpose of this chapter is to bring to the fore and to unpack some overarching issues, which will be taken up in following contributions from different vantage points. The focus will be on foreign aid, and development theory and practice in the contemporary social, political, and economic environment.

This chapter sets the scene for a critical evaluation of how and why assessing the impact of foreign aid is both essential and complex. These themes are taken up in more detail in Chapter 2.

AID, ODA, AND RESOURCE FLOWS TO THE DEVELOPING WORLD

Foreign aid or development aid covers a vast array of resource flows (cash, commodities, and services) to and between "developed" and "developing" countries. For a better understanding, these terms are used to convey a general split between OECD and non-OECD countries. Where required the terms Least Developed Countries or low, medium, or high human development countries are used as per UN Human Development Index categorization.

ODA forms the most commonly used measure of flows to developing countries and incorporates

...flows to developing countries and multilateral institutions provided by official agencies, including state and local governments, or by their executive agencies, each transaction of which meets the following test: a) it is administered with the promotion of the economic development and welfare of developing countries as its main objective, and b) it is concessional in character and contains a grant element of at least 25% (calculated at a rate of discount of 10%)' (OECD, 2015b, Definition of ODA).

ODA makes up one component of overseas capital flows. However, in terms of relative contribution of aid, there are two further and important considerations to be noted. These are Foreign Direct Investment (FDI) and remittances.

As can be seen in Fig. 1.1, Net ODA reached an all-time high in 2013 and 2014. Figures for 2013 are $135.1 billion, and $135.2 billion in 2014, although this represents a 0.5% decline in real terms (OECD - DAC, 2015). These somewhat impressive figures represent a 66% increase in ODA since 2000 when the Millennium Development Goals (MDG) were agreed (OECD - DAC, 2015). However,

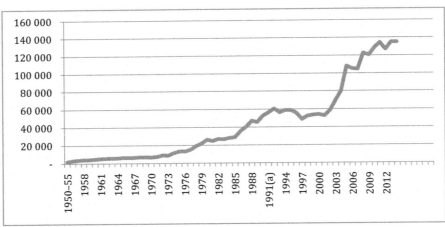

FIGURE 1.1 Net Official Development Assistance Flows from DAC Member Countries

Source: Compiled from OECD Data, http://www.oecd.org/dac/stats/data.htm, accessed May 26, 2015.

it falls short of the 0.7% GNP committed to by "economically advanced countries" since the 1970s when it was firstly raised by UN General Assembly. In effect, it represents 0.3% of DAC donors Gross National Income (GNI). The United Kingdom achieved 0.7% of GNI in 2013 and appeared to be retaining this level of spending. In contrast, recent Australian budget cuts to Aid Flows have reduced Australian aid commitments from a high of 0.35% of GNI in 2012/13 to a historic low of a planned 0.22% aid/GNI ratio in 2016/17. The current context for foreign assistance is more complex than just ODA flows. Private flows and Other Official Flows (OOF) are non-ODA flows from DAC member countries. Total OOFs for 2013 were around US$7 billion, or 5% of ODA (OECD, 2015c). There are also increasing flows from nontraditional, or non-DAC donors. Although there are a number of countries within this category, the principle source of south–south transfers comes from the so-called BRICS (Brazil, Russia, India, China, and South Africa).

Estimates of foreign assistance from BRICS countries vary widely. For example, OECD estimate (based on direct reporting or indirect assessment of likely flows) US$5.1 billion in flows in 2013. PR China contributed two-thirds, and a further 25% came from India (OECD, 2015a). Nontraditional donors operate outside existing donor mechanisms, including effectiveness and accountability reporting, co-ordination, and aid modalities. Xu and Carey (2015) conclude that there are considerable policy implications of the increasing importance of nontraditional donors, specifically China, which is likely to become the world's largest supplier of finance to developing countries. Given the predominance of western concepts and intellectual centers in the existing aid architecture (particularly Bretton Woods institutions) Xu and Carey (2015) argue that there is likely to be both divergences – in terms of new thinking in the institutional landscape of aid, and convergence as new institutions "seek to establish their reputation for promoting effective and sustainable development" (p. 4). This may be clearly seen in the setting up of the Asian Infrastructure Investment Bank (AIIB). In other words, the impact of China's development work is hard to judge, due primarily to little clear data. However, legitimacy and accountability may see this change. The emergence of new aid institutions, structures, and modalities will potentially challenge existing aid architecture and institutions. There will potentially be increased pressure on donors to demonstrate an impact of foreign aid. Such pressure will affect both, donors and more importantly recipients, particularly of nongrant resource flows.

In addition to ODA, OOFs, and nontraditional donor assistance, there is also substantial resource flows through other mechanisms. Of particular note in lesser-developed country financial flows are migrant remittances and FDI (Driffield and Jones, 2013). World Bank estimates of migrant remittances to the developing world in 2013 were US$414 billion. There was a strong growth in 2014 (US$435 billion est.), and in 2015 (US$454 billion) (World Bank, 2013, 2014). The link between FDI and poverty alleviation and sustainable development is complex and debated. FDI does contribute to economic growth. There is some evidence that FDI can contribute to poverty alleviation under certain conditions (cf. Fowowe and Shuaibu, 2014; Klein et al., 2001; Krajewski, 2013). The potential impact of FDI is, however, difficult to measure and critics point to issues of rising inequality (Basu and Guariglia, 2007). FDI flows to developing countries estimates in 2013 reached $759 billion (UNCTAD, 2014). This represents over half of global FDI inflows (greater than developed countries). The figures for 2014 reached an all-time high of more than $700 billion (UNCTAD, 2015). Private flows through philanthropic sources are also growing exponentially. The Gates Foundation disbursed US$3.6 and US$3.9 billion in 2013 and 2014, respectively. In broad terms then it can be seen that ODA to developing countries is one aspect of a much broader series of financial flows at the global level. The focus of this book is firmly on ODA. However, it must be seen in the context of the broader resource flows, which impact on poverty and sustainable development. This is of particular importance given substantial changes in the global aid architecture, which make it increasingly difficult to make generalizations. Contemporary development is characterized by complex and varying partnerships between multilateral agencies, bilateral donors, civil society and private and philanthropical organizations to pursue shared goals. As Lele et al. (2006) note

> ...they differ widely in goals, size, age, governance structures, and modalities. But they reflect a broadly shared view that today's global challenges are too wide ranging and complex for single actors to address alone, and primarily through traditional country focused assistance programs (p. 1).

In addition to the total resources flows through ODA to the developing world, it is important to understand changes in flows, within and between countries. One point of considerable importance in assessing resource flows are geographical, political, and economic changes in aid flows. There are considerable changes occurring in aid flows within the larger picture of the overall quantity of aid. In reviewing the practices of DAC members, the OECD (2015b) notes that donors are getting more strategic in aid allocation, in response to self-interest and an increasingly securitized agenda for aid. However, a focus on results and effectiveness of aid by donors can change allocations, in particular to multilateral agencies. Aid flows via bilateral channels can also be reduced in cases where human rights and democracy records are poor (Diettrich, 2010). There has been a drop in bilateral aid to the least developing countries (LDCs) of 16% in the 2014 aid figures (OECD - DAC, 2015). Although bilateral aid can be very volatile in response to changing aid flows for disaster and conflict, and discounting debt relief within these bilateral figures, the OECD still interprets this as a downward trend in aid to LDCs (OECD - DAC, 2015). The implications for poverty reduction and sustainable development in LDCs seem unlikely to be positive.

BACKGROUND TO FOREIGN AID

Prior to embarking on the contemporary debate surrounding Impact Assessment (IA) in the context of foreign aid, let us, however briefly, note the evolution of aid and development. ODA as we understand it today emerged in the 1940s as a perceived economic and political necessity to rebuild Europe after the World War II through the implementation of the Marshall Plan. The concept was simply to provide capital funding for development combined with promoting skill training. The aid system institutional structures emerged from the WW II postwar period. Today it still forms the basis of much of the current aid systems including namely The United Nations (UN) and Bretton Woods Institutions namely the IMF and World Bank. Subsequently, economic and political challenges that influenced the aid environment such as the effects of the Cold War and the colonial legacy in the newly independent developing countries focused these institutions increasingly on economic and social development and brought new players into the aid development game from the 1960s. This includes entities such as various UN agencies and a number of regional aid agencies such as the Asian Development Bank (ADB), African Development Bank (AfDB), EuropeAid, and bilateral aid agencies such as USAID (Engel, 2014), JICA among many, and a range of NGOs.

An analysis of changes in aid architecture since this time shows a highly fragmented system, with multiple agencies and overlapping agendas. Kharas (2007) highlighted the 233 multilateral agencies at that time, with the creation of 25 new multilateral agencies between 2000 and 2005 with little or no disbanding of existing or outdated institutions. This increases issues of aid fragmentation, coordination, economies of scale, and institutional knowledge that are some core benefits of the multilateral system (cf. Kharas and Blomfeld, 2013). There have long been calls for reform of aid architecture (often focused on the UN). Much of this debate has fed into the "aid effectiveness agenda" discussed later.

Theoretical and practical underpinnings of aid have evolved from this early context to a contemporary system of diverse aid modalities, implemented by the complex aid system noted above. International and in some countries domestic financial, political, and economic circumstances have significantly impacted development thinking. For example, since the early 1950s development aid theories have been underpinned by practices such as import subsidies, industrialization, large investment stimulus for sustainable economic growth, and the importance of implementing free-market (neo-liberal) economic policies in developing countries. This modernization paradigm faltered when the link between economic growth and poverty alleviation crystallized by the early 1970s (UNICEF, 1996). The 1970s and 1980s saw the rise of the poverty-focused development agenda, coming in alongside unanticipated shockwaves, in the form of oil shocks, Latin American debt crises, together with trade imbalances, demographic challenges, and the emergence of new technologies, all of which affected the global economic system (Groves and Hinton, 2004). Thus, to a large extent the aid-development focus shifted toward new challenges such as investment in people including primary, secondary, and technical education, health and household priorities, reducing government intervention into markets through deregulation, governance, and legal system improvements, trade tariffs barriers reduction, implementation of macroeconomic policies such as debt management and inflation attentive monetary policy. Structural Adjustment Loans was the buzzword of the 1980s.

In the 1990s ODA was strongly influenced by the forces of Globalization. The end of the cold war, and the rise of the free market drove a development agenda increasingly focused on the aid for increased global trade liberalization, free market access to domestic industry and enterprises, privatization, and decentralization (cf. Groves and Hinton, 2004). The overarching focus was on the "Washington Consensus" values. Subsequently in 2000 the thinking underpinning the MDG took root. The main MDG framework included nationally developed, implemented, and owned strategies for poverty reduction, good governance, and workable macroeconomic policies. Within this framework, MDG goals to be reached by 2015 were provisions of universal primary education, reducing extreme poverty by half, combatting hunger, HIV/AIDS, malaria, and other diseases, reducing child mortality, and improving maternal health, attaining gender equality, ensuring environmental sustainability, and promoting global partnerships for development. Thus, ODA would seem to have shifted more from economic rationality to poverty reduction and health. Shleifer (2009) argues that this is a shift from economic growth to welfare… In a post-Washington development environment there is increasing emphasis on resilience to economic crises, albeit tied to free market economics but with substantially more focus on reducing social disruption, and with greater regulation of financial sectors (Birdsall and Fukyama, 2011). This needs to be seen in the context also of new players in the development sector, particularly as noted previously in Brazil, Russia, India, and most particularly China, who do not necessarily subscribe to similar ideals, approaches, or even purpose. However, events such as the Global Financial Crisis (GFC) and the subsequent European Monitory Crisis of the latter half of 2000 and beyond has led to renewed politico-economic, socio-economic, and socio-political tensions globally and thus the ODA arena. Despite early calls that the GFC heralded the end of neoliberalism (Kotz, 2009), it seems that it is an enduring economic paradigm, which has survived with minimal damage (cf. Mirowski, 2013).

The MDGs are worthy of some more detailed mention. Progress on reaching the MDGS is partial, and very uneven, although frequently hailed as a success. The United Nations (not dated) hailed them "the most successful global anti-poverty push in history." However, others (Lockwood, 2012) argue that the impact of the MDGs (not in terms of the progress or lack of progress, but in the impact of the MDGs in reaching the result achieved) is unclear due to the lack of clear strong evidence. Of course, the focus is now firmly on the "Post MDG" agenda, or the Sustainable Development Goals (SDGs). There were 17 SDGs as of May 2015. The first is to end poverty in all its forms everywhere. Addressing inequality, food security, and economic growth are also embedded in the 17 goals. Unsurprisingly Willian Easterly is critical – particularly of the notion of the development of goals by consensus, while Jeffrey Sachs is more optimistic, while noting the need to fund the activities required to achieve the SDGs. It remains to be seen exactly what the final version of the SDGs will be, how they will be received, and how they will be met.

The above is but a brief summary of key points of relevance to this chapter (cf. Kingsbury, 2013; Peet and Hartwick, 2009). It is fair to say that ODA was over time influenced by the prevailing thinking of the day. It changed from a purely economic development perspective in the 1940s and 1950s to an investment in human resources including education and health in the 1980s. This moved toward trade liberalization, privatization, and decentralization in the 1990s and universal primary education, poverty alleviation, and reduction in the spread of HIV/AIDS in early 2000. However, and somewhat due to the GFC and the EMC the pendulum swung back to economic considerations in the late 2000s. The changes, however, did not bring about any significant changes in the economic thinking within aid agencies. There was and still is a strong belief within aid agencies that the neoliberal economic policies would lead to economic development, prosperity, and growth. The changes are observable along the political and social parameters, such as corruption, human rights, good governance, environment, gender, social access, and equity to name a few. There is a visible and ever-increasing focus on market-based solutions to complex or "wicked" problems, in conjunction with a growing focus on country ownership, resilience, and a good governance agenda (and of course a securitization of the aid agenda). New forms of partnership are emerging, particularly with private sector involvement in development, and the flow of funds is increasingly filtering through ever more complex "aid chains" (Wallace et al., 2007). Given that there is little empirical evidence of the impact of aid policy and practice to date we are yet again entering a relatively uncharted territory in terms of approach and potential impact of development interventions.

Although we are now firmly in the "post GFC" phase, austerity measures impacted on aid budgets in some areas. IrishAid, for example, increased its aid from 0.39% GNI in 2003 to 0.58% in 2008 back to 0.45 in 2013 (OECD, 2015c) Australia as noted earlier has implemented significant cuts to aid flows. Overall 15 of the DAC members recorded a fall in % GNI for 2014. Notable increases include the United Kingdom, Germany, United States, and New Zealand. However, it is clear that one of the results of the GFC and EMC has been a renewed focus on aid budgets, and an increased focus from donor governments on "value for money" (DFID, 2011). The fact that the United Kingdom managed for the first time to achieve the 0.7% GDP target in 2013 drives some of this recovery. However, it may well be a fragile recovery as Provost and Jones (2014) noted there was no fanfare associated with this "achievement" and aid budgets are at the mercy of domestic and international political concerns.

OECD - DAC (2015) noted a point of unease with reference to the shift in aid allocations away from the poorest countries to world's middle-income countries. The potentially improving fiscal situation within DAC members may provide some respite for stretched aid budgets but the underlying reform movement driven by the notion of "value for money" is highly likely to remain, with aid allocations to middle-income countries in the form of loans providing an attractive option to donors (OECD) and providing ever tighter conditions for aid disbursement. Aid to humanitarian crises has grown significantly, but the gap between met and unmet needs in humanitarian funding has increased by 10% between 2007 and 2011, which still falls well short of need according to Global Humanitarian Assistance (2012).

So, at the current time there are signs of life in the global economy, albeit driven by a raft of austerity measures, and accommodative fiscal policies. However, there have been some readily identifiable shifts in donor approaches, such as the increasing link between ODA and trade. Conservative governments in Australia and Canada collapsing their Aid Departments into Foreign Affairs and Trade of course exemplify this. The UK Department for International Development provides an exception here, both in ring-fencing its aid budget, but also in retaining its International Development Department. Several other factors are likely to impact ODA flows and focus, including the post MDG agenda, the emergence of middle-income countries (BRICS), and the rise of business models for development and the growing role of the private sector. Within this increasingly complex aid environment there is little factual data and information available on the impact of rapidly changing political and economic environment on ODA, and in reality what the fallout and future directions of ODA are likely to be. What is available is to a large extent speculative in nature.

CONTEMPORARY DEBATES, AID EFFECTIVENESS, VALUE FOR MONEY, AND AID FOR TRADE

The previous discussions, albeit very circumscribed, would seem to indicate an aid system that has flourished over three-quarters of a century. This could be perceived as proof that aid works and that it promotes "good change" (Chambers, 2004, p. 3). The reality of both global political and economic forces shaping the aid and development discourse highlights some key areas in relation to both aid design and delivery.

Against the assumption of success built into donor and key stakeholder actions in ODA, there is a consistent increase in the chorus of foreign aid critique, mainly claiming that many aid projects and programs are ineffective. This includes claims that ODA at times obstructs development. This discourse was ignited in the 1970s, initially by Bauer (1972). An advocate of property rights and free trade, he posited that aid was an inappropriate mechanism to speed up development, and potentially could even delay development outcomes. There are arguments advanced by ODA critics that aid agencies' operative and field staff contribute to the lack of impact due to their pursuit of quick funds disbursement and associated advancement and promotion within the organization. Others have pointed out that in order to complete a project or program in the fastest possible time, aid agencies' field and operational project staff have a pronounced risk aversion (Buchanan-Smith and Scriven, 2011). This has the tendency to discourage implementation of new ideas and strategies and at the same time it is assumed that operative and field staff members know best when it comes to deciding what may or may not succeed. To sum up, from this perspective, it can be claimed that ODA is potentially administratively costly and cumbersome. This is, among other factors, due to risk adversity and the requirement to follow the established procedures, irrespective if they have been proven successful or otherwise. This may be difficult to explain to recipient countries and appear seldom transparent to the general public in the donor countries (cf. Moyo, 2009; Boone, 1996; Foreman, 2013).

Notwithstanding the above and irrespective of aid an agency's prevailing policies and practices, there is a general acceptance by stakeholders that the success or otherwise of ODA programs or projects is determined on bases of its impact(s). Thus, it follows that when a project or program fails, it can be traced back to a wide range of factors, such as inadequate knowledge, inappropriate policy, performance of aid agencies, their staff, consultants, executing and implementing agencies, and their staff in recipient countries, and/or a combination of these entities.

This brings to the fore difficulties in determining aid impact at theoretical as well as practical levels. Thus, it is not surprising that scholarly literature, impact assessment practices, and various reviews of impact assessments have to a large extent been less than successful to sway or impress those who may provide funding for aid and to provide evidence that aid works. The same can be said of those who oppose development aid in its current form(s), for they have not been able to provide evidence to the contrary (cf. Birdsall and Savedoff, 2009 Cohen and Easterley, 2009; Easterly, 2003, 2008; Sachs, 2005; Riddell, 2008). Thus after more than 50 years of ODA the jury is still out if and to which extent development aid has contributed to its development goals.

A further point of debate is the inclination of a number of ODA aid agencies to argue that "aid works" because aid promotes (economic) development, and therefore ODA has a positive impact. For example Atwood (2012) as chair of DAC claims the success of ODA on the basis of generating an environment in which private enterprise can develop and expand, and where governance systems are established to reform economic policies and to create a workforce capacity through education and healthcare. These are purely neoliberal economic arguments, and using these as measures of ODA success the conclusion that ODA works is relatively easy to substantiate.

Others argue that economic development may happen without aid, and at best ODA may quicken development (cf. Riddell, 2008). In either case, it is not uncommon for aid agencies or organizations to adopt a taken-for-granted attitude and reduce IA to a minimum within their project and program portfolio.

One of the many reasons for questioning the success of ODA is that multilateral and bilateral aid agencies do not make their findings regarding success or otherwise of the projects readily accessible to general public. In other words, there is an absence of evidence that ODA is generally successful. However, this absence of evidence must not be construed as proof that ODA is unsuccessful.

Some of the skepticism regarding success can be traced back that IAs are not carried out for every project and program. Some of the explanations given are that impact assessments are time and resource consuming, difficult to execute, and costly (cf. Baker and Bank, 2000). This may be true, but then what are the alternatives to ascertain the impact of a project, especially in a climate where donor governments are seeking clarification on the impact the taxpayer money had on identified beneficiaries in the recipient country. Many of these debates are taking place at the macro level. The capacity of aid to create good change does need to be perceived across a range of levels. There is the high (or macro) level of global human development as measured and debated by metrics such as the Human Development Index, and the MDG. There is a meso level – of specific country programs, or sectoral programs, and finally the micro level of individual programs or projects. The following sections debate the notions of aid effectiveness, development effectiveness, and value for money. Much of this chapter is focusing on global or macro level. However, this sets the scene for a more in-depth analysis of the impact at the meso and micro levels, which is the focus of this volume. Understanding the macro level debates and complexity that contextualizes development is essential to understanding both issues and opportunities in assessing the impact of foreign aid.

AID EFFECTIVENESS

The aid effectiveness agenda has provided one specific impetus to respond to challenges of shortcomings in aid and development. The effectiveness of aid and development is a current core point of discussion, debate, and contention within development aid. The 2005 Paris Declaration on Aid Effectiveness emerged from the 2002 Monterrey Consensus, which agreed to increased funding, and the 2003 High-Level Forum on Harmonization in Rome (convened by the OECD). This focuses not so much on the impact of aid but the effectiveness of the delivery of aid, based on the multitude of diverse approaches, and requirements imposed by donors on countries, and organizations implementing ODA. This particular aid effectiveness agenda is of course equally driven by value for money, and impact and underpinned allocations of ODA. It is important to be clear on the relationship between IA and aid effectiveness as a policy agenda. An initial point of concern in 2002 and 2003 was the idea of making aid more effective through aid harmonization, with donors discussing the need for reform of ODA to become more streamlined and coordinated. The Paris Declaration on Aid Effectiveness (OECD, 2005) focused on country ownership of development policy and strategy, donor alignment and harmonization, mutual accountability, and most importantly for this discussion, managing for results. There was a follow-up meeting in Accra in 2008. The managing for results aspect of aid effectiveness noted the requirement for citizens and taxpayers in both the donor and recipient countries to see a demonstrable impact (Killen, 2011). The aid effectiveness agenda shifted focus to a partnership discourse at the 4th high-level Forum in Busan putting aid effectiveness in a broader context of development effectiveness and incorporating new actors. These included Non-DAC Donors (NDDs), the private sector, and civil society. Despite considerable discussion on what effective aid and development may be, Hall-Matthews (2014) argues that there is a major disconnect between what is agreed to be an effective aid, and what actually happens on the ground. Aid impact is also strongly linked to statistical data – providing yet more impetus for quantitative impact assessment. The link between aid effectiveness and aid impact is, therefore, problematic, in that the Aid Effectiveness agenda is just that – an agenda, or as Ssewakiryanga (2011) calls it, "efficient disbursement procedures" (p. 1). Killen (2011) raised the questions of what impact the aid effectiveness discourse is having on aid, as well as what the impact of aid is. These according to Killen (2011) are problematic questions due to the lack of a "clear long-term causal link between the Paris principles and development outcomes" (p. 2).

Of course, the link between aid effectiveness and development effectiveness brings us back to some of the earlier focus on diverse resource flows to non-OECD countries. The move from a focus from aid alone, to poverty reduction, through the Busan "partnership discourse," reaffirms the focus of development on economic growth and enhanced productivity, endorsing the role of the private sector (cf. Mawdsley et al., 2013). This reaffirms the link between aid and trade, as well as demonstrates results, and value for money, in an increasingly complex aid and development environment. The UKs Independent Commission for Aid Impact argues that effectiveness and Value for Money cannot be disentangled, arguing that effectiveness necessitates impact sustainability for intended beneficiaries. In this context, ICAI (2011) suggests that value for money is the best approach to ensure the desired impact.

VALUE FOR MONEY

Buzzwords abound in development and Value for Money (VfM) is no exception. VfM is now firmly embedded in development discourse. It is partly related to aid effectiveness (Davis, 2012), but more broadly related to the interconnected concepts of economy, efficiency, and effectiveness (The Three Es) (Jackson, 2012). The UKs Independent Commission for Aid Impact adds a further "E" that of equity (ICAI, 2011). The UKs Department for International Development identifies the purpose of VFM as "maximizing the impact of each pound spent to improve poor people's lives" (DFID, 2011, p. 2). It notes an explicit requirement for increased transparency and accountability to achieve the "desired quality at the lowest price." VfM originates from business discourse with a clear purpose particularly in the procurement of goods and services (Davis, 2012). In development discourse, VfM, like many of the key concepts discussed in this book is far from clear. There are some fundamental tensions inherent in the VfM discourse. For example, development assistance funded by public funds may be perceived as being exempt from the same levels of scrutiny and is somehow different from other areas of public spending (Jackson, 2012).

Given recent fiscal woes, it is not surprising that donor governments are cognizant of the need to ensure that the "taxpayer" money is spent far sightedly and that the aid funds have the desired sustainable impact. This puts an onus on multilateral, and bilateral aid agencies not only to document ODA project and program impacts, but also to ensure transparency of the findings. As DFID (2013) notes, its 2013 evaluation policy

… comes at a crucial time as the external scrutiny of UK assistance, how it is delivered and what the money is spent on is increasing. The public, as taxpayers and the media take a strong interest in the aid budget and its impact, and thus it is vital that DFID has a clear transparent framework for the independent evaluation of its work. (p. ii)

This is not a unique situation. In particular in the post-GFC world, not only the public but also the political decision-makers, are asking questions about how much is being spent for domestic aid and how much for development aid for developing countries? What are the advantages of providing funding for a range of multilateral and domestic bilateral aid agencies? What impact can be attributed to the tax dollar allocated for development aid and how can the impact be verified?

Apart from the moral arguments in applying VfM logic to foreign aid, there is also the issue of value for money for whom, and of what, and by when? (Jackson, 2012). These questions raise associated issues of accountability, transparency, timeframes, and level of focus (macro–meso–micro). There is also the possibility of a VfM focus increasing a culture of risk-averse, and quantifiable priorities in designing and delivering development aid.

AID, DEVELOPMENT, RESULTS, AND IMPACT

There is an apparently a clear divide at the macro level as to whether aid works, as epitomized by the "great debate" between the "aid radicals" and "aid reformers" (Gulrajani, 2011). This divide is frequently epitomized best in the best-selling tomes by Easterly (2008) and Moyo (2009) versus Sachs

(2005) and Collier (2007). However, Engel (2014) argues that this is a "not so great" debate as it is in essence based on out-dated notions of aid and national development, privileging the idea of development guided by outside institutions. This chapter has analyzed some core changes in contemporary development that have contributed to an evolving and disputed aid discourse and practice. The changing aid flows, evolving and fragmenting aid architecture, diverse aid modalities all have implications for both how money is disbursed, to whom, and for what purposes.

Riddell (2014) argues that currently the determining factor of whether aid should be given is whether it can be clearly shown to work, but that we need also to reassess what success or failure is, and over what time frame, given the highly complex context within which aid is allocated. Similar questions are being asked in recipient countries, which are obtaining loans from aid agencies and where the loan has to be paid back with interest. Donor countries, which are experiencing intimidating fiscal and debt difficulties on the basis of self-imposed or externally dictated austerity measures, emphasize the need for maximizing the impact of their aid spending, ensuring validity and affordability of foreign aid. The question of the impact of aid support has turned to a large extent, if not completely, to quantitative aspects of aid. This does not take into consideration the potentially significant differences of quality between projects, programs, and donors (cf. Garbarino and Holland, 2009). But this is not surprising, because, as Taylor (2012, p. 3) argues, aid agencies

...do not widely publish the success they have sustained in terms of democratic process, economic growth, institution building and budgetary support; these are the largest budget lines of donors and it is significant that there is little conclusive evidence on these indicators.

There is little analytical work being published on the impact of aid and authentic practices of different aid organizations and long-term effectiveness of project or program impact. With this in mind, it is difficult to draw a conclusion if and how donor agencies use IA practices and procedures, which would allow for a transparent and open analysis and reporting.

The rhetoric behind investments in international or foreign aid is of course that there is a positive and significant impact on the lives of the people in the regions that receive foreign aid. The basic underpinning of human development, as understood and practiced by the architecture of the international development Goliath in all its form depends on this one basic assumption; that aid promotes human development. An approach that addresses the impact of a particular development intervention must, therefore, take account of impacts across multiple facets of human development, social, economic, and cultural as key aspects. It should be noted that although environmental concerns are core components of any intervention, the environmental dimension is included here as part of a sustainable human development discourse, rather than with any specific focus on Environmental Impact Assessment (EIA). There is significant literature surrounding EIA, and the next section addresses diverse origins and perspectives of Impact Assessment.

Let us try to explain IA from a broad ODA perspective. In this context IA can be understood as an activity to identify expected or authentic impacts of an ODA –project's intervention on social, political, cultural, economic, legal, and environmental aspects within a framework of predetermined intervention.

In the broadest sense, IA can be defined as

> ...the systematic analysis of the lasting or significant changes - positive or negative, intended or not – in people's lives brought about by a given action or series of actions (Roche, 1999, p. 21).

This definition may be applied to all forms of ODA IA such as Regulatory Impact Assessment (RIA), Poverty and Social Impact Analysis (PSIA), EIA, Strategic Environmental Assessment (SEA), Health Impact Assessment (HIA), Integrated Impact Assessment (IntIA), and Inequality Impact Assessment (IneIA). For the purpose of this book, we are concentrating specifically on Impact Assessment of development-aid related policy and programming – with a particular focus on social sector activity.

Our thesis is that IAs should be at the center of each ODA project or program with the purpose to determine to what extent the intervention has led to the desired impact. This thesis is underpinned by the assertion that a project or program can only be justified by its (positive) impact on the beneficiaries. One of the important general challenges in the area of social sector ODA is that the project or program supports a range of activities, yet impacts remain ambiguous, for a number of reasons, but exacerbated by a lack of IA. Thus, the capacity to show positive impacts to donors becomes a first-rate instrument to secure future ODA funding. It also supports the argument against IA as being costly, cumbersome, and time consuming. O'Flynn (2010) notes the potential disconnect in the purpose of IA, suggesting that it must simultaneously demonstrate success as the basis for further funding (value for money), as well as provide a mechanism for what can be done better. These multiple purposes are "not necessarily happy bedfellows" (O'Flynn, 2010, p. 2). Correspondingly, if the IA shows negative, or no ODA project or program impacts the question of possible consequences and remedies can be articulated. Be this as it may, a main challenge of IA in ODA is the linking of project or program interventions to specific impacts. That is, one cannot ascribe all the impacts, be they positive or negative, to the project or program interventions alone. Some impacts may be due to external interventions, that is, not related to the project or program interventions. Thus, one of the fundamental challenges of any ODA program or project IA is the attribution of interventions. In other words, there is a challenge to the nexus between interventions and impacts (Oldsman and Hallberg, 2001). As noted earlier, moves toward a partnership dialog, increasing focus on trade, and non-ODA activities under this partnership dialog all add significant complexity to the task of assessing the impact of foreign aid.

CONCLUSION

There is, and has been for some time, increasing pressure on government and non government agencies to provide an evidence-based effectiveness of development expenditure. Twin pillars of fiscal pressure on governments, and a significant and public debate about the effectiveness of aid drive this. It is generally an accepted truth that the global economy will continue to impact aid flows through traditional mechanisms. Aid is also very strongly impacted by political concerns and an increasing link between trade and aid, both through the AfT agenda, and through the self-interest of bilateral donors driving aid budgets increasingly from a trade perspective. This in conjunction with new donors, and new aid architecture are driving a need to demonstrate not only expenditure, but also results. Results are often perceived in a linear quantifiable form, driven by the much-maligned log frames. However impact has become the driver of aid justification. As a scholarly pursuit and practical field, Impact Assessment for development aid in its various forms, including RIA and PSIA, as a scholarly pursuit and practical field endeavor, is relatively new. However, a robust impact assessment can contribute both to securing funding and in providing learning for better impact. The rationale of assessing the impact of aid is robust. There is, however, a wide range of questions to be asked about how IA is conceptualized, across a range of contexts, how it is operationalized, and what core challenges exist. This volume seeks to address these from a range of perspective across the social sector. The following chapter unpacks impact assessment as the field of enquiry and practice, setting the scene for the remainder of the volume.

REFERENCES

Atwood, J.B., 2012. Creating a Global Partnership for Effective Development Cooperation. Center for Global Development, October 2012, Washington DC.

Baker, J.L., Bank, W., 2000. Evaluating the Impact of Development Projects on Poverty: A Handbook for Practitioners, First ed. World Bank Publications, Washington, DC.

Basu, P., Guariglia, A., 2007. Foreign direct investment, inequality, and growth. J. Macroecon. 29 (4), 824–839.

Bauer, P.T., 1972. Dissent on Development. Harvard University Press, Cambridge, MA.

Birdsall, N., Fukuyama, F., 2011. The Post-Washington Consensus: Development After the Crisis. Center for Global Development, Washington, DC, (Working Paper 244).

Birdsall, N., Savedoff, W.D., 2009. Ca$h on Delivery: a New Approach to Foreign Aid: With an Application to Primary Schooling. Center For Global Development, Washington, DC.

Boone, P., 1996. Politics and the effectiveness of foreign aid. Eur. Econ. Rev. 40, 289–330.

Buchanan-Smith, M., Scriven, K., 2011. Leadership in Action: Leading Effectively in Humanitarian Operations. ALNAP, London.

Chambers, R., 2004. Ideas for development: Reflecting forwards. IDS Working Paper 238. Institute for Development Studies, Sussex. Available from: <http://www.ids.ac.uk/publications/ids-series-titles/ids-working-papers/page Publication/12>.

Cohen, J., Easterley, W. (Eds.), 2009. What Works in Development?: Thinking Big and Thinking Small. Brookings Institution Press, Washington, DC.

Collier, P., 2007. The Bottom Billion: Why the Poorest Countries are Failing and What can be Done About it. Oxford University Press, New York, NY.

Davis, T.W.D., 2012. ACFID and 'Value for Money' Discussion Paper. Australian Council for International Development, Canberra, Available from: <http://www.acfid.asn.au/resources-publications/files/acfid-and-value-for-money>.

DFID, 2011. DFID's Approach to Value for Money (VfM), UK Department for international Development, London. Available from: <https://www.gov.uk/government/uploads/system/uploads/attachment_data/file/67479/DFID-approach-value-money.pdf> (accessed 24.06.2015).

DFID, 2013. International Development Evaluation Policy, UK Department for International Development. Available from: <https://www.gov.uk/government/uploads/system/uploads/attachment_data/file/204119/DFID-Evaluation-Policy-2013.pdf> (accessed 24.06.2015).

Diettrich, S., 2010. Does donor selectivity in aid delivery help the poor? In APSA 2010 Annual Meeting Paper. Available from: <http://ssrn.com/abstract(1644727>.

Driffield, N., Jones, C., 2013. Impact of FDI, ODA and migrant remittances on economic growth in developing countries: A systems approach. Eur. J. Dev. Res. 25 (2), 173–196.

Easterly, W., 2003. Can foreign aid buy growth? J. Econ. Perspect. 17 (3), 23–48.

Easterly, W., 2008. The White Man's Burden Why the West's Efforts to Aid the Rest Have Done so Much Ill and so Little Good. Penguin Group USA, New York, NY.

Engel, S., 2014. The not-so-great aid debate. Third World Q. 35 (8), 1374–1389.

Foreman, J., 2013. Aiding and Abetting: Foreign Aid Failures and the 0.7% Deception. Civitas, United Kingdom.

Fowowe, B., Shuaibu, M.I., 2014. Is foreign direct investment good for the poor? New evidence from African countries. Econ. Change Restructuring 47 (4), 321–339.

Garbarino, S. Holland J., 2009. Quantitative and qualitative methods in impact evaluation and measuring results. Governance and Social Development Resource Centre Issues Paper. Available from: <http://www.gsdrc.org/docs/open/EIRS4.pdf>.(accessed June 24, 2015).

Global Humanitarian Assistance, 2012. Global Humanitarian Assistance Report 2012. Development Initiatives. Available from: <http://www.globalhumanitarianassistance.org/wp-content/uploads/2012/07/GHA_Report_2012-Websingle.pdf.>.

Groves, L.C., Hinton, R.B., 2004. Inclusive Aid: Changing Power and Relationships in International Development. Earthscan, London.

Gulrajani, N., 2011. Transcending the great foreign aid debate: Managerialism, radicalism and the search for aid effectiveness. Third World Q. 32 (2), 199–216.

Hall-Matthews, M., 2014. Open aid and the road to 2015. BlogPost on Global Partnership for Effective Development Cooperation Blog (GPEDC), January 27th 2014. Available online: <http://devcooperation.org/2014/01/27/open-aid-and-the-road-to-2015-3/> (accessed 26.08.2015).

ICAI, 2011. ICAI's approach to effectiveness and value for money. Independent Commission for Aid Impact. Available from: <http://icai.independent.gov.uk/reports/icais-approach-effectiveness-value-.money> (accessed 24.06.2015).

Jackson, P., 2012. Value for money and international development: Deconstructing myths to promote a more constructive discussion. OECD Development Co-operation Directorate. OECD.Available from: <http://www.oecd.org/development/effectiveness/49652541.pdf.>.

Kharas, H., 2007. Trends and Issues in Development Aid. Available from May 29, 2015: <http://www.brookings.edu/research/papers/2007/11/development-aid-kharas.>.

Kharas, H., Blomfeld, M., 2013. Rethinking the role of multilateral institutions in an ever-changing aid architecture. In: Besada, H., Kindornay, S. (Eds.), Multilateral Development Cooperation in a Changing Global Order. Palgrave Macmillan, Houndmills.

Killen B., 2011. How Much Does Aid Effectiveness Improve Development Outcomes? Lessons from Recent PracticE. Busan Background Papers. OECD. Available from: <http://www.oecd.org/development/effectiveness/48458806.pdf.>.

Kingsbury, D. (Ed.), 2013. Critical Reflections on Development. Palgrave Macmillan, United Kingdom.

Klein, M., Aaron, C., Hadjimichael, B., 2001. Foreign Direct Investment and Poverty Reduction. World Bank Policy Research Working Paper 2613 (pp. 2–3). World Bank.

Kotz, D.M., 2009. The financial and economic crisis of 2008: A systemic crisis of neoliberal capitalism. Rev. Radical Polit. Econ. 41 (3), 305–317.

Krajewski, M., 2013. Investment guarantees and international obligations to reduce poverty: A human right perspective. In: Krista Nadakavukaren, Schefer (Eds.), Poverty and the International Economic Legal System: Duties to the World's Poor. Cambridge University Press, Cambridge, MA.

Lele, U., Sadik, N., Simmons, A., 2006. The changing aid architecture: can global initiatives eradicate poverty. (OECD) DAC News. Available from: <http://www.oecd.org/dac/37034781.pdf.>.

Lockwood, M., 2012. What have the MDGs achieved? We don't really know [From Poverty to Freedom, OxfamBlogs]. Available from: <http://oxfamblogs.org/fp2p/what-if-we-applied-the-results-agenda-to-the-mdgs-quasi-heretical-guest-post-from-matthew-lockwood/>.

Mawdsley, E., Savage, L., Kim, S.-M., 2013. A 'post-aid world'? Paradigm shift in foreign aid and development cooperation at the 2011 Busan High Level Forum. Geographical J. 180 (1), 27–38.

Mirowski, P., 2013. Never let a Serious Crisis go to Waste: How Neoliberalism Survived the Financial Meltdown, First ed. Verso Books, London.

Moyo, D.F., 2009. Dead Aid: Why Aid is not Working and how There is a Better Way for Africa, First ed. Farrar, Straus and Giroux, New York, NY.

O'Flynn, M., 2010. Impact assessment: Understanding and Assessing our contributions to change. M&E Paper 7. INTRACAvailable from: <http://www.intrac.org/data/files/resources/695/Impact-Assessment-Understanding-and-Assessing-our-Contributions-to-Change.pdf.>.

OECD - DAC., 2015. Development aid stable in 2014 but flows to poorest countries still falling. Technical Note. Available from: <http://www.oecd.org/dac/stats/documentupload/ODA%202014%20Technical%20Note.pdf.>.

OECD, 2005. Paris Declaration on Aid Effectiveness, OECD.

OECD, 2015. OECD international development statistics. OECDStat. Available from: <http://www.oecd-ilibrary.org/statistics>.

OECD., 2015b. Official development assistance – definition and coverage. Available March 24, 2015 from: <http://www.oecd.org/dac/stats/officialdevelopmentassistancedefinitionandcoverage.htm.>.

OECD, 2015c. Other official flows (OOF) (indicator). Available from: <https://data.oecd.org/drf/other-official-flows-oof.htm.>.

Oldsman, E., Hallberg, K., 2001. Framework for evaluating the impact of small enterprise initiatives. Nexus Associates, Inc. 2001. Available ftom: <http://www.value-chains.org/dyn/bds/bds2search.details2?p_phase_id=403&p_lang=en&p_phase_type_id=4.>.

Peet, R., Hartwick, E., 2009. Theories of Development, Second Edition Guilford Publications, United States.

Provost, C., Jones, S., 2014. Shh, don't tell anyone, but UK government meets foreign aid target, The Guardian, Friday 4th April, 2014.Available from: <http://www.theguardian.com/global-development/2014/apr/03/uk-meets-foreign-aid-target> (accessed 20.06.2015).

Riddell, R.C., 2008. Does Foreign Aid Really Work? Oxford University Press, Oxford.

Riddell, R.C., 2014. Does foreign aid really work? An updated assessment. Discussion paper 33. Development Policy Centre, ANU, Canberra.

Roche, C., 1999. Impact Assessment for Development Agencies: Learning to Value Change. Oxfam, United Kingdom, Oxford, 1999.

Sachs, J.D., 2005. The End of Poverty: Growing the World's Wealth in an Age of Extremes. Penguin Press, New York, NY.

Shleifer, A., 2009. The age of Milton Friedman. J. Econ. Literature 47 (1), 123–135.

Ssewakiryanga, R., 2011. From aid effectiveness to development effectiveness. DEVEX. Available from: <https://www.devex.com/news/from-aid-effectiveness-to-development-effectiveness-76786.>.

Taylor, H., 2012. To what extent do the arguments against development aid outweigh the case for aid in poor countries. HiiDunia. Available from: <http://www.hiidunia.com/2012/07/to-what-extent-do-the-arguments-against-development-aid-outweigh-the-case-for-aid-in-poor-countries> (accessed 24.06.2015).

UNCTAD, 2014. Global FDI Rose By 11%; Developed Economies Are Trapped In Historically Low Share. Global Investment Trends Monitor (No. 15). Available from: <http://unctad.org/en/PublicationsLibrary/webdiaeia2014d1_en.pdf.>.

UNCTAD, 2015. Global FDI Flows Declined In 2014: China Becomes The World's Top FDI Recipient. Global Investment Trends Monitor (No. 18). Available from: <http://unctad.org/en/PublicationsLibrary/webdiaeia2015d1_en.pdf.>.

UNICEF, 1996. The State of the World's Children 1996 (State of the World's Children). Oxford University Press for UNICEF, United Kingdom.

Wallace, T., Bornstein, L., Chapman, J., 2007. The Aid Chain: Coercion and Commitment in Development NGOs. Practical Action Pub, LONDON.

World Bank, 2013. Developing Countries to Receive Over $410 Billion in Remittances in 2013, Says World Bank. World Bank Press Release. No: 2014/115/DEC. Available from: <http://www.worldbank.org/en/news/press-release/2013/10/02/developing-countries-remittances-2013-world-bank>.

World Bank, 2014. Remittances to Developing Countries to Grow by 5 Percent This Year, While Conflict-Related Forced Migration is at All-Time High, Says WB Report. World Bank Press Release. No: 2015/148/DEC. Available from: <http://www.worldbank.org/en/news/press-release/2014/10/06/remittances-developing-countries-five-percent-conflict-related-migration-all-time-high-wb-report.>.

Xu, J., Carey, R., 2015. China's Development Finance: Ambition, Impact and Transparency. IDS Policy Briefing 92. Institute of Development Studies, Brighton.

CONCEPTUALIZING IMPACT ASSESSMENT IN FOREIGN AID

Max Kelly

School of Humanities and Social Sciences, Faculty of Arts and Education, Deakin University, Warrnambool, Australia

INTRODUCTION

Impact Assessment has evolved across a number of diverse disciplines and areas of human activity. In its broadest form IA is "the process of identifying future consequences of a current or proposed action. The impact is the difference between what would happen with the action and what would happen without it" (IAIA, 2009, p. 1). Another commonly used definition is from Roche (1999) "The systematic analysis of lasting or significant change –positive or negative, intended or not – in people's lives brought about by an action or a series of actions" (p. 21). This second definition incorporates some acknowledgment of the complexity of the concept of impact in a development, or humanitarian context. The differentiation between a significant, and a lasting impact may be substantial. The OECD-DAC definition of impact is "The positive and negative changes produced by a development intervention, directly or indirectly, intended or unintended" (OECD, n.d.). The need to understand the impact of development activities is hardly new. For example, the OECD-DAC included impact as one of the five criteria for evaluation in their 1991 report on principles of evaluation for development (OECD-DAC, n.d.). The imperative to demonstrate impact is however growing (see Chapter 1). Bamberger (2010) argues that it is important to differentiate between a "technical-statistical definition" and a "substantive definition." The broader definitions of Roche (1999) and the OECD-DAC are based on understandings and values embedded in aid and development discourse, and are substantive, including recognition of shifts in stakeholder relationships – such as the partnership discourse of Busan, and effective aid. At this broad conceptual level, IA is relatively easy to grasp, and the benefits of understanding the impact of any development intervention are attractive. Of course, a more cynical view may be that if an agency is unsure of whether they are having a positive impact they would be much less keen on measuring the impact. This chapter analyses the role and evolution of impact assessment in the context of foreign aid, and unpacks some conceptual and operational challenges in the design and implementation of impact assessment in development activities.

RESULTS AND IMPACT

In terms of measuring results, the normal causal chain is shown in Fig. 2.1.

This results chain is of course predicated on a framework of understanding often best encapsulated by Results Based Management (RBM). Results in this chain can be seen as output, outcome, or impact. Of course, there is a substantial difference between these three diverse types of results. Outcome and impact are considered the higher order results. Hatton and Schroeder (2007) raised some key issues with RBM, including a failure of many evaluations to get past activities. They argue that moving forward from "managing for inputs" (p. 428) is a key challenge. A review of different uses of the terms outcome and impact reveals significant confusion. The outcome is frequently noted as being a more concrete concept – finite, often predefined, and, therefore, measurable (Harding, 2014). Using this understanding of the outcome, the impact is, therefore, a broader effect. Assessing impact or benefits from any interventions can arguably require a value judgment, based on a normative valuation. Another way of conceptualizing impact versus outcome is time. Hatton and Schroeder (2007) identify output as being short-term results, an outcome the medium term, and impact the long-term result. Penna (2012) highlights this complexity when noting that although we hope for impact, outcomes are actually what we work for. This echoes Brewer (2011) in identifying outcomes as much easier to focus on, in that outcomes can be much more easily measured. However, there is also significant overlap between the usage of outcome and impact. O'Flynn (2010) delineates activities and outputs related to monitoring, the outcome as the focus of evaluation, and impact as the change in peoples' lives that is related to the results from monitoring and evaluation. USAID (2010) identifies impact evaluation as "an evaluation that looks at the impact of an intervention on ..outcomes.. rather than outputs.." (p. 1). Roche (1999) notes that although the difference between outcome and impact can be useful it is imprecise, or blurred.

As raised in Chapter 1, our understandings of whether aid works or how it could work better, based on a clear, robust evidence base is lacking. The Centre for Global Development convened a working group on this "evaluation gap," namely the lack of rigorous impact evaluations of social development programs (The Evaluation Gap Working Group, 2006). This evaluation gap is best demonstrated by systematic reviews or evaluations of evaluations. The Evaluation Gap Working Group (2006) identified a number of reports highlighting this gap. In a systematic review of UNICEF programs, only 15% of reports included impact. Similarly, a review by the ILO found that only 2 of 127 studies of

FIGURE 2.1 The Results Chain

258 community health-financing programs demonstrated robust conclusions on the impact of the programs (Baeza et al., 2002). More recently a review by the Office of Development Effectiveness (ODE) of DFAT of 87 evaluations conducted on Australian Aid in 2012 concluded that half of evaluations failed to consider Impact. Evaluations that considered impact were often very weak (ODE, 2014a). However, the overall growth in impact studies was recently highlighted by Cameron et al. (2015) who found that from the mid 1990s impact studies were published steadily, increasing from around 25 per year in 2000 to over 350 in 2012. Health, nutrition, and population have been the sectors with the highest level of impact studies. However, education and social protection, and agriculture have demonstrated modest increases in impact studies, according to the Impact Evaluation Repository underpinning Cameron et al. (2015) research. Therefore, there has been some movement in addressing the "evaluation gap."

Despite this, underinvestment in impact studies is the norm. Pritchett (2002) conducted a political economy analysis of this underinvestment in rigorous research of impact concluding that if a program can already generate sufficient support to be adequately funded then "knowledge is a danger ..... endless, but less compelling controversy is preferable to certainty" (p. 268). This kind of strategic ignorance contrasts with the increasing push for transparency and accountability, particularly in public funds. There can be a public good aspect to impact studies that transcend the kind of self-interest identified in Pritchett's (2002) work. However, issues of attributability complicate this. The difficulty of identifying sole attribution of impact in complex development spaces is high, but the benefit (and cost) of understanding impact in these spaces is equally high (see for example Bell and Alttahir, this volume).

Some of the arguments raised against the use of impact assessment include human and financial resources available to conduct the studies, buy-in required from various stakeholders, including government; difficulties of assessing impact in complex situations, lack of understanding of the importance of impact versus other lower order results (cf. ADB, 2006). A significant concern is timing, in that an *ex-post* impact assessment needs to be carried out at an appropriate time after the completion of the work that makes it difficult to fund, difficult to justify (this kind of *ex-post* IA has more of a public good aspect), and also, at what point is the timing appropriate to conduct the assessment (ADB, 2006).

A further issue is the link between implicit or intuitive understandings of change, often incorporated through visions, missions, goals, objectives, and so on, and explicit analysis of change. Progressions from logical or linear thinking encapsulated in Logical frameworks and similar have evolved a focus on "Theory of Change" (ToC). Although it can be many things to many people, the underlying focus of ToC is

> ...a big picture analysis of how change happens in relation to a specific thematic area; an articulation of an organisation or programme pathway in relation to this; and an impact assessment framework which is designed to test both the pathway and the assumptions made about how change happens. (O'flynn, 2012, p. 2).

The original rationale as outlined by Connell et al. (1995) was the lack of articulation of assumptions that drive programs. Although much of the ToC literature promotes the link between activities and outcomes, the basic premise has much to offer impact assessment in that ToCs can be a mechanism whereby organizations refocus on what needs to be changed, rather than what needs to be done. There is also the potential for ToCs to be "eroded by fashionable reductionism" (O'flynn, 2012, p. 2). If ToC is so eroded then it is likely to revert to a narrow extension of the risks and assumptions of the logical framework, rather than providing an opportunity for higher-level engagement with social change and research-based evidence (Stein and Valters, 2012).

There are significant obstacles to Impact Assessment. However, there is also a very strong pressure for increased accountability of funds disbursed in the name of development, as detailed in Chapter 1. Some examples include the World Bank Independent Evaluation Group, charged with evaluating the activities of the World Bank group. There are similar groups within the ADB, AfDB, and other multilateral institutions. Bilateral Agencies have, or have had a focus on Impact Studies such as the UK Independent Commission for Aid Impact (ACAI). NGOs are also under more pressure to identify the difference they have made to the beneficiaries of development. The UK Charity Commission requires NGOs to report against their strategic objectives (O'Flynn, 2010). However, even when Impact Studies are conducted they are not always readily available, reliable, or acted upon (cf. ODE, 2104b; O'Flynn, 2010). These competing pressures for and against impact assessment are contextualized by some of the challenges and opportunities embedded in the impact assessment debate.

In a rapidly changing aid and development environment, it is interesting to note the ebb and flow of impact assessment in various quarters. The Australian ODE review previously mentioned (ODE, 2014a) was critical of the level of engagement with impact as well as the reliability of the evaluations that did attempt to cover impact. A resulting final report presenting recommendations from the Operational Evaluations of Australian Aid unfortunately contained no reference at all to assessing impact, despite the previous findings in one of the two contributing reports to the recommendations (ODE, 2014a). A new Australian development policy and performance framework was launched in 2014, which excluded any discussion on impact (despite a commitment to maximize impact of the aid program generally – whatever this may mean) and made reference only to managing risk via mandatory safeguard policies in environment, resettlement and child protection (DFAT, 2014a). The performance framework for this development policy identifies as need for gender-disaggregated data to understand the impact on women and girls (DFAT, 2014b). This in effect returns IA to the regulatory risk mitigation role embodied in EIA and SIA discourse. A 2012 discussion paper on Impact Evaluation released for comment prior to the merging of AusAid into DFAT is no longer available on the DFAT site and no reference to impact evaluation or impact assessment outside of mitigation of environmental and social impacts via mandatory safeguards, is now made within DFAT, leaving an impression of a retreat from impact studies.

O'Flynn (2010) noted that impact is a fairly well-understood term but when used in the context of foreign aid and development "it seems to take on a mysterious complexity which leaves practitioners feeling unsure and lacking in confidence as to what is really meant" (p. 1). This confusion around what impact means, why it is important, and therefore what constitutes good practice, or useful approaches to IA is echoed by a range of other stakeholders (cf. AusAid, 2012a, b), and is discussed in many ways throughout this volume. This can be perhaps related to its diverse origins and the resulting lack of clarity as to its current role, and purpose. Earlier discussions centered on the diverse meanings of outcome and impact. This kind of confusion adds to the overall lack of clarity of what exactly constitutes impact studies in development.

THE EVOLUTION OF IMPACT ASSESSMENT

It is necessary to explore, however briefly, the emergence and evolution of Impact Assessment relevant to the international development context. Impact Assessment initially surfaced in response to the nature and scale of environmental change occurring as a result of human actions. Environmental Impact Assessment (EIA) was formally incorporated legislatively in 1970 in the US National Environment Policy Act (Morgan, 2012). EIA initially focused on the biophysical environment, with the social and economic impacts of development proposals later emerging.

IA from this disciplinary perspective has evolved considerably since this time. IA now occurs in a wide diversity of forms – Social IA, Health IA, Ecological IA, or Biodiversity IA (IAIA, 2009). Impact Assessment at the strategic (decision making) level evolved Strategic Environmental Assessment (SEA) (IAIA, 2009). Each of these forms is perceived by one strand of thinking in IA discourse as evolutions of EIA (cf. IAIA, 2009; Morgan, 2012). Sustainability Assessment within this field is essentially an integrated form of IA (IAIA, 2009) or an evolution from EIA, through SEA to Sustainability Assessment, or what Bond et al. (2012) refer to as the "third generation" of IA. However, Bond et al. (2012) also note the simultaneous emergence of the notion from other fields.

Social Impact Assessment emerged in the 1970s and 1980s in response to the critique of the biophysical nature of EIA, and its lack of capacity to cover social impacts (Morgan, 2012). SIA in its early form focused on a more technocratic prediction of likely impacts from a social perspective, with particular relevance to large-scale construction projects. However, Vanclay and Esteves (2012) argue that SIA has evolved from this narrow application to be a process of managing social aspects of development interventions. This places SIA well outside its regulatory, and primarily *ex-ante* origin and much more into the realm of a proactive process, or even a paradigm for research and practice, and methodology (Vanclay, 2006). There is still a bias in the literature around SIA toward resource-focused interventions, and physical infrastructure projects. While there is much of relevance, particularly perhaps in the new directions of SIA theory and practice, there is a need to consider the applicability of the often very diverse contexts and intentions of foreign-aid programming, and the potential opportunities, and limitations of SIA. Vanclay and Esteves (2012) further identify the range of good practice in the area of social development that operates far outside the scope of SIA.

One perhaps defining factor in IA is that often EIA (and SEA) is legislatively mandated whereas other forms of IA, in particular, IA in the development sector (not legislatively requiring EIA/SIA or SEA) are more often a requirement of the funder or other stakeholders. Vanclay and Esteves (2012) argue that the "old" view of EIA and SIA as predicting impacts in a regulatory context needs to be challenged as SIA is of benefit not only the regulatory agencies, but also to the communities, governments, and the private sector and by implication in this context the development organizations, donors, and even perhaps the beneficiaries. However, Anis and Beddies (2012) note the shift to a more holistic focus within SIA discourse but contend that in practice a majority of SIA is still focused on physical projects.

A review of available literature on Impact Assessment will invariably throw up significant volumes relating to EIA, and SIA. However, it is to the evolution and practice of assessing the impact from diverse perspectives that we now turn. The terminology surrounding IA in the context of ODA is rather convoluted, for a number of reasons. EIA and associated forms of IA have been widely used and debated, as noted above. Sustainability Assessment is heavily related to the EIA strands of thinking but also encompasses significant aspects of other disciplinary areas related more strongly to sustainability. SIA, as outlined above, is the term often associated with a more traditional impact-assessment discourse. However, SIA has evolved a long way from the regulatory and predictive context of *ex-ante* IA. The notion of assessing impact in social development programming is easily associated with SIA, however, this is not a straightforward endeavor. Perhaps a seismic shift in the Impact Assessment literature is from a focus on the minimization of impacts to a much more holistic focus on positive impact, and enhancement of social, ecological benefits (cf., Gibson, 2006; Bond et al., 2012; Vanclay and Esteves, 2012). However, Social Impact is still strongly associated with "identifying and managing the social issues of project development, and include the effective engagement of affected communities, in participatory processes of identification, assessment and management of social impacts" (Vanclay et al., 2015, p. iv). Although the message is driven by a focus on SIA as a process and not a product, the underlying focus is still on risk mitigation and managing social change.

Roche (1999) explored some of the contributing approaches to appraisal and evaluation to the 1990s (drawing on previous work by Howes, 1992). He links EIA, SIA, Logframes (as well and cost-benefit analysis) and Impact Analysis to a modernization paradigm, with more participatory process in the evaluation and appraisal sphere including Participatory Rural Appraisal, and other forms of evaluation that can promote structural or transformative development (p. 19). He identifies Impact Analysis as a specific *ex-post* analysis carried out several years after the project ending.

Impact Assessment within the development context draws from a range of thinking from IA literature but probably emerges more heavily from the monitoring and evaluation heritage of development. Social Soundness was an early attempt by USAID to determine, *ex-ante*, potential impacts on different and marginalized social groups (Kedia and Van Willigen, 2005). Most organizations have implicit or intuitive understandings of change (O'Flynn, 2010). Given the diversity of institutions and organizations involved in the international development industry it is unsurprising that the evolution of a focus on the "impact" of the work has been equally diverse.

Impact Evaluation is a term frequently encountered in development discourse and forms the basis of the International Initiative for Impact Evaluation (3ie). Impact Evaluation sits firmly in the project monitoring and evaluation framework (as indicated by the Results Chain in Fig. 2.1). There is some considerable breadth of understanding of impact within this framework. ADB (2006) identified Impact Evaluation as comprising both outcome and impact measurement, as differentiated from process evaluation and project monitoring (p3). 3ie defines Impact Evaluation studies as the "measure the net change in outcomes amongst a particular group, or groups, of people that can be attributed to a specific program" (3ie, undated). This replicates other work that identifies impact as the measurement of difference in outcome with or without the activity, with specific reference to two key concepts – the counterfactual, and attributability, both of which are discussed in more detail. White (2009) draws a strong distinction between impact evaluations, based on the understanding of attribution. He argues that the difference is in the definition, and, therefore, much of the misunderstandings on methodology could be avoided if the definition of impact evaluation, encompassing attribution, were made upfront.

Impact Evaluation according to the World Bank is an approach that measures whether an intervention

…had the desired effects on individuals, households, and institutions and whether those effects are attributable to the program intervention. Impact evaluations can also explore unintended consequences, whether positive or negative, on beneficiaries.' (Baker and Bank, 2000, p. 1).

Impact evaluation in this context is the final part of a comprehensive evaluation strategy. The key conceptual difference between an evaluation of outcomes and the measurement of impact is the estimation of the counterfactual. White (2009) argues that attribution requires dealing with counterfactuals (implicitly or explicitly). A further point on attribution is that attribution itself is not necessarily a "sole" attribution (White, 2009), but should or could explore contribution. The counterfactual has become the defining aspect of impact evaluation as promoted by 3ie and others. The use of a Randomized Controlled Trial approach as the experimental option for the research design of Impact Evaluation has become the "gold standard" of "Rigorous Impact Evaluation." However, experimental and quasi-experimental design is the hub of yet another development "impasse" or what Easterly (2009) refers to as the "civil war in development economics" between the "experimentalists" offering the "illusory certainty of numbers" and the "best fit institutionalists and complexity people" (Green, 2012: final paragraph). Although a detailed discussion of research design for impact assessment is beyond the scope of this book, there has been a substantial debate in this quarter (cf. Cohen and Easterley, 2009; Deaton, 2010).

Impact Evaluation has grown exponentially in interest within international development and is a much more frequently used terminology than impact assessment. It raises the question of what is the difference between them? The strong focus on a quantifiable and "rigorous" evidence base for development is arguably part of both terminologies. However, 3ie is a very strong proponent of randomized evaluation. Aside from the debate around research design, however, there is relevance in addressing some theoretical underpinnings of impact studies, which have a direct relevance to the role and approach used.

IMPACT ASSESSMENT IN THEORY AND PRACTICE

There are a number of points of concern around both the theory and practice of impact assessment. These are offset somewhat by the twin proponents – the vocal impact assessment practitioners (as evinced by Vanclay and Esteves, 2012) as well as the ubiquitous framing of development results through the lens of impact. The usefulness of IA often hovers at the edge of many discussions. Roche (1999) argues that IA needs to be useful and relevant not only to the organization engaged in the development activity but also to local staff and partner organizations. Vanclay argues that it should also be of benefit to the participants. The underlying purpose of IA, therefore, comes into play. Reasons to assess the impact of development activities fall under a number of headings, accountability (to whom), transparency, learning, effectiveness, efficiency, and so on. Basically, O'Flynn summarizes well that "impact assessments need at the same time to demonstrate success and to learn about what we could do better. These ideas are not necessarily happy bedfellows" (p. 2). Success and learning are bounded by underlying philosophies of what we are trying to achieve and what success looks like.

Traditionally IA has been associated with the positivist paradigm, with a strong quantitative element. The messy reality and multiple diverse and complex contexts in which international development assistance takes place provide a significant challenge in assessing impact. This is particularly important when trying to identify less tangible impacts (cf. Adams, 2001). Morrison-Saunders et al. (2014) also note that the benefit of impact assessment itself can appear intangible, as changes potentially brought about through IA, such as institutional learning, are not immediately apparent.

Adams (2001) also notes the difficulty methodologically relating to confusion between outcome and impact.

As we alluded to above, there are at least two different views on ODA effectiveness. One is governed by the economic paradigm the other by the sociopolitical paradigm. Like in any other endeavor paradigms govern the "world view" and thus the methodology, method, and questions asked. In essence, the ODA business is to a large extent focusing on a paradigm aligned with a focus on homo economicus. Thus, in this case, IA criteria are based on, and the impact is measured by economic achievements. In contrast, there is the other paradigm, which focuses on homo sociologicus. In this case, the emphases are on the social dimension of ODA. But here we have to sound a cautionary note. For example, education as a focus of ODA can be seen from both an economic perspective (e.g., production of human resources, increased income, employability, etc.) as well as social perspective (e.g., participation in governance, democratization, improved self-esteem, health and quality of life).

Let us take a step back here. Even a cursory of literature from aid agencies shows that proponents of economic "impact" indicators rely to a large extent on conventional empirical economic data such as disbursement levels, rates and ratios, and availment rates. Such data have often been used by aid agencies as a substitute for the performance of different projects and programs. Subsequently it was only a small step to argue that if the project or program was implemented successfully, as measured by economic indicators that a positive impact will follow. This type of argument may lead to the *a priori* conclusion that *ipso facto* IA may be considered as a self-fulfilling prophecy and thus is superfluous.

Social dimensions of ODA, of course, raise a completely different set of challenges and opportunities. The range of theoretical discourses that could or should be relevant to assessing social impact are noted by Howitt (2012) as including (but are not limited to)

> ...power, the state, community, culture, place, difference, sustainability and scale .... Along with methodological questions of participation an social responsibility. (p. 82)

Engagement with the less quantifiable concepts encapsulated in social development obviously requires more focus on qualitative approaches to assessing impact.

So the purists in the economic camp will argue for a purely economics-based IA indicators and quantitative methods. Their counterparts in the social camp argue for qualitative methods and indicators. Despite that battle lines are drawn between the proponents of the economic agenda, and the proponents of the social and socio-political agenda, there are no particular reasons for an argument of mutual exclusivity. Given the wide spectrum to which IA is applied within the ODA sector such as the environment, infrastructure, education, health, agriculture, governance, energy, transportation, and industry to name a few it is not surprising that there is much debate in the relevant literature and deliberations about the methods to be used for IA. In short for every sector and every IA, there is a range of methods being used. In many cases, the choice of methods depends on the underpinning disciplinary paradigm or preference of the assessor. However, and more importantly, IA methods are used according to the precise purpose of the assessment. It also depends on the socio-economic, socio-political, and politico-economic context within which the ODA project or program is set. At a more pragmatic level, the budgetary and time constraints as well as ethical considerations and the research capacity of the assessor(s) will influence the method(s) to be used for IA.

However, the methodologies, methods, and techniques for IA are hotly debated in the academe, as much as amongst practitioners (Deutscher and Fyson, 2008). On the one end of the spectrum in this debate are the proponents of the "cult of efficiency" with a focus on empirical measurements and audit mentality. On the other side are the proponents of effectiveness. To put it differently, on the one side there is a focus on "explaining" impact in quantitative terms, and on the other side there is a focus on "understanding" impact in qualitative terms. For us the point is what type of information shall IA provide to stakeholders, such as donor agencies and recipient countries, so that they may have a thorough understanding of the impact their aid budget has achieved in the context of contemporary development activities. Central to this discourse is an explicit focus on contemporary development activities, and the social, economic, and political context, as well as the theory of change. Subsequently this should enable stakeholders to determine the impact and enhance activities.

In the broadest sense, there are two basic methods that have been and are used by aid agencies for ODA projects or programs. These are, as we said (i) quantitative statistical methods; (ii) qualitative methods. However, a combination of these two, namely the mixed method has significant advantages for IA. Participatory methods can raise a whole new spectre from a methodological perspective – that of transformative development. Not surprisingly there are arguments for and against all these methods. However, the potential answer to the question as to which method is more suitable for a project or program IA, will depend on a number of factors, such the epistemological grounding of the specific sector, aims and objectives of the project or program, what are the expected or projected impacts, who are the beneficiaries and stakeholders, and what type of interventions are planned and or have been introduced during the implementation of the project or program. Thus, it is not unexpected that the battle lines are drawn between the proponents of the quantitative methods and the proponents of the qualitative methods. We argue that given the complexity of the paradigms, and methodologies of development, there is a requirement to overcome traditional boundaries of technique or method. Easterly (2009) "civil war" needs to move past the current "impasse" and acknowledge the context-specific nature of research design in impact assessment.

TRANSPARENCY AND ACCOUNTABILITY

Impact assessment as a mechanism for accountability is a complex area. Accountability, as demonstrated by IA should logically be both to those who are the focus of an intervention ("beneficiaries") but also to those who fund the interventions. Herein lies the problem. The aid chain starts with the public, whose tax dollars fund the interventions (or perhaps who make direct contributions to various organizations voluntarily). As Roche (1999) notes, this has two significant disadvantages. The issue of demonstrable impact or effectiveness is the first. Support for foreign aid requires an acceptance of its effectiveness by the public (the moral case for funding based on impact) and the difficulties in assessing the effectiveness or impact of considerable amount of development interventions leaves organizations open to criticism and "polemic attack" (p. 3). The second issue of considerable importance, which often appears lost is that aid is not the only, or indeed even the main mechanism for supporting human development. Driffield and Jones (2013) found that

…both FDI and migrant remittances have a positive impact on growth in developing countries. In addition, this is attenuated by a better institutional environment, in that countries that protect investors and maintain a high level of law and order will experience enhanced growth. In contrast, the relationship between aid and growth is not clear-cut. On its own aid appears to have a negative impact on growth and it appears to be poorly targeted. However, when there is enough bureaucratic quality, aid does begin to make a difference (p. 189).

Therefore, there is an explicit requirement to understand how development thinking has evolved and matured, in particular with relevance to the economic foundations of human development, and the interrelationships with foreign aid. McKay (this volume) addresses the complex and evolving nature of economics and development aid from which all of the proceeding chapters must be contextualized. DFAT makes the clear and upfront demand that aid spending is accountable to taxpayers (Bishop, 2014). Two further criteria are put forth by New Rules for Global Finance (2014) namely, responsibility and inclusiveness.

EX-ANTE AND *EX-POST* IA

Linking significant debates on the meaning of impact, and on the philosophical stance of the various stakeholders in designing impact assessment is the overall sense of where impact assessment sits within programme or project design, and implementation. EIA evolved as an *ex-ante* process (both as a tool, and a procedure), primarily legislatively mandated, to determine, and therefore mitigate effects of development proposals "prior to major decisions being taken and commitments made" (IAIA, 2009, p. 1). Bond et al. (2012) go so far as to say that "Impact assessment is predictive" (p. 1). IA's origins as a risk identification and mitigation strategy locate IA as an essential precursor to the activities – or *ex-ante* IA. The debate in the literature surrounding the approach to IA (or IE) specifically in a development context is heavily biased toward *ex-post* IA but carried out at a specific point in time. According to O'Flynn (2010) this is an external assessment conducted at or after the completion of the study, and assumes a linear approach to change, assessing changes related to, and attributability of changes from an intervention. Hatton and Schroeder (2007) in linking a temporal factor to results identify impact as a long-term result and, therefore, call for more *ex-post* impact studies. This kind of thinking unequivocally relegates impact assessment to *ex-post*. It is often the practice that impact is to be conducted some years post project completion.

This stands to reason if one accepts the notion that there are only *ex-ante* and *ex-post* IAs. This also tends to relegate IA to a product. However, there is no logical reason to reject the idea of IA to be conducted in between *ex-ante* and *ex-post*-IA, moving IA from a product to a process. This conceptual shift has strongly emerged from the SIA camp (Vanclay and Esteves, 2012). A much more holistic approach to assessing impact that is integrated as a process is more likely to contribute to learning, and to have the potential to benefit a much wider range of stakeholders, including communities engaged in development activities. This raises the questions of whether impact assessment can contribute to transformative development through innovation in understanding change and impact of activities beyond basic justification and accountability to donors. This has particular relevance in moving from the rhetoric of success embedded in a competitive development industry, and the reality of what is being achieved (Roche, 1999).

There is significant confusion regarding what impact is, and how it can be assessed. The diverse conceptual underpinnings of the impact assessment contribute to this, along with a tendency for diverse understandings to be contentions (cf. White, 2009). Bond and Pope (2012) argue that the country context is critical, with a need to take account for diverse stakeholders views about what works, being a key to effective IA. The counterargument that IA can increase VfM needs to be unpacked more.

As it has been highlighted in the preceding discussion there is a long history of debate about the effectiveness of IA in EIA, SIA, and SEA. However, over time there has been a move from a positivist theoretical basis to a "post positivism," which provides more complex understandings of the influence and role of IA, but perhaps little consensus on the theoretical lens through which to view IA (Bond and Pope, 2012, p. 2). The final topic issue, raised by Bond and Pope (2012) is the importance of knowledge and learning, as the basis for critical reflection, for successful IA.

CONCLUSION

Impact assessment as it is theorized and practiced today is an unfinished project. Notwithstanding, the given uncertainties surrounding IA, such as its characteristics in the form of process against a tool, there is a need to acknowledge that approaches to ODA have evolved and changed. However, the institutions and fundamental philosophy of ODA are still in place. Historically, approaches to and of IA have to a certain extent changed. For example, the previously entirely dominant quantitative methods have made way to mixed mode methods, and in some quarters even purely qualitative methods have emerged. But the major paradigm in use is still the statistical quantitative method. The underpinning notion of assessing impact for both accountability, and for institutional learning underpins most IA discourse. However, IA must be understood as a process, encompassing theoretical discourse on aid and development, methodological and philosophical approaches to development, and the methods and techniques on which IA relies.

To conclude, the goal of any development intervention is by definition to realize a positive impact on human development. Unfortunately it is far from straightforward to determine what the impact of any given intervention is. We have 70 years of development assistance to draw on to determine how effective development interventions can be across a wide range of contexts. However, the lack of attention to what the impact of aid spending is, is likely to contribute to further mixed, uncertain, or indefensible claims for positive impact of effective aid. Politically, and economically ODA needs to produce results and therefore assessing impact must be the basis of future expenditure. Development aid is also one part of the puzzle of tackling poverty, and development globally. Understanding the impact of development aid, and its interrelationship with the wide variety of complicating and contributing factors to changes in peoples socio-economic condition is vital.

The discussion in the following chapters will delve into many of the issues, challenges, and opportunities raised above, and will contribute to a much deeper understanding of the role or IA in ODA in the contemporary global economic, and political context.

REFERENCES

Adams, J., 2001. NGOs and impact assessment, NGO Policy Briefing Paper No. 3, INTRAC. Available from: <http://www.intrac.org/resources.php?action=resource&id=39>.

ADB, 2006. Impact evaluation; methodological and operational issues. Manila: Economic Analysis and Operations Support Division Economics and Research Department, Asian Development Bank. Available from: <http://www.adb.org/sites/default/files/institutional-document/33014/files/impact-analysis-handbook.pdf>.

Anis, D., Beddies, S., 2012. The World Bank's Poverty and Social Impact Analysis. In: Vanclay, F., Esteves, A.M. (Eds.), New Directions in Social Impact Assessment: Conceptual and Methodological Advances. Edward Elgar Publishing Ltd, Northampton, MA.

AusAid, 2012. Impact evaluation: A discussion paper for AusAID practitioners, Australian Department of Foreign Affairs and Trade (Formerly AusAID). Available from: <http://www.alnap.org/resource/9831> (accessed 24.06.2015).

AusAid, 2012. Impact evaluation: A discussion paper for practitioners. Canberra: Office of Development Effectiveness. Available from: <http://r4d.dfid.gov.uk/pdf/outputs/misc_infocomm/ImpactEvaluationDiscussionPaper FINALSept%202012.pdf.>.

Baeza, C. (Ed.), 2002. Extending social protection in health through community based health organisations. Evidence and challenges. Discussion Paper, Universitas Programme. Geneva, International Labour Office. (ISBN 92-2-113271-4).(http://www-ilo-mirror.cornell.edu/public/english/universitas/download/publi/cbhostudy.pdf).

Baker, J.L., Bank, W., 2000. Evaluating the Impact of Development Projects on Poverty: A Handbook for Practitioners, 1st ed. World Bank Publications, Washington, DC.

Bamberger, M., 2010. Institutionalising impact evaluation. In: Segone, M. (Ed.), From Policies to Results. Developing Capacities for Country Monitoring and Evaluation Systems. UNICEF, New York, NY.

Bishop, J., 2014. The New Aid Paradigm. Presented at the National Press Club, Canberra, June 2014.

Bond, A., Pope, J., 2012. The state of the art of impact assessment in 2012. Impact Assess. Project Appraisal 30 (1), 1–4.

Bond, A., Morrison-Saunders, A., Pope, J., 2012. Sustainability assessment: The state of the art. Impact Assess. Project Appraisal 30 (1), 53–62.

Brewer, J.D., 2011. The impact of impact. Res. Evaluation 20 (3), 255–256.

Cameron, D.B., Mishra, A., Brown, A.N., 2015. The growth of impact evaluation for international development: how much have we learned? J. Dev. Effectiveness, 1–21.

Cohen, J., Easterley, W. (Eds.), 2009. What Works in Development?: Thinking Big and Thinking Small. Brookings Institution Press, Washington, DC.

Connell, J., Kubisch, A., Schorr, L., Weiss, C. (Eds.), 1995. New Approaches to Evaluating Community Initiatives: Concepts, Methods, and Contexts. The Aspen Institute, Washington, DC.

Deaton, A., 2010. Instruments, randomization, and learning about development. J. Econ. Lit. 48 (2), 424–455.

Deutscher, E., Fyson, S., 2008. Improving the effectiveness of aid. Finance Development, 2008 45 (3.), .

DFAT, 2014a. Australian aid: promoting prosperity, reducing poverty, enhancing stability, Department of Foreign Affairs and Trade, Canberra. Available from: <http://dfat.gov.au/about-us/publications/Pages/australian-aid-promoting-prosperity-reducing-poverty-enhancing-stability.aspx> (accessed 24.06.2104).

DFAT, 2014b. Making performance count: Enhancing the accountability and effectiveness of Australian Aid. Department of Foreign Affairs and Trade, Canberra. Available from: <http://dfat.gov.au/about-us/publications/Pages/making-performance-count-enhancing-the-accountability-and-effectiveness-of-australian-aid.aspx> (accessed 24.06.2015).

Driffield, N., Jones, C., 2013. Impact of FDI, ODA and migrant remittances on economic growth in developing countries: A systems approach. Eur. J. Dev. Res. 25 (2), 173–196.

Easterly, W., 2009. The civil war in development economics, Aidwatch Blog. Available from: <http://aidwatchers.com/2009/12/the-civil-war-in-development-economics/> (accessed 25.06.2015).

Gibson, R.B., 2006. Sustainability assessment: Basic components of a practical approach. Impact Assess. Project Appraisal 24 (3), 170–182.

Green, D., 2012. Lant Pritchett v the Randomistas on the nature of evidence – is a wonkwar brewing? Presented at the From Poverty to Power, Blog. Available from: <http://oxfamblogs.org/fp2p/lant-pritchett-v-the-randomistas-on-the-nature-of-evidence-is-a-wonkwar-brewing/>.

Harding, J., 2014. What is the difference between an impact and an outcome? Impact is the longer term effect of an outcome. [London School of Economics Impact Blog]. Available from: <http://blogs.lse.ac.uk/impactofsocialsciences/2014/10/27/impact-vs-outcome-harding/>.

Hatton, M.J., Schroeder, K., 2007. Results-based management: friend or foe? Dev. Practice 17 (3), 426–432.

Howes, M., 1992. Linking paradigms and practice: Key issues in the appraisal, monitoring and evaluation of British NGO Projects. J. Int. Dev. 4 (4), 375–396.

Howitt, R., 2012. Theoretical foundations. In: Vanclay, F., Esteves, A.M. (Eds.), New Directions in Social Impact Assessment: Conceptual and Methodological Advances. Edward Elgar Publishing, Northampton, MA.

IAIA, 2009. What is Impact Assessment. Available March 17, 2015 from: <http://www.iaia.org/publicdocuments/special-publications/What%20is%20IA_web.pdf>.

Kedia, S., Van Willigen, J., 2005. Applied Anthropology: Domains of Application. Praeger Publishers, United States.

Morgan, R.K., 2012. Environmental impact assessment: The state of the art. Impact Assess. Project Appraisal 30 (1), 5–14.

Morrison-Saunders, A., Bond, A., Pope, J., Retief, F., 2014. Demonstrating the benefits of impact assessment for proponents. Impact Assess. Project Appraisal 33 (2), 108–115.

New Rules for Global Finance, 2014. Governance and Impact Report, 2014. Available from: <http://www.new-rules.org/storage/global_financial_governance_and_impact_report_2014.pdf>.

O'Flynn, M., 2010. Impact assessment: Understanding and assessing our contributions to change. M&E Paper 7. Oxford: INTRAC. Available from: <http://www.intrac.org/data/files/resources/695/Impact-Assessment-Understanding-and-Assessing-our-Contributions-to-Change.pdf.>.

O'flynn, M., 2012. Theory of change: What's it all about? Ontrac (No. 51 May 2012). INTRAC. Available from: <http://www.intrac.org/data/files/resources/741/ONTRAC-51-Theory-of-Change.pdf>.

ODE, 2014a. Learning from Australian aid operational evaluations; Office of Development Effectiveness Briefs. Available from: <http://dfat.gov.au/aid/how-we-measure-performance/ode/Documents/ode-brief-learning-from-aust-aid-op-evaluations.pdf.>.

ODE, 2014b. Quality of Australian aid operational evaluations; Office of Development Effectiveness BRIEFS. Available from: <http://dfat.gov.au/aid/how-we-measure-performance/ode/news/Pages/ode-briefs.aspx>.

OECD-DAC, n.d. DAC Criteria for Evaluating Development Assistance. Available June 2015 from: <http://www.oecd.org/dac/evaluation/daccriteriaforevaluatingdevelopmentassistance.htm>.

Penna, R.M., 2012. The Nonprofit Outcomes Toolbox: A Complete Guide to Program Effectiveness, Performance Measurement, and Results. Wiley, Hoboken, New Jersey.

Pritchett, L., 2002. It pays to be ignorant: A simple political economy of rigorous program evaluation. J Policy Reform 5 (4), 251–269.

Roche, C., 1999. Impact Assessment for Development Agencies: Learning to Value Change. Oxfam, Oxford, United Kingdom.

Stein, D., Valters, C., 2012. Understanding theory of change in international development. Justice and Security Research Programme Paper 1. London School of Economics and Political Science (LSE). Available from: <http://www.theoryofchange.org/wp-content/uploads/toco_library/pdf/UNDERSTANDINGTHEORYOFChangeSteinValtersPN.pdf.>.

The Evaluation Gap Working Group, 2006. In: Savedoff, W., Levine, R., Birdsall, N. (Eds.), When Will we Ever Learn; Improving Lives through Impact Evaluation. Center for Global Development, Washington, DC.

USAID, 2010. Performance monitoring & evaluation tips: Rigorous impact evaluation, TIPS, NUMBER 19, United States Agency for International Development. Available from: <http://pdf.usaid.gov/pdf_docs/pnadw119.pdf> (accessed 24.06.2015).

Vanclay, F., 2006. Principles for social impact assessment: A critical comparison between the international and US documents. Env. Impact Assess. Rev. 26 (1), 3–14.

Vanclay, F., Esteves, A.M., 2012. Current issues and trends in social impact assessment. In: Vanclay, F., Esteves, A.M. (Eds.), New Directions in Social Impact Assessment: Conceptual and Methodological Advances. Edward Elgar Publishing Ltd, Northampton, MA.

Vanclay, F., Esteves, A.M., Aucamp, I., Franks, D., 2015. Social impact asssessmnet: guidance for assessing and managing the social impacts of projects. International Association of Impact Assessmet. Available from: <http://www.iaia.org/pdf/IAIA%202015%20Social%20Impact%20Assessment%20guidance%20document.pdf.>

White, H., 2009. Theory-based impact evaluation: Principles and practice. J. Dev. Effectiveness 1 (3), 271–284.

COMPETING DEVELOPMENT PARADIGMS AND ALTERNATIVE EVALUATIONS OF AID EFFECTIVENESS: CHALLENGING THE DOMINANT NEOLIBERAL VISION

John McKay

Analysis International & Honorary Professor in Development Studies, Deakin University, Geelong, Australia

CHAPTER OUTLINE

INTRODUCTION

In the period since the Second World War dominant ideas on the nature and genesis of the very processes of development – and therefore on the role of aid and the criteria by which aid effectiveness needs to be judged – have gone through a series of transformations, in response to the major trends, conditions, and prevailing ideologies within the emerging global system. But in each case strong counterarguments have also emerged constantly. Thus, the history of ideas on development can be characterized as a series of revolutions and counter-revolutions, and in many cases the key ideas from a particular period have re-emerged in a new guise at a later date (McKay, 2012). In this chapter, I want explore the potential role of aid in each of the main development paradigms that have emerged in the last half 60 years or so, and therefore the appropriate criteria under each mode of thought for judging the forms of aid that might be desirable and for evaluating effectiveness of aid. In particular the place of aid within the dominant neoliberal paradigm since the 1980s, and the implications for aid policy, will be analyzed.

In this study it must be remembered, of course, that while particular ideas about development and the role of aid may be fashionable at specific times not all development and aid initiatives will adhere neatly to these dominant ideologies. Aid has always been given for a wide range of motives, some of them noble and altruistic and others merely involving brazen self-interest. Similarly, while dominant paradigms generally relate to economic considerations, aid as will be emphasized below, is frequently driven by political and strategic factors. However, it is still useful to examine these changing sets of priorities. I will argue that ideas dominant at particular junctures have rarely if ever originated with donor governments or international organizations but become amplified by these groups through their large funding programs. As I have stressed elsewhere (McKay, 2014), Official Development Aid Assistance (ODA) is only responsible for some 27% of global financial flows but the influence of ODA on government policies on development is very considerable, and there are also strong linkages between flows of aid and the operations of the financial organizations that are responsible for the overwhelming share of global money. Also of great significance is the role of international institutions, and notably the International Monetary Fund (IMF) and the World Bank, whose influence on governments and the private sector extends far beyond their modest contributions to the finances of the developing world. These organizations have essentially set the policy agendas in virtually all countries, and this has determined the ways in which aid coming from individual donors has been utilized. In all of these ways dominant paradigms have been both amplified and maintained, hence the importance of understanding these influential discourses, the ways they have originated, and how they have been eventually replaced by alternative discourses and policy prescriptions.

A POLITICAL ECONOMY BACKGROUND

It is particularly important to recognize that most fundamental changes take place in response to crises of various kinds that challenge accepted paradigms, and the Global Financial Crisis (GFC) has since 2007 shaken the foundations of the global economy and has had a major impact on our thinking about competing theories of development. For some, the entire edifice of neoliberal thought, which has been dominant since the 1980s, has been shown to be worthless or even reckless and dangerous, and has brought the entire global financial and economic system to the brink of disaster (McKay, 2013). However, there have been concerted attempts by many with a strong vested interest in retaining the pre-GFC system – with the finance houses of Wall Street and the City of London very much to the fore – to drag public opinion and policy makers back to "business as usual" (McKay, 2014). The economics profession in particular has shown itself to be generally unwilling to rethink any aspects of neoliberal orthodoxy and has carried on as if nothing had happened: as Mirowski (2013) has put it, economics makes no pretence to describe the world as it is but rather the world as some important vested interests would prefer it to be. But at the very least, as Robert Wade (2009) has put it, even if there are strong pressures from powerful elites to return us to the familiar ways of thought and action, it is now more possible to consider some alternative paradigms and policy agendas. For some, the basic problem is that although neoliberal approaches have been roundly attacked, no well articulated alternatives have so far emerged, however as Streek (2014a) has argued it is possible that the current system may collapse under the weight of its own contradictions even in the absence of any clear new direction. What we are certainly now seeing is a healthy reappraisal of the entire architecture of development theory, with important implications for aid policy.

However, we also need to ask whether an ultimately successful overthrow of neoliberalism seems to be possible. There are a number of core problems that neoliberalism does not seem capable of solving, and in particular the extreme levels of inequality that prevail in most nations around the world, and the challenge of creating sufficient jobs, in particular for young people in both the industrial and developing nations (Piketty, 2014; World Bank, 2012; Dabla-Norris et al., 2015). Thus, in the final part of this chapter I will consider some new ideas that seem to be emerging for an alternative development policy in direct opposition to neoliberalism, the vision for aid within this new framework, and the most appropriate criteria for evaluating aid policy and its effectiveness within this possible new paradigm.

THE QUEST FOR MODERNIZATION: THE NEOCLASSICAL FOUNDATIONS

The complexities, counterarguments, and self-doubts that have been a feature of recent debates about development issues, including the role of foreign aid, were not allowed to cloud the simple but powerful message espoused by the proponents of the modernization theory in the period immediately after the end of the Second World War. During the 1960s and part of the 1970s in particular, a simple and beguiling promise was made: all nations however poor were able, with the implementation of "correct" policies, to achieve a modern standard of living by following exactly the same growth path as that pioneered by the western nations. The seminal work from this period was *The Stages of Economic Growth* by Rostow (1960) in which he proposed that the path to modernity involved the movement by any nation through a series of stages. Traditional societies, he argued, can achieve "take-off" – a particularly evocative image – then eventually mature into mass consumption societies. The subtitle of the book – "a non-communist manifesto" – written at a time when Communist expansion was feared in all parts of the underdeveloped world, emphasized that successful development could be achieved without revolution. The most important mechanism in the whole process, the fuel needed to achieve take-off, was investment derived principally from domestic savings: if the savings rate could be moved from the normal 5% of GDP to 10% or more for a sustained period, then take-off could proceed.

There was much discussion in policy circles about the need to escape the "vicious cycle of poverty": low rates of growth meant that savings and investment rates were low, ensuring that low levels of growth persisted. Funds were not available for better schools, universities, or hospitals, ensuring that the nation could not find a way out of its poverty through investment in its human resources. Lack of investment in roads, ports, and other infrastructure kept the economy working at low levels of efficiency. A way out of this persistent cycle of poverty was needed, and the modernization theorists provided a hope that this might be possible.

So far I have concentrated on theories that attempted to account for growth within single countries but in fact international trade and investment have become increasingly important in the global economy and hence have also attracted a great deal of attention. Adam Smith is recognized as the creator of the concept of absolute advantage, according to which nations should concentrate on the production of goods in which they hold some kind of cost advantage. But it was Ricardo who extended this argument to include the case for specialization in national exports that had such an advantage, and who argued that partner nations in trade would all benefit from this kind of exchange.

The emphasis on modernization within economics was mirrored by a range of other studies in other social sciences. In politics, for example, there was much research on political modernization and the generation of more effective political institutions, inevitably made in the image of the West.

In geography, a number of studies concentrated on "spatial modernization," involving the spread of infrastructure and other symbols of modern life, and the gradual expansion of the *core* into the more backward *periphery*. In psychology, too, there was an attempt to explore the ways in which more "modern" personality traits could be engendered and fostered. Perhaps most influential was the work going on at this time in sociology, especially that of Talcott Parsons (1937, 1951), who has become known as "the theorist of modernity" (Robertson and Turner, 1991). He attempted to develop a grand theory of "social action," seeing human activity as voluntary and intentional but set within a symbolic realm and a natural environment. He identified four major functional subsystems – the economy, the polity, the social community, and the fiduciary system – and argued that as societies modernize these systems become more elaborate and the roles of individuals are increasingly differentiated.

Some assumptions in the rather optimistic modernization framework were questioned by Gunnar Myrdal (1957) and Albert Hirschman (1958); both of who demonstrated that "virtuous" as well as "vicious" cycles could operate simultaneously to produce growth in some areas and stagnation in others. Earlier economic theory suggested that inequalities would not persist because labor would migrate from low-wage areas to regions where rewards were higher. Similarly, capital would move to regions where the returns were higher, usually in areas, which were currently backward but had high investment potential. Thus, growth would take place in the more backward areas, removing the initial inequalities. Both Myrdal and Hirschman attacked this kind of equilibrium analysis. Myrdal suggested that two kinds of forces would be at work. *Spread* effects would serve to distribute growth from richer to poorer regions or countries, while *backwash* effects tended to intensify existing inequalities. The relative strength of these two forces would depend on a range of circumstances and policy frameworks: thus processes of *circular and cumulative causation*, could often lead to ever-deepening levels of inequality.

Many of Hirschman's idea were quite similar, but he argued that development is by necessity an unbalanced process, and it would also be unrealistic to expect government planners to invest in various sectors of the economy in a finely balanced way. In particular, he considered the balance between investment in *directly productive activities,* such as factories or plantations, and the infrastructure needed to support these facilities, which he termed *social overhead capital.* Growth may occur by concentrating on the development of infrastructure, thereby reducing production costs and encouraging further investment in production, or the reverse may be preferred. If production is privileged, inefficiencies in infrastructure will appear, forcing catch-up investment. Either strategy might work, and the choice of the more appropriate would depend on local circumstances.

The role of foreign aid in this blueprint for enhanced development is very clear. The major bottleneck is seen as the low level of savings and investment, and aid could be used to enhance these local resources. In many cases this role was fulfilled through the supply of infrastructure, which was seen as being an essential pre-requisite for increased investment in directly productive activities. The widely used textbooks on economic development from this period certainly identify such a role for aid. In his *Economic Development*, Benjamin Higgins (1968) noted that the most obvious thing that foreign aid can do is to "fill the gap between capital requirements for a take-off into sustained growth and domestic capacity for savings and investment" (p. 579). However, he stressed that the absorptive capacities of recipient countries placed limits on the amount of capital that should be provided in this way: an ideal aid policy to support economic growth would make it possible for all countries to invest annually an amount equal to their maximum absorptive capacity. Hopefully as development proceeds and local infrastructure and institutions are improved then the capacity for productive investment can be increased, and with this mind he saw a role for technical assistance – a particular focus of President Truman's 1949 Point Four Program. The Marshall Plan had facilitated dramatic increases in European productivity, and Higgins hoped that a similar aid effort could bring similar results in the developing world. However, he did admit that a primary aim for aid was to assist in the stabilization of the countries concerned and reduce the threat to national security.

Charles Kindleberger (1958), in his *Economic Development* (1958), was even more skeptical about the economic merits of foreign aid, on the grounds that it was hard to make the case that the development of underdeveloped countries will result in economic benefits for the developed world. He too then falls back on the advantages of fostering stability and orderly political development, but suggests that there is little merit in grants for this purpose. "Development is a business matter" (p. 299), and while grants can be justified for national reconstruction after wars or natural disasters, only loans should be made available for economic development.

DISSENTING VOICES FROM THE SOUTH: THE CHALLENGE OF THE DEPENDENCY THEORY

During the 1960s it became clear that inequalities were not being narrowed as conventional economic theory had predicted: rather, the world was becoming increasingly divided between the powerful *core* regions and the impoverished *periphery*. One of the regions where this reality was most pronounced was in Latin America, and it was from here that an influential set of new theories began to emerge – what became known as the *dependencia* or dependency school.

Much of the initial impetus for this mode of thought came from the work of the United Nations Economic Commission for Latin America, and in particular from the work of Raul Prebisch (1950). The central argument – now known as the "Prebisch thesis" – was that the basic assumptions of neo-classical economics did not exist in the real world: the economic landscape did not primarily consist of small producers and buyers, each operating in a perfect marketplace with none able to exert power over these market processes. Rather, global commerce took place between the rich and powerful developed economies and the weaker peripheral countries, and not surprisingly, the rules of the trading system were systematically manipulated in favor of the powerful western-based corporations. In particular, Prebisch rejected the orthodox Ricardian arguments in favor of each nation specializing in the output of goods for which it had a particular comparative advantage, and trading these goods through the international system. He argued that none of the "late industrializers," such as the United States, Germany, and Japan, had been able to use such a strategy for their development: rather, they had gone through the early stages of industrialization behind protective tariff walls until they felt competitive enough to confront the global market on equal terms. Specialization would not encourage industrial development of the kind needed in Latin America: instead the region would be condemned to a peripheral position as a supplier of primary products.

These arguments were taken a stage further, and given much greater exposure in the English-speaking world, by Andre Gunder Frank, who in 1967 produced his classic *Capitalism and Underdevelopment in Latin America*. Development and underdevelopment are simply two sides of the same coin: the rich countries achieved growth by systematically exploiting their colonies and the rest of the underdeveloped world and this process had been going on for several centuries, at least since the Spanish penetration of the New World. By the twentieth century, no part of the globe was too remote to remain untouched by the impacts of the international economic system of imperialism and domination. Thus it was nonsense to regard, as Rostow had done, the underdeveloped world as in some kind of pristine initial state. The poor countries had in fact been *underdeveloped* in the process of incorporation into the global system, and the structural changes that had been imposed upon them made future development of a real and autonomous kind much less likely. Latin America as a whole, he suggested, had progressed most during the two world wars when the countries at the core of international capitalism had been otherwise engaged and the periphery was left to develop in its own way.

Many similar ideas were developed at roughly the same time by Celso Furtado (1964), who also dealt with the class implications of the structures of underdevelopment: particularly lacking in most cases is an elite committed to the generation of autonomous industrialization, and institutional arrangements would need to be flexible enough to allow such a group to assume power – a crucial advance in development thought that we will take up again with reference to the successful industrialization of East Asia.

Furtado's analysis of the internal structures of underdeveloped countries was taken a stage further by Samir Amin (see, e.g., Amin 1976, 1977). Areas involved in export activities, usually of primary products, would have higher wages than found in the rest of the economy, but the multiplier effects of these investments would be far less than in developed economies. Most of the supplies of specialized machinery would come from core countries, as would even some of the food and more luxury items consumed by the labor force, thus the two parts of the economy were quite isolated from each other. The export sector would in fact have its closest relationships with the areas to which its output was exported, again in the core countries, a characteristic which he termed *disarticulation*. The obvious gaps between the rich and poor would inevitably cause deep resentments and, to ensure the maintenance of order, large sums would have to be spent on the import of military hardware and on rewards to local elites and the military forces to ensure their loyalty. This would exacerbate a balance of payment situation already made dire by the progressive decline in the relative value of the primary products being exported. The shortfall in hard currency could only be met by opening up yet further mines, plantations, or other export activities, but this would lead to yet another spiral of deepening disarticulation and internal inequality.

As we have seen, in much of the dependency theory there was the assumption that external forces were all-powerful and simply swept away any lingering remnants of the old structures. As a number of critics pointed out, this is clearly too extreme, and even in the newer versions of modernization theory important interactions between the modern and traditional sectors were postulated. A number of the later dependency writers attempted to remedy this shortcoming, notably Fernando Cardoso (Cardoso and Faletto, 1979; Cardoso, 1982), who pointed to the complex configuration in various Latin American countries of competing or cooperating groups and classes, each influenced by external forces and each attempting to use these external elements to their own advantage, although no class or group is strong enough to control this environment.

Given that the major policy prescription of the dependency school was that links with the global economy should be minimized, or at least carefully controlled, the role of foreign aid for this group of theorists was extremely limited. Tamás Szentes (1971), one of the most strictly Marxist of the writers on dependency, argued that foreign aid and other forms of financial support available externally would serve only to bind its recipients even more tightly into the inherently exploitative global economic system, resulting in a complete loss of independence. The only way forward for underdeveloped countries was to fully use their internal resources, but given the weakness of national private capital only state accumulation could provide the large amount of investment needed. Foreign loans might also be used but only if channeled through the state to ensure that they were used in the national interest.

Similar points were made by Andre Gunder Frank (1969) in a chapter entitled "Aid or Exploitation." US "assistance" to Latin America has in fact had negative consequences, he suggests: any aid flows are more than offset by the outflow of profits. Aid and investment are deliberate vehicles for obtaining access to the riches of Latin America and for maintaining the present structure of the American economy, and in the process Latin America's economy remains underdeveloped and dependent. Importantly, Frank suggests in a not-entirely tongue-in-cheek concluding paragraph, a serious cause of Latin America's continued backwardness is that the United States continues to supply graduates from the region trained in economics and in the ideology that accompanies that discipline: these economists try to pretend that the existing exploitative relationships are really necessary and desirable!

BASIC NEEDS

For a short period during the 1970s and early 1980 attention turned to a rather different set of priorities, with a focus on what were defined as the basic needs of any society. While earlier approaches had been concerned particularly with economic aspects of development, and especially with the need to increase incomes in the developing world, supporters of this new paradigm argued that what was needed was a broader approach to the fundamental needs of the individual and the changes that would be needed to produce better lives, especially for the most disadvantaged groups in society, a number of writers advocating that special attention now needed to be given to women and children and their pressing needs (e.g., Streeten, 1979). For this brief period both bilateral aid and the support of World Bank shifted to the provision of better health and education services. Streeten, who at that time occupied a senior position within the World Bank, put forward a list of priority indicators for the whole basic needs approach (Hicks and Streeten, 1979) and the items given prominence there formed the core of the policy and aid initiatives. There was particular attention given to extending life expectancy, education, reducing infant mortality, the provision of safe drinking water, and the improvement in the supply of adequate and healthy food. This was another period of simple prescriptions for development, and hence some clear ways of targeting aid and assessing its effectiveness, but Streeten (1984) did raise some important unanswered questions about the entire approach, issues that are still highly relevant today. In particular, he asked, who is to determine what exactly constitutes basic needs in particular situations, and what kind of participation is needed in various societies? Similarly, is the whole approach about forms of income redistribution, and will this just require some palliative measures or a fundamental shift in the economic and political system? As a result, what policies will be required to deal with income inequalities? How is international support for such an approach most appropriately utilized?

I will return to all of these questions, still they are still startlingly relevant in the current debate about neoliberalism, and in particular the widespread concern with the origins and impacts of the enormous levels of inequality that have emerged it would appear as an inevitable component of neoliberalism itself. These issues also highlight what I would see as the essential relationships between improved development and the provision of security, in the broad sense of the term, to all sections of society, a concern that has also been expressed by Frances Stewart (2001), one of the pioneers of the basic needs approach.

THE RISE OF NEOLIBERALISM: GLOBALIZATION AND DEVELOPMENT THEORY

Since the 1980s, development thought and policy have been dominated by what has become known as the neoliberal thought, or what Toye (1991) has called the New Political Economy, a movement that gained much momentum from the fall of the Soviet Union, and the consequent discrediting of socialist alternatives to capitalism. A more self-confident West became willing to reassert many of the elements of the old modernization model. In the core countries of the developed world the rise of neoliberalism followed the election of Ronald Regan in the United States and Margeret Thatcher in Britain (Peck, 2010), but these ideological currents also flowed into the developing world (McKay, 2013).

Certainly, there are many elements that demonstrate a simple return to modernization, notably the often-unstated belief that there is one path to development that all nations can follow in a series of stages. The goals of development are also portrayed as unproblematic, involving a simple movement toward modernity that is portrayed as so successful in the West. All good comes from external sources, with outside norms and methods being essential to the breaking down of traditional barriers to growth. Many of the core mechanisms for growth are also similar to those cited in the earlier period. Savings rates are still a central element, supported by foreign investment. But the role of government is simply dismissed: politicians are uniformly portrayed as rent-seeking villains, willing only to look after their own narrow interests rather than the good of the entire society (Toye 1991). Thus, while markets may not be perfect, they are portrayed as infinitely preferable to governments controlled by a "kleptocracy." Government services, even including health and education, must be pared back in the interests of balancing the budget and creating an environment conducive to foreign investment, and where possible government-owned services and assets should be privatized in the interests of efficiency. Similarly, foreign exchange rates must be managed (i.e., devalued) to encourage export competitiveness. Many of these policy measures have been promulgated by international institutions, notably the IMF, to deal with the periodic crises that have plagued much of the underdeveloped world.

While there are certainly some elements of this old agenda based on neoclassical economics that have returned to the fore, there are also some important ways in which neoliberalism has departed from these older traditions. We should certainly note that the very term "neoliberalism" is not one that is generally used by its adherents, rather it is a label adopted by its critics. It must also be emphasized that while there does exist what Mirowski (2013) has called the "Neoliberal Thought Collective" its members are far from united on all questions of theory and policy, however, it is possible to identify some key areas of general agreement and to highlight some important ways in which neoliberalism differs from neoclassicalism. From the outset it must be recognized that for neoliberals the aim is not a return to the *laissez faire* of some earlier periods of free trade and capital movements: rather the ideal society must be actively and painstakingly constructed. To this end the role of an active state is central, but not the kind of interventionist government proposed by the adherents of industrial policy. The state needs to allow the market to exert its total control, and protect it from those seeking to impose undue regulations. In some situations, as we saw at the height of the GFC, it may even be essential for the government to save the neoliberal society from itself. But this raises the important issue of what the market is and the roles that it performs for neoliberals. Markets, as I have noted, have an almost mystical quality in this paradigm. They are the supreme vehicles for the delivery of all kinds of information, and for some true believers they exist in a realm that is beyond the capacity of mere mortals to understand. Markets should simply be constructed and allowed to fulfill their almost sacred destiny. Such tenets go well beyond the narrow economic focus of neoclassicism, of course, and bring in many aspects of politics, sociology, and other disciplines. One area in which this broad perspective is certainly seen is in the attitudes of neoliberal proponents to the basic ideas of individual freedom and democracy. While Friedrich Hayek, one of the founding fathers of neoliberalism, always stressed the imperative of avoiding tyranny and serfdom (see, e.g., Hayek, 1944, 1960), he had what can only be described as an ambivalent attitude toward democracy and individual thought and action. Rather, adherents to the faith need only to follow the teachings of the chosen few that have understood the real needs of the society, and pure democracy is certainly not what is needed in his ideal society. The focus for the individual should be on the creations of his or her own human capital, to take advantage of the myriad new opportunities created in this new society.

In the neoliberal era the focus for aid suggested by the IMF, the World Bank, and others – at least until recently, as we will see – has been the support of essential efforts to restructure all developing economies to align them more effectively with the needs of the global economy. The real hope for enhanced development, it is argued, is to become ever more tightly enmeshed in global trade and the emerging global production networks. This can be achieved through the realignment of government structures and priorities, a reduction in government spending through programs of austerity in order to balance budgets, and the privatization of most government agencies and functions. In some cases it may be necessary to recast the whole form of government in order to achieve an effective administrative and policy system. At the same time, human resources need to be upgraded to take advantages of the new opportunities offered by globalization, and improved infrastructure of all kinds is needed to reduce the costs of integration into global markets. All of this is summed up in the so-called "aid for trade" agenda (Razzaque and te Velde, 2013).

THE GLOBAL FINANCIAL CRISIS AND EMERGING CHALLENGES TO NEOLIBERALISM

As was noted earlier, the GFC and its numerous aftershocks that are continuing right down to the time of writing have given rise to much criticism of neoliberalism but the dominant paradigm still survives, at least for the present, in part because no clear alternative has yet been fully articulated. Most of the economics profession, as well as the ever-expanding finance industry, has tried to pretend that nothing serious has happened and that the world can return to business as usual, but some serious challenges have been mounted, and these continue.

However, the inherent superiority of market mechanisms for the allocation of resources and in the design of a whole range of policy instruments in all areas of development is now under serious question. It is not just that markets were patently incapable of dealing with the crisis of 2007 – and for many critics they were seen as being central to the problem – but some key theoretical constructs backing up long-held assumptions about the role and efficiency of markets have been shown to be shaky to say the least.

Related to this point, the neoliberal slogan that governments were part of the problem rather than the solution has also been challenged. With the widespread and catastrophic failure of markets, governments were the only line of defence against complete system failure, and were forced to pump billions of dollars into their economies. This has generated widespread taxpayer anger, and there have been many calls for much stronger regulation regimes. Just how far this political process goes depends upon how much longer the crisis continues – at the time of writing continued fears about Europe suggest that the instability still has a long way to go, with unpredictable consequences – but it is clear that the debate about the appropriate role of the state in the whole process of development has returned to centre stage (Tanzi, 2011). The intense examination of neoliberalism that has taken place in the aftermath of the GFC has shown that in fact the whole edifice of neoliberal thought and action depends on the existence of a powerful and active state, but one that is diametrically opposed to the aims and methods of the developmental state that has been so vital to the emergence of the Asian powerhouses. Thus, the debate is now not about whether state action is vital, but rather about what kind of state serving whose interests. The UNDP (2013) has made its position on this issue quite clear, arguing that progress in developing nations is ultimately dependent on the presence of a proactive and responsible developmental state with a long-term vision and the ability to design shared norms, values, rules, and institutions.

One other clear dimension of the developments leading directly to the global crisis was the "unhitching" of the financial sector from the "real" economy. Both Satyajit Das (2011) and Costas Lapavitsas (2013) have noted that once upon a time economies were about making useful things, but now we construct immense and artificial financial structures that give untold riches to a few but put at the risk the vast majority of the population. Virtually all aspects of the economy – and indeed the society more generally – have been "financialized" and brought within the realm of the market (OECD, 2015). Goods and services that were once thought of as unambiguous public goods – for example, water supplies – have been privatized in many countries. Similarly, many food staples now traded on world markets have attracted the interest of speculators, and speculation on wheat, rice, and other basic items has been seen by many as being a major contributor to the rapid increases in food prices in the last few years.

A number of authors have raised the wider question of the impact of the dominance of neoliberalism on the psychological health of individuals and on the texture of entire societies. Sandel (2012) has suggested that societies are significantly weakened in a moral and psychological sense because nonmarket norms have been crowded out by market values in almost every aspect of life. Even more provocatively, Paul Verhaeghe (2014) has argued that the market-driven world is one of atomization, loneliness, and unbounded selfishness, bringing out the worst in all of us.

Overall, it could be argued, the world is now much more unstable than it has been for some time, and this is creating a lack of security across many dimensions for many millions of people, but especially the most vulnerable. As part of the debate about the causes and consequences of the GFC it has been argued that the processes of financial sector growth and the increasing reach of the market have exacerbated degrees of inequality at all levels, and this inequality has been a major contributor to the rise of instability and crisis (Vandermoortle, 2009). The recent publication of a detailed study by the French economist Thomas Piketty (2014) has stirred enormous interest. He argues that current levels of inequality have not been seen since the latter part of the nineteenth century, the era of the unbridled "robber barons" in the United States and some parts of Europe. Wealth, he stresses, is not determined by income alone but more importantly by possession of a wide range of assets, including housing and land, many of them inherited. As Christine Lagarde, the head of the IMF, is fond of pointing out, the 85 richest people in the world now control as much wealth as the poorest half of the global population – that is 3.5 billion people!

This incredible level of polarization in the global economy has been made worse by the inability of most countries to create nearly enough well-paid jobs, so that the World Bank (2012) is arguing that jobs, and in particular jobs for vast numbers of unemployed young people, are now a key global priority. As the Bank stresses, jobs not only provide income but also largely define who people are, and contribute enormously to the maintenance of social and political stability. Similarly, the use of austerity measures to balance the budgets of many nations that had spent vast sums to ameliorate the impacts of the GFC by bailing out their banking systems has had an serious effect on the poorer segments of society while not achieving any of the benefits predicted by supporters of neoliberal policies (Blyth, 2013).

One important component in the growing skepticism about the neoliberal position especially as it relates to developing countries is the shift in the priorities of some key international institutions, notably the World Bank and the IMF. Changes in the position of the World Bank have been particularly interesting to observe, and recent appointments to senior positions, and in particular those of the President and the Chief Economist, seem to be at the center of this change in policy. One crucial area in which the Bank's new priorities have become manifest is in the emphasis on job creation already noted. Thus, the Bank argues, governments need to approach development policies through a lens of job creation. Certainly the task ahead is enormous. It is estimated that in the shadow of the GFC some 200 million people worldwide are unemployed, including 75 million under the age of 25. Increasingly these unemployed or underemployed people are congregating in the burgeoning cities of the developing world, where youth unemployment is of particular concern. A central role of government then should be to create the conditions conducive for the private sector to expand employment.

At a more general level, the GFC has forced everyone to think about the politics involved in financial and economic policy issues: the need to take what some regard as the old-fashioned field of political economy seriously may be one of the most important consequences of the crisis in terms of development theory and policy. In considering the new global political economy one key impact of these recent events has been the hastening of the transfer of global power from the West, and in particular the United States, to the rising powers of Asia, and notably China. It has always been clear that dominant paradigms can only be established and maintained with strong pressure from a major global power. The United States exerted the power necessary to establish and defend the neoliberal orthodoxy, but with the decline of Washington and the rise of Beijing things may be very different. China is of course actively promoting its interests and the strengths of its development model with a deliberate campaign to enhance its "soft power" through a well-financed "charm offensive" (Kurlantzick, 2007).

A key consequence of this renewed attraction of Asian approaches to development policy and planning is that the state has returned as a central issue of our age. The fact that China's economy is still under very direct control of the state, that a significant proportion of the economy is still state-owned, that the nature of China's links with the global economy are tightly constrained, and that the country was able to weather the GFC so well, has not gone un-noticed in the rest of the developing world (Subrahmanian, 2011). The need to strengthen state capacity and regulatory reach has emerged as one of the key lessons of the GFC: markets unaided simply cannot be relied on to deliver the benefits of development. This lesson is certainly being heeded in a wide range of countries where various kinds of "state capitalism" have been established. Aware of the economic power of capitalist systems but unwilling to trust the operations of uncontrolled markets, several countries are using carefully regulated markets to create wealth but are ensuring that the funds are used as the government sees most appropriate (Bremmer, 2010).

This re-evaluation of the role of the state also raises questions about the future of democracy. If the dominant model of capitalism is concerned more about profits than the creation of jobs, and as we have seen is now producing incredible levels of inequality at all levels of the economy, it may be that capitalism and democracy are not really compatible. As Wofgang Streek (2014a,b) has argued, we may be witnessing a conflict between capitalism and democracy, and if as he predicts capitalism will be the victor in this battle then the future may be extremely unstable. Halper (2010) fears that with the rise of China authoritarian forms of government will again become more attractive, but Dani Rodrik (2011) presents a rather different kind of argument about the future of democracy. He suggests that after the GFC we now realize that the simultaneous pursuit of democracy, self-determination, and economic globalization is not feasible. If nations need the ability to defend their own economies and citizens at times of financial crisis, and if the frequency and impacts of such crises are to be lessened, then it is the nature of globalization that must be redefined: we must return to the idea that international economic rules need to be subservient to domestic policy, not the other way round. A less ambitious globalization would be better for the vast majority.

CONCLUDING THOUGHTS: TOWARD A NEW DEVELOPMENT PARADIGM AND A NEW ROLE FOR AID

For the first time for several centuries developing Asia is replacing the North Atlantic region as the main driving force of the global economy, and the G8 and the other cosy clubs of the rich nations are challenged by newer groupings such as the BRICS (Brazil, Russia, India, China, South Africa). Will the old imperial relationship between the rich and powerful be re-established, albeit in a revised form, or are, for example, China's relationships with Africa and Latin America very different from British or French colonialism, and will China emerge as the champion of the developing world rather than just the latest superpower? Many African leaders believe that China is not just interested in economic exploitation – offering generous assistance with infrastructural, health, and educational development – and see China as offering a way out of the restrictive lending practices of the older international institutions such as the IMF (Ampiah and Naidu, 2008; Michel and Beuret, 2009). However, there is some evidence of popular resentment against Chinese practices in Africa, resulting in anti-Chinese riots in Madagascar and Zambia (Lee, 2014).

Perhaps the most fundamental question of all for development theory relates to the whole nature of the debate – if indeed the developing economies are now poised to become the main driving force of global growth while the West is entering a prolonged period of austerity and low growth. Nancy Birdsall (2011) has even asked whether the GFC might mark the end of "development" as an idea to be replaced by a more global agenda for cooperation. Certainly, if the developing world is to escape from what it sees as the tyranny of the neoliberal world order, and the dominance of the large multinational corporations and the escalations in inequality that go along with it, the revival of what for long was known as "Third World Solidarity" will be essential. Unless developing countries form a united front then each of them can be used in turn by international corporations to provide cheap labor and resources, in a cut-throat competition that in the long-run will harm all of them. Vijay Prashad (2012) has presented a detailed history of cooperation between developing nations, and argues that it is both essential and possible for some of the old momentum to be recaptured. Clearly, he suggests, neoliberalism has failed the developing world but under the leadership of China, India, and other members of the BRICS a completely new narrative for the Global South is possible.

Flowing from this vision of a new paradigm for development, and a key role for development theory as the focus for a sustained attack on neoliberalism, should be a new conception for what aid can and should try to achieve. Elsewhere I have argued that the neoliberal focus on what they call "good governance" and "rational economics" has produced a range of results that are neither good nor rational (McKay, 2014). The dominant mode of development policy formulation has benefited the few at the expense of the many and what we need to seek is a new paradigm that can support the greater good. We need to recognize that the world has changed and that some elements in the new global economic and political situation can be utilized for the common good, but some key elements of the earlier critiques from the dependency and basic needs approached need to be taken seriously and updated. A concern with issues of human security, one of the key initiatives in modern development thought, is surely well overdue.

This surely also needs to be the focus for a new aid policy. In part the need is for a practical concern with reducing inequalities and creating many more good jobs, but what is also required is a concern for goals that go far beyond "economic rationalism." At its best, aid policy can focus attention on joint concerns with creative co-operation in policy formation and project delivery, and the case studies contained in this book can hopefully be an important step in a vital and constructive dialog.

REFERENCES

Amin, S., 1976. Unequal Development. Monthly Review Press, London.

Amin, S., 1977. Imperialism and Unequal Development. Harvester, Hassocks.

Ampiah, K., Naidu, S., 2008. Crouching Tiger, Hidden Dragon? Africa and China. University of KwaZulu-Natal Press, Cape Town.

Birdsall, N., 2011. The global financial crisis: The beginning of the end of the "development" agenda. In: Birdsall, N., Fukuyama, F. (Eds.), New Ideas on Development After the Financial Crisis. Johns Hopkins University Press, Baltimore, MD, pp. 1–26.

Blyth, M., 2013. Austerity: The History of a Dangerous Idea. Oxford University Press, Oxford.

Bremmer, I., 2010. The End of the Free Market. Portfolio, New York, NY.

Cardoso, F., 1982. Dependency and development in Latin America. In: Alavi, H., Shanin, T. (Eds.), Introduction to the Sociology of Developing Countries. Monthly Review Press, New York, NY, pp. 112–127.

Cardoso, F., Faletto, E., 1979. Dependency and Development. University of California Press, Berkeley, CA.

Das, S., 2011. Extreme Money: The Masters of the Universe and the Cult of Risk. Penguin, London.

Frank, A.G., 1969. Latin America: Underdevelopment or Revolution. Monthly Review Press, New York, NY.

Furtado, C., 1964. Development and Underdevelopment. University of California Press, Berkeley, CA.

Halper, S., 2010. The Beijing Consensus: How China's Authoritarian Model Will Dominate the Twenty-First Century. Basic Books, New York, NY.

Hayek, F., 1944. The Road to Serfdom. University of Chicago Press, Chicago, IL.

Hayek, F., 1960. The Constitution of Liberty. University of Chicago Press, Chicago, IL.

Hicks, N., Streeten, P., 1979. Indicators of basic needs: The search for a basic needs yardstick. World Dev. 7, 567–580.

Higgins, B., 1968. Economic Development: Principles, Problems and Policies. Constable, London, (revised edition).

Hirschman, A., 1958. The Strategy of Economic Development. Yale University Press, Yale, CT.

Dabla-Norris, E., Kochhar, K., Suphaphiphat, N., Ricka, F., Tsounta, E., 2015. 'Causes and consequences of income inequality: A global perspective', IMF Staff Discussion Note SDN/15/13, International Monetary Fund, Washington, DC.

Kindleberger, C., 1958. Economic Development. McGraw-Hill, New York, NY.

Kurlantzick, J., 2007. Charm Offensive: How China's Soft Power is Transforming the World. Yale University Press, New Haven, CT.

Lapavitsas, C., 2013. Profiting Without Producing: How Finance Exploits us All. Verso, London.

Lee, C.K., 2014. The Spectre of Global China. New Left Rev. 89, 29–65.

McKay, J., 2012. Reassessing development theory. In: Kingsbury, D., McKay, J., Hunt, J., McGillivray, M., Clarke, M. (Eds.), International Development: Issues & Challenges. Second ed. Palgrave Macmillan, London, pp. 53–78.

McKay, J., 2013. After the Washington Consensus: Rethinking dominant paradigms and questioning "one size fits all" orthodoxies. In: Kingsbury, D. (Ed.), Critical Reflections on Development. Palgrave Macmillan, London, pp. 50–68.

McKay, J., 2014. Development: "good governance" or development for the greater good. In: Steger, M., Battersby, P., Siracusa, J. (Eds.), The Sage Handbook of Globalization. Sage, Los Angeles, CA, pp. 505–523.

Michel, S., Beuret, M., 2009. China Safari: On the Trail of Beijing's Expansion in Africa. Nation Books, London.

Mirowski, P., 2013. Never Let a Serious Crisis Go to Waste: How Neoliberalism Survived the Financial Meltdown. Verso, London.

Myrdal, G., 1957. Economic Theory and Underdeveloped Regions. Duckworth, London.

OECD, 2015. How to restore a healthy financial sector the supports long-lasting inclusive growth. Paris, OECD Economics Department Policy Note No. 27.

Parsons, T., 1937. The Structure of Social Action. Free Press, New York, NY.

Parsons, T., 1951. The Social System. Free Press, New York, NY.

Peck, J., 2010. Constructions of Neoliberal Reason. Oxford University Press, Oxford.

Piketty, T., 2014. Capital in the Twenty-First Century. The Belknap Press of Harvard University Press, Cambridge, MA.

Prashad, V., 2012. The Poorer Nations: A Possible History of the Global South. Verso, London.

Prebisch, R., 1950. The Economic Development of Latin America and its Principal Problems. United Nations, New York, NY.

Razzaque, M., te Velde, D.W. (Eds.), 2013. Assessing Aid for Trade: Effectiveness, Current Issues and Future Directions. Commonwealth Secretariat, London.

Robertson, R., Turner, B., 1991. Talcott Parsons: Theorist of Modernity. Sage, Thousand Oaks, CA.

Rodrik, D., 2011. The Globalization Paradox: Democracy and the Future of the World Economy. W.W. Norton, New York, NY.

Rostow, W.W., 1960. Stages of Economic Growth. Cambridge University Press, Cambridge, MA.

Sandel, M., 2012. What Money Can't Buy: The Moral Limits of Markets. Allen Lane, London.

Stewart, F., 2001. Horizontal inequalities as a source of conflict. In: Hampson, F., Malone, D. (Eds.), From Reaction to Prevention. Lynne Rienner, London.

Streek, W., 2014a. How will capitalism end? New Left Rev. 87, 35–64.

Streek, W., 2014b. Buying Time: The Delayed Crisis of Democratic Capitalism. Verso, London.

Streeten, P., 1979. Basic needs: Premises and promises. J. Policy Modelling 1, 136–146.

Streeten, P., 1984. Basic needs: Some unsettled questions. World Dev. 12, 973–978.

Subrahmanian, A., 2011. The crisis and the two globalisation fetishes. In: Birdsall, N., Fukuyama, F. (Eds.), New Ideas on Development After the Financial Crisis. Johns Hopkins University Press, Baltimore, MD, pp. 62–82.

Szentes, T., 1971. The Political Economy of Underdevelopment. Akadémiai Kiadó, Budapest.

Tanzi, V., 2011. Government Versus Markets: The Changing Economic Role of the State. Cambridge University Press, Cambridge, MA.

Toye, J., 1991. Is there a new political economy of development? In: Colclough, C., Manor, M. (Eds.), States or Markets? Neo-Liberalism and the Development Policy Debate. Oxford University Press, Oxford.

Vandermoortle, M., 2009. Within-Country Inequality, Global Imbalances and Financial Instability. ODI, London.

Verhaeghe, P., 2014. What About Me? The Struggle for Identity in a Market-Based Society. Scribe, Melbourne.

Wade, R., 2009. From global imbalances to global reorganisations. Camb. J. Econ. 33, 539–562.

World Bank, 2012. Jobs: World Development Report 2013. World Bank, Washington, DC.

United Nations Development Program, 2013. Human Development Report 2013: The Rise of the South – Human Progress in a Diverse World. UNDP, New York, NY.

AID FOR TRADE: A CRITICAL ANALYSIS

4

Viktor Jakupec

School of Education, Faculty of Arts and Education, Deakin University, Warrnambool, Australia

CHAPTER OUTLINE

INTRODUCTION

Improving human development outcomes, through trade liberalization, forms the basis for the development of Aid for Trade (AfT). Based on a recognition that many developing countries are not well positioned to directly benefit from trade liberalization, AfT was introduced into Official Development Assistance (ODA) in 2005 by the ministerial meeting of the World Trade Organisation (WTO) in Hong Kong (Hühne et al., 2014). Its core intention is to assist developing countries to participate in global trade. Since its inception, AfT has gained significant political importance. AfT now makes up around one third of ODA flows (OECD – WTO, 2013). However, this discourse begets one important question, namely how to define AFT? One answer is "Aid for Trade is hard to define and its nebulousness can allow it to be all things to all people" (Negin, 2014).

To elucidate, WTO (2015a) states "…[b]ecause trade is a broad and complex activity, AfT is broad and not easily defined" (p. 1). WTO (2015b) explains "Aid for Trade helps developing countries, and particularly least developed countries, trade" (p. 1). Not dissimilar the IMF "defines AfT as comprising: …aid that finances trade-related technical assistance, trade-related infrastructure, and aid to develop productive capacity" (Dorsey, 2007, p. 1). The above cited international organizations are well equipped to explain what AfT "does" or is supposed to "do" but are unable to define what it "is." Given the lack of clarity around AfT, it seems appropriate to start our discussion with "unpacking" some key issues.

UNPACKING "AID FOR TRADE" WITHIN A CONTEXT OF ODA

Originally AfT was envisaged as a new and supplementary funding stream to ODA and became a classification within the existing ODA scheme. It encompasses technical and financial assistance focusing on trade capacity in developing countries (Razzaque and te Velde, 2013). AfT is unashamedly a trade-focused construct, but for whose benefit is a question increasingly asked.

The existing and growing dominance of the AfT concept, claiming that it reduces poverty through economic growth via trade is not surprising, especially as there is an increased demand by donor governments for aid accountability and "value-for-money" (VfM). Both these issues support the notions of AfT and will be discussed below. However, AfT is also heavily critiqued by the economic "Right" arguing for "Trade not aid" *and* the "Left" that opposes the neoliberal ideology embedded in the AfT practices.

As noted in Chapter 1 there is increasing pressure to demonstrate accountability and value for money in aid disbursement. As OECD (2011) notes

> At a time when aid budgets are under pressure and scrutiny, there is a need to improve accountability. This is especially true in the case of aid for trade, which has become an increasingly important priority in development co-operation. (p. 11)

OECD (2011) argues further that in order to ascertain the value and achievements of aid there is a need for a thorough evaluation of an aid project or programme from its beginnings, citing *ex-ante* as well as *ex-post* "assessment." In the first instance there is a need to establish the intent of what is to be achieved and subsequently to determine what has been achieved, as well as drawing lessons about what worked and what did not. In other words, establishing a Theory of Change from which intended impacts (*ex-ante*) and establishing what the real intended or unintended impacts (*ex-post*) are.

However, the underlying confusion surrounding Impact Assessment (IA) (see Chapter 2) is equally true in the AfT literature. Impact Assessment in the AfT sector is highly problematic. The World Bank (cited in OECD, 2011) pointed out that, in comparison to other forms of aid, impact assessment for AfT depends markedly on obsolete methods, including a need for development of AfT impact assessment methodologies, methods, and tools. Cadot et al. (2014) strengthen this argument, noting in a review of evaluation of AfT initiatives that "there is substantial scope for adapting methods to the particular context of trade interventions" (p. 527). The EU claims that the vast array of indicators for AfT militates against a comprehensive and reliable method to determine the success or otherwise of AfT programs and projects (EU, 2013). Cadot et al. (2014) note that robust policy conclusions are highly problematic due to confounding factors. The problem encountered in the relevant AfT literature is that the IA represents broad generic foci, such as gender and social equity, good governance, environmental protection, financial sustainability rather than AfT specific criterion. This is not to say that these foci cannot be defined within AfT parameters, but are seldom delineated within a context of AfT. Furthermore, IA in terms of AfT is given inadequate financial and human resources and thus the results do not give an accurate in-depth picture of impact for either learning or accountability purposes. IA also faces incentive constraints as well as resource constraints. Incentives to conduct IAs are limited by agency factors (long-term results that may not be beneficial for the project). A cost factor is also significant with often relatively small-scale budgets of AfT projects against a relatively fixed cost for a feasible impact assessment (Cadot et al., 2014).

In other words, proponents of AfT would like the ODA community to believe that AfT is "good" and "effective" and at the same time claiming that because of the huge range of variables and indeterminable factors it is difficult, if not impossible to determine what impact (if any) the AfT project or programs may have. This brings to the fore the issue of accountability. Or to put it differently, how may it be possible to increase scrutiny of AfT programs and projects within an atmosphere of increased demand for improved accountability.

THE INCREASED QUEST FOR ACCOUNTABILITY

Aid funding became less motivated by philanthropic or social welfare concerns and more by economic self-interests of donors. Tax-payers, donors, and potentially beneficiaries are increasingly demanding assurances that they are receiving value for money. The quest for improving accountability is directly related to evaluation and assessment. As discussed in Chapter 2, the methodologies, methods, and tools for IA are contentious (Deutscher and Fyson, 2008). Although, IA in a context of trade-related support is not a new phenomenon, in the context of AfT it remains a complex undertaking. One of the major reasons is the existence of diverse conceptual political and economic factors relating to AfT that need to be overcome. However, if there is an absence of AfT conceptualization even the best IA methods and techniques will deliver poor results. In other words if an aid program or project is based on an AfT premise, the design and implementation of IA needs to be embedded in the AfT conceptualization and practice at macro as well as micro levels. Against these shortcomings it is usually difficult, if not impossible to determine how far AfT works, if at all.

AfT FROM THEORETICAL UNDERPINNINGS TO CONCEPTUALIZATION

AfT at the theoretical level is defined by principles of trade-based capacity and infrastructure building, supply side economics, and facilitation of short- and medium-term trade-based adjustments (Cali and te Velde 2008; Cali et al., 2011). Furthermore, the AfT theory reinforces the belief that developing *cum* aid-recipient countries shall be setting their own trade policy agenda. They also should be able to partake as equal partners in multilateral trading schemes, enabling them to negotiate and implement trade treaties and agreements, and to use international legal mechanisms to settle trade disputes. From such a perspective it is evident that AfT is a persuasive mechanism for sustainable economic growth and poverty reduction in developing countries.

Similarly, AfT reinforces the principled argument of trade-based poverty reduction. It enhances trade-based development, increased production, employment, income, profitability, and export capacity.

It reduces poverty and provides opportunities for greater regional and global economic integration, benefitting individuals, enterprises, and the nation. With reference to the national benefits, production increases have the tendency to encourage added investment in pro-poor social programs and projects. This in turn leads to economic empowerment of individuals and communities. (González, 2013; Fields, 2013).

Prior to exposing AfT to a critique let us look at its basic premise; that there is a level playing field between donor cum developed countries and recipient cum developing countries.

Although the general literature on AfT places it within the parameters of ODA, we should point out that AfT is also an integral component of Other Official Flows (OOF), which is defined by OECD (2009) as

> [consisting] of i) grants or loans from the government sector not specifically directed to development or welfare purposes (e.g., those given for commercial reasons); and ii) loans from the government sector which are for development and welfare, but which are not sufficiently concessional to qualify as ODA (p. 180).

Having made the distinction between ODA and OOF, we can now outline the underpinning principles of AfT in ODA from a conceptual perspective. ODA's AfT agenda is being driven by WTO and OECD. According to WTO (2015a) AfT has the aim of supporting developing countries to foster their trade ability and infrastructure with the purpose to profit from regional and global trade opportunities. However, the WTO goes further by stating that AfT is an integral part of ODA, for AfT projects and programs may attract grants and concessional loans, but within the limitations of trade-based activities. In the same context AfT as an ODA activity attracts funding for technical assistance, infrastructure building, industrial development, and adjustment assistance. However, it falls short of direct relevance for any social sector, such as education, health, gender equity and participation, or environmental issues. Having said that it could be argued that the aforesaid social equity issues may be subsumed implicitly in AfT activities.

A vexing question is – Why should an organization such as the WTO be involved in AfT at the ODA level. One could understand such involvement at the OOF level, but how can one justify the former? The issue is that the WTO cannot deliver aid, it cannot influence directly aid delivery. Yet it imposes itself on multi and bilateral aid agencies. Let us take a step back. WTO is a global trade organization, which has been established by developed countries under the "globalization" political and economic agenda. WTO emerged from the 8th Round of the General Agreement on Trades and Tariffs (GATT), the so-called Uruguay Round, and has been given the mandate to advance global economic and trade policy development (cf. Finger and Schuler, 2000; Scott, 1994), and in doing so to collaborate closely with the IMF, the WB, and other multilateral economic actors to ensure coordinated international trade policies. Within these parameters, the WTO claims, however curiously that AfT is an integral part of its mandate.

There are however two major problems facing AfT. Firstly, if one sees AfT from the WTO's point of view then there is a need to adhere to the principles of globalization, which in turn is grounded in neoliberalism. Secondly, globalization is an unfinished business and as such needs to "liberate" trade (i.e., advancement of free trade agreements). However, to achieve this much of protectionism still needs to be reduced. The WTO Doha round commenced in 2001 and had improvement of the trading prospects of developing countries as a fundamental objective. This round stalled primarily due to the inability of various OECD members to cede any trade advantage to lesser developed countries. Despite some progress in a Bali ministerial meeting in 2013 the WTO remains a system of "competitive bargaining among unequals ….. [and is therefore] unlikely ever to yield symmetrical outcomes" (Wilkinson et al., 2014, p. 1046). Interestingly, since the GFC globalization in terms of international trade and industrial production has slowed (cf. CPB Netherlands Bureau for Economic Policy Analysis, 2015; Constantinescu et al., 2015).

A CRITIQUE OF AfT

Much of this section (particularly the critique of the neoliberal agenda) builds on the substantial discourse in Chapter 3 on the continuing domination of the neoliberal paradigm. The purpose here is not to replicate but to summarize relevant aspects that contextualize and contribute to a critique of AfT. There is much literature that critiques aid and its effectiveness generally. There is a general consensus amongst donor and recipient countries that aid in its current format, despite the claims to the contrary (see Riddell, 2014; Sachs 2006, 2009, 2012), is not working (see Easterly 2006, 2008, 2014; Friedman, 1995). There is a growing discontent amongst donor and recipient governments, respectively with aid programs generally and AfT especially (Birkbeck, 2009). With reference to the latter, there is much evidence suggesting the need for substantial change to AfT. There is a necessity to expose AfT's theoretical and conceptual underpinnings to external critical examination. This critique can, to a certain extent, be found in the academic literature, but is lacking within the dominant AfT protagonist organizations such as the WTO and the IMF. In other words, AfT has been to a large extent protected by powerful institutional interest.

In this section of the chapter, AfT critique will be presented from two vantage points. On the one side of the spectrum are those opposing aid in its entirety and the "trade-not-aid" advocates and on the other are those opposing the neoliberal agenda of the existing ODA ideology. The former see ODA as a mechanism to strengthen the power of bureaucrats, officials, and governments at the expense of free market enterprise and competition. The latter see or critique ODA as an instrument of neoliberal ideologues and global identities such as the WTO, IMF, WB, and other similar organizations, whereby not the poor in the recipient developing countries, but the donor countries are the real beneficiaries. The polarized debate does little to advance theory and practice of AfT, and little exists to substantiate either argument. Most aid agencies show deficiency in facilitating independent sustainable impact assessments and make often excessive claims (based usually on single one-off evaluation) concerning impact(s) of their aid projects and programs. Findings from the Millennium Village project effectiveness as advocated by Jeffrey Sachs (cf. Clemens and Demombynes, 2011), or scientific statistical impact assessment of *"specific"* aid as proposed by William Easterly (2008, 2014) cannot be used as generalizable mechanisms for determining sustainable aid impact assessment.

If the above stands to reason and taking into consideration the two opposing camps, the critique of AfT raises two questions. One is: Why provide aid to developing countries at all? The other one is: How can AfT make foreign aid more effective? Both these questions turn AfT on its head. Those ascribing to the "why" question will argue that trade not aid will bring about economic growth in developing countries. Those asking the "how" question, refer to effectiveness based on a combination of political, social, and economic perspectives rendering the purely economic AfT paradigm impotent (Rogerson, 2005; Kingsbury et al., 2004). The effectiveness position is crass opposition to the AfT efficiency argument. We shall refer to the former as a "aid-not-trade" critique and the latter as "critique of the neoliberal ODA agenda" to be discussed below.

A general critique of AfT is its unproblematic nature, namely that by providing developing nations access to trade with developed countries, there will be economic growth and thus poverty alleviation (cf. OECD – WTO, 2013). However, the critics suggest that AfT is characterized by conditionality, which overtly or covertly favors the donors (Hühne et al., 2014). Donor countries are accused of exporting or imposing their cultural, social, political and economic, and commercial values and ideals on recipient countries. In doing so, the needs and desires of the developing recipient countries are set aside.

Others have critiqued AfT on the basis of its distributive effects. That is, trade liberalization not necessarily fosters a pro-poor agenda (Meschi and Vivarelli, 2009). Evidence of the impact of trade liberalization on poverty reduction in recipient countries is problematic, and indicates that results are uneven at best (Winters and Martuscelli, 2014). Even in countries where trade liberalization has been implemented there remain distributive matters, such as equitable trade, to be considered. The crux of the problem with AfT is the need to safeguard additional, foreseeable, and devoted resources, which effectively address the existing and potential supply-side constraints within the developing economy. In other words, there is a need to ensure the capacity to produce goods and services competitively and the ability to export these at a reasonable competitive cost, without conventional assistance and without trade barriers and tariffs.

Subsequently, the paramount aim of AfT, namely to reduce poverty in developing ODA recipient countries has to a large extent not been achieved. For this reason alone there is a compelling argument to be made for balancing poverty reduction and trade liberalization.

TRADE NOT AID

Trade-not-Aid notions and ideologies emerged prominently in 1968 as the theme for the Second United Nations Conference on Trade And Development (Van Bilzen, 2015). The Trade-not-Aid approach emphasized the mercantile nexus between developed and developing countries. Its proponents argue for the former countries to forego the idea of channeling all profits back to their own economy, but to allow a however small part of the profit to remain or be channeled back to the developing countries, as a development aid. However, over the last few decades the argument has shifted, if not advanced.

Proponents of trade-not-aid ideologies have often rallied in favor of abolishing protectionist trade policies. On this point, at least there are synergies between trade-not-aid and AfT ideologies. However, the arguments are somewhat different. Trade-not-aid proponents argue that protectionism in donor countries is for developing countries much more costly in comparison to foreign aid that the latter may receive. Perhaps, a more contentious trade-not-aid argument is that trade may well advance the efficiency and effectiveness of a developing country's economy. In contrast, so the argument goes, aid may create tenacious incentives such as rent seeking and lead to corruption (Balls, 2015).

The problem with this approach is that it relies on an "either-or" logic. There is however little evidence, if any, to show that increased trade would remove the need for aid, or to put it differently the argument in favor for increased trade between developed and developing economies, would bracket the aid agenda. If one takes the distributional trade impact into consideration, it may be shown that it differs substantially from the distributional impact of aid. Unless it can be shown that those who are poorest in a socio-economic strata of a developing country are likely to be the foremost beneficiaries from trade, the "either trade -or aid" argument lacks nuance.

However, the proponents of trade-not-aid argue for an orthodox neoliberal position akin to a laissez-faire-liberalism, namely, if there are barrier-free trade mechanisms in place between the wealthy developed and poor developing nations, the latter would gain economic benefits due to export income. Thus they would have lesser or no need for development aid to finance their economic and social development. Free multilateral trade, so the argument goes, would enhance living standards especially in developing countries. This is due to the ability of developing countries to export their goods and services to wealthy developed countries and trading blocks. From this perspective the "trade-not-aid" theorem is a poverty reduction paradigm, only if the theory of "trickle down" works. Given the increased complexity of aid chains, and aid investment in and through the private sector, assumptions around poverty impact are entirely at odds with a VfM and accountability agenda. This may however, stand to reason if the underlying proposition of the demand for goods and services, which the developing countries are able to export, exists and is sustainable. In an ideal situation this requires the creation of a viable labor force and competitive export markets to increase economic development, as well as removal of government subsidies in developed countries.

Unfortunately, ideal situations do not readily exist. Despite numerous free trade agreements a significant number of trading blocks such as the EU, and wealthy developed nations maintain tariffs on imports from poor developed countries. This issue has stalled the Doha development round since 2001, and the lack of agreement, on protection of agriculture as a vital sector politically and economically to both developed and developing countries, remains a significant global stumbling block to the WTO free trade agenda. Thus the question of how developing countries can mobilize sufficient domestic resources or appropriate investments to produce goods for exports remains to a large extent unanswered.

CRITIQUE OF THE NEOLIBERAL ODA AGENDA

Proponents of the neoliberal ideology are as any other ideologues utopian. As far as the ODA agenda is concerned there is a romantic belief of a "beautiful" new free market world where all nations, be it developed industrial or developing and less industrialized nations are embracing the same cultural, social, political, and economic values. The underpinning postulate is that all nations embrace the cult of economic competitiveness, brought about by the free market enterprise. More to the point, in terms of ODA neoliberals asserted that (i) the government cum state is in principle is unable and incompetent to solve the problems encountered in developing countries and (ii) market forces are the most efficient institutions and if left to their own devices lead to wealth creation. However, conditions under which an unbridled free market produces such wealth generation were not articulated. Market failures are only mentioned in passing.

Issues raised by the critics of the neoliberal aid agenda focus on the premise that free trade and neo liberal ideologies are socially, culturally, and economically unsustainable. Thus the perception of neoliberal economic development as a foundation for poverty alleviation often shifted from orthodox neoliberalism (Hayek, 1973; Friedman, 1995) to reformist neoliberalism (Orenstein, 2013; Lane, 2006) or a return to ordoliberalism (Bonefeld, 2012; Dullien and Guérot, 2012) making a case for increased reforms allowing for a shift away from the predominance of private enterprise in favor of a government influence. This, so the argument goes may offer social protection of the poor in terms of poverty in developing aid recipient countries – protection that private enterprise is ill equipped to offer.

To conclude, critics of the neoliberal agenda point to the flawed and unsubstantiated argument that a free-market economy is inevitably better than other forms of economy when it comes to economic developments in aid-recipient countries as far as poverty alleviation is concerned. The argument that in neoliberal economies capital, goods and services, and human resources can be more efficiently moved and distributed than government agencies can, has thus far not been proven as being correct as a contributor to poverty alleviation in developing countries. The whole premise rests on the notion of competition. But, as noted throughout, there is no level playing field globally when it comes to global competition in trade. As UNDP (2013) noted that there is considerable evidence that shows growths in economic development inequality over the last 20 years. These were primarily due to financialization (Jakupec and Kelly, 2015), trade, and globalization practices that debilitated the bargaining arrangement between developed and developing countries. Thus there is a compelling argument to be made for increased regulation of trade and financialization, and not less.

TOWARD A PARADIGM SHIFT IN AfT

Based on the above critique, there is, within the neoliberal economic agenda governing AfT, a prima facie case for a paradigm shift to be made. Orthodox neoliberal AfT ideologies based on low level of government interventions and deregulation of markets, can be reshaped through acceptance or rejection of certain ODA policies and procedures. Perhaps the question is not so much about when, but how a paradigm shift may occur. With reference to the former, we may invoke Thomas Kuhn (1962) and his work relating to paradigm shift in scientific disciplines. He argues that significant changes do not come about measured and persistent analysis, but rather swiftly when a number of practitioners and academics recognize that established methods are not unraveling the problems confronting the discipline.

As shown above the critique of contemporary development aid paradigms is its adherence to the limited and narrow economic concepts and an ideology that, at the exclusion of alternatives, relies extensively on neoliberalism. In addition, the ODA practices, procedures, and ideals are predominantly conceptualized, defined, determined, and implemented by donors. Inevitably this leads to a self-perpetuating vicious circle and a failure to bring about changes by which the recipient countries have their interest considered.

The failure of many existing multilateral aid agencies with their neoliberal AfT agenda is leading to potential paradigm shifts with the aim to favor developing countries. The emergence of the China-led Asian Infrastructure Investment Bank (AIIB) and the Russia-led BRICS (Brazil, Russia, India, China, and South Africa) Bank, are the potential signs of ideological paradigm shifts. AIIB is being established against the will of the USA who is the traditional stalwart of neoliberalism in the development arena. Yet despite all the attempts by the USA, to dissuade allies from joining the AIIB, some 35 countries applied to become founding members. How far the establishment of the AIIB as a potential competitor to the WB and IMF will erode the neoliberal ideological dominance of the USA-led MDBs is to be seen. However, speculatively, the prospect that China will exchange its "socially oriented market economy" for a neoliberal economy with minimal state intervention is highly unlikely (Pennay, 2015; Keqiang, 2014). South–South cooperation and trade is increasing – reaching 25% of the world trade in 2013, with Asian countries key areas of growth – and Africa not faring so well (UNCTAD, 2013).

Given new donors, new institutions, and new partnerships in the development arena it remains to be seen what the impact will be on the old order. If nothing else, AIIB will force the major MDBs to pursue a more level playing field. In order to achieve this within the AfT arena a paradigm shift from orthodox neoliberal AfT with its cult of economic efficiency to a value laden AfT approach would be required.

PARADIGM SHIFT: AfT AS A SUBSET OF VfM

For the purpose of this discussion VfM is defined as "…the best use of resources to deliver the desired impact" (Independent Commission for Aid Impact, 2011, p. 1). But the question of impact is the crux. From a purely AfT perspective, impact is measured in trade terms like balance of payment, counter-trade, quotas, export performance measure, export competition, trade-balancing measures, to name a few. The missing points are impacts measured on the basis of "…transformational, positive and lasting impact on the lives of the intended beneficiaries" (Independent Commission for Aid Impact, 2011, p. 1). The afore-said indicators, may positively affect the economy of an aid recipient country and the economic elite, but do not necessarily benefit the poor.

If this stands to reason and taking into consideration the economy and economic conditions in the post-GFC era a new picture emerges. Firstly, since the GFC many donor countries are faced with formidable debt and fiscal difficulties there is a justifiable accent being placed on VfM and on maximizing the impact of AfT and other ODA spending. Secondly, traditional donor nations such as EU are experiencing demographic changes, such as an aging population, which impact on their productivity and need to change their economic policies. Thirdly, countries previously considered to fall under the developing country definition, such as Brazil, India, China, and South Africa, have advanced their economies and have themselves become AfT providers. These and other factors contribute to paradigm shifts in terms of trade generally, which is starting to impact on AfT and VfM. This contributes to the argument for paradigm shift. Accountability and a push for VfM have strengthened the requirements for aid agencies to demonstrate AfT (and other interventions) are effective.

Many European governments and indeed EU itself are trying to link AfT and VfM. It is however the dominance of the VfM agenda that now drives ODA and thus AfT, being an integral component of ODA. There is a swing toward inclusive economic growth, which moves away from the traditional AfT structures, which rarely benefit the poorest in any country. There is a tendency among donor countries to establish and enhance an environment in which entrepreneurial interests may be included in AfT. But if the entrepreneurial interests are from a private enterprise, then the question surely must emerge if this inclusion provides VfM for the private sector. Promoting a stronger agenda for private sector engagement includes a number of non-AfT activities such as support for recipient countries counterparts in negotiating development aid as an equal partner or establishing HRD infrastructures through education and training, and other social agendas.

Thus, there is recognition amongst ODA donor agencies for a paradigm shift from a focus on "hard infrastructure" to an attention being given to "soft infrastructure" (see World Bank, 2015), or from the aforesaid orthodox neoliberalism to ordoliberalism. In other words, the argument has shifted toward a potential necessity to assessing VfM's overall benefit (social, economic, political, etc.). If this stands to reason AfT needs to be balanced within the overall VfM social, political, and economic costs and private investment framework (Commonwealth of Australia, 2014). In essence, from an IA point of view this requires putting qualitative values on *ex-ante* and *ex-post* impact and sustainability.

However, AfT, as a vehicle for economic growth in terms of VfM, remains an elusive concept. There are some signs of change. The WTO-based AfT agenda couched in orthodox neoliberalism is changing. In the new highly promising "fighting poverty" rhetoric the focus is on the proposition or conditionality of self-determination of the recipient government and its civil society. This means that recipient governments are required to develop their own strategies for the fight against poverty, driven by principles of aid effectiveness. Notions such as "ownership" and "participation" became the guiding principles and thus there was arguably less conditional and more self-determining (see Chapter 1).

This shifts the focus of AfT inadvertently toward the institutional importance because given the free-market ideology, private enterprise and not governments have the responsibility for preparation and implementation of development strategies for economic growth and thus poverty alleviation. Thus it is not surprising that a paradigm shift had to take place. Namely, the assertion that economic development is in essence a technical problem that can be overcome with trade liberation and financial means shifted toward the recognition that the AfT strategies need to consider a recipient country's social and political organizational structures and civil society requirements, so as to enable developing countries to advance their economic growth and poverty alleviation and yet maintain if not advance VfM through social and political "ownership" and "participation" in recipient countries (Bassnet and Engel, 2013; House of Commons International Development Committee, 2012; Niebel, 2011; OECD, 2008).

The notions of social and political "ownership" and "participation" in recipient countries, is in stark contrast to the concept of globalization as it is advocated by the WTO and to a lesser extent by other MDOs. In any case, there is an unholy alliance between neoliberalism and globalization. To elucidate, at the end of the 1980s, neoliberalism and globalization, as its ideological derivative, became the validating orthodox neoliberal constructs, as instituted in Fukuyama's (1992) self-decreed "end of history." However, history has proven Fukuyama's thesis drastically inadequate. The neoliberal argument against the economic role of national governments in a globalized world in favor of orthodox neoliberal free market enterprise as advocated by Hayek (1973) and Friedman (1995) was seen as problematic, if not dubious (see Stieglitz, 1998). However it would be wrong to portray the pre-GFC situation as purely in Hayek's or Friedman's terms (see Jones, 2012). Others, such as Claassen (1999) maintain that globalization has successfully coexisted with international markets and thus there is no valid a priori argument to be made that globalization automatically must bring about the lessening of nation state governments' role in economic or social politics or indeed polity. History has demonstrated once again that there is a possibility for a new foundation for globalization outside the orthodox neoliberal economic paradigms.

From this point of view globalization may well exist within a context of "social contract" rather than "trade contracts." That is, trade contracts based globalization agenda driven by a speculative profit-generating agenda needs to be changed so as to include a public-movement with an aim to provide socio-economic services as to advance social progress and thereby eliminate the existing historical, geo-political regional, and structural economic inequalities between donors and recipient countries. Thus there is a need to negotiate a transition from a purely "trade contracts"-based AfT to a "social contract"-based AfT with an emphasis on VfM, not only in crude profit terms but more so in socioeconomic terms. As far as IA within a context of AfT as a subset of the concept of VfM is concerned, there is a need to address specific approaches and advance for its implementation within a national as well as global context.

AROUND AND AROUND; BACK TO ASSESSING IMPACT AND AID FOR TRADE

As noted in the Introduction, it is extremely problematic to demonstrate the impact of AfT initiatives, yet the ideological framework, driven by powerful vested interests, appears unstoppable. It is useful to repeat a few cautionary notes here. Firstly, from an econometric point of view it is problematic to establish the counterfactual, namely which would have been the impact if given AfT projects or programs would not have been implemented? Secondly, there are no universal IA methods or techniques for AfT. Thirdly, different aid agencies use different delineations and have diverse aims and objectives in relation to AfT, which may vary from project to project and program to program. Fourthly, donors have different IA resources to be used for AfT, which may differ from time to time. Fifth, many AfT projects and programs lack well-defined baseline data against which IA can be undertaken.

Let us take a step back by pointing out again that AfT is not a new phenomenon. It is also noteworthy that evaluations of ODA projects and programs have been around in one or another form since the beginning of ODA in the late 1940s. However these evaluations and subsequently IA mechanisms did not necessarily focus on AfT activities. There are a number of possible reasons; one is that AfT had until recently not been explicitly articulated as an aid objective. It emerged as we have seen through the makings of the WTO. Assessing the impact of free market economics has hardly been a policy priority in much of the OECD. Another potential reason is that the complexity of methodologies, methods, and techniques required for AfT evaluation and assessment within a context of ODA have not been adequately developed.

With the growth of political importance of AfT and its enlargement of interest or encompassment of social issues such as gender and social equity, education and training, governance, etc., the criteria for establishing and formulating IA determinants grew proportionally. From a critical point of view this creates a cascade model of IA indicators with an equally long list of conditions attributed to loan disbursement. This enables IA to be conducted in stages on bases of rates of implementation. The danger is that IA becomes either subsumed by, or an exercise in monitoring and evaluation (M&E) with a focus merely on outputs, rather than fulfilling the critical function of assessing impact. The other danger is that as the list of indicators becomes longer and the scope more complex, the IA activity and execution becomes more demanding. Without adequate funding, IA for AfT projects and programs may be even further undermined. As noted the resources and incentives for IA in AfT are problematic at best.

These and other reasons are sufficient to suggest that there are compelling arguments for introduction of more concise IA procedures for AfT, procedures that focus on the scope of trade as a significant paradigm of ODA. If this stands to reason, then it could be argued that there is a need for developing new knowledge about and understanding of IA interventions for ODA focusing on AfT. This should apply to both, *ex-ante* and *ex-post* IA. However, it appears that there is not much being done in relation to the former and the main focus is on the latter. Main IA literature and AfT activities are preoccupied with the question if the expectations of AfT programs and projects have been met and that the expected impacts have been achieved. This sounds simple enough, would it not be for the fact that it is the *ex-ante* IA that provides or should provide base data, indicators, methodologies, methods and techniques, target audiences, etc. which are the foundations for *ex-ante* IA. Higgins and Prowse (2010) note the need for an assessment and mitigation of risks, as well as a clear focus on impacts for inclusive growth and poverty reduction.

From this vantage point, it seems reasonable to argue for a more comprehensive and focused IA mechanism that addresses the specifics of ODA within a context of AfT – a mechanism that provides an appropriate evaluative regime for policy makers, project and/or program management practitioners, and stakeholders from inception through implementation to completion and beyond. This may include independent, participatory, joint, and other forms of IA for AfT ODA, based on a clear Theory of Change, and conceptually and theoretically critically located with trade, aid, and development discourse.

CONCLUSION

AfT initiatives are now firmly entrenched in foreign-aid funding activities, with little clear understanding of either what AfT is, and what the impacts of AfT interventions are. This discussion has underscored the necessity to bring about changes to the existing narrow perception of the AfT approach as a mode to improve the results of ODA in developing countries. Thus far these improvements have been shown to be mostly intractable. The discussion here was intended to bring to the fore new understandings of ODA, especially to the dynamics of AfT as one of the many forms of potential reform agendas for ODA. Here, it could be said that a more detailed and politicized, if not a politico-social, approach to AfT is required. Within a context of AfT-based ODA, this approach should lead to informed political decision-making about and understandings of inequalities between donor and recipient countries and the desired and/or unintended impact of the aid program or project.

As we have seen there are significant contradictory discourses about trade as a tool for aid provisions. There is the "trade-not aid" movement as an opposing paradigm to the AfT movement, which in turn is critiqued by the opponents of the AfT neoliberal agenda. Thus it is not surprising that there are ongoing discourses between donors, recipient governments, and other stakeholders. Yet to a large degree these discourses continue to be polarized, unexamined by practitioners, academics, policy makers, and aid agencies. The problem is that the dominant neoliberal ideologies that underpin AfT and trade-not-aid paradigms remain unopposed and devoid of a critical analysis, and a global quest for the "right answer" to "trade" within ODA continues.

The demand for IA results of foreign aid, be it AfT within a context of VfM or any other paradigm is of paramount importance. To provide such results there is a need to develop and implement complex and innovative approaches supported by relevant IA instruments at *ex-ante* and *ex-post* macro, meso and micro levels. At the policy level there is a need to develop a well-founded understanding of international relations between donor and recipient countries. In short, unless demonstrable and sustainable impact assessment results become evident the taxpayers in donor countries will not, nor should not support the AfT agenda. Until such times that there is a strong grass-root support for AfT and in donor countries AfT will become increasingly volatile and complex.

Perhaps to untangle IA of AfT, it may be appropriate to develop a two-level methodology: (i) a macro-level IA, to assess the general impact of AfT on the donor and recipient countries' trade capacity; and (ii) a micro-level IA to assess the AfT impact at the project level. The former IA may include indicators such as sector-base policies, good governance, regulatory parameters, supply-side constraints, market access and tariff barriers, preferential trade arrangements and other international market access provisions, national and international economic tendencies, to name but a few. As far as the latter is concerned a mixed-mode IA method may well be useful, whereby the indicators must be based on the project-specific Theory of Change.

In conclusion, it may be said that AfT is here to stay, but under which conditions is difficult to decide. Whether it will play an important or dominant role with its neoliberal economic agenda remains to be seen. There is an option for change, embracing diverse socio-economic and socio-political rationales for a trade-aid nexus. As it stands AfT will remain open to criticism from the economic right and the economic left. Given the significant ODA invested in the name of AfT, the exceptionally limited current understanding of the impact of this approach runs against increasing drives for value for money, accountability, and effectiveness.

REFERENCES

Balls, A., 2015. Corrupt governments receive no less foreign aid, National Bureau of Economic Research. Available April 10, 2015 from: <http://www.nber.org/digest/nov99/w7108.html.>.

Bassnet, Y., Engel, J., 2013. Aid for trade in practice: Addressing political economy barriers to improve development outcomes. In: te Velde, D., Razzaque, M. (Eds.), Assessing Aid for Trade: Effectiveness, Current Issues and Future Directions. Commonwealth Secretariat, London, pp. 128–150.

Birkbeck, C.D., 2009. Reinvigorating debate on WTO reform: The contours of a functional and normative approach to analysing the WTO system. In: Steger, D.P. (Ed.), Redesigning the World Trade Organisation for the Twenty-first Century. Centre for International Governance Innovation, Ottawa, pp. 18–42.

Bonefeld, W., 2012. Freedom and the strong state: On German ordoliberalism. New Political Econ. 17 (3), 1–24.

Cadot, O., Fernandes, A., Gourdon, J., Mattoo, A., de Melo, J., 2014. Evaluating aid for trade: A survey of recent studies. World Econ. 37 (4), 516–529.

Cali, M., te Velde, D.W., 2008. The effectiveness of aid for trade: Some empirical evidence. Commonwealth Trade Hot Spots Issue 50, Commonwealth Secretariat, London.

Cali, M., Razzaque, M., te Velde D.W., 2011. Does Aid for Trade work for Small Vulnerable Economies? In Trade Negotiations, Insights, Vol. 10, No. 2. Available April 10, 2015 from: <http://www.ictsd.org/bridges-news/trade-negotiations-insights/news/does-aid-for-trade-work-for-small-vulnerable-economies>.

Claassen, C., 1999. The state, globalisation and education. In: Lemmer, E. (Ed.), Contemporary Education: Global Issues and Trends. Heinemann, Sandton.

Clemens, M.A., Demombynes, G., 2011. When does rigorous impact evaluation make a difference? The case of the Millennium Villages. J. Dev. Effect. 3 (3), 305–339.

Commonwealth of Australia, (DFAT), 2014. Australian aid: Promoting prosperity, reducing poverty, enhancing stability. Commonwealth of Australia, Canberra.

Constantinescu, C., Mattoo, A., Ruta, M., 2015. The Global Trade Slowdown: Cyclical or Structural? IMF Working Paper. IMF Strategy, Policy and Review Department, Washington, DC.

CPB Netherlands Bureau for Economic Policy Analysis, 2015. CPB Memo: CPB World Trade Monitor December 2014. CPB NBEPA, Den Haag.

Deutscher, E., Fyson, S., 2008. Improving the effectiveness of aid. Fin. Dev.-IMF 45 (3), 15–19.

Dorsey, T., 2007. What is Aid for Trade? IMF Policy Development and Review Department, Washington, DC, Available March 26, 2015 from: <https://www.imf.org/external/pubs/ft/survey/so/2007/POL0523A.htm>.

Dullien, S., Guérot, U., 2012. The long shadow of ordoliberalism: Germany's approach to the Euro crisis. In: Policy Brief. European Council on Foreign Relations, London, pp. 1–11.

Easterly, W., 2006. The White Man's Burden: Why the West's Efforts to Aid the Rest Have Done So Much Ill and So Little Good. Oxford University Press, Oxford.

Easterly, W. (Ed.), 2008. Reinventing Foreign Aid. MIT Press, Cambridge, MA.

Easterly, W., 2014. The Tyranny of Experts: Economists, Dictators, and the Forgotten Rights of the Poor. Basic Books, New York, NY.

EU, 2013. Aid for Trade Report 2013. Brussels, EU.

Fields, D., 2013. A band-aid solution to economic development: The false promise of 'fair trade'. In: The Hampton Institute, December 12, 2013. Available April 10, April 2015 from: <http://www.hamptoninstitute.org/false-promise-of-fair-trade.html#.VSd6AqYxaOU>.

Finger, J.M., Schuler, P., 2000. Implementation of Uruguay round commitments: The development challenge. The World Economy 24 (4), 511–525.

Friedman, M., 1995. Foreign Economic Aid: Means and Objectives. Stanford University Press, Stanford, CA.

Fukuyama, Y., 1992. The End of History and the Last Man. Penguin, London.

González, A., 2013. Why economic empowerment is crucial to climbing the development ladder. Available April 10, 2015 from: <https://www.devex.com/news/why-economic-empowerment-is-crucial-to-climbing-the-development-ladder-82208>.

Hayek, F.A., 1973. Economic freedom and representative government. The Institute of Economic Affaires, London.

Higgins, K., Prowse, S., 2010. trade, growth and poverty: Making aid for trade work for inclusive growth and poverty reduction. Overseas Development Institute, London. Working Paper 313.

House of Commons International Development Committee, 2012. EU Development Assistance – Sixteenth Report of Session 2010-12. House of Commons, London.

Hühne, P., Meyer, B., Nunnenkamp, P., 2014. Who benefits from aid for trade? Comparing the effects on recipient versus donor exports. J. Dev. Studies 50 (9), 1275–1288.

Independent Commission for Aid Impact, 2011. ICAI's approach to effectiveness and value for money. Available April 9, 2015 from: <http://icai.independent.gov.uk/wp-content/uploads/2010/11/ICAIs-Approach-to-Effectiveness-and-VFM.pdf.>.

Jakupec, V., Kelly, M., 2015. Financialisation of Official Development Assistance. Int. J. Econ. Commerce Management Vol. III (2), 1–18, Feb 2015.

Jones, D.S., 2012. Masters of the Universe: Hayek, Friedman and the birth of neoliberal politics. Princeton University Press, Princeton, NJ.

Kingsbury, D., Remenyi, J., Mc Kay, J., Hunt, J., 2004. Key Issues in Development. Palgrave Macmillan, New York, NY.

Kuhn, T.S., 1962. The Structure of Scientific Revolutions. University of Chicago Press, Chicago.

Lane, J.F., 2006. Bourdieu's Politics: Problems and Possibilities. Routledge, Milton Park.

Keqiang, L. 2014. On deepening economic reform. Qiushi, (4), 5–27.

Meschi, E., Vivarelli, M., 2009. Trade and income inequality in developing countries. World Dev. 37 (2), 287–302.

Negin, J., 2014. Understanding Aid for Trade part one: A Dummy's Guide. Development Policy Centre. Australian National University, Canberra.

Niebel, D., 2011. Minds for Change – Enhancing Opportunities. Federal Minister for Economic Cooperation and Development, Bonn.

OECD, 2008. Public-Private Partnerships: In Pursuit of Risk Sharing and Value for Money. OECD, Paris.

OECD, 2011. Strengthening Accountability in Aid for Trade, The Development Dimension. OECD Publishing, Paris.

OECD, 2009. Better Aid – Managing Aid: Practices of DAC Member Countries. OECD, Paris.

Orenstein, M.A., 2013. Reassessing the neo-liberal development model in Central and Eastern Europe. In: Schmidt, V.A., Thatcher, M. (Eds.), Resilient Liberalism in Europe's Political Economy. Cambridge University Press, Cambridge, MA, pp. 374–400.

Pennay. P., 2015. China says Western rules may not be best for AIIB. In: China Spectator. Available April 9, 2015 from: <http://www.businessspectator.com.au/news/2015/3/23/china/china-says-western-rules-may-not-be-best-aiib.>.

Razzaque, M., te Velde, D., 2013. Aid for trade: Effectiveness, current issues and future directions – an overview. In: te Velde, D., Razzaque, M. (Eds.), Assessing Aid for Trade: Effectiveness, Current Issues and Future Directions. Commonwealth Secretariat, London, pp. 1–12.

Riddell, R.C., 2014. Does foreign aid really work? Keynote address to the Australasian Aid and International Development Workshop, Canberra13th February 2014. Available March 22, 2015 from: <http://devpolicy.org/2014-Australasian-Aid-and-International-Development-Policy-Workshop/Roger-Riddell-Keynote-Address.pdf>.

Rogerson, A., 2005. Aid harmonisation and alignment: bridging the gaps between reality and the Paris Reform Agenda. Dev. Policy Rev. 23 (5), 531–552.

Sachs, J.D., 2006. The End of Poverty: Economic Possibilities for Our Time. Penguin Press, New York, NY.

Sachs, J.D., 2009. Common Wealth: Economics for a Crowded Planet. Penguin Press, New York, NY.

Sachs, J.D., 2012. The Price of Civilization: Reawakening American Virtue and Prosperity. Random House, New York, NY.

Scott, J., 1994. The Uruguay Round: An Assessment. Institute for International Economics, Washington, DC.

Stieglitz, J.E., 1998. Towards a New Paradigm for Development Strategies, Policies and Processes, Prebisch Lecture. UNSTAD, Genf.

UNCTAD, 2013. UNCTAD Handbook Of Statistics, 2013, United National Conference on Trade and Development, Geneva. Retrieved June 15, 2015 from: <http://unctad.org/en/pages/newsdetails.aspx?OriginalVersionID=673>.

UNDP, 2013. Humanity Divided: Confronting Inequality in Developing Countries. UNDP Bureau of Development Policy, Washington, DC.

Van Bilzen, G., 2015. The Development Aid. Cambridge Scholarly Publishing, Cambridge, MA.

Wilkinson, R., Hannah, E., Scott, J., 2014. The WTO in Bali: What MC 9 means for the Doha Development Agenda and why it matters. Third World Q. 35 (6), 1032–1050.

Winters, A.L., Martuscelli, A., 2014. Trade liberalization and poverty: What have we learned in a decade? Annu. Rev. Resource Econ. 6 (1), 493–512.

World Bank, 2015. *What is the World Bank doing on Aid for Trade?* Available April 3, 2015 from: <http://siteresources.worldbank.org/INTRANETTRADE/Resources/AfTbookletFINAL.pdf.>.

WTO, 2015a. Development: Aid for trade: Factsheet. Available February 15, 2015 from: <https://www.wto.org/English/Tratop_E/devel_e/a4t_e/a4t_factsheet_e.htm>.

WTO, 2015b. Development: Aid for trade. Available February 15, 2015 from: <https://www.wto.org/english/tratop_e/devel_e/a4t_e/aid4trade_e.htm.>.

THE RHETORIC AND REALITY OF RESULTS AND IMPACT ASSESSMENT IN DONOR AGENCIES: A PRACTITIONERS' PERSPECTIVE[1]

5

Simon Milligan*, Steve Bertram*, and Alwyn Chilver[†]

*Independent Consultant, UK
†Growth, Private Sector & Livelihoods, GRM International, Canberra, Australia

CHAPTER OUTLINE

---

[1]Disclaimer: The views expressed in this chapter are those of the authors. They should not be attributed to any organisation with which the authors might be affiliated. The authors would like to thank those who have provided comments on earlier drafts.

INTRODUCTION
THE CHANGING AID ENVIRONMENT

The issue of whether or not aid works has been hotly contested for some time. Revisiting his seminal publications from 1987 and 2007, Riddell recently asked, "does aid make a significant contribution to reducing the numbers in developing countries living in extreme poverty; does it make a significant contribution to a country's economic growth and development? Does aid work in this sense? What does the evidence tell us?" (Riddell, 2014, p. 12). More pertinently, perhaps, is the question of whether or not aid might work better. Is there a gap between what aid currently delivers and what it might deliver? And, if so, what should be done to close the gap?

The need for answers – the need for evidence – is greater than ever. Aid to developing countries has reached record levels. Despite the prevailing economic pressures, net official development assistance (ODA) in 2013 amounted to USD 135 billion – a new record (OECD, 2014). The same year the United Kingdom met, for the first time, the international target of giving 0.7% of gross national income (GNI) as development assistance, becoming the first G8 country to do so.

Behind the headlines a new aid environment is unfolding. Aid budgets are in a state of flux. A number of donor governments have recently frozen or cut their budgets (e.g., Canada, Netherlands) and/or have folded their aid agencies into their ministries of foreign affairs (e.g., Australia, Canada, and New Zealand). In parallel, there is growing recognition of the emergence of new donors, including Middle Eastern countries, philanthropic foundations, and the so-called BRICS – Brazil, Russia, India, China, and South Africa.

For some, ODA is no longer seen as the principal or default source of funding for development, with many Western Governments looking "beyond aid" to the private sector as *the* driver of sustainable development (Barder and Evans, 2014). Increasing attention is being placed on the role and potential of alternative sources of finance for development (e.g., remittances) and on the need for better policy coherence for development (e.g., concerning taxation, market access, and climate change). This is understandable. In 2012, workers' remittances to low income countries were worth USD 32billion whilst net ODA to the same countries was worth USD 30billion (EU cf. Booth, 2014).

In this context those managing and implementing aid programs frequently need to demonstrate to taxpayers and to politicians that aid can and does make a difference.

THE PURSUIT OF SUCCESS

Results matter. In the United Kingdom, aid "investment" options are now carefully scrutinized for their likely "returns" and ambitious "reach targets" are set and tracked. Concerted effort is made to capture, amongst other things, the number of rural men and women whose incomes are raised, the number of additional people with access to financial services, and the number of children under five, breastfeeding and pregnant women reached through DFID's nutrition-relevant projects (DFID, n.d.a).

In 2011, the UK Prime Minister stated that "without being hard-hearted, we will also be hard-headed, and make sure our aid money is directed at those things which are quantifiable and measure-able... ...so we really know we are getting results" (Cameron, 2011). Two years later, in February 2013, the UK Minister for International Development, states

... essentially, I think when it boils down to it, people need to see that we are targeting our spend effectively. Spend needs to be in the right places, on the right things and done in the right way. People need to have a clear sense that when a pound of British taxpayers money is spent, it is a pound that takes the country that we are working with further along the path of development. Our money should not be invested in simply maintaining the status quo. We want to invest in long-term progress. (Greening, 2013; "right places"; para 1)

The business-like framing of the aid budget, and the implicit "contract" with the domestic taxpayer, is not unique to the United Kingdom. In December 2013, it was announced that EuropeAid, in collaboration with the European External Action Service, would set up its own Results Framework to enable reporting of the EU's contribution to the development results achieved in partner countries (European Commission, 2014). Elsewhere, when Australia's Foreign Minister launched the country's new aid policy and performance framework – a "new aid paradigm" – in 2014, she declared that "Australians are a generous people but they expect Government to impose the same rigors and tests of value for money on our aid program [sic] as we do on areas of domestic spending and they want to see results" (Bishop, 2014; para 14).

It is difficult to argue with the intent. Public expenditure should – must – be subjected to scrutiny. Aid should be regarded as an investment, upon which returns are generated (whether they be developmental in nature or extended to include the donor's foreign policy-related objectives – something that is likely to be increasingly the case). Projects and programs, which are commonly regarded as having performed badly, should be reformed or cancelled.

Laudable sentiments but the reality is more complex. The environment within which aid and development objectives are framed and pursued is messier than we might like. Drawing on their experience of working in donor agencies or as consultants to the same, we explore the current framing of aid, results, and impact assessment. Focusing on UK Department for International Development (DFID) but making reference to other donor agencies, we examine the extent to which the emergent targets culture leads us to the pursuit of the "right" results and in the "right" way. In fusing research evidence with "clinical experience," we explore what this means for the framing, assessment, and communication of impact, and we identify opportunities for reshaping the impact and accountability agenda.

UNDERSTANDING THE "RESULTS CULTURE"

The 0.7% target dates back at least 50 years, though it was only formally recognized in 1970 when the UN General Assembly adopted a Resolution that contained a goal that "each economically advanced country ... [would] exert its best efforts to reach a minimum net amount of 0.7% of its gross national product at market prices by the middle of the Decade" (cf. Booth, 2014, p. 5). Having missed the goal, the UN Financing for Development meeting in Monterrey in 2002 again called on developed countries to "make concrete efforts" to see its attainment (Booth, 2014).

In 2004, the Labour Government announced its commitment to spend 0.7% of GNI on aid by 2013– the first time-bound target since the UK Government first adopted the 0.7% target in principle in 1974

(Booth, 2014). The introduction of time-bound targets was a central tenet of the "New Labour" platform (one consequence of which was a proliferation of league tables across much of the public sector; see Morrissey, 2002; Pellini, 2013). Critically, however, the new "results culture" did not disintegrate when the Coalition Government took power in 2010. In fact on his appointment in 2010, the then UK Secretary of State for International Development announced that, "my top priority will be to secure maximum value for money in aid through greater transparency, rigorous independent evaluation and an unremitting focus on results" (Mitchell, 2010). Key to this would be the need for greater "civil service DNA and business DNA" in DFID (Mitchell, 2009).

The basis for the results culture can be explained with reference to at least two agendas: one concerning accountability and transparency; the other, learning and efficacy.

THE ACCOUNTABILITY AND TRANSPARENCY AGENDA

Transparency is increasingly regarded as being a critical driver of accountability (and of aid effectiveness). The emphasis on transparency and accountability in the United Kingdom comes at a time when public skepticism about the value of overseas aid is rising. A recent poll found that 57% of the UK population is of the view that "too much" is spent on aid to developing countries; the same proportion felt that most financial aid to developing countries is wasted (Niblett, 2011).

The Coalition Government's shielding of the aid budget during a period of widespread domestic spending cuts motivated by the global financial crisis (and possibly political ideology) has likely compounded negative public perceptions of aid. Recent polls show that a slim majority now favors a reduction in UK aid spending (though polls also show that the public tends to considerably over-estimate government's spending on international aid and development; Glennie et al., 2012). This reality is reflected in DFID's communications. In the foreword to its operational plans for 2011–2015, DFID states

> In the current financial climate, we have a particular duty to show that we are achieving value for every pound of UK taxpayers' money that we spend on development. Results, transparency and accountability are our watchwords and guide everything we do. (DFID, 2011, p. 1)

Such pubic commitments are not restricted to the UK Government. The Australian Government has recently felt the need to reassure domestic tax-payers that their money is not being wasted; that results will be achieved:

> At the project level, we will ensure that funding is directed to projects making a difference. When projects don't deliver the results we expect, we will cut our losses. When they do well, we will look for ways to expand or replicate them.
>
> The new performance framework will ensure that funding is linked to performance at all levels of the aid program. This will ensure that taxpayers' money spent through Australia's aid program is achieving the greatest possible development impact (DFAT, 2014a, p. 3).

Internationally, the commitment to better track what aid is being used for can be illustrated by the 2009 launch of, and then subsequent expansion to, the International Aid Transparency Initiative (IATI). The IATI now represents a coalition of donors, developing countries, and NGOs that seek to release regular, detailed, and timely information on aid programs for the benefit of recipients, partners, and domestic taxpayers.

THE LEARNING AND EFFICACY AGENDA

Beyond transparency and accountability-related requirements, it is commonly accepted that it is imperative for decision-makers to understand what works, where, why, and how so as to enable improved programming and policy-making. All aid agencies want to be fulfill their objectives (however framed) and therefore the challenge is one of identifying, supporting, and championing good ideas, of learning and innovating, and of applying proven practice. That requires an informed understanding of results and the processes by which they are achieved.

With improved understanding comes the opportunity to make informed investment decisions (DFID, n.d.a). That opportunity is rightly recognized. For example, when introducing its new performance framework in mid-2014, Australian Department of Foreign Affairs and Trade states

[The framework] is simple; it links performance with funding; and it ensures a stronger focus on results and value-for-money.... Where aid investments perform well, we will look for ways to increase their funding or replicate them in other countries or sectors. (DFAT, 2014b)

The principle is sound but inevitably the reality is more nuanced. Yes, funding decisions are often linked to expected and actual performance; successful initiatives often attract additional investment and are taken to scale, and; poor performers are often reformed, scaled back, or cancelled. However, it is also a truism that funding decisions are not based on technical performance alone. Domestic politics and bilateral relations all matter. As Vince Cable – the Secretary of State for Business, Innovation and Skills in the UK's Coalition Government of 2010–2015 – noted in 2004, five "s"s tend to limit evidence-based decision-making: speed, superficiality, spin, secrecy, and scientific ignorance. Whilst external scrutiny and demands for greater accountability may be encouraging policy-makers to place increasing emphasis on the use of evidence (Cable, 2004; Dhaliwal and Tulloch, n.d.), the role of evidence in decision-making processes should not be overstated (Pellini, 2013).

A FLY IN THE OINTMENT?

A somewhat skeptical public frequently requires a clear, compelling narrative about its aid investment. As a consequence, donor agencies frequently feel obliged to feed the perceived hunger with "good news stories" on what the investment has "bought": how many teachers have been trained, how many children are enrolled in the schools it has built, how many lives have been saved, etc. Unfortunately, not least for those designing, implementing, evaluating, and overseeing aid programs, the reality is more complex. As the problems we seek to address and the numbers we seek to reach become more ambitious, the number and complexity of the drivers increases sharply, their interconnectedness more frequent (and often less apparent), and the trajectory and timing of change less certain. It also holds that aid expenditure cannot and should not be perceived in the same light as areas of domestic public expenditure: put simply, DFID and other donors cannot be held accountable for the meeting of high-level targets in partner countries in the same way a government agency might be held accountable at home.

In a challenge to those calling for increased levels of aid expenditure (e.g., Sachs, 2005) and those searching for a silver bullet, there is an increasing body of literature (and a more vocal lobby) that challenges the linear, mechanistic models and assumptions on which aid programs are often designed. This perspective argues that development challenges and opportunities are highly context specific and often political in nature and it therefore cautions against the championing of simple problem–solution equations that can be solved by more aid dollars. It concludes that rigid planning within aid and development should be eschewed in favor of adaptive and flexible approaches (cf. Andrews et al., 2012; Barder and Ramalingam, 2012; Ramalingam, 2013; also Harford, 2011).

With an acceptance that developmental change is complex and that the full array of results and opportunities cannot be predicted, the key challenge becomes one of how to support adaptive management, internal learning, and adjustment (cf. Ballan, this volume). That necessarily requires tight feedback loops that permit rapid learning and ongoing performance management and adaptation (Andrews et al., 2012). It also requires a reconsideration of how results are framed, measured, and communicated. As Gibson recently noted in his critique of the current aid environment, it is "much easier to talk of lives saved, to proffer images of kids in school, etc., than attempt to communicate the progress of something as apparently amorphous as the development of self-reliant functional systems. Not impossible – but more difficult" (Gibson, 2014; "Reason 3" point 1).

THE PUSH FOR IMPACT ASSESSMENT

Until the 1970s there was little interest in the impact and effectiveness of aid. As Riddell notes, "the (assumed) need for aid was seen as a sufficient basis for providing it" (Riddell, 2009, p1). For many donors that era has passed. The pressure to predict, to plan, to measure, and to understand the impact of aid continues to grow. The United Kingdom is no exception. Following the challenge outlined in the Center for Global Development publication, *When Will We Ever Learn?* in 2006, DFID has steadily increased its investment in impact assessment (see Box 5.1). This has taken a number of forms, such as the appointment of an expanded cadre of Evaluation Advisors (often appointed from other ministries), the establishment of the Independent Commission for Aid Impact (ICAI) in 2011, the release of DFID's inaugural Annual Evaluation Report in 2013 (DFID, 2013), and the provision of support to key international partners, such as the International Initiative for Impact Evaluation (3iE).

The rise in prominence of impact assessment is consistent with a broader agenda: that of evidence-informed or evidence-based decision making (EBDM) (Gertler et al., 2011). In the United Kingdom, the notion of evidence-based decision making has been part of public discourse for a number of years but it has risen to particular prominence since the 1990s. Impact assessment and EBDM are natural bed-fellows, sitting neatly as they do with the accountability, transparency, and learning agendas described above. As the UK Secretary of State for International Development

---

BOX 5.1 MONITORING, EVALUATION AND IMPACT EVALUATION

Monitoring is the regular and systematic collection and analysis of data to determine what progress is being made, most notably at *activity* and *output* levels. It seeks to establish whether the intervention "is doing things right." As such, it helps program managers and other stakeholders to understand whether intended deliverables are being realized and if results are being achieved as planned (e.g., in terms of exposure to new information, availability of new technology, receipt of policy recommendations).

Evaluation, by contrast, is the systematic collection and objective assessment of data and information at *outcomes*-level, that is, where behavioral change is manifest (e.g., in changed practices, in the application or utilization of new technology, in policy change). It seeks to establish whether the intervention is doing "the right things." As such, it helps stakeholders understand why and how intended results were or were not achieved and explores any unintended results, with a view to supporting learning processes and for making improvements to program performance.

Impact assessment does not focus on the interventions themselves but on the effect of them, that is, it seeks to establish the difference made by the investment to particular groups. As such, it helps stakeholders understand the size, nature, and distribution of the impacts associated with a particular investment.

The OECD rightly notes that "the term *'impact'* continues to be used in two ways in the literature: (i) as the last stage in a chain of results, i.e. the ultimate objective of the intervention; and (ii) the assessment or analysis of the whole results chain". Whereas the OECD opts for the latter, the authors favor the former and regard "impacts' as the (net) long-term effects produced by an investment, directly or indirectly, intended or unintended. Whilst these are typically synonymous with the long-term welfare effects on individuals, households, and communities (e.g., in terms of poverty rates and income levels), government aid agencies may increasingly frame aid investments by their expected or actual impacts within economic and political spheres (e.g., in terms of access and political support).

---

announced in 2012, DFID needs to know "that what we're funding will actually work as we intend" (Greening, 2012).

Rigorous impact assessment has been heralded by some organizations (e.g., DFID, JPAL, 3iE) as a critical component of the aid machinery's armory. The appeal is obvious: with better evaluation and rigorous impact assessment come the opportunity to infuse lessons from past investments and to revisit the rationale for ongoing investments. As a recent DFID Business Case for the Impact Evaluation Support Facility (2013) notes

Impact evaluation provides the evidence needed to make decisions such as scaling up, scaling down or adjusting policies and programmes. Making decisions based on robust evidence of what works in specific contexts increases the value for money of interventions and reduces the risk of failure. [With investment in IE there should be] improved awareness, demand for and use of evidence in decision-making in key sectors, as evidenced by the scaling up, scaling down and midcourse correction of policies and programmes, [and] improved effectiveness and impact of new and existing development interventions by DFID and the wider development community. (DFID, n.d.b)

That we – policy-makers, partners, recipients, practitioners – want results and evidence is not in question (though, there is considerable space for debate about who defines what success looks like and who captures the benefit). In principle, the prevailing results culture should offer considerable opportunity. For example, it should allow for:

- Greater scrutiny of investment options, improved decision-making, and greater efficiency and aid effectiveness.
- A clear line of sight on agreed objectives and a better understanding of how performance should be tracked, assessed, and evaluated over time.
- The setting of simpler targets that domestic tax-payers can understand but which are nested within a more sophisticated and ultimately more accurate presentation of how, when, and why change occurs.
- Greater preparedness to identify and address failure.

But does it?

THE CHANGING FACE OF IMPACT ASSESSMENT

The emergence of impact assessment has been met with uncertainty and, at times, misunderstanding, fear, and hostility within the aid community. Let us therefore start with the facts. First, the number of known impact evaluations commissioned by the global aid community has grown steadily – from about 10 in 2002, to about 40 in 2007, and then to about 120 in 2011 (Savedoff, 2013). Secondly, their use in the period 1985–2013 was concentrated in several sectors, most notably social protection (and particularly conditional cash transfers), health, and education (Savedoff, 2013). Thirdly, Random Control Trials accounted for about 50% of the impact assessments conducted in 2012–2013 (followed by Difference-in-Difference, Instrumental Variable, and Regression Discontinuity in declining order of frequency; Savedoff, 2013). Finally, the overall use of impact assessment, when considered alongside the number of evaluations commissioned each year, is still very limited.

We do not seek to describe the ongoing methodological debates (see Chapter 1 for some discussion on this). Nevertheless, three observations are necessary at this point. First, the debate about the emergence and use of impact assessment has frequently been polarized, though thankfully it is increasingly accepted that many interventions do not lend themselves to experimental or even quasi-experimental methods. Secondly, debate about impact assessment should not be focused on which one approach offers the best sight of the "uncontested truth." There is no "gold standard" – instead thought must be given to appropriateness and cost-effectiveness. Thirdly, it is increasingly acknowledged (and rightly so) that practitioners require a better, more varied "tool-kit" that is "fit for context" and this necessarily requires investment in mixed methods and in innovative, qualitative approaches; for example, ongoing innovation in response to cases where $n = 1$ (White and Phillips, 2012; Masset, 2013).

In our view, it is important that debate about approaches and methods does not overshadow other important issues; issues that concern the framing and communication of aid and its impact. For example, there remains a perception that a hierarchy of evidence exists, even if guidance on the matter suggests otherwise (cf. DFID, 2014). Perception and reality matter, for it affects professional judgment and decision-making about, for example, the quality of the evidence-base that underpins investment choices and the framing of any projected or actual results. Moreover, there is a risk that the current focus on impact assessment might actually lead us away from good practice; good practice that is built upon monitoring and adaptive management. For the authors, key questions necessarily arise. How is evidence used? Who defines what is acceptable or sufficient? What are the incentives and disincentives to the capture, use and reporting of results, and does the prevailing culture inhibit or stifle adaptive program management?

RESULTS REPORTING AND IMPACT ASSESSMENT IN A CONTESTED, DYNAMIC, AND POLITICAL ENVIRONMENT

That managers and practitioners require a clear line of sight on objectives is not in question. Equally, the pursuit of efficacy and learning and the need for accountability and transparency is well understood. However, risks remain and challenges exist. Whilst evidence remains patchy and often anecdotal (cf. Eyben, 2014), attempt is made in the following sections to look at the risks associated with the (mis) application of the results agenda and impact assessment within that. It does so by examining the key stages of a programme cycle.

PROGRAM DESIGN

For the UK Prime Minister, results matter. Naturally, therefore, aid money should be "directed at those things which are quantifiable and measureable… …so we really know we are getting results" (Cameron, 2011). This should not be a surprise. As Stern recently noted, donors tend to drift toward things they can do, to things they can achieve, and to things they can measure (Stern, 2013). Policy-makers are fearful of scandal. They typically favor the minimization of transaction costs and waste over risk-taking. In that context an emphasis – intended or otherwise – on short-term, low-risk, and quantifiable gains is likely to have unintended consequences. The pressure to disburse and to deliver tangible results creates a risk that direct deliverables are pursued at the expense of support to necessary changes in governance structures and processes, and to the improved functioning of markets. That would be a mistake for systemic change offers opportunity to reach large numbers of a target population in such ways that should unlock enduring benefits for many people over the long term (cf. Ballan, this volume).

So is the risk of missed opportunity real or imagined? A recent paper by a former Administrator of USAID outlined the role of the "counter-bureaucracy" in shaping – distorting – the US aid programme (Natsios, 2010). Natsios argued that "obsessive measurement disorder" – a belief that the more an activity can be quantified, the better the policy choices and management of it will be – has led to a shift in investment to those initiatives that are easily quantifiable and which are measureable after only a short period of time. Natsios is not alone in noting his concerns. Bob McMullan, Australia's former Parliamentary Secretary for International Development, recently commented on an "enduring concern' of his: "the tyranny of the measurable" (McMullan, 2015; para 12). He argued that "it is difficult to win support for measures which seem important but where the results are not measurable. This distortion is a by-product of the very welcome focus on results and outcomes. But we need to guard against ignoring important issues where measurement may be difficult" (McMullan, 2015; para 12). Practice-based evidence supports McMullan's concerns. A recent commentary on the experience of grant-holders that received funding from the DFID-financed Governance and Transparency Fund in Africa points to an apparent risk that the current climate of impact and evidence may mean that some implementing agencies may simply option not to deliver certain kinds of interventions (KPMG, n.d.).

PROGRAMME DELIVERY AND MANAGEMENT

Results, particularly at outcome and goal levels, are influenced by a range of external factors, often in combination with each other. Programmes are delivered in real time, in the real world, and by people and institutions with different and sometimes fluid interests. Inevitably, therefore, the programming context rarely plays out in an expected, stable, and linear manner. Instead, constraints emerge, assumptions prove misplaced, lessons are learned, and opportunities arise. This creates at least two challenges: how can programmes adapt and respond to new circumstances? And how can impacts (as defined in Box 5.1) be tracked, measured, and reported when welfare gains may only be realized over the long term?

From a performance assessment perspective, there is emerging concern amongst some practitioners that insufficient attention is being paid to monitoring and performance management at an output and intermediate outcome level (cf. Ticehurst, 2012). The concern may be justified. In its recent review of DFID nutrition projects, the UK's Independent Commission for Aid Impact (ICAI) noted that "some projects do not monitor adequately short-term results" and observed that "monitoring systems often focus on producing 'reach' figures" (ICAI, 2014a). In the case of two DFID postconflict programs in Somalia, the ICAI pointed to an "absence of monitoring data" altogether (cf. DFID, 2013).

The causes of these cases and the extent to which they are representative of DFID's broader portfolio are not known. Nevertheless, they remain insightful. It would be a perverse outcome if the current emphasis on *ex-post* impact assessment has devalued the "M" within M&E, thereby increasing the risk of programme failure (Ticehurst, 2012). Managers require (or should require) a "drip-feed" of timely, relevant, and actionable information about programme performance. They need a nuanced understanding of how change *might* happen and timely access to program performance information that compares actual with expectation. They should also require a nuanced understanding of how broader sectoral change – for example, within the policy environment, to sector financing, etc. – may have bearing on the results, relevance, and sustainability of their programme so that results can be maximized, opportunities can be exploited, and risks can be managed.

Several donors, including DFID and DFAT, have responded to such challenges by investing in quasi-independent performance and oversight components to large-scale programmes. Such investments can be beneficial but only in certain circumstances. For example, their utility is dependent on there being a desire by programme managers to get the most out of such components and a preparedness to make changes to programme design and to seek continuous improvement in programme relevance and effectiveness. Secondly, the contracting of external monitors and assessors must not absolve the "day-to-day managers" from maintaining a clear line of sight on overarching objectives, of conducting high-quality monitoring and of appraising risk. This is particularly important should *ex-post* impact assessments be driven by an accountability agenda – did the programme work or not? Can the service provider be paid or not? The need for continuous learning about "the what, the why and the how" and for adaptive programme management must not be forgotten or sidelined.

Are there reasons for optimism? Quite possibly. DFID has recently undertaken to improve its ability to commission and manage adaptive, flexible programmes so that it can better respond to changing contexts and opportunities in a timely and flexible manner (Vowles, 2013). Whilst challenges remain – for example, individuals sometimes have personal financial incentive to meet spending targets (Gibson, 2014) – this is a positive development and one other donor agencies would do well to follow.

REPORTING, ACCOUNTABILITY, AND (IMPACT) EVALUATION

The production and use of evidence – of impact, for example – is informed by the context within which it occurs. Inevitably, the pressure to demonstrate results creates risk of over-reporting actual change. The extent to which this occurs or is systemic is unknown but there is evidence of its occurrence.

In 2014, the UK ICAI found that DFID had "over-estimated" some results in its nutrition portfolio (explicitly noted in, e.g., ICAI, 2014a, p. 1). This finding chimes with those outlined in other ICAI reports. For example, in its assessment of DFID's private sector development portfolio in 2014, ICAI noted that, at present, "the target culture arguably provides incentives to report large numbers for impact wherever possible" (ICAI, 2014b, p. 27). It found that

> [R]eporting against targets encourages the appearance of precision, even though the margin for error when measuring impacts in more complex programmes may be large. The numbers are presented to the nearest person, even though their calculation is often based on a number of assumptions and approximate multipliers making such claimed precision meaningless.....The margin for error is, therefore, very large, yet unacknowledged. (ICAI, 2014b, p. 26)

In addition to the prevailing pressure to demonstrate results, there is an attendant risk that programmes and donors overstate *their actual contribution* to the changes described. DFID's target culture means that country offices are required to capture results and impact in measurable terms (ICAI, 2014b; e.g., in terms of children completing primary school). In its recent assessment of "How DFID learns," the ICAI argued that "the emphasis on results can lead to a bias to the positive" (ICAI, 2014c, p. 1) and suggested that "DFID staff often feel under pressure to be positive. This applies to assessing both current and future project performance" (ICAI, 2014c, p. 9).

The extent to which donors frequently claim achievements as entirely theirs is unknown; in fact, key DFID statements are often careful in declaring that they have "helped," not directly caused, notable achievements. For example, 2.7 million children and pregnant women helped to get better nutrition, 21 million children immunized with DFID help, and 5.9 million children put into school with DFD help (Greening, 2013). Nevertheless, there is probably truth in the suggestion that DFID's "reach targets" frequently sit at the cusp of what could be plausibly attributed to them and what is dependent on a range of external drivers. For example, DFID's Level 2 Results Targets, which "measure the outputs that can be *directly linked* to DFID programmes and projects" (DFID, n.d.a, p. 3), include the

- Number of people achieving food security through DFID support (target: 4 million)
- Number of children per annum completing primary education supported by DFID (no target provided)
- Number of people who vote in elections supported by DFID (no target provided).
- Number of neonatal lives saved through DFID support (target: 250,000 newborn babies; DFID, n.d.a).

With ambitious "results pledges" made to Ministers, parliaments, and the public come questions. To whom are managers and implementers accountable? Who sets the targets and who participates in the analysis? To whom are impacts reported? Who decides if an investment is a success? Which impacts are valued and by whom?

DFID's former Chief Social Development Advisor, Rosaline Eyben, has argued that, despite the spirit and principles captured in the Paris Declaration, domestic pressure has required donors to "claim achievements as entirely theirs, rendering invisible to their domestic audience the contribution of recipient government staff and others" (Eyben, 2014, p. 138). What is equally at risk is that with the need to deliver a public aid program that represents value for money, which delivers tangible, quantifiable results and which meets disbursement and ambitious "reach targets," accountabilities to partners governments and end beneficiaries may be underplayed. Equally, the pressure to demonstrate and be accountable for measurable, high-level results may erode or threaten relationships of openness and honesty between donor agencies and implementing partners.

Anecdotal evidence points to a number of cases in which prospective and actual implementing partners "spin" the results story to satisfy what they believe the donor expects of them, to supply "good news stories" or to comply with what they believe will secure a good review. This may not be restricted to implementing partners. Findings of a 2014 DFID Evidence Survey found that staff report to feeling under pressure "to provide selective evidence that would justify decisions" (cf. ICAI, 2014c, p. 20).

LESSON LEARNING AND APPLICATION

It is clear that the current results and impact assessment agenda is informed by many and diverse drivers. As Barder recently noted, different drivers might take us in broadly the same direction but they might not necessarily take us to the same destination (Barder, 2012). One major driver is the assumption that organizations have the capacity, willingness, and incentives to act upon findings. Recent evidence casts a cautionary note. A recent synthesis review of lessons and reflections from 84 Sida evaluations concluded that "we have yet to overcome institutional hurdles and develop sufficient mechanisms to learn from experience in general and evaluations in particular" (Christopolos et al., 2014, p. 19). Sida is not alone. DFID allocated at least GBP 1.2 billion for research, evaluation, and personnel development for the period 2011–2015. Nevertheless, the previously mentioned ICAI (2014) survey found that DFID placed "insufficient priority… on learning during implementation" (ICAI, 2014c, p. 1). It argued that DFID does not "'fully ensure that the lessons from each stage of the delivery chain are captured, particularly in relation to locally employed staff, delivery agents and, most crucially, the beneficiaries" (ICAI, 2014c, p. 1). The ICAI found that "knowledge within many evaluations is still not fully utilised" (ICAI, 2014c: 13) and argued that DFID's failure to use available knowledge was to the "detriment of DFID's impact and value for money" (ICAI, 2014c, p. 1).

DFID's overall performance in relation to "learning" was rated as "amber-red," signaling that "'significant improvements should be made" (ICAI, 2014c, p. ii). Whilst the ICAI assessment acknowledged the steps DFID has taken, it also identified a number of institutional constraints to improved learning and evidence-informed decision-making. This includes the existence of a "culture where staff have often felt afraid to discuss failure" (ICAI, 2014c, p. 9). The ICAI also pointed to there being insufficient provision of "time and incentives [for staff] to learn from success and failure while they are doing their jobs" (ICAI, 2014c, p. 24). This raises important questions about the use of and growing (financial) commitment to impact assessments and whether staff is able to process, synthesize, and use the growing number of impact assessments it has commissioned.

AN EVOLVING CONTEXT?

There are other changes on the horizon that are relevant to the aid effectiveness and impact assessment agenda. Canada, New Zealand, and Australia have recently merged or reintegrated their aid agencies into ministries of foreign affairs. The United Kingdom remains the exception but a UK Parliament International Development Select Committee enquiry in 2014 is seeking to form conclusions about the future UK approach to development, and whether a stand-alone DFID has a long-term future. As has been noted, "it is hard not to imagine a scenario after the [2015] election in which a Prime Minister decides to square political commitment to 0.7% with hostile benchmark opinion on aid spending by merging it back into the Foreign Office" (Barder and Evans, 2014). With aid administered within a foreign affairs portfolio it will inevitably be considered, at least in part, as a tool for economic and political diplomacy. That raises questions for performance reporting and impact assessment. For example:

- Will reductions to aid expenditure and the folding of aid agencies back into ministries of foreign affairs placate any existing public skepticism about the aid budget? If so, it is probable that the relative importance of the accountability agenda might wane, as might the demand for impact assessments.
- Are embassies and departments of foreign affairs comfortable with external bodies, such as consultants, providing critical comment on the appropriateness and effectiveness of their investment decisions? If not, that might reduce the number of assessments commissioned. It might also increase the pressure to put a positive gloss on any findings.
- Where aid programs are conceived from a development perspective *and* from a (more explicit) national interests' perspective, on what basis should evaluators judge a program's performance? Put simply, should evaluators view impacts through the lens of both developmental objectives *and* foreign policy interests?

LOOKING FORWARD

So where from here? We concur with the view that the results agenda debate should be much less around whether we want to see results of course we want to see results. However, we need to know how we can measure these results without adverse effects. We also contend that we must be sure not to miss important opportunities.

THE IMPLICATIONS FOR AID INVESTMENTS AND THE FRAMING OF RESULTS

Political rhetoric about "cutting our losses" when programmes fail to deliver measurable and quantifiable results is ultimately unhelpful *should* it stifle innovation and foster the pursuit of short-term measurable "wins" over long-term systemic change. If agencies are to support innovation and to pursue high returns, then there must be an acceptance of the possibility that some initiatives might fail altogether whilst others might be "slow burners"; slow burners that offer considerable long-term benefits.

Aid is an inherently risky business. As such, it is critical that donors conceive and regard their investments as portfolios. Where failure occurs, there must be a genuine desire to acknowledge and learn from such experience. There must also be attendant commitment to accept and explain risk. This means that practitioners, managers, and politicians must effectively communicate the complex and often uncertain reality of development processes and aid's role within that environment.

Should aid agencies be committed to the pursuit of the "big wins" they must necessarily accept that aid programmes will interact with complex and dynamic political-institutional systems. That requires at least two responses. First, it requires a rejection of any mechanistic view of systems and of aid programmes as having clear cause-and-effect relationships. In turn, that creates a challenge to the culture of control that some feel has crept in to development programming in recent years. Secondly, it requires acknowledgment of the political, institutional, and other dimensions that frequently make development and aid successes highly context specific. That necessarily creates a challenge for those seeking easy wins through "replication." Solutions have to be "fit the context." At best they might be *adapted* from other locations. Rarely will straightforward *adoption* work.

Managers need to find an appropriate balance between delivering "good news stories" whilst articulating the bigger picture. Set against those realities and the political imperative for "good news stories," it might be prudent for aid agencies to adopt a twin track aid programme, with one part devoted to achieving quick, political wins, whilst the other focuses on long-term engagement in the riskier "game" of development.

With an acceptance that development is complex and that long-term aid investments do not necessarily offer "easy wins," comes a requirement for investment in high-quality monitoring and performance management systems that provide timely information about programme performance and its broader context. That should help meet the necessary communication and advocacy requirements. After all, managers need to work within their domestic political framework and defend the aid program (Natsios, 2010). However, high-quality monitoring and performance management systems also enable programmes to adapt. For managers, that requires that they be prepared to act upon incomplete information – information that is "good enough" – for ultimately there is a trade-off between the quality and completeness of information and there being enough time left within a programme to make corrections and to exploit emerging opportunities.

In turn, that requires critical reflection about how success is framed and reported. The overwhelming tendency towards measurable, quantifiable results and targets can create a skew towards averages. Development is not about averages, particularly if issues of equity and equality are of concern (which surely they must). Indeed, it is relevant to note that there is emerging evidence that where Payment-by-Results (PbR) contracts do not have an explicit focus on equity, suppliers may "avoid supporting marginalized groups or complex cases as the added cost is not rewarded" (BOND, 2014, p. 1). As that would suggest, managers and decision-makers need to reconsider who defines impact and to whom they are accountable. A culture in which beneficiaries are seen as passive, grateful recipients of donor "help" must be avoided. It reinforces the notion of development assistance as charity. It promotes the notion that aid on its own will solve the problem, and it downgrades the need for managers to be responsible and responsive to their partners (be they governments, civil society groups, or individuals).

THE IMPLICATIONS FOR IMPACT ASSESSMENT

Donors in general recognize that impact assessment in international development is an emerging field, with diverse views on the appropriate application of impact assessment and what constitutes a rigorous approach (Stern et al., 2012). The importance of "context" within aid programming has been noted by DFID (DFID, 2013). This is welcomed. Steps must be taken to ensure that this is reflected in design, review, and evaluation processes.

With acceptance of complexity and nonlinearity, and with a commitment to support systemic or transformational change, comes both uncertainty and opportunity. The prevailing culture of targets and results necessarily places attention on capturing *intended* impacts. It is important, however, that assessments also seek to capture and understand unintended impacts, be they positive or negative. Inevitably that raises question marks about the suitability and application of the current impact assessment toolkit. It is a challenge to which practitioners must continue to respond.

It is increasingly accepted that impact assessment should not be limited to experimental and quasi-experimental methodologies (Stern et al., 2012). It is also increasingly accepted that the most appropriate approach depends on the policy or practice question in question. Again, this is welcomed. However, it is also the case that decision-makers often endorse – tacitly or otherwise – a "hierarchy of evidence"; one that prioritizes "hard data" stemming from experimental and quasi-experimental methods over others (Court et al., 2006; Taylor, 2013). Without consistent recognition that qualitative evidence is of equal weight staff may draw the "logical" conclusion and likely avoid commissioning innovative and potentially high reward programmes should the case not be supported with hard evidence.

Aid investment decisions are frequently pragmatic and negotiated, and based on a range of considerations, including political expediency. It is necessary to acknowledge, as Natsios did in 2010, that foreign policy objectives may shape or drive some [or all] aid investments. That raises the thorny issue of whether impacts should be judged against development *and* political objectives. Whether foreign ministries have the appetite for such scrutiny and for such forthright acknowledgment of their foreign policy objectives remains to be seen.

CONCLUSION

Throughout this chapter, we have sought to describe and examine the interplay between the results agenda and the emergence of impact assessment. It is ironic that much of our critique of the current environment draws on findings of the ICAI: a child of that very culture. The relationship between programming, results, evidence, and impact assessment is a topic of considerable and sometimes polemical debate. It is undeniable that the setting of ambitious targets and the associated use of evidence is not value-free. It sends signals that have bearing on what is funded, how implementation proceeds, what results are pursued, how they are measured, and how they are framed. We have pointed to the risks and challenges that this creates. But we have also pointed to opportunities for future programming and the associated implications for impact assessment. Without doubt, impact assessments can offer a rich source of data and information. However, they must be promoted for the right reasons, and agencies must have the willingness and capacity to respond to their findings. Moreover, they must not be promoted at the expense of performance monitoring and adaptive management, such that managers are able and encouraged to make decisions that will better safeguard the ongoing relevance, effectiveness, and sustainability of current investments.

REFERENCES

Andrews, M., Pritchett, L., Woolcock, M., 2012. Escaping capability traps through problem-driven iterative adaptation (PDIA). CGD Working Paper 299. Washington, D.C.: Center for Global Development. [ONLINE]. Available from: <http://www.cgdev.org/content/publications/detail/1426292> (accessed 25.03.2015).

Barder, O., 2012. What are the results agenda? [ONLINE]. Available from: <http://www.org/blog/5228> (accessed 14.11.2014).

Barder, O., Evans, A., 2014. Future UK development policy. Memorandum to the UK International Development Select Committee.

Barder, O., Ramalingam, B., 2012. Complexity, Adaptation, and Results [ONLINE]. Available from: <http://www.cgdev.org/blog/complexity-adaptation-and-results> (accessed 10.01.2015).

Bishop, J., 2014. The New Aid Paradigm. [ONLINE] Available from: <http://www.foreignminister.gov.au/speeches/Pages/2014/jb_sp_140618.aspx?ministerid=4> (last accessed 20.08.2014).

BOND, 2014. Payment by results: What it means for UK NGOs. BOND.

Booth, L., 2014. House of Commons Library Standard Note: SN/EP/3714.

Cable, V., 2004. Evidence and UK Politics. Research and Policy in Development: Does evidence matter? Meeting Series. London: ODI. [ONLINE]. Available from: <http://www.odi.org/sites/odi.org.uk/files/odi-assets/publications-opinion-files/206.pdf> (last accessed 26.03.2015).

Cameron, D., 2011. PM's Speech on Aid, Trade and Democracy. [ONLINE] Available from: <https://www.gov.uk/government/speeches/pms-speech-on-aid-trade-and-democracy> (last accessed 01.07.2014).

Christopolos, I., Hedqvist, A.L., Rothman, J., 2014. Lessons and Reflections from 84 Sida Decentralised Evaluations 2013 – A Synthesis Review. SIDA Studies in Evaluation. Sida, Stockholm, *2014:1*.

Court, J., Mendizabal, E., Osborne, D., Young, J., 2006. Policy Engagement How Civil Society Can be More Effective. ODI, London.

DFAT, 2014a. Australia's New Development Policy and Performance Framework: A summary. [ONLINE]. Available from: <http://www.aid.dfat.gov.au/Publications/Pages/aid-policy-summary.aspx> (last accessed 14.10.2014).

DFAT. 2014b. Making Performance Count: Enhancing the accountability and effectiveness of Australian aid. [ONLINE]. Available from: <http://www.aid.dfat.gov.au/Publications/Pages/framework-making-performance-count.aspx> (last accessed 14.10.2014).

DFID, n.d.a. DFID's Results Framework: Managing and reporting DFID's results. [ONLINE] Available from: <https://www.gov.uk/government/uploads/system/uploads/attachment_data/file/175945/DFID-external-results.pdf> (last accessed 10.11.2014).

DFID, n.d.b. Intervention summary (for a business case). Title: Impact Evaluation Support Facility. [ONLINE]. Available from: <http://www.iati.dfid.gov.uk/iati_documents/4323282.docx> (last accessed 07.12.2014).

DFID, 2014. Assessing the strength of evidence. How to note [ONLINE]. Available from: <https://www.gov.uk/government/uploads/system/uploads/attachment_data/file/291982/HTN-strength-evidence-march2014.pdf> (last accessed 27.11.2014).

DFID, 2013. Annual Evaluation Report. DFID, London.

DFID, 2011. Operational plan 2011-2015 DFID Bangladesh. April 2011. [ONLINE]. Available from: <https://www.gov.uk/government/uploads/system/uploads/attachment_data/file/67555/Bangladesh-1.pdf> (last accessed 27.11.2014).

Dhaliwal, I., Tulloch, C., n.d.. From Research to Policy: Using Evidence from Impact Evaluations to Inform Development Policy. J-PAL, Department of Economics, MIT.

European Commission, 2014. A culture of results: Change is possible. [ONLINE] Available from: <http://capacity4dev.ec.europa.eu/article/culture-results-change-possible> (last accessed 10.11.2014).

Eyben, R., 2014. International Aid and the Making of a Better World: Reflexive Practice, first ed Routledge, London.

Gertler, P.J., Martinez, S., Premand, P., Rawlings, L.B., Vermeersch, C.M.J., 2011. Impact Evaluation in Practice. World Bank, Washington, DC.

Gibson, A., 2014. If we want better development, cut the UK aid budget' [ONLINE]. Available from: <http://www.springfieldcentre.com/resources/soap-box/> (last accessed 10.11.2014).

Glennie, A., Straw, W., Wild, L., 2012. Understanding Public Attitudes to Aid and Development. IPPR/ODI.

Greening, J., 2013. Justine Greening: Development in transition. [ONLINE] Available from: <https://www.gov.uk/government/speeches/justine-greening-development-in-transition> (last accessed 10.09.2014).

Greening, J., 2012. Speech for Conservative Party Conference.

Harford, T., 2011. Adapt: Why Success Always Starts with Failure. Farrar, Straus and Giroux, New York, NY.

ICAI, 2014a. DFID's contribution to improving nutrition. [ONLINE]. Available from: <http://icai.independent.gov.uk/wp-content/uploads/2014/07/ICAI-REPORT-DFIDs-Contribution-to-Improving-Nutrition.pdf> (last accessed 09.09.2014).

ICAI, 2014b. DFID's private sector development work. [ONLINE]. Available from: <http://icai.independent.gov.uk/wp-content/uploads/2014/05/ICAI-PSD-report-FINAL.pdf> (last accessed 09.09.2014).

ICAI, 2014c. How DFID learns. [ONLINE]. Available from: <http://icai.independent.gov.uk/wp-content/uploads/2014/04/How-DFID-Learns-FINAL.pdf >(last accessed 14.11.2014).

KPMG, n.d. Governance and Transparency Fund Briefing Paper: The Evidence Agenda in Practice.

Masset, E., 2013. Impact evaluation when N = 1. Centre for Development Impact Practice Paper No. 4. Brighton: IDS. [ONLINE] Available from: <http://opendocs.ids.ac.uk/opendocs/bitstream/handle/123456789/2796/CDI%20PP4%20Final.pdf;jsessionid = AB6B1367BB50B21D15A0153C87AB2750?sequence = 1> (last accessed 15.12.2014).

McMullan, B., 2015. Julia and the four challenges [ONLINE]. Available from: <http://devpolicy.org/in-brief/julia-and-the-four-challenges/?utm_source=Devpolicy&utm_campaign=6ce5f208c7-RSS_EMAIL_CAMPAIGN&utm_medium=email&utm_term=0_082b498f84-6ce5f208c7-308440093/> (last accessed 31.03.2015).

Mitchell, A., 2010. Andrew Mitchell appointed Secretary of State. [ONLINE]. Available from: <http://www.dfid.gov.uk/news/latest-news/2010/andrew-mitchell-appointed-secretary-of-state> (last accessed 20.09.2014).

Mitchell, A., 2009. Transcript of Development Drums Episode 13 – Andrew Mitchell. [ONLINE]. Available from: <http://www.developmentdrums.org/wp-content/DD13transcript.pdf> (last accessed 10.11.2014).

Morrissey, O., 2002. British aid policy since 1997 is DFID the standard bearer for donors? [ONLINE]. CREDIT Research Paper No. 02/23, University of Nottingham. Available from: <https://www.nottingham.ac.uk/credit/documents/papers/02-23.pdf> (last accessed 25.03.2015).

Natsios, A., 2010. The Clash of the Counter-bureaucracy and Development. [ONLINE]. Available from: <http://www.cgdev.org/sites/default/files/1424271_file_Natsios_Counterbureaucracy.pdf> (last accessed 10.09.2014).

Niblett, R., 2011. The Chatham House–YouGov Survey 2011: British Attitudes Towards the UK's International Priorities Survey Analysis. London, Chatham House/YouGov.

OECD, 2014. Aid to developing countries rebounds in 2013 to reach an all-time high. [ONLINE]. Available from: <http://www.oecd.org/newsroom/aid-to-developing-countries-rebounds-in-2013-to-reach-an-all-time-high.htm> (last accessed 10.10.2014).

Pellini, A., 2013. The limits of evidence. [ONLINE]. Available from: <http://www.thebrokeronline.eu/Blogs/Human-Security-blog/The-limits-of-evidence> (last accessed 26.03.2015).

Ramalingam, B., 2013. Aid on the Edge of Chaos: Rethinking International Cooperation in a Complex World, first ed. Oxford University Press, Oxford.

Ramalingam, B., 2012. ODI Background Note. Learning How to Learn: Eight Lessons for Impact Evaluations that Make a Difference. ODI, London.

Riddell, R., 2009. Is aid working? Is this the right question to be asking? Open Democracy. Available from: https://www.opendemocracy.net/roger-c-riddell/is-aid-working-is-this-right-question-to-be-asking (accessed 6.10.2015.).

Riddell, R.C., 2014. Does foreign aid really work? [ONLINE] Available from: <http://devpolicy.org/2014-Australasian-Aid-and-International-Development-Policy-Workshop/Roger-Riddell-Background-Paper.pdf> (last accessed 20.09.2014).

Sachs, J.D., 2005. The End of Poverty: Economic Possibilities for our Time. Penguin Press, New York, NY.

Savedoff, W.D., 2013. Impact Evaluation? Where Have we Been? Where are we Going. Paper presented at the CGD-3iE Conference, Washington, DC. 17 July 2013. [ONLINE]. Available from: <http://www.cgdev.org/sites/default/files/savedoff> (last accessed 10.10.2014).

Stern, E., 2013. The Problem with 'Impact Evaluation': Balancing Precision and Generalisation in a Complex World. Keynote speech at the 'Conference on Impact Evaluation', Wageningen University, 25 March 2013.

Stern, E., Stame, N., Mayne, J., Forss, K., Davies, R., Befani, B., 2012. Broadening the Range of Designs and Methods for Impact Evaluations. DFID Working Paper 38, DFID, London.

Taylor, B., 2013. Evidence-Based Policy and Systemic Change: Conflicting Trends? Springfield Working Paper Series # 1. Durham: Springfield Centre. [ONLINE]. Available from: <http://www.effective-states.org/the-role-and-politics-of-evidence-in-development> (last accessed 15.11.2014).

Ticehurst, D., 2012. Who is Listening to Who, How Well and With What Effect? [ONLINE]. Available from: <http://www.mande.co.uk/blog/wp-content/uploads/2013/02/2012-Who-is-listening-to-Whom> (last accessed 15.10.2014).

Vowles, P., 2013. DFID Bloggers: Adaptive Programming. [ONLINE]. Available from: <https://dfid.blog.gov.uk/2013/10/21/adaptive-programming> (last accessed 12.11.2014).

White, H., Phillips, D., 2012. Addressing Attribution of Cause and Effect in Small Impact Evaluations: Towards an Integrated Framework. International Initiative for Impact Evaluation Working Paper No. 15.

BEYOND AID DISTRIBUTION: AID EFFECTIVENESS, NEOLIBERAL AND NEOSTRUCTURAL REFORMS IN PACIFIC ISLAND COUNTRIES

6

Amerita Ravuvu and Alec Thornton

School of Physical, Environmental and Mathematical Sciences, University of New South Wales, Canberra, Australia

CHAPTER OUTLINE

INTRODUCTION

The aid effectiveness discourse is a recurring theme that has generated considerable discussions globally (Killen, 2011; McGillivray, 2004). In practice, the role of development aid in addressing development challenges has been negligible where the recurring outcome of the so-called trickle-down effects of project aid often do not live up to expectations at the commencement of development projects. Aid effectiveness forums have recognized the challenges with the value for money agenda and although these two agendas seek to complement each other, in practice, the two agendas seem polarized (Manuel, 2011). In the last decade, concerns have increased regarding the priorities of actors and beneficiaries and whose priorities aid serves. Given the power relations that do exist between donor agencies, NGOs and recipient governments, there are valid concerns about striking a balance between the efficiency and effectiveness of aid in the context of the value for money agenda (Jackson, 2012). Critiques of aid have often blamed the donor–recipient bureaucracy relationship that exists in the process of committing, delivering, and managing aid to the failure of aid in achieving impact. In the context of Pacific island countries facing considerable development challenges, the aid effectiveness discourse looms large in discussions concerning the quality of life and the future livelihoods of Pacific island communities.

There are continuous roundtable discussions for changes in policy and practice. While neostructural reforms have been heralded to bring forth participatory and decentralized aid modalities in the Pacific islands, there are criticisms that neoliberal reforms still dictate the way donors distribute aid.

This chapter is concerned with Official Development Assistance (ODA) to the Pacific islands and will discuss the relationship between aid impact and neoliberal and neostructural reforms in the Pacific island countries. The chapter aims to provide a critical assessment of the nexus between these reforms and Pacific island governments' capacity to prioritize, deliver, and manage aid and how this relationship ultimately contributes to the effectiveness and sustainability of discrete development projects. It will examine, in particular, how these reforms impinge on governments' capacity to prioritize and deliver ODA, and how donors and governments approach and manage impact assessment of ODA projects. The chapter concludes by examining selected case studies from Fiji and Samoa, providing analyses of their appropriateness and effectiveness. These case studies will address the unique challenges involved in aid and supporting progress in these countries, where there is a very complex interplay of governance, development, poverty, and instability issues. The cases highlight the lack of country ownership and the existing disconnect between what beneficiaries expect and what aid agencies and recipient governments prioritize.

OVERVIEW OF DEVELOPMENT AID

Since its inception after the Second World War, the key proclaimed purposes of foreign aid have been development and poverty alleviation. Broadly speaking, foreign aid can be classified into three separate categories: humanitarian or emergency aid, charity-based aid, and systematic aid (Moyo, 2009), conventionally known as development aid. Besides ODA, flows from the private sector of a donor country and private grants from nongovernmental organizations (NGOs), development aid also includes other official flows as defined by OECD (2009, p. 180) including "…loans from the government sector which are for development and welfare, but which are not sufficiently concessional to qualify as ODA."

The foreign aid agenda has evolved enormously in the last five decades. Prior to the 1970s, the aid agenda was targeted at the restoration and reconstruction of the fractured European countries in the postwar years under the Marshall Plan, also known as the European Recovery Program, and the reviving of development in these countries measured in terms of rising per capita incomes. This focus shifted to include the funding of large-scale industrial projects such as roads and railways during the period of industrialization in the 1960s following the success of the Marshall Plan (Willis, 2005). The evolution of the aid agenda then shifted its focus to relief of poverty in developing countries in the 1970s, followed by the promotion of neoliberal development policies encapsulated in the structural adjustment programmes of the 1980s. In the 1990s and 2000s, the aid agenda has shifted to promote sustainable development, democracy, and improved governance, and the funding of social sector activities, all of which are prominent in the present international development aid discourse. Chapters 1 and 3 discuss this area in much more depth. The following analysis directly relates to this research.

Research over the last few decades has provided inconclusive findings to the question "Does aid work?" Many studies examining the link between aid and economic growth have had contradictory results. Up until the 1990s, research on the macroeconomic impact of aid was either of the "It Works or It Doesn't Work camp" (McGillivray et al., 2006, p. 1032). This impact of aid on economic growth was positive, negative, or neutral depending on who one chose to cite (see Chapter 1). However, from the late 1990s onwards, much of the macroeconomic debates on aid effectiveness have concluded that aid effectiveness is contingent on political stability, policy environment, and climatic conditions (McGillivray et al., 2006).

In assessing the effectiveness of micro or project-related aid studies, the general finding seems to lean toward the negative end of the continuum – that aid is not effective with only a few projects benefitting specific groups of people in specific settings, yet, on the whole, aid has been ineffective (Kosack, 2003). In Europe, for example, the effecting of the Marshall Plan funneling assistance worth US$13 billion from the United States over the period 1948 to 1952 brought about political stability, a revived economy, and restored derelict infrastructure for the 14 European countries that were assisted. These include today's leading industrialized economies and G7 members of Great Britain, France, Italy, and Germany. However, the aid agenda and its effectiveness have, to a large extent, been questionable for other parts of the world. This is conspicuous in the African continent where US$1 trillion in development aid has flowed into the region in the last five decades, but millions of people in Africa remain poorer today (Moyo, 2009).

For the South Pacific region, aid has not helped Pacific island countries in reaching their development objectives. While it has contributed to some economic growth and development, there have been a number of macroeconomic studies (Fielding, 2007; Feeny, 2007, 2010), which have highlighted the negligible impacts of ODA to the Pacific island economies. In the Pacific Islands, as well as other developing regions, the aid agenda has largely been shaped by western models of development (Scheyvens, 1999). These development models are underpinned by neoliberal and neostructural policies that have been incorporated into the Pacific island economies and supported via ODA. Since 1970, the Pacific has received approximately US$50 billion in aid and Australia has been the largest donor (Hughes, 2003).

ECONOMIC REFORMS IN PICS: KEY ISSUES

Despite large volumes of aid in support of neoliberal and neostructural policies, there has been criticism on the appropriateness of these for Pacific island economies and whether they yield sound impacts in practice (Bertram, 1993; Jayaraman and Ward, 2006). In the past three decades, the Pacific region has been characterized as a collection of remote and struggling economies, a misfit of small-scale and large-scale development projects promoted by governments and aid agencies where the striking contrasts between urban and rural development and the widening gaps between rich and poor are closely linked to, if not a direct consequence of, the critical global forces that are at play (Slatter, 2006; Jones, 2013). These include the region-wide economic reforms adopting globally integrated economic models, trade liberalization agreements, and the implementation of neoliberal market policies that were introduced to decrease the very problems that they have now exacerbated.

Small island economies like those in the Pacific, have had limited success in benefitting from region-wide economic reforms and trade liberalization agreements (Pacific Island Forum Secretariat, 2014). A key driver of the region's economic development supported by ODA is the Aid for Trade (AfT) paradigm – a paradigm that is now an integral part of development assistance concerned with trade negotiations, commitments, and opportunities in the region. AfT covers a range of activities as defined by the Pacific Island Forum Secretariat (2014) as a "subset of development assistance that boost a country's capacity to create and take advantage of expanded trade opportunities" (p. 6). AfT to the region has been lauded for its efforts in bringing about transformative development through trade capacity building, strengthening export capacity, attracting foreign direct investment, and the vast improvements to the development of infrastructure, such as airports and telecommunication services (Pacific Island Forum Secretariat, 2014). However, developing countries are often at a significant disadvantage when they are integrated into the global trading system and bound by trade commitments. For instance, commitments associated with World Trade Organisation (WTO) accession have had negative implications for countries, such as Nepal, Cambodia, and Tonga, whose governments were urged to make WTO-plus commitments (Legge et al., 2013; Wallis, 2010). In Vanuatu, there have been concerns expressed regarding the demanding requirements of accession needed prior to obtaining WTO membership in 2012. For example, criticisms during the last round of Least Developed Countries (LDC) accession guidelines on agricultural products were expected to impact Vanuatu and other LDCs negatively (Toohey, 2012). As Allee and Scalera (2012) point out, international bodies like the WTO "can have a significant effect on state behavior through the accession process" (p. 246).

From the mid-1990s, bilateral and multilateral donor aid programs in the Pacific islands eagerly sought to lend money to Pacific island governments to assist with economic reforms and the public sector reform of several countries, including Cook Islands, the Federated States of Micronesia, Fiji, the Republic of the Marshall Islands, Vanuatu, Tonga, and Samoa (Slatter, 2006). Consensus in policy circles saw the implementation of these as the best fit for delivering sustained economic growth and stimulating development. Yet, despite the aid aimed at ensuring such maximum returns, these heightened lending programs are now being strongly criticized for the accumulated burdensome debts that Pacific islands are grappling with and the aid-dependence cycle that it has perpetuated in the islands. In practice, aid flowing in, particularly for public sector reforms, has enabled the public sector to dominate the island economies and remain the largest employer. Undoubtedly, the high levels of public sector wages and salaries have and continue to be supported directly or indirectly by aid receipts (Siwatibau et al., 1991; Hughes, 2003). While the public sector is growing bigger, private sector development is undermined.

The influence and roles that aid agencies and governments play in the process of delivering and managing aid go beyond simply delivering development plans and projects. These institutions are also "key vehicles for setting the context in which projects and policies evolve and for determining which projects or policies will or will not be supported or delivered" (Roche, 1999, p. 234). As lamented by aid critiques that decry aid conditionalities, one of the ways in which donors have tended to tie aid is via their imposition of preselected projects and policies that their aid will support. PIFS, for example, is a regional agency advancing donor programmes concerned with the economic restructuring of the Pacific region and is a "think-tank" that has been responsible for the dissemination of liberalization policies and plays a critical role in advising Pacific island leaders on best economic policy options.

In the new millennium, PIFS has become increasingly focused on trade liberalizing agreements supported and regulated by OECD donors such as the Pacific Island Countries Trade Agreement (PICTA), the Pacific Agreement on Closer Economic Relations (PACER), PACER-Plus and the Economic Partnership Agreement (EPA). Significant concerns remain about these AfT initiatives and whether they bring about the value for trade reforms and the potential benefits that the stated objectives of these agreements profess to do. As Narsey (2004) has pointed out, these agreements pertain to increased economic integration and minimizing barriers of trade on one hand, but there are significant costs as far as trade liberalization is concerned (Narsey, 2008). Evidence from research over the years has widely acknowledged that the implementation of such reforms in the Pacific region brings a range of costs that are far-reaching (Slatter, 2006; PANG, 2008). The benefits of these trade liberalizing agreements may include cheaper imports that will benefit consumers, increased investment, increased competition that will attract new enterprises and a healthy commercial trading environment with improvements in efficiency that will benefit Pacific business and service suppliers. On the other hand, costs include a loss of government revenue, particularly through the reduction in import tariffs that are a major source of revenue for Pacific island governments, loss of jobs, the undermined access to essential services for the poor and rural people, and a loss of "policy space" to governments to steer development (PANG, 2008).

OECD countries have delivered millions of dollars of preparatory work under the AFT initiative to these free trade agreements. Despite more than a decade of work by PIFs and a decade of trade negotiations with various stakeholders, the potential value and benefits of these free trade agreements for Pacific island countries remain doubtful (Narsey, 2004). To put this into perspective, following a decade of negotiations with EPA, there are pressing concerns about the benefits of EPA for Papua New Guinea. Recent developments in PNG's tuna fishery show that besides changing the rules of origin, the outcomes of EPA for development have been questionable (Havice and Reed, 2012). Under EPA, the European Union is demanding that access to fisheries be part of the trade negotiations. This will allow PNG to export canned tuna to the European Union at a zero duty tariff regardless of the origin of the tuna. As a result, tuna fleets from the Philippines who now have access to PNG waters with a state-of-the-art tuna canning factory in PNG, can their tuna using cheap labor and then sell the tuna back into the European markets that are essentially PNG's export target (Havice and Reed, 2012). Although there are economic spin-offs for PNG, there are also questions about socio-economic outcomes. Research by Anderson (2008) highlights that the average weighted income for road sellers was four times the weighted average income for those employed in the tuna factories.

In the late 1990s and the early 2000s, the global aid architecture has been driven by the poverty agenda and the good governance agenda. Both these agendas are fundamentally in a neostructuralist language (Murray and Overton, 2011a, 2011b). These agendas have been furthered by the MDGs and shaped by the Paris Declaration for Aid Effectiveness 2005. For the Pacific, even though development policies, recipient state development plans and donor efforts are focused on neostructural policies concerning poverty alleviation and sustainable economic development, "neoliberal conditionalities regarding economic restructuring and public sector reform" are still dominant (Murray and Overton, 2011a, 2011b, p. 280). It has been observed that the heavy involvement of government agencies in the wider aid process in the name of "country ownership" and "harmonisation of work programmes" – both tenets of neostructuralism, has brought about new conditionalities and donor interference that do not necessarily augur well for development effectiveness in the region (Murray and Overton, 2011a, 2011b).

In theory, the benefits of a transition toward neoliberal and/or neostructural market-based policies heavily geared toward increasing production, national wealth, and sustainable development seem to make sense. However, these fundamentally ignore social dimensions of development that ultimately impact the sustainability and effectiveness of development aid on people's lives in the region. Moreover, in impact assessments of many aid projects implemented in the region, the focus of donors and national governments has largely been on how foreign aid supporting economic neoliberal and neostructural policies has improved the overarching themes of sustainable development, democracy, and governance at the macrolevel.

The World Bank (WB), a major multilateral donor in the region, produced a report (World Bank, 2011) on its performance and aid effectiveness agenda ahead using the Paris Declaration survey – a tool monitoring and tracking development partner performance against a set of macro-indicators focused on institutional strengthening, country ownership, alignment of programs, and development partnerships. The report proclaims that this global survey has value and is widely recognized given the growing number of countries that participate in it annually. Among these partner countries are Fiji, Solomon Islands, Samoa, Tonga, Vanuatu, and Papua New Guinea. According to the report, the survey is a "good tool to track progress [however] it is only a partial measure of achievements: it tracks only selected Paris Declaration commitments, it does not cover many Accra Agenda for Action commitments" (World Bank, 2011, p. 7). The loopholes in this survey call for a "global-light, country-focused approach" going forward. This sort of quantitative monitoring is prevalent in many donor–recipient states tracking of development projects and often gives the erroneous impression of aid's success and the success of liberalization reforms versus qualitative evaluation of implemented projects.

THE LIMITATIONS OF ECONOMIC REFORMS

The Burnside and Dollar (1997) hypothesis contends that aid is effective for spurring economic growth in countries where the macroeconomic policy environment is stable. This premise was widely supported by the World Bank (1998) study *Assessing Aid*, arguing that aid will be effective for poverty alleviation in countries founded on good economic policies. These liberalization policies, launched between the 1980s and 1990s, have been integrated into developing countries including Pacific island economies. Many Pacific island economies are undergoing structural adjustment as conditioned by multilateral agencies such as the WB and the Asian Development Bank, and bilateral donors such as AusAID (Maclellan, 2001). These "tied aid" conditions have been highly influential in the way Pacific island governments have rapidly adopted and implemented reforms, which now make them inevitably much more dependent on developed global markets.

For the region, external pressures have largely dictated structural adjustment policies and financial reforms from donors and the global market, as well as internal pressures from different political groupings and economic uncertainties looming in the islands. The effective implementation of these reforms has been heavily dependent on the political stability of each country. Fiji, for example, has adopted various structural adjustment policies centering on the privatization of public enterprises, private sector-led development, public sector management, and market-led policies. In Vanuatu, structural adjustment policies focused on decentralization reforms in the early years of postindependence and now on market-centered reforms including the more recent Asian Development Bank-sponsored Comprehensive Reform Program (CRP). The five-point action plan of the CRP was aimed at strengthening public institutions and the governance framework, restructuring of the public service, strengthening of Parliament as an institution, strengthening of the legal sector, and an extensive financial and economic reform. Assessments of the CRP (Nari, 2000; Gay, 2004) show that implementation was unsuccessful and this was constrained by political instability, amongst other issues. For Samoa, donors have lauded a track record of good macroeconomic management over the last 20 years, followed by successful reforms, such as the ADB-sponsored economic reform program (Maclellan, 2001). Despite this optimistic economic outlook, poverty in Samoa is an increasing concern. In particular, the rural–urban drift is contributing to expanding urban poverty in Samoa, which include emerging issues such as "urban landlessness" (alienation from customary land rights) and social problems, described as "suburban dystopia," meaning substance abuse, domestic violence, street crime, and suicide (Thornton et al., 2010, 2013). In Papua New Guinea, the WB has been the lead multilateral agency financing public sector reforms. As mentioned earlier in the chapter, the WB, the ADB, and other major bilateral donors to the region have also driven financial and public sector reforms in other Pacific island countries.

Despite the huge ODA loans driving these restructuring programs, these programs have resulted in backlash from various groups including public sector employees, antiglobalization protestors, civil society groups, and nongovernmental organizations. The impacts of these structural adjustment reforms have included but are not limited to, job losses, monopolies, high cost of essential services, urban-based growth, neglected rural development, and negligible emphasis on social and cultural issues of development. As highlighted by Maclellan (2001), these restructuring programs impacted the working population the most. In Marshall Islands, for example, a 3-year wage freeze was experienced. For Papua New Guinea, these reforms seemed to benefit a few people only, particularly the elites, with increases in salaries for high-end public service employees in the year 2000 while the basic wage remained at the levels set in 1992 for the populace. In Fiji, the privatization of water resulted in a 40% rise in water rates in 1998 and increased taxes on foodstuffs and other essential services. There was also a huge downsizing of the public sector waiting to happen with the move to privatize government services from 1993 to 1998.

It is clear that the inclusion of these reforms has brought about far-reaching social costs that has enriched a few and impoverished the masses. The notion that the so-called "trickle down" effects of aid supporting these reforms to bring about economic growth for the benefit of those in rural areas is, arguably, far-fetched (Gibson-Graham et al., 2013). In 2001, the Ecumenical Centre for Research, Education and Advocacy (ECREA), a civil society group based in Fiji, remarked "current economic policies operate above the heads of the people, marginalizing many from the decision-making processes of governments, and particularly those shaping and directing our economy and its impact on our lives" (cited in Wendt, 2001, p. 11). The failure of development aid to strengthen rural economies in PICs has resulted with unintended impacts, seen in increasing urban densities and squatter or informal settlements, where living conditions for the urban poor reflect conditions typically found in other developing countries (Thornton, 2009, Thornton et al., 2013). Jones asserts, "in the next 15 years, squatter and informal settlements will comprise the main urban form in Pacific towns and cities." Although squatter settlements at levels experienced in the Melanesian context do not yet exist in Samoa, an urbanizing trend does indeed exist and related urban poverty is increasing (Thornton et al., 2013, p. 359).

As the following case studies indicate, market-driven policies largely benefit urban-based growth and the formal sector of the economy, while neglecting the nonformal sector and the rural areas where the majority of island populations reside. Yet even with this contrast, donors and national governments continue to emphasize a neoliberal view on aid effectiveness and economic impacts of development projects in the region.

CASE STUDY 1: SOVI BASIN CONSERVATION AREA IN FIJI

Consideration for the environment has become increasingly prominent in the sustainable development of Pacific islands. The conservation area at Sovi Basin in the interior of Viti Levu, takes on a participatory management plan approach in achieving the preservation of this biological and landscape heritage. With over 25 years of wide consultation with landowning communities, relevant government departments, and donor representation through the Conservation International, the Sovi Basin was successfully leased to the National Trust of the Fiji Islands (a statutory body cofunded by the Government of Fiji, independent donors, and multilateral projects) in 2011 for conservation purposes. The 99-year lease signed by landowners covers an area of approximately 16,300 hectares (Sovi Basin, 2013).

Shortly after the formalizing of this long-term conservation lease, the Namosi Joint Venture (NJV) – a joint venture exploration between three different mining companies (Nittetsu Mining Co Ltd and Materials Investments (Fiji) Ltd from Japan, and Newcrest Limited from Australia commenced with exploration activities focusing on copper–gold deposits at Namosi and proposed to mine in the Sovi Basin despite the area being set aside as a protected rainforest heritage. Along the western boundary of the Sovi Basin is the Wainavadu catchment area, where the NJV proposed to convert into a site for mine waste (NatureFiji - Mareqeti Viti, 2012). In August 2011, the Office of the Prime Minister called off the processing of the lease document for the Sovi Basin. This resulted from several correspondences sent through by the Namosi Joint Venture on their redefined boundary of the Conservation Area, which excluded the Wainavadu catchment area. Due to the halt in processing of lease documents, conflicts between the landowners and conservation stakeholders have been escalating and there have also been grave concerns from the international conservation community (*ibid*). To add to challenges of preserving the Sovi Basin Conservation Area, Fiji's Water Authority also proposed the construction of a hydrodam within the protected area to cater for the water needs of the Suva/Nausori corridor.

Based on a study by Keppel et al. (2012), the Sovi Basin Conservation Area has been listed as a successful conservation program of green aid where a trust fund was set up in 2005 for the landowning communities. This was to compensate them for a temporary 5-year conservation lease to protect the Sovi Basin and the wide array of endemic and native flora and fauna that thrived in the area. The interest accumulated by this trust fund, which is financially supported by the largest exporting bottled water company Fiji Water, has facilitated the payment of lease premiums, compensated foregone timber royalties from a logging concession that was revoked by the Fijian *itaukei* Land Trust Board after consultation with landowners, allowed for development opportunities, and enabled the implementation of the management plan devised by a steering committee and working group of relevant government departments, the multilateral donor agency Conservation International and the landowners. Through the trust fund a scholarship programme was also established and has provided scholarship opportunities for school leavers pursuing tertiary education from the area.

Despite these benefits from a community-driven initiative centered on biodiversity conservation and sustainable development, the ongoing challenges faced by the Government of Fiji recognizes the need to promote economic growth through major economic investment and development on one hand, and at the same time, abiding by sustainability principles it has committed itself to through several international conventions and agreements, and national policy commitments. These include the Convention on Biological Diversity, the Millennium Development Goals, the World Heritage Convention, and the Fiji National Biodiversity Strategy and Action Plan to name a few.

In pursuing the use of the Wainavadu catchment area as their waste dump site, the Namosi Joint Venture invested FJ$4m for its Environment Impact Assessment for a decision to be made on the use of the Wainavadu area in 2013. It must be noted that a stakeholder involved in the steering committee and working group concerned with the protection of the area carried out the EIA. This conflict of interest illustrates another issue prevalent in Pacific island settings, and that is the limited capacity and expertise to carry out technical tasks as such. Being spread too thin or merely lacking capacity often results in stakeholders representing both parties involved. Moreover, the role played by the donor agencies in this example is unclear. While Conservation International has been instrumental in the setup of a management plan to conserve the Sovi Basin and has entered into a grant agreement with Fiji Water on the setup of a Trust Fund to compensate the landowning communities, their role in the mitigation of the conflicts at hand is unclear.

Following this, the Government of Fiji also approved a feasibility study to look into the feasibility of establishing the proposed dam in the area and its potential impacts despite lacking the expertise and capacity to carry this study out properly. Moreover, this was carried out even though it was not within the requirements of the management plan for the Sovi Basin Conservation Area that the Government of Fiji had already agreed to via its relevant departments who played key roles in the devising of the management plan. The Sovi Basin Conservation Area conflict addresses four dilemmas that Pacific island governments constantly struggle with when striving for sustainable development: (i) the maximum returns of conservation planning and initiatives at the expense of major investment and development, (ii) economic growth and investment taking precedence over all other national priorities, (iii) pressure from foreign investors, and (iv) the role played by donor agencies in mitigating such dilemmas.

For the Pacific islands, the impacts of large-scale mining and logging on local communities have been well documented. Despite the obvious, advocates of mining, including Pacific island governments and donors who support these, as important contributions to economic stability tend to overestimate the national and regional economic benefits of these activities. One only has to cite examples of large-scale mining from Papua New Guinea and excessive logging from the Solomon Islands to grasp the environmental and social costs and impacts that these activities exacerbate.

CASE STUDY 2: ONGOING ADB REFORM "PROMOTING ECONOMIC USE OF CUSTOMARY LAND" IN SAMOA

Perhaps the most controversial land for development reform of recent-years in the Pacific region has been that from Samoa promoting the economic use of customary land. This small island country has experienced low and volatile economic growth buffeted by a series of major external shocks in recent years (MFEPD, 2012). With a vision to bring about robust economic growth and improve the quality of life for all, Samoa had launched its Strategy for Development (SDS) for the period 2005 to 2007 with a six-point action plan heavily centered on economic development. This document reflected a continuation of reforms that were implemented over the past SDS periods. As part of its second goal relating to promoting investment, the document outlined "land for development" as a key SDS activity to be rigorously pursued. According to the document, a broad review of the economic use of customary land would be undertaken "with the view to opening opportunities for landowners and facilitating both external and domestic investment without jeopardizing the social ownership of land" (MFEPD, 2005, p. 8). Under the proposed SDS, the Asian Development Bank provided technical assistance worth US$300,000 to support Phase I of III for the project.

Research undertaken highlights that this joint effort between the ADB and the Government of Samoa to mobilize and securitize customary land has been in process for at least 15 years (Lameta et al., personal communication, December 19, 2013), with previous ADB land and financial sector reforms namely the "Samoa Agribusiness Support Project" in 1998, and the "Small Business Development" and the "Capacity Building of Financial and Business Advisory Services' projects in 2000" (Asian Development Bank, 2005). These series of projects are all under the reform called "Promoting Economic Use of Customary Land" (PREUC), formerly known as "Facilitating Land Mobilization and Securitization."

With the amendment of the Alienation Customary Land Act 1965 and the passing of two new bills, the Land Titles Registration Act Bill 2008 and the Customary Land Advisory Commission Bill 2012, both established under Phase II of the PREUC, there has been growing concerns from various stakeholders including disgruntled titleholders, NGOs, and political groups. In an interview with the Samoa

Umbrella for Non-Governmental Organisations (SUNGO) in 2008, they "believed the government was under pressure by international funders to free up land for development and that was the end goal of the controversial bills" (Tait, 2008). Signatories of a complaint report to the ADB Pacific Subregional Office in Fiji lamented, "these land tenure reforms are incompatible with the indigenous culture and political institutions of Samoa, and are inconsistent with the needs and aspirations of the Samoan people" (Lameta et al., personal communication, December 19, 2013). Members of the Tautua Samoa Party echoed similar sentiments that the government was only proceeding with leasing customary land for economic development as per the advice and recommendation of ADB in 2006 to have the customary lands leased (Tupufia, 2012). Conversely, the ADB technical assistance report (2005) for the PREUC highlights that the government requested their assistance in mobilizing and securitizing customary land.

The implementation of reforms in Phases I and II was viewed as successful with concrete actions carried out. To achieve impact in this project, ADB's design and monitoring framework highlighted that the reforms would bring forth increased levels of economic activity on customary land. Outputs 1 and 2 were achieved with the amendment of the Alienation Customary Land Act 1965 and the establishment of two new Land Bills. There has also been successful streamlining of administrative processes involved in the leasing of customary lands. For Output 3, the development of a comprehensive communication strategy to disseminate public information materials and increase awareness on the key issues involved for landowners and investors have proven less successful.

The issues surrounding the controversial ADB-backed reforms can be summarized as threefold: (i) there has been no meaningful consultation with stakeholders, consulting as widely as possible to gain landowner approval and acceptance, (ii) the implications of these reforms in the name of promoting economic development and investment without the provision of complete and accurate information to affected communities on the social costs, and (iii) the ADB's ignorance to fathom the cultural significance of these customary lands for the Samoan people and noncompliance of their own policies and procedures in the implementation of these reforms. Although the ADB was aware of social issues and concerns that they identified during their fact-finding mission citing "fears of alienation of customary ownership of lands," "the rights of titleholders and heirs," "rights of access to leaseholds," and "the role of Government in the negotiation of leases" (Asian Development Bank, 2009), it seems that these concerns were not dealt with appropriately.

With more than 80% of land held under customary ownership, alternative approaches need to be undertaken to make landowners fully aware of the implications of acquisitions as such given the sacrosanctity of customary land for Samoans. It appears that the ADB and the Government of Samoa need to devise mitigation measures to resolve the current conflict and accept that any efforts to promote the economic use of customary land need to be done with full acknowledgment and understanding of its importance as "land is at the very core of everything connected to the *fa'a Samoa* (Samoa way) – culture, titles, language, *aiga* (extended family) and people" (Tu'u'u et al., 2003, p. 1).

CONCLUSION

Approaches to the disbursement and utilization of aid in the Pacific have evolved to recognize the socioeconomic, political, and cultural environments at the national and regional level, and the global transition toward the idea and practice of sustainable development. With that being said, this chapter has shown that Pacific islands and their governments continue to struggle to keep up with the tides of globalization and adopting reforms to fit in with the globalized economy while at the same time striving to uphold practices of sustainable development that meet cultural and socioeconomic needs.

The AfT paradigm alluded to earlier in this chapter highlights the value of trade reform and areas in which AfT programs have made progress, yet there are significant concerns that remain about its impact on developing countries and the lack of a level playing field for these countries to negotiate their terms on. Besides the WTO regulations that developing countries struggle with, significant concerns also remain about other AfT initiatives in the region including the PICTA, PACER, PACER Plus, and EPA free trade agreements. Problems relating to food security and increasing poverty, particularly at the grassroots level will be affected if Pacific island economies totally commit to unfavorable requirements such as those pertaining to agreements on agriculture cited in this chapter. This problem is not unique to the Pacific and as research has shown is evident in other developing countries such as Nepal and Cambodia. Under the heading of neoliberal structural adjustment programmes and AfT, various initiatives have been explored and implemented by Pacific island governments, bilateral donors, and development agencies. In embracing globalization and the "new consensus" on the logic of free trade, the costs and challenges associated with these reforms bring to question the value for money agenda and whether OECD donors represent complimentary agendas where AfT addresses both macro and micro effects of these agreements ensuring that there is robust economic and social development, or whether they represent divergent agendas such as those where OECD countries are protecting their own trade interests.

For the Sovi Basin Conservation Area, the case study has examined the conflicts emerging from a successful green aid conservation programme now undermined by a mining proposal that is anticipated to boost development for the locality of the mining area. Although relevant stakeholders recognize the significance of protecting this biological and landscape heritage and are fully aware of the negative impacts of mining, a feasibility study is currently being carried out given that economic development and investment is also a key priority for the Government of Fiji. To add to this, the role played by donors contributing to Fiji's coffers for development plans that concern mining and other economic activities is also unclear in the Sovi Basin issue. In the Samoan case study, there has been backlash from landowners and titleholders who have lodged complaints with the ADB Sub-Regional Office in Fiji and the Head Office in the Philippines. There have also been complaints made on the way the ADB has carried out this project with disregard of its own policies, compliance procedures, and engagement requirements. It seems that the Samoan Government has its hands tied as well – on the one hand striving for increased investment and economic development, and on the other, dealing with potential displacement of indigenous peoples.

While the highlighted case studies have benefits for economic development, their appropriateness and effectiveness for sustainable development and addressing socioeconomic needs concerning the livelihoods of the island communities is negligible. The pressure imposed on the Fiji Government by the NJV shows that little attention is paid to the negative impacts that mining will have on sustainable practices of the affected communities and direct commercial benefits that landowners currently enjoy such as royalty from land leases. The extraction of mineral resources and the waste-dumping activities proposed does not take account of the subsistence economic activities, the culture, and traditions of the affected communities.

Many aid programs backing Pacific government programs focused on land projects, persist with the idea that customary land must be reformed, and mobilized to bring forth rapid growth and development in the Pacific. The Government of Samoa, with backing from the ADB, has progressed with the implementation of the land reform process to make more land available for development. The idea behind this reform to open up more land for development is a rather narrow conceptualization of land that limits it to its commodity value with a gross disregard for the significance of customary land to the Samoans and its role in sustaining its communities for thousands of years.

These case studies highlight the dilemmas facing Pacific island governments in their efforts to carry out economic and income generating activities. These examples of neoliberal attempts to reform the Pacific island economy often undermine the value of natural resources such as customary lands to the indigenous peoples. In many instances, market-driven policies like the ones outlined in this chapter largely benefit urban-based growth and the formal sector of the economy, while neglecting the nonformal sector and the rural areas where the majority of island populations reside. Yet even with this contrast, donors and national governments continue to emphasize a neoliberal view on aid effectiveness and economic impacts of development projects in the region.

There is no doubt that donors' approaches to development in the region are closely aligned with strategies for economic growth and policies largely driven by neoliberalist and neostructuralist language. These approaches are evident in the way "tied aid" is disbursed to the region with conditions of reforms promoting capitalist development. Despite the recognition of agreed principles of aid effectiveness outlined in various international agreements such as the Paris Declaration 2005, Accra Agenda for Action 2008, and the Busan Partnership for Effective Development Cooperation 2011 – all defining principles of ownership, transparency, and sustainable partnerships, the fact in the Pacific islands is that donors have a strong influence on how aid funds are used and still dictate the terms of the sectors in which they deem the use of aid funds as being most appropriate and effective. In many instances, Pacific island governments have limited capacity and clout in intervening on aid funded state-wide programmes and projects.

There have been no signs that the Fiji and Samoa people and those across the Pacific are becoming less concerned about reforms aimed at increasing economic prosperity at the cost of their resources over time – quite the opposite. There is a great need for Pacific island governments to take heed of the interests of local people and to enable community-driven projects funded by aid, with assistance from relevant stakeholders. Conditions for the release of funds over the years have become overwhelmingly controlled by donors and governments who decide which projects are to be funded and which are not to. In addition to this, donors and recipient-state government representatives, who also decide on measures that determine the success of projects, overwhelmingly coordinate the design and monitoring frameworks of development projects. In doing so, these decisions further disengage those at the bottom-end of the aid delivery structure who are, ultimately, beneficiaries of development projects.

REFERENCES

Allee, T.L., Scalera, J.E., 2012. The divergent effects of joining international organizations: Trade gains and the rigors of WTO accession. Int. Organ. 66, 243–276.

Anderson, T., 2008. Women roadside sellers in Madang. Pacific Econ. Bull. 23 (1), 59–73.

Asian Development Bank, 2005. Technical assistance to the independent state of Samoa: Promoting economic use of customary land. Technical Assistance Report (Project 37234). Available from: <http://www.adb.org/projects/documents/promoting-economic-use-customary-land-financed-japan-special-fund-0>.

Asian Development Bank, 2009. Independent state of Samoa: Promoting economic use of customary land, Phase II. Technical Assistance Report (Project 41173-01). Available from: <http://www.adb.org/sites/default/files/project-document/64634/41173-sam-tar.pdf>.

Bertram, G., 1993. Sustainability, aid, and material welfare in small South Pacific island economies, 1900–90. World Dev. 21 (2), 247–258.

Burnside, C., Dollar, D. 1997. Aid, Policies and Growth. Policy Research Working Paper 1777. World Bank, Washington.

Feeny, S., 2010. Aid and growth in small island developing states. J. Dev. Studies 46 (5), 897–917.

Feeny, S., 2007. Impacts of foreign aid to Melanesia. J. Asia Pacific Econ. 12 (1), 34–60.

Fielding, D., 2007. Aid and Dutch disease in the South Pacific, 2007. (Report No. 2007/50). Available from: http://www.wider.unu.edu/publications/working-papers/research-papers/2007/en_GB/rp2007-50/.

Gay, D., 2004. The emperor's tailor: An assessment of Vanuatu's Comprehensive Reform Program. Pacific Econ. Bull. 19 (3), 22–39.

Gibson-Graham, J.K., Cameron, J., Healy, S., 2013. Take Back the Economy. University of Minnesota Press, Minneapolis, MN.

Havice, E., Reed, K., 2012. Fishing for development? Tuna resource access and industrial change in Papua New Guinea. J. Agrarian Change 12 (1&2), 413–435.

Hughes, H., 2003. Aid has failed the Pacific. Issue Anal. (33), 1–31.

Jackson, P., 2012 Value for money and international development: Deconstructing myths to promote a more constructive discussion. Available from: <www.oecd.org/dac> (accessed 16.03.2015).

Jayaraman, T.K., Ward, B.D., 2006. Aid effectiveness in the South Pacific island countries: A case study of Vanuatu. Discussion paper, no 110. Commerce Division, Lincoln University. New Zealand.

Jones, P., 2013. 'Aid to PNG and the Pacific should focus on fixing cities'. The Conversation, 12 September. Available from: <http://theconversation.com/aid-to-png-and-the-pacific-should-focus-on-fixing-cities-18079> (accessed 25.03.2015).

Keppel, G., Morrison, C., Hardcastle, J., Rounds, I., Wilmott, I., Hurahura, F., Shed, P., 2012. Conservation in tropical Pacific island countries: Case studies of successful programmes. Int. J. Protected Areas Conservation 18 (1), 111–124.

Killen, B., 2011. Aid effectiveness and value for money aid: Complementary or divergent agendas as we head towards HLF4. PowerPoint presentation. Available from: <http://www.odi.org/sites/odi.org.uk/files/odi-assets/events-presentations/823.pdf> (accessed 14.03.2015).

Kosack, S., 2003. Effective aid: How democracy allows development aid to improve the quality of life. World Dev. 31 (1), 1–22.

Legge, D., Gleeson, D., Snowdon, W., Thow, A.M., 2013. Trade agreements and non-communicable diseases in the Pacific Islands. Available from: <http://www.who.int/nmh/events/2013/trade_agreement.pdf>.

Maclellan, N., 2001. Pacific Islands troubled by trade. Focus on the Global South. Available from: <http://focusweb.org/publications/2001/Pacific-islands-troubled-by-trade.html>.

Manuel, M., 2011. Aid Effectiveness and Value for Money Aid: Complementary or Divergent Agendas as we Head Towards HLF4. PowerPoint presentation. Available from: <http://www.odi.org/sites/odi.org.uk/files/odi-assets/events-presentations/823.pdf> (accessed 14.03.2015).

McGillivray, M., 2004. Is aid effective? Mimeo. Helsinki, UNU-WIDER.

McGillivray, M., Feeny, S., Hermes, N., Lensink, R., 2006. Controversies over the impact of development aid: it works; it doesn't; it can, but that depends…. J. Int. Dev. 18, 1031–1050.

MFEPD, 2005. Strategy for the Development of Samoa 2005-2007. Apia. Available from: <http://www.mof.gov.ws/Portals/195/sds_2005_-_2007_-_english.pdf>.

MFEPD, 2012. Strategy for the development of Samoa 2012-2016. Apia. Available from: <http://www.mcit.gov.ws/Portals/0/Publications/Policy/SDS%202012%20-%202016_English%20version.pdf>.

Moyo, D., 2009. Dead aid: Why aid is not working and how there is another way for Africa. Penguin Group, London.

Murray, E.W., Overton, J.D., 2011a. Neoliberalism is dead, long live neoliberalism? Neostructuralism and the international aid regime of the 2000s. Prog. Dev. Studies 11 (4), 307–319.

Murray, E.W., Overton, J., 2011b. The inverse sovereignty effect: Aid, scale and neostructuralism in Oceania. Asia Pacific Viewpoint 52 (3), 272–284.

Nari, R., 2000. Comprehensive reform program in the Republic of Vanuatu: a major challenge, through the eyes of ni-Vanuatu. Paper presented at the Pacific Updates on Solomon Islands, Fiji and Vanuatu, National Centre for Development Studies, Canberra, Australia: The Australian National University. Available from: <https://digitalcollections.anu.edu.au/bitstream/1885/40179/3/nari2000.pdf>.

Narsey, W., 2004. PICTA, PACER AND EPAs: Where are we going? Tales of fags, booze and rugby. Working paper 6. University of the South Pacific, Suva.

Narsey, W., 2008. 'PICTA, PACER and EPAS: Where are we going?'. Islands business, April. Available from: <https://narseyonfiji.wordpress.com/2012/03/28/picta-pacer-and-epas-where-are-we-going-appeared-in-islands-business-april-2004/> (accessed 14.03.2015).

NatureFiji - Mareqeti Viti, 2012. Position statement on the Namosi Mine, Viti Levu, Fiji. Available from: <http://www.naturefiji.org/downloads/news/NFMV%20Namosi%20Mine%20Position%20Statement_19_Jun_520120619214324.pdf>.

OECD, 2009. Better Aid Managing Aid: Practices of DAC Member Countries. Paris OECD Publishing.

Pacific Island Forum Secretariat, 2014. Aid for trade. Available from: <http://www.forumsec.org/pages.cfm/economic-governance/aid-for-trade/> (accessed 26.06.2015).

Pacific Network on Globalisation PANG, 2008. Making waves: Opportunities for reclaiming development in the Pacific. Report prepared by PANG for the 2008 Annual Pacific Civil Society Organisation Forum, Auckland, New Zealand. Available from: <http://www.oxfam.org.nz/resources/PANG%20MAKING%20WAVES%20Informing%20CSOs%20response%20to%20the%20free%20trade%20agenda.pdf>.

Roche, C., 1999. Impact assessment for development agencies: Learning to value change. Oxfam.

Scheyvens, R., 1999. Culture and society. In: Overton, J., Scheyvens, R. (Eds.), Strategies for Sustainable Development: Experiences from the Pacific. University of New South Wales Press, Australia, pp. 48–63.

Siwatibau, S., Bauer, P., Kasper, W., 1991. Aid and development in the South Pacific. The Centre of Independent Studies, Sydney.

Slatter, C., 2006. Treading water in rapids? Non-governmental organisations and resistance to neo-liberalism in Pacific island states. In: Firth, S. (Ed.), Globalisation and Governance in the Pacific Islands. ANU E Press, Canberra.

Sovi Basin, 2013. Available from: <https://www.facebook.com/video/video.php?v=490286354370245> [Video file].

Tait, M., 2008. Customary Land Excluded from Samoa Bill. The New Zealand Herald. Available from: <http://www.nzherald.co.nz/world/news/article.cfm?c_id=2&objectid=10509553>.

Thornton, A., 2009. Garden of Eden? The impact of resettlement on squatters' 'agri-hoods' in Fiji. Dev. Practice 19 (7), 884–894.

Thornton, A., Binns, T., Kerslake, M.T., 2013. Hard times in Apia? Urban landlessness and the church in Samoa. Singapore J. Tropical Geography 34 (3), 357–372.

Thornton, A., Kerslake, M., Binns, T., 2010. Alienation and obligation: Religion and social change in Samoa. Asia-Pacific Viewpoint 51 (1), 1–16.

Toohey, L., 2012. Barriers to universal membership of the World Trade Organisation. Austr. Int. Law J. 19, 97–115.

Tupufia, L., 2012. Samoa opposition queries land leases to foreign institutions. [Source: Samoa Observer]. Pacific Islands Report. Available from: <http://pidp.eastwestcenter.org/pireport/2012/November/11-02-09.htm>.

Tu'u'u, I., Taule'alo, S., Fong, D., Patea, M.S., 2003. Samoa Customary Lands at the Crossroads: Some Options for Sustainable Management. Proceedings of the 2002 National Environment Forum, No. 4, Ministry of

Natural Resources and Environment, Apia, Samoa. Available from: <http://www1.mnre.gov.ws/documents/forum/2003/2003.pdf>.

Wallis, J., 2010. Friendly islands in an unfriendly system: Examining the process of Tonga's WTO accession. Asia Pacific Viewpoint 51 (3), 262–277.

Wendt, N., 2001. Inquiry into Australia's relationship with Papua New Guinea and other Pacific island countries. Submission to the Senate Foreign Affairs, Defence and Trade References Committee by the Australian Council for Overseas Aid. Available from: <http://www.acfonline.org.au/sites/default/files/resources/submisson_to_senate_inquiry_on_png_and%20pacific_relations.pdf>.

Willis, K., 2005. Theories and Practices of Development. Routledge, London.

World Bank, 1998. Assessing Aid: What Works, What Doesn't and Why? Oxford University Press, New York, NY.

World Bank, 2011. The World Bank and Aid Effectiveness. Performance to Date and Agenda Ahead. The World Bank, Washington, DC.

REGULATORY IMPACT ASSESSMENT: THE FORGOTTEN AGENDA IN ODA

Viktor Jakupec* and Max Kelly†

*School of Education, Faculty of Arts and Education, Deakin University, Warrnambool, Australia
†School of Humanities and Social Sciences, Faculty of Arts and Education, Deakin University, Warrnambool, Australia

CHAPTER OUTLINE

INTRODUCTION

Although Regulatory Impact Assessment (RIA) has attracted significant attention from OECD, the EU, and governments in developed and developing countries, little is known about its application within the domain of foreign aid. To clarify this claim: There is extensive evidence in the public sphere that countries that are donors of Official Development Assistance (ODA) are using RIA as a tool for improving their regulatory framework within a context of their development assistance. There is evidence that Multi Lateral Development Banks (MDB) provide technical assistance (TA) to recipient governments for the development and application of RIA systems and structures (see ADB 2010, 2012). In many cases, RIA has been used as a mechanism for ODA concerning "good governance" projects. However, there is a lack of published documents showing the application of RIA within a general framework of projects, which have "regulatory conditionality" attached to them. There is however interest within the academic community to discuss, analyse, and critique RIA for ODA, with some of the notable work in the English speaking countries coming from *the Institute for Development Policy and Management* (see Kirkpatrick and Parker, 2007) at *the University of Manchester* (see also Kirkpatrick, 2014).

Given these different levels and foci of interest, our thesis is that there is a compelling logical argument to be advanced that the concept called RIA needs to be critically analyzed with particular attention to ODA projects, which have regulatory and/or policy-oriented conditionality attached. This should include *ex-ante* and *ex-post* RIA.

Having said this, it is important to note that RIA has been addressed by many developing countries. According to Kirkpatrick (2014, p. 165):

> RIA helps to improve the quality of new regulatory proposals by providing a methodological framework for analyzing the problem that the regulation is intended to solve, identifying alternative ways of dealing with the problem, and assessing the likely positive and negative impacts of adopting the proposed regulation.

Here Kirkpatrick is referring clearly to *ex-ante* RIA and subsequently turns to *ex-post* RIA, which

> ...can be used to review the net benefits of existing regulations and to ensure that regulations remain consistent with their intended policy objectives (p. 165).

If this stands to reason, there is a compelling case to be made for both *ex-ante* and *ex-post* RIA within the ODA arena.

DEFINING RIA

A cautious note may be in place: replicating the confusion in terminology throughout impact assessment in foreign aid, RIA means different things to different organizations and different stakeholders in the development aid arena. These differences may be summarized under the following three perceptions: (i) RIA as a tool for regulatory reform to be achieved by recipient countries, such as deregulation or reduction of new regulations, governing or impacting on the macro, meso, or micro environment as it relates to the aid funding; (ii) a mechanism for ensuring accountability of and political control over the recipient country's public service that creates and administers regulations; (iii) the third area of potential understanding is characterized by its advocacy for improving regulatory decision-making, based on rational-analytical analysis. The common denominator is however that irrespective of which stance one may take, RIA is critical.

This raises the question of methods and depth of analysis in RIA. These may vary in significance and the likely impact of existing and/or proposed future regulations on aid programs and projects.

For the purpose of this chapter and prior to developing our thesis let us, however briefly, define RIA. OECD (2015) defines RIA as

> ...a systemic approach to critically assessing the positive and negative effects of proposed and existing regulations and nonregulatory alternatives. As employed in OECD countries it encompasses a range of methods. It is an important element of an evidence-based approach to policy making. (n.p.)

Thus, we see RIA includes evaluation of policies, regulations, decrees, and any other government proclamation. However, this needs to be set within a contemporary context.

Let us take a step back. For a better understanding and for the purposes of this discussion RIA is perceived as setting out the potential effects (positive or negative) of the regulations to be implemented (*ex-ante*) or assessing the impact (positive or negative) of the newly introduced regulatory requirements (*ex-post*) on the beneficiaries. More specifically as far as *ex-ante* RIA is concerned there are questions concerning the aims and objectives of the regulation(s), the mechanisms to be employed to achieve the desired regulation(s), alternative options and regulations(s), and the assessment of the impact of each option from a donor's as well as recipients' perspective.

This brings us to the question of purpose. Very few Multilateral Development Organizations (MDOs) have articulated the purpose, namely, and being in danger of oversimplification, that RIA shall make regulations, imposed on recipient countries as a conditionality of a loan or grant, so as to contribute and enhance the effectiveness and efficiency of the aid at macro-, or meso-, or micro levels. Such regulations must be measured against the social, economic, and other benefits to the aid recipient nation and society as a whole. Furthermore, there is also the question of a basic RIA rationale. In essence, RIA shall be used to ensure that all regulatory proposals under the aid conditionality are such as to advance the aid objectives agreed to between the donor agency and the recipient country, as efficiently and effectively as possible.

If we are not mistaken currently there is much evidence permeating from Multilateral Development Banks (MDBs) that aid should be based on principles of Value for Money (VfM) and Aid for Trade (AfT) (cf. ICAI, 2011; Chapter 4 this volume). Thus "regulation" within ODA becomes a catalyst for economic development and advancement in developing countries. Due to the prevailing neoliberal ideology of the major MDBs this means *inter alia* to consider issues concerning market failures, which may be especially pronounced in developing countries. In such cases regulation is seen as a tool to rectify market failures with the aim to reinforce free-market efficiency and effectiveness and thus economic advancement (IFC, 2010; Chapter 3, this volume). This, according to OECD (2011) means that under the umbrella of RIA we may include all forms of regulatory policies and processes.

Let us turn to the rationale for RIA in ODA. Our claim is that the basic rationale for RIA in ODA is to guarantee that all regulatory requirements and proposals imposed by donor organizations, for example, conditionality, be scrutinized with the aim to establish how far conditionality serves political, economic, and social objectives of the recipient government as effectively and efficiently as possible. RIA as a method for analyzing *ex-ante* the likely consequences of proposed and/or actual regulation RIA has the potential to assist policy-makers and decision-makers in donor organizations and recipient countries' governments in designing, implementing, and monitoring of regulatory systems improvements, or otherwise.

However, as our research has shown, although many governments and organizations use RIA, it has seldom been used for the purposes of development aid.

A CRITICAL ANALYSIS OF MDB'S CONTEMPORARY APPROACHES TO RIA

Multilateral Development Organizations such as the UNDP, OECD, EU, the World Bank, and ADB promote *ex-ante* RIA. However, according to Renda (2011) RIAs in many developing countries are patchy at best.

There is significant evidence to show that donors intervene into recipient countries' regulatory reforms. This is however mainly in form of Technical Assistance and other measures. Interestingly enough, these interventions are focusing mainly on business and free-market development and trade. Some typical examples have been identified by Kirkpatrick (2014, p. 164) and include UNDP technical assistance in writing the Enterprise law in Vietnam; IFC's project on reforming business inspections in Uzbekistan; World Bank's project for Business registration, and licensing in Brazil and RIA in Albania.

Notwithstanding the potential benefits of these undertakings, there appears to be little evidence that MDOs are indeed utilizing RIA systematically to enhance regulatory outcomes at program or macro-, meso-, or micro-levels. As Kirkpatrick (2014, pp. 164–165) observes

> Ideally, we would like to have direct evidence on the impact of donor-supported regulatory reform measures. However, there is a paucity of statistical data on development assistance for regulatory reform, and as a result, it has not been possible to test the impact of donor support for regulatory reform directly.

Concurring with Kirkpatrick we found that there exists a poverty of publically available data on RIA in the ODA arena.

Thus we are facing a problem of dichotomy. On the one hand international organizations and MDBs are keen to impose processes of RIA on recipient countries, but are reluctant to impose the same requirement on the conditionality of ODA loans or grants. To put it differently, when MDBs impose conditionality on recipient countries they seldom, if at all, undertake *ex ante* RIA to ascertain the potential impact. It seems that the set conditionality is a given because an MDB dictates so.

Eurodad (2006) identified the situation as follows:

> ...impoverished countries still face an unacceptably high and rising number of conditions in order to gain access to World Bank and IMF development finance. On average poor countries face as many as 67 conditions per World Bank loan. However some countries faced a far higher number of conditions. (p. 3)

Furthermore, the propagation of WB and IMF conditionality imposed on developing countries in return for aid funding frequently force exceedingly contentious economic policy and regulatory reforms on recipient countries including trade liberalization and privatization of essential services. These imposition do not necessarily comply with the views of either the recipient countries social, political, and economic agenda, nor on the society itself. This, of course, may have the opposite effect, namely increasing poverty amongst the poor, rather than alleviating it (Eurodad, 2006 Chapters 3 and 4, this volume).

From this viewpoint there is a compelling case to be made for major ODA fundings to be subjected to RIA. In essence the *ex-ante* questions such as how will the regulatory requirements proposed by the donor impact on the economic, political, environmental, and social agenda of the recipient country (if at all) is seldom asked and even more seldom answered.

A critique of MDB's approach to RIA may be presented from two vantage points. One refers to the ideology and politics, the other to implementation.

THE NEOLIBERAL AGENDA

Following in the footsteps of a neoliberal economic ideology RIA has risen during the Regan and Thatcher era to new heights. It was based on the proposition that economic growth at national levels could be mired by undue or disproportionate government regulations. Thus, it is not surprising that a significant number of OECD and other countries adopted RIA as a mechanism to improve the quality of existing regulations as well as exposing new regulations to scrutiny. In other words, regulatory reforms became subject to RIA, which in turn is a mechanism for analyzing policies and/or regulations, with the purpose of enabling policy makers to improve content, framework, evaluating, monitoring, and implementing institutional, sectoral, and systemic regulatory provisions. Thus, the aim of RIA is to ascertaining probable consequences of proposed regulations or policies, as well as tangible consequences of prevailing regulations or policies.

From a neoliberal economic perspective RIA was originally perceived as a tool for determining the cost of regulations in the free-market business enterprises. It usually followed a call for deregulation in order to minimize the regulatory "red tape" and thus cut the regulatory load on private enterprise and thus foster competitiveness. However, following the Regan–Thatcher era RIA became more sophisticated. RIA was broadened from being a tool for crude measurement of regulatory cost on free-market market enterprise to a mechanism for establishing costs and benefits. Over times, tables were turned on Regan's and Thatcher's neoliberal economic legacy and it was acknowledged that regulations are intrinsically not "evil," but that every regulation needs to be assessed individually as to ascertain how it affects public plans and desired aims, objectives, and outcomes. Further it was recognized that public plans and desired aims, objectives, and outcomes to which regulations may contribute can be broadened. That is by using RIA as a tool it is possible to bring to the fore tangible positive as well as negative impacts of an existing or proposed regulation within a framework of sustainability be it economic, social, political, or environmental, etc. Thus RIA progressed from a focus on "minimal regulations" to a focus on "improved regulations."

The precipitous acknowledgment of the importance of RIA contributed to more wide-ranging public sector management reform processes and "good governance" in many OECD countries as well as the EU.

A BRIEF IDEOLOGICAL CRITIQUE

Prior to presenting a critique of the dominant neoliberal ideology as it relates to ODA, we see it as important for a better understanding to review the theoretical basis of ideology critique. Here we draw heavily on Jürgen Habermas' writings. Our point of departure is the proposition that ideological critique functions within a framework of finding "consensual truth" within a context of authentic socioeconomic and sociopolitical conditions. The problem here at the theoretical level is that, as we will show below, MDBs do not subscribe to "consensus" but impose their ideology and dogma on the recipient countries via conditionality. Returning to theory, truth according to Habermas has an eminence of "myth." In other words there is no absolute truth. If this stands to reason then the claims of any ideology are pockmarked by "false clarity." Furthermore, the socioeconomic and sociopolitical acts like imposition of conditionality without consensus that an ideology justifies and claims to be true are frequently intimately associated with powerful social and economic interests of the donor organizations.

Focusing on the specific example of RIA in ODA there are prevailing myth and validity claims, which need to be demystified, especially the claim that developing countries can prosper by adopting free-market ideologies. This is further supported by the assumption that social and institutional change is inspired with recipient countries adherence to a number of fixed free-market "laws."

Over a number of years now, every MDB subscribes to the notion of fostering a better regulatory framework in connection with its aid programs and projects (see ADB, 2012; World Bank Group, 2010; Jacobs, 2006). This, however is mainly governed by enhancing regulations that foster neoliberal aid agendas such as deregulation, privatization, and free-market economic structures, competition, reduction of trade barriers. These regulatory frameworks are often enshrined as loan or grant conditionality.

However, conditionality is usually based on an MDB economic ideology and as such has the potential to bring about an economic colonization of the social life within the recipient country – an imposition of values, which may be alien to the recipient country's society. The imposition of a free-market ideology on recipient countries, for example, has not led to free-market development, but at best to an emergence of ordoliberalism (Bonefeld, 2012; Dullien and Guérot, 2012). At the same time donor organizations establish their firm grip on politicoeconomic control, which in many cases led to financial failure of aid projects. The politicoeconomic control has been used by MDBs simply for imposition of free-market ideologies for specific goals, such as value-for-money and aid-for-trade approaches in ODA.

Drawing on writings of Easterly (2009) the ideology present within the MDBs such as WB and ADB as these relate to conditionality there is a dominance of the neoliberal "free-market" dogma. The danger with this approach (as it is with any other dogma) is the belief that there is only one correct answer. Thus developing recipient countries are obliged to follow the doctrine. Yet many developing and developed countries do not subscribe to this ideology. As Easterly (2009) observed

...one of the best economic ideas of our time, the genius of free markets, was presented in one of the worst possible ways, with unelected outsiders imposing rigid doctrines on the xenophobic unwilling. (n.p.)

Of course there are other views, like those expressed by Jeffrey Sachs (2006, 2009, 2012), where ideology is replaced by a technocratic approach. Yet the replacement of ideology by technocraticism is an ideology itself.

We argue that even the simplest definition of economic development is linked to social dimensions and as such will be governed by ideology. The choice of recipient governments to include or exclude privatization and free-market ideologies from an ODA loan or grant conditionality for example, will impact on types of economic and social policies governments espouse to implement. This requires flexibility from donors and a freedom of choice of ideologies of conditionality to the recipient governments. However, as we have seen the dogmatic approach by WB, IMF, ADB, etc., militates against the potential wished of the recipient countries.

To conclude, like any other ideology, neoliberalism as defined by WB, ADB, and other MDBs is too inflexible to prophesize via *ex-ante* RIA what impact a project or program may have and yet sufficiently flexible to escape falsification of its ideology in Kuhnian terms. The fallacy is the doctrine enunciated however overtly by MDBs that the same ideology can yield different development aid policies as long as these policies adhere to the dogma of neoliberalism with all its trappings of privatization, free-market enterprise, democratization, etc. This is but a brief enunciation of varying critiques of development policy via a neoliberal ideology, which is given much more attention in Chapters 3 and 4 (this volume).

A BRIEF IMPLEMENTATION CRITIQUE

Setting aside issues concerning ideologies there are other critical concerns, namely the implementation of RIA. These include unsatisfactory institutional financial and administrative backing and personnel with suitable abilities to conduct RIA at donor and recipient levels. If this stands to reason, then RIA is problematic to realize especially if donors and recipients and their staff have not dealt with it before. Thus it could be argued that during the RIA implementation process, technical difficulties are faced, potentially leading to a lack of efficiency and effectiveness of the project or program. If the RIA in the policy-making process does not actively involve financial and administrative support, there is an elevated risk of having an onerous bureaucratic process instead of a useful tool for analysis.

In other words, our critique is that the lack of implementation of aid projects and programs on the basis of *ex-ante* RIA militates against the socioeconomic and sociopolitical contradictions that may arise from competing vantage points of the donor organization vis-à-vis the recipient country's values. Thus our critique is contrary to the principles of values proposed unilaterally by the donor organization. Perhaps it may be useful for donor organizations to subject their own dogmas and ideologies to internal critique with the aim to implement via *ex-ante* RIA projects and programs, which are in line with other, at times, competing, values of the recipient society.

INFERENCE: THE POLICY CYCLE AND THE PROJECT CYCLE

From the above discussion and critique two cycles emerge. From the ideology point of view there is the "policy cycle" and from the implementation vantage point there is a "project cycle" to be considered in the overall RIA agenda for foreign aid. These may be seen as follows:

THE POLICY CYCLE

At the simplest level a policy cycle may be described as an interactive and progressive interaction of (a) policy agenda setting; (b) policy formulation; (c) policy implementation; (d) policy monitoring; (e) policy enforcement; (f) policy sustainability. If we were to superimpose RIA into the policy cycle, (i) *ex-ante* RIA would be implemented between (a) policy agenda setting and (b) policy formulation processes, whereas *ex-post* RIA would be conducted after (e) policy enforcement leading to new (a) policy agenda setting. Thus within a policy cycle RIA includes both the *ex-ante* and *ex-post* assessment of public policies and regulations. Furthermore, RIA within the policy cycle includes analysis of processes underpinning distinct policy measures and the status of the existing body of legislation and the politico-economic ideologies of the recipient country without unnecessary dogmatic conditionality of the donor organization, for conditionality may render the policy cycle invalid.

THE PROJECT CYCLE

Given that a "good" design and implementation of the policy cycle is indisputable, implementing them within a framework of RIA efficiently and effectively may be challenging. To be sure even though formal acceptance of regulatory policy reforms may be an important milestone in the overall RIA process, actual change does not transpire until policies based on *ex-ante* RIA are implemented.

Let us take a step back. The project cycle consists of input–output–outcome–impact cycles. RIA at project cycle level is a progressive activity starting as an *ex-ante* activity prior to program or project inception. That is, it will be conducted prior to (a) input phase and shall be used as a monitoring guide for (b) the output phase. Within the (c) outcomes phases via (d) effectiveness analysis, RIA may be used to establish the need for changes to or introduction of new policies. It may also confirm the sustainable effectiveness of the existing body of policies and regulations.

With the policy cycle – the project cycle approach it is possible to make RIA a central component of a policy cum regulatory management structure, for RIA incorporates (a) the results of sound analytical processes and (b) indicators for analyzing the impacts as an ongoing process.

A POINTER TO PROCEDURES: TRANSCENDING POLICY AND PROJECT CYCLE

Being in danger of oversimplification the questions that potentially address RIA procedures may be synthesized as follows: (i) Are existing regulations, policies, and laws limiting the achievements (outcomes, effects, and impacts) of an ODA program or project? (ii) Have government and institutional regulatory features been taken into account in the design of the program or project, focusing especially on the role of the recipient government and its instrumentalities? (iii) Does the ODA intervention actually change, or needs to change the regulatory framework in order to overcome barriers to sustainable long-term achievement of the impact(s)? (iv) Are there mechanisms in place to allow donor agencies and recipient government to implement necessary regulatory changes or strengthen existing regulations to ensure that the impacts are achieved? These questions can of course be posed for *ex-ante* as well as *ex-post* RIA.

APPLYING RIA FOR ODA PROJECTS AND PROGRAMS

The activities identified within the policy cycle suggest two paradigms, that is, the *technical* paradigm and the *political* paradigm (see Easterly vs. Sachs). However, the processes adopted by MDOs are mainly focusing on the former. On the other hand the academic literature focuses mainly on the *political* paradigm. In very few practical cases can one find both simultaneously and the academic literature stereotypically features either one or the other, rarely both concurrently. The proponents of the *technical* paradigm perceive RIA as an activity consisting of "correct" technical (quantitative) analysis, leading to an optimal solution to a complex problem. They use "instrumental rationality" or (*empirical) analytical* methodologies, methods, and techniques. The proponents of the *political* paradigm see RIA as a process by which support for a policy through the however burdensome legislative process can be achieved. They perceive RIA as an instrument for reaching compromise and consensus –building using "value rationality" and qualitative (*hermeneutic) political* methodologies, methods, and techniques. Our argument is that both paradigms are interrelated and necessary.

Let us clarify this. One, we can perceive RIA as the advancement of acceptable and effective sequences of action for addressing issues, which are on the policy agenda. It is now possible to allocate the *technical* paradigm to effectiveness of RIA and the *political* paradigm to *acceptability* of RIA. Let us take this argument a step further. Using *technical* paradigm within a context of effectiveness means that a RIA of an policy or regulatory proposal needs to show *technical validity* and *reliability*. However irrespective of the strengths of its *validity* and *reliability* an RIA needs to show that the policy or regulation is also *politically* implementable and acceptable to the majority of stakeholders and the authorities, which legitimize, implements, and monitor the adherence to such policies or regulations. Taking a step back, this means that a proposed course of action like proclamation and subsequent implementation needs to be authorized by legitimate legislature and executive. This requires a consensus and majority-building; the policy or regulation must be politically feasible. In a case where a consensus has not or cannot be reached the propositions included in the RIA, irrespective of its technical *validity* and *reliability*, become "*impractical.*"

Now let us try to formulate a potential supposition. If our argument stands to reason, then the two aspects to RIA (the *technical* and the *political* approaches) each have their own methodologies, methods, and techniques. So the challenge is to combine these two into a coherent RIA. At pragmatic levels, firstly an effective technical RIA, which can be shown to have reliability and validity must be articulated. Second, building on the findings of the *technical* RIA, a political RIA can be formulated. That is, political (value laden) choices amongst the technical alternatives must be addressed. Both phases comprise the RIA. In other words, neither the technical nor the political RIA by itself will produce a valid outcome. A mixed technical–political or quantitative–qualitative approach is required.

At a pragmatic level RIA may be delineated through a Weberian division of labor. On the one hand there is the function of the RIA analyst(s) and there is a separate role of the RIA formulator(s). However despite the Weberian division of labor there is a need to integrate these two distinct roles. This integration is best demonstrated through the fact that the professional RIA analyst and the formulator(s) use (or at least should use) basically the same "tools" to examine an issue and to formulate policy and regulation alternatives, which address the regulatory or policy issue at hand. This brings theoretical concepts into the domain of practical application.

PROBLEMATICS OF *EX-ANTE* RIA

We have mainly focused on *ex-ante* RIA. Although *ex-ante* IA of proposed regulation within OECD member countries has become a standard procedure, the same cannot be said to have been adopted by donor countries and bilateral and multilateral organizations with reference to ODA. Our argument is that as new regulations and laws in OECD countries are subjected to an *ex-ante* analysis of their potential impact (including economic, environmental, and social cost and benefits) before these are enacted, the same principles of *ex-ante* analysis shall apply to regulatory and policy requirements of donor countries and organizations that are to be enacted by recipient governments. For example, new regulatory requirements such as privatization, financialization, democratization, free-market economy, good governance, etc., are often imposed on recipient governments through the mechanism of loan or grant conditionality (Jakupec and Kelly, 2015).

However, such conditionality is often lacking in evidence-based policy decisions. Here *ex-ante* RIA fulfills a useful function, by enabling donor policy makers to integrate vertical and horizontal policy aims and objectives into different, but not necessarily mutually exclusive loan and/or grant policies and thus responding conditionality. To restate, interestingly, most OECD member countries acknowledge that there is a need for *ex-ante* assessment as far as their domestic policies are concerned, they do seldom, if at all, use the same approach for ODA. In other words, there is much evidence that although most OECD member countries governments acknowledge that there is a need for *ex-ante* assessment of ODA, there is little evidence that there is a common approach with regards to specific aims and processes for RIA. Thus it could be argued that there is a need for a broad common ground delineating the practices of *ex-ante* RIA as well as IA generally. In this context it should be noted that OECD member countries and other donors acknowledge that the implementation of RIA for the social sector, at least, is a challenging undertaking. In this way there is a potential overlap between Poverty and Social Impact Assessment (PSIA) and RIA (World Bank, 2009).

However, there are also marked differences between RIA for ODA and PSIA. For example, the latter may in addition to the above issues be used to develop the ability of governments and government instrumentalities for designing their overall national development strategies.

CONCLUSION: A CASE IN FAVOR OF RIA IN ODA

Our argument is obvious by now. We strongly advocate that *ex-ante* and *ex-post* RIA should be an integral part of the ODA project and program at macro-, meso-, and micro levels. It should be part of the project cycle and policy cycle but within the social, political, and economic values of the recipient country. This requires a comparative analysis of linkages between, and impact on the economic, social, and political landscape of the recipient country, the stakeholders, and beneficiaries. By comparing these linkages, impacts and regulatory changes as well as the effects of different and competing interests, RIA can help to integrate multiple economic sociological and political ideologies and the possible regulatory responses.

To take this further. RIA in ODA should encompass a systematic evaluation of the regulatory provisions, which impact on an ODA program or project. This includes evaluations of the aforesaid economic, social, political, environmental, and other benefits associated with proposed new regulation and policies. So far, most academic research has been concerned with the adoption of RIA in OECD countries and to a lesser extent with ODA. This chapter focuses on the input that RIA can make to improve ODA project and/or program regulation in developing and transition recipient countries. There are some indicators that point to the fact that an increased number of ODA recipient countries and donor agencies are using regulatory assessment for ODA loans, grants, and other technical assistance. However, the methods used are limited and fragmented in their application.

RIA can be seen as a strategic method focusing on development performance from a regulatory perspective, with the aim to enhance sustainable outcomes and effectiveness. RIA provides a coherent framework for development effectiveness in which regulatory functions are analyzed and such analyses are used, strengthened, modified, or newly articulated with the aim to improve regulatory and policy decision-making.

To put it differently, ODA needs to provide not only the financial and human resource (inputs), but also needs to provide input in the form of a regulatory framework that will contribute to the achievement of the outcomes and impacts *ex-ante* and *ex-post*. Thus RIA pays an important role in the political and regulatory dialog between donor agencies and recipient government and their relevant agencies. From this point of view, RIA becomes an important component for assessing ODA effectiveness. The success or otherwise of RIA is only achievable if aid agencies and recipient governments are willing to look beyond the technical approaches (input–output–outcome) to project or program impact assessments and are prepared to set up the necessary procedures and RIA human resources.

Notwithstanding the advantages of RIA for ODA there may be various reasons for RIA not being widely used in ODA technical assistance, loans, and grants. For a better understanding of RIA the following question may be in place: What contribution may RIA make to understanding a success or otherwise of ODA? An answer may be that like in any other form of IA – be it *ex-ante* or *post-ante* – RIA has the potential to provide information on what and how law, policies, and regulations may affect a proposed program or project or how the project or program may affect existing laws, policies, and regulations and what changes may be necessary in order to achieve the overall desired impact in a sustainable manner beyond the life span of the program or projects.

REFERENCES

ADB, 2010. Kingdom of Cambodia: CREST Project – Regulatory Impact Assessment Subproject. ADB, Manila.

ADB, 2012. Lao People's Democratic Republic: Implementing Regulatory Impact Assessment. ADB, Manila.

Bonefeld, W., 2012. Freedom and the Strong State: On German Ordoliberalism. New Political Econ. 17 (3), 1–24.

Dullien, S., Guérot, U., 2012. The long shadow of ordoliberalism: Germany's approach to the Euro crisis. Policy Brief. European Council on Foreign Relations, London, pp. 1–11, February 2012.

Easterly, W., 2009. The ideology of development. Available June 30, 2015 from: <http://foreignpolicy.com/2009/10/13/the-ideology-of-development/>.

Eurodad (European Network on Debt and Development), 2006. World Bank and IMF conditionality: A development injustice. Eurodad Report. Available June 12, 2015 from: <http://www.eurodad.org/uploadedfiles/whats_new/reports/eurodad_world_bank_and_imf_conditionality_report.pdf.>

Independent Commission for Aid Effectiveness (ICAI), 2011. ICAI's Approach to Effectiveness and Value for Money. ICAI, London.

International Finance Corporation (IFC), 2010. Making it work: 'RIA light' for developing countries. Better regulation for Growth. Investment Climate Advisory Service/World Bank Group, Washington, DC.

Jacobs, S., 2006. Current Trends in Regulatory Impact Analysis: The Challenges of Mainstreaming into Policy-Making. Jacobs & Associates, Washington, DC.

Jakupec, V., Kelly, M., 2015. Financialisation of ODA. Int. J. Econ. Commerce Management III (2), 2015.

Kirkpatrick, C., 2014. Assessing the Impact of Regulatory Reform in Developing Countries. Wind Energ. 34, 162–168.

Kirkpatrick, C., Parker, D. (Eds.), 2007. Regulatory Impact Assessment: Towards Better Regulation? Edward Elgar, Northampton, MA.

OECD, 2011. Regulatory Policy and Governance: Supporting Economic Growth and Serving the Public Interest. OECD Publishing, Paris.

OECD, 2015. Regulatory impact assessment. Available April 12, 2015 from: <http://www.oecd.org/gov/regulatory-policy/ria.htm>.

Renda, A., 2011. Law and Economics in the RIA World. Intersentia Ltd, Cambridge, UK.

Sachs, J.D., 2006. The End of Poverty: Economic Possibilities for Our Time. Penguin Press, New York, NY.

Sachs, J.D., 2009. Common Wealth: Economics for a Crowded Planet. Penguin Press, New York, NY.

Sachs, J.D., 2012. The Price of Civilization: Reawakening American Virtue and Prosperity. Random House, New York, NY.

World Bank, 2009. Poverty and social impact analysis (PSIA): Reviewing the link with in-country policy and planning processes, Synthesis Report. Report Number: 4844-GLB, Social Development Department. World Bank Group, Washington, DC.

World Bank Group, 2010. Better Regulation for Growth: Governance Frameworks and Tools for Effective Regulatory Reform-Making it Work: 'RIA Light' for Developing Countries. World Bank Group, Washington, DC.

CAN WE ASSESS THE OVERALL IMPACT OF DEVELOPMENT AGENCIES? THE EXAMPLE OF CORPORATE RESULTS FRAMEWORKS IN MULTILATERAL DEVELOPMENT BANKS

8

Marc M. Cohen[1]

CHAPTER OUTLINE

[1]Disclaimer: *The opinions expressed in this paper are those of the author only and in no way reflect those of the Agencies quoted herein, their Board of Directors or the Governments they represent.*

SETTING THE STAGE: PRESSING FOR RESULTS

Most Multilateral Development Banks (MDBs) including the African Development Bank (AfDB), the Asian Development Bank (AsDB), and the World Bank (WB) rely on two main sources of finance: (i) the hard or nonconcessional lending window, typically in the form of loans provided on market-based terms to middle income countries, and (ii) the soft or concessional window, essentially in the form grants or loans (at zero or below market rates and with long maturity periods) to their lower income member countries. The soft windows are the African Development Fund (AfDF), the Asian Development Fund (AsDF), and the International Development Association (IDA) in the case of the World Bank. While MDBs borrow on international markets to relend to developing countries for the hard lending window, they depend essentially on contributions to these Funds from donor countries (essentially but not exclusively OECD countries) for their concessional window. The policy leverage that donor countries exercise over MDBs' strategic agenda is essentially exercised through the regular replenishments of these funds.

The policy discussions that drove the Funds' replenishment exercises were in fact very similar across the three MDBs. Negotiations between representatives of OECD donor countries and multilateral agencies typically focused on cross-cutting development themes deemed critical in donor countries such as gender equality, environmental safeguards, climate change, good governance, engagement in fragile and conflict-affected situations. In all substantive policy discussions that took place between MDBs and their richer shareholders, impact assessment was an overriding concern. Since the early 2000s thus, the successive replenishments of concessional lending windows have provided an essential platform for rich countries to voice demands for a rigorous assessment of the impact of development interventions, particularly with regards to MDB contributions to poverty reduction and the Millennium Development Goals (MDGs). The set of sustainable development goals (SDGs) that will replace the MDGs in the post 2015 development agenda will certainly play a similar role in benchmarking the impact assessment efforts.

While different concepts with slightly different meaning are often used – results, efficiency, development effectiveness, value for money, etc. – the constant and underlying questions raised by donor countries to MDBs were both unusual and straightforward: What are we buying exactly? Is it worth it? Are we putting our money in the best place? These concerns were obviously fueled by growing budget constraints in the traditional donor countries as well skepticism toward the role of aid in development; both factors resulting in a declining aid appetite in many OECD countries.

In parallel, the series of high-level forums on aid effectiveness (Rome in 2003, Paris in 2005, Accra in 2008, and Busan in 2011) largely echoed these demands from rich countries on the international development scene. Five "principles" of effective aid were adopted through the 2005 Paris Declaration on Aid Effectiveness: "Alignment," "Ownership," "Harmonization," "Managing for Results," and "Mutual Accountability." In particular, the focus on results management radically changed the way

MDBs as well other development agencies measure, report and communicate their performance. They had to equip themselves to perform new functions related to corporate impact assessment; results or development effectiveness organizational units were established, essentially tasked with developing corporate reporting tools and in some instances implementing reforms to promote principles of results-based management. The so called "results agenda" emerged and evolved as a major response to the aid effectiveness concerns. Indeed, a tangible demonstration of results on the ground achieved by development agencies could justify aid to taxpayers, improve the management of aid interventions and also enhance the functioning of institutions viewed as excessively bureaucratic and inefficient (Barder, 2012a)

Particularly innovative and influential in the development scene has been the formulation of Results Frameworks used to assess and periodically report corporate performance around a structured set of key indicators. Currently, the AfDB has developed a "One-Bank Results Measurement Framework" (African Development Bank, 2013a), the AsDB has its "Corporate Results Management Framework" (Asian Development Bank, 2013a), while the WB is using a "Corporate Scorecard" (World Bank, 2013). In this chapter, we refer to these tools with the generic term of Corporate Results Framework (CRFs).

WHAT ARE CORPORATE RESULTS FRAMEWORKS?

The CRF can be defined as a management tool that helps monitor institutional performance toward goals set out in a corporate strategy. The explicit purpose of the CRFs developed by the AsDB and the AfDB is to assess progress in implementing the long-term strategies that guide their interventions: "Strategy 2020" by AsDB and the "Ten-Year Strategy" by AfDB. The WB is currently revisiting its CRF to fully align it with its new corporate strategy.

The first attempt to develop a framework of quantitative indicators to monitor corporate performance appeared in 2002 with the adoption by the WB of the Results Measurement System for the 13th replenishment of its soft lending window (International Development Association, 2002). This framework covered IDA countries only and was developed as part of the Fund replenishment dialog with donors, illustrating the donor-initiated nature of the exercise.

The IDA system consisted of two tiers: country outcome indicators on the one hand, and IDA's contribution to country outcomes on the other hand. Tier 1 included about 15 indicators capturing the economic growth and human development priorities of IDA and consistent with MDG monitoring. Tier 2 included a small set of four indicators of corporate performance: number of results-based country strategies, percentage of country strategies rated satisfactory at completion, percentage of operations with satisfactory rating at entry, and percentage of operations with satisfactory rating at completion (International Development Association, 2002).

This two-level rudimentary CRF offered little potential for impact assessment and little relevance to the key questions of performance management raised by donors. Its conceptual underpinning appeared insufficient with a very weak (if any) causality between the two tiers and in the absence of corporate efficiency metrics.

The CRF, in its current prevailing structure, was developed by AsDB's results unit in 2007 as part of an AsDF replenishment exercise (Cohen, 2007). The framework was expanded to cover both AsDB and AsDF operations and reviewed in 2012 to take its current forms (Asian Development Bank, 2012).

While the AsDB model was later adopted by other MDBs and refined over years, it has remained virtually unchanged in its basic principles, structure, and even key constituent indicators. The AfDB introduced its results measurement framework in 2010 (African Development Bank, 2010) and the WB followed with the release of its Corporate Scorecard in 2011 covering operations from the International Bank for Reconstruction and Development (IBRD), IDA, and trust funds (World Bank, 2011).

The CRF is typically organized around a four-level structure that groups key performance indicators along a results chain. It monitors, at an aggregate or corporate level, whether the institution is functioning efficiently (level IV), with a view to managing its operations effectively (level III) in order to deliver results defined as outputs and intermediate outcomes (level II) that contribute to broader development objectives (level I).

Despite slight differences in headings, dimensions, or indicators, the CRFs developed by the three MDBs reflect an identical chain of causality that rests on similar assumptions or theories of change.

This linear results chain can be simply depicted in Chart 8.1.

Level I of the results framework tracks overall development progress achieved in MDB client countries, that is, Africa for AfDB, Asia and the Pacific for AsDB, or worldwide for the WB. Indicators at this level are long-term development outcomes that provide the general context for development assistance. Progress toward targets cannot be attributed to any particular institution(s) as countries and their development partners jointly contribute to these achievements through their interventions,

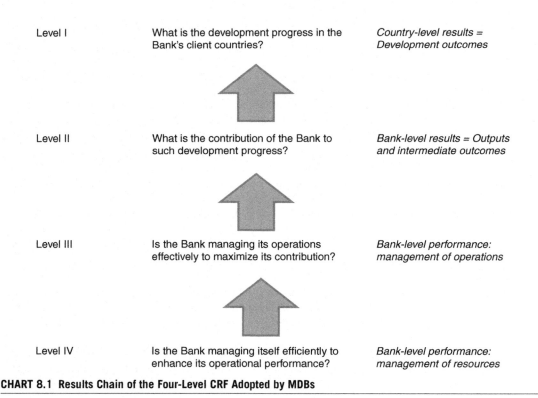

Level I	What is the development progress in the Bank's client countries?	*Country-level results = Development outcomes*
Level II	What is the contribution of the Bank to such development progress?	*Bank-level results = Outputs and intermediate outcomes*
Level III	Is the Bank managing its operations effectively to maximize its contribution?	*Bank-level performance: management of operations*
Level IV	Is the Bank managing itself efficiently to enhance its operational performance?	*Bank-level performance: management of resources*

CHART 8.1 Results Chain of the Four-Level CRF Adopted by MDBs

programs, policies, etc. Performance at this level is thus understood as the product of collective action over the long term. Progress is also ultimately and fundamentally dependent upon a multitude of external factors, out of the control of any agent(s) and not easily predictable (financial crises, external shocks, weather conditions, price of commodities, security situation, etc.).

Key results reported under level I of the CRF tend to reflect a consensus in the international development community on "what" development is about. They are typically pegged to the MDGs, largely prioritizing social development and fully aligned with the poverty reduction mandates of MDBs. For memo, let us recall here that the eight MDGs are: MDG 1: eradicate extreme hunger and poverty; MDG 2: Achieve universal primary education; MDG3: promote gender equality and empower women; MDG 4: reduce child mortality; MDG 5: improve maternal health; MDG 6: combat HIV/AIDS, malaria and other diseases; MDG 7: ensure environmental sustainability; and MDG 8: develop a global partnership for development. In its scorecard, the WB adds specific references to its postcrisis directions (PCD), which also reflect equity concerns: (1) Target the poor and vulnerable. (2) Create opportunities for growth. (3) Promote global collective action. (4) Strengthen governance. (5) Manage risks and prepare for crisis.

Growth and poverty reduction seem inevitably associated in this framework: dominant economic thinking sees economic growth as a prerequisite for reducing poverty and improving income distribution. However, CRF indicators have evolved over time to better capture the "inclusive" and "green" dimensions of growth, bringing issues of equity and sustainability at the forefront of the strategic agenda of MDBs. Dimensions of good governance and private sector development are also captured through specific indicators at this level. More adjustments at this level can be anticipated in order to reflect the new set of SDGs under development.

Data sources of level I are specific to each indicator and usually originate from specialized international agencies or other institutions in the concerned area. They include for instance UNESCO for education statistics, FAO for agricultural data, UNCTAD for trade indicators, WHO for water and sanitation access, Mo Ibrahim Foundation or Transparency International for governance related indicators, WB/IMF for growth and income poverty data, and so on.

Level II measures operational results delivered by MDBs that contribute to country outcomes identified in level I. It does so by aggregating key outputs (typically quantified physical realizations) and intermediate outcomes (essentially indicators of access to goods and services or numbers of beneficiaries) of interventions. Indicators are organized around core sectors that reflect MDBs' priority areas of intervention: transport, energy, education, water and sanitation, private sector development, finance, regional integration, etc. (Asian Development Bank, 2013b). As for level I, MDBs have tended to harmonize those core sector indicators in their respective CRFs. This is obviously true to the extent that they are engaged in similar operational areas; the WB for instance covers a wider range of sectors than the regional banks (World Bank, 2013). The following indicators, to name a few, are used by the three Banks: kilometers of roads built, power capacity installed in megawatts, number of micro credits granted, hectares of land whose use has been improved, number of teachers trained, number of people with new or improved access to water and sanitation, etc.

Those sector outputs or intermediate sector outcomes are direct, tangible, and measurable results of the assistance provided through MDB financing. Their "attribution" to the institution can thus be expressed with a high level of confidence. Level II data are extracted from the consolidation of operational reports undertaken at project completion. As long as the definitions of indicators are harmonized, allowing aggregation across projects and countries, figures reported can be considered as reliable proxies for MDB results.

Level III indicators provide information on the effectiveness of the portfolio of operations (lending and nonlending as well as knowledge products) that generate the goods and services reported under level 2 of the CRF.

The rationale behind this relationship is that by better managing its operations, an institution can make a greater contribution to its results on the ground. For instance, improving project design, shortening project preparation and approval periods, accelerating the delivery of goods and services, cancelling poorly performing operations, mobilizing additional resources, developing access to knowledge, better monitoring operational results, etc. all contribute to the timely and successful delivery of the intended outputs and outcomes of development interventions. Level III indicators thus essentially monitor the quality of operations and country strategies throughout the operational lifecycles – that is, at entry, during implementation, and at exit or completion.

Again, despite differences in terminologies and methodologies for deriving indicators, the three MDBs have adopted a core of similar measures: percentage of operations rated satisfactory at entry, percentage of operations rated satisfactory at completion, percentage of country strategies with satisfactory evaluation rating, percentage of operations at risk, average number of months from approval to first disbursement of operations, overall disbursement ratio, etc.

Data used to monitor the performance of the operational portfolios are extracted internal from reports, self-assessments, and in some instances independent evaluation studies carried out by MDBs' evaluation offices.

Level IV focuses on internal reforms implemented to enhance the functioning of the institution and ultimately expected to enhance portfolio performance reported under level III of the CRF. While different terms are used by the three MDBs – organizational efficiency for AfDB, organizational reforms for AsDB, and organizational effectiveness for WB – indicators at this level essentially capture dimensions of skills mixes and human resources (especially their alignment with the corporate strategy), budget utilization (including unit costs to prepare and administer operations), business processes (including aspects of procurement), and responsiveness to clients (for instance through decentralization). Indicators at this level aim at capturing progress in implementing specific internal reform agendas of the institutions.

Data sources of level IV are internal, usually provided from organizational units in charge of human resources, budget management, procurement services, and information technology.

HOW ARE CORPORATE RESULTS FRAMEWORKS USED IN PRACTICE?

This section provides an assessment of the experience gained so far with CRFs. Have CRFs lived up with their expectations? What are the main advantages and concrete applications of the CRF? Can they actually be used as impact assessment tools? Are they contributing to instill a culture of performance and results in MDBs?

FOCUS ON AGENCY RESULTS AND PERFORMANCE

From a practitioner's point of view, CRFs have unambiguously contributed to change the nature of the dialog between MDBs and their shareholders, focusing it on strategic results and corporate performance. Performance has been increasingly gauged in terms of outputs and outcomes of development interventions as opposed to financial flows and inputs. Thanks to corporate frameworks, MDB shareholders and clients are provided with a set of metrics to compare actual achievement against baselines and targets. Over time, indicators are used to signal trends, successes, risks, and weaknesses. The needs for further analysis can be identified as well as the areas for action. Mainstreaming results-based assessment, the intended benefit of CRFs, has thus been achieved. The focus on results (outputs and outcomes) and efficiency indicators constitutes a fundamental departure from past practice and probably an irreversible trend in the way corporate performance is apprehended.

POWERFUL COMMUNICATION TOOLS

CRFs have proven to be a very effective way to present and communicate corporate performance in a simple, coherent, and user-friendly manner. Byproducts of CRFs such as the Development Effectiveness Reports produced annually by MDBs are broadly disseminated, available online, effectively reaching out an audience never reached so far by MDBs (African Development Bank, 2013b; Asian Development Bank, 2013c). The reporting systems built around CRFs thus played an essential advocacy role for MDBs who were keen to establish that aid in their hands provided good value for donors' money. The need to convince skeptical donor governments and public opinions does come with some risks though. MDBs are more prone to celebrate success than report failures through their reports; they are also less inclined to develop complex messages or technical contents. The purpose becomes to convince through smart communication rather than to manage through robust assessment. This has clearly hampered the actual use of CRFs as genuine management tools.

SIMPLICITY AND ECONOMY

The introduction of the CRF helped consolidate and harmonize the parallel and sometimes duplicating corporate reporting systems of the past. Annual corporate reports, budget and planning reviews, internal reform agendas, or other results frameworks have become subsidiary sources of information. The CRF has imposed itself as the single and unified source of corporate-level performance. Getting internal consensus and clarity on what should be measured to assess corporate performance, when and how, has been an important factor of economy and positive synergies across organizational units in MDBs.

STRATEGIC ALIGNMENT AND FOCUS

We know that "what gets measured usually gets done." Undoubtedly, the overall strategic focus and selectivity of MDBs interventions has improved by systematically measuring progress toward a small set of indicators. Specific CRF indicators assess the extent to which MDB resources and skills are geared toward core operational priorities and reflect the specific mandates and comparative advantages of MDBs. The performance dimensions identified at the various levels acted *de facto* as a way to screen operations and corporate initiatives. CRFs have thus become the essential tool to monitor the level of alignment of MDBs with their institutional priorities as well as with the global development agenda.

FLEXIBILITY

The four-level structure adopted at the corporate level can be conveniently expanded by sources of fund, subregions, countries, sectors, organizational units, etc. making it a uniquely flexible tool for performance assessment. To complement the production of their periodic (corporate-wide) Development Effectiveness Reports, MDBs have regularly produced a series of thematic or country-focused development effectiveness reports, also built around the CRF (African Development Bank, 2014; Asian Development Bank, 2014). More focused results frameworks have been developed in parallel to assess progress toward specific strategies or agenda; gender, governance, regional integration, infrastructure, or even results management have their own results measurement systems based on specific indicators. Because of their limited scope and analytical depth, these by-products of CRFs can offer more potential as management and decision-making tools.

DEFINING LIMITATIONS

Notwithstanding their popularity, CRFs cannot be taken as panaceas for corporate results management. They suffer from a number of conceptual flaws that limit their robustness as impact assessment tools and therefore their actual use as instruments that support sound results management.

THE ASSUMED GLOBAL CAUSALITY

In the CRF model, progress at one level is supposed to contribute to overall progress at the level immediately higher. The relationship between levels is a simple one of (unquantifiable and unspecific) contribution. It is understood that a multitude of factors are at play and can interfere into progress from one level to another; it would be impossible thus to measure the extent to which progress in one level can generate progress at another level there (no attribution can be derived). Causality is thus assumed to take place "globally" across levels, rather than through causality relationships linking specific indicators of the various levels. This is true along the CRF results chain as described below.

FROM CORPORATE RESULTS TO COUNTRY RESULTS

There are no attempts to link specific agency-level outputs (say core sector indicators in education) with country level results (say education-related MDGs). The mechanisms by which outputs in the core operational areas contribute to country outcomes rest on a series of simplistic, generic, and often undemonstrated assumptions or theories of change. It is for instance, assumed that investing in the transport sector and delivering transport outputs (level 2 indicators) may contribute to development outcomes (level 1) by (a) increasing access of the poor to markets and raising their incomes (MDG 1), (b) promoting access to education and health facilities, especially by women and disadvantaged groups (MDGs 2–6), and (c) improving physical connectivity and boosting trade, etc. Investing to enhance access to water supply (level 2 indicators) could contribute to development outcomes (level 1) by (a) raising agricultural productivity and incomes of poor farmers (MDG 1), (b) improving hygiene and health status and helping combat diseases that affect infants and children (MDGs 2–6), and (c) reducing numbers of slum dwellers and improving the urban quality of life (MDG 7), etc. Such reasoning can apply to other sector/operational areas of level 2 of the CRFs. It is clear though, that while relationships between level 1 and 2 can be tested and substantiated in specific contexts (at the country level and for particular operational areas), their validity at the corporate multicountry multisectoral can only be assumed.

FROM OPERATIONAL PERFORMANCE TO CORPORATE RESULTS

The assumption that portfolio performance (at entry, during implementation at exit) improves the delivery of outputs only holds under certain conditions. Two such conditions are critical: (i) the operational rating system must be candid and evidence-based; (ii) quality must remain unaffected by reduced resources and time inputs. These two conditions are the subject of debates in MDBs. Indeed, the perception that operational ratings tend to be inflated (excessively biased toward satisfactory assessment) is widespread. To promote the level of confidence in project ratings, MDBs are developing improved rating systems based on evidence (quantifiable and verifiable from reliable date source) and focused on results (delivery of intended outputs and outcomes). There is an equally widespread perception that pressures to compress project processing time and to accelerate disbursements, with the intention of achieving efficiency gains, have actually resulted in a lower quality of design or at entry. Quality at entry has thus received much attention from MDB with recent efforts to set quality standards and monitoring compliance with such standards.

FROM INSTITUTIONAL REFORMS TO OPERATIONAL PERFORMANCE

No direct linkage can be established with a high level of confidence between specific indicators of the two lower levels of the CRF. It is assumed that for instance more decentralization (e.g., a growing share of operation handled by field offices), improved staffing gender balance (e.g., share of women in professional staff), or reduced unit costs (e.g., cost for preparing a loan) will jointly, naturally, and harmoniously contribute to improve the performance of the portfolio of operations. The underlying assumptions are not tested or based on evidence from evaluation studies. They can even be counterintuitive and ignore possible tensions between performance indicators. For instance, reducing the cost of preparing an operation can be achieved as part of an efficiency enhancement effort but bears some risks on the project design quality and its readiness for implementation, possibly undermining portfolio performance.

ISSUES OF DATA AGGREGATION

The aggregation of results has been an essential driver for developing CRFs. Donors rightly insisted on getting precise and reliable figures of key outputs delivered by MDB interventions at a time where these outputs were not systematically reported and most agencies were not equipped to capture them. Level 2, where core sector indicators are aggregated and reported, was seen as the essential piece of the CRF and continues to attract most of the attention. Obviously, indicators such as number of kilometers of roads built, number of classrooms built, number of households with access to water, etc. can speak easily to any audience. They directly measure "what" shareholders are buying through their contributions; they allow rough comparisons across agencies. However, this aggregation appears as a weak proxy for capturing effectiveness. Caution is indeed required in interpreting figures of aggregated outputs for a number of reasons.

In the first place, to be meaningful or to provide an indication of the magnitude of the aid effort, the values of the outputs reported should be compared with the total needs of the country(ies), which are rarely assessed with sufficient reliability (and never alluded to in the CRF). Improving access to safe water for XXX thousands people is an interesting piece of information, but how many more people must be reached out to ensure universal access? How do YYY additional megawatts of power generated satisfy the electricity needs of the concerned population? What share of the planned network of primary roads do ZZZ kilometers represent? etc.

Second, the selection process leading to the identification of those outputs that are considered as "core" is necessarily subjective. A natural tendency is to focus on what can be easily measured. Interventions where sound measurements of results or cost–benefit analysis are difficult to generate – or interventions in areas where statistics are scarce – may lose out as a whole. The aggregation thus bears the risk of creating perverse incentives (Barder, 2012b). Some output indicators may not be essential or cost-effective in certain contexts; yet, they may be "forced" into development interventions with a view to inflating results and merely for aggregate reporting purpose. This aggregation process can also conflict with country priorities and policies. "More" is not necessarily "better" as quantitative increases do not systematically imply improved effectiveness. In certain settings for instance, a rationalization of facilities – say school or health facilities – and hence a reduction in physical outputs may be a desirable outcome in order to enhance sector efficiency. The natural tendency however, would be to dismiss such interventions that offer no tangible results in the CRF.

Third, the intrinsic features of the outputs delivered (e.g., the content and durability of textbooks or the norms of road construction) and therefore the likelihood of their actual use or beneficial impacts on beneficiaries are not considered. Only the volume of outputs delivered matters in assessing performance. This increases the risk of prioritizing quantity at lower cost, possibly at the expense of quality.

Last, the physical output aggregation approach is not well suited to capturing the less tangible and nonphysical results of assistance. Institutional development, regulatory reforms, and policy changes that are supported by economic, sector, and thematic work of MDBs are not adequately captured and reported through CRFs. Yet, they are essential manifestations of development effectiveness and constitute important areas of MDB contributions to country outcomes.

RESULTS VERSUS RISKS

As CRFs gauge success through the ability to reach the amount of outputs and outcomes initially planned, the system is likely to create a bias toward those countries, sectors, or activities that can yield stronger quantitative results. A feature of any performance-based system is indeed to exacerbate the tension between risks and results. The performance-based system adopted by MDBs to allocate concessional funding across member countries exemplifies this tension: countries with sound macroeconomic policies, a good governance record, and strong portfolio performance are "rewarded" through complex resource allocation formula. The effect of this system however, needs to be mitigated through the allocation of special resources devoted to regional operations, small economies, or countries termed "fragile."

For the sake of enhancing performance, or in order to demonstrate their commitment to achieve planned targets, MDBs may be tempted to disengage from countries or work areas where operational risks are known to be higher. Countries prone to political instability, leading unorthodox macroeconomic policies, where institutions are dysfunctional, or with higher level of corruption, etc. would naturally receive a lower share of resources as they do not provide settings for achieving quick results. Yet, it is arguably in countries where the risk of failure is higher that aid is most needed and that success has most national and regional spillovers (Chauvet and Collier, 2005).

SHORT-TERM VERSUS LONG-TERM IMPACT

By definition, development interventions – unlike humanitarian or emergency assistance – are of a long-term nature and take several years to bear fruit. A typical MDB country strategy programming or a typical project cycle is 5–6 years, with most benefits occurring after the completion of the program or project. These timeframes are usually beyond the electoral cycles and the Fund replenishment exercises; MDBs have thus been pressed to demonstrate progress in timespans that do not correspond to their usual business cycles.

The search for quick gains and quick results has indeed tended to be prioritized in the design of CRF, possibly at the expense critical development outcomes. The long-term developmental perspective – for example, strengthening institutions and country systems, enhancing the quality of basic services, supporting the resilience of economies, developing adaptation modalities to climate change, etc. – has received insufficient attention in CRFs while supply side interventions that generate quick gain in terms of coverage and accessibility have been prioritized access – for example, building new classrooms, roads, or power plants, etc.

OWNERSHIP AND POLITICIZATION OF THE AGENDA

CRF formulation exercises, through extensive discussions at MDB Boards meetings and fund replenishment meetings, have become increasingly complex and politically charged processes. The selection of indicators has been the subject of debates that reflect competing agendas and priorities of the various shareholders. Target setting for different indicators – an area that would normally require specialized expertise and careful planning – has also tended to be discussed in open forum. The question of the inclusion of indicators of climate change and governance in particular opposed different constituencies. Emerging economies that depend on cheap fossil fuel resources for their growth were reluctant to monitor CO_2 emissions as part of level I indicators. Other constituencies objected to the inclusion of composite governance indicators published by nongovernmental sources and capturing aspects of human rights and freedoms unrelated to MDB mandates. Other MDB constituencies insisted on including specific gender equality indicators throughout the results chain, etc.

It is clear that the perspective of traditional OECD donors has so far been prevalent in the dialog on results and in the formulation of CRFs. Donors' involvement in technical matters has been so high that a form of micromanagement of CRF has taken place. Fundamentally, the donor-driven aspects of the results agenda has raised legitimate questions regarding its ownership.

NEW AVENUES FOR NEW REALITIES

We must keep in mind that CRFs can only be imperfect and partial representations of corporate performance. MDBs are large and complex institutions that follow a variety of internal and external motives and are subject to a diversity of influences. However, we argue in this section that the corporate results measurement systems adopted by MDBs and other development agencies need to be revisited to adjust to a rapidly changing aid environment. Some directions for further work are proposed to enhance the robustness of CRFs as well as their practical applications for MDBs and their shareholders. In particular, the directions proposed in this section could contribute to unfold the potential of CRFs as impact assessment and management tools.

IMPROVED CONCEPTUAL UNDERPINNING

A number of work directions can be proposed to strengthen the results chain of the CRF, that is, to build a more robust causality chain between levels. This requires primarily more efforts to generate relevant knowledge including better use of evaluation studies and techniques. MDBs, for a variety of reasons including costs and skills gaps, have so far made very little use of impact evaluations to gauge the success of their operations. Operation completion reports as well as postevaluation studies essentially draw their conclusions on observed changes on the beneficiary group without reference to any counterfactual or control group. Changes in the identified results areas are assumed to be attributable to the intervention; other possible causalities are ignored; unplanned outcomes are neglected. While it would be unrealistic to expect MDBs to systematically integrate impact evaluation methods in the design of their operations, the selective use of impact evaluations would considerably increase the level of confidence we have in the assumed causality between levels 1 and 2. In particular, the assumed intersectoral linkages could be better understood. Findings would also help selecting those core sector indicators for which evidence of contribution to country outcomes can be established with more certainty.

In the same vein, specific investigations are necessary to establish more firmly the linkages between other levels of the framework. More insights are needed on the relationship between results on the ground and operational performance. Does portfolio performance support delivery of results? What level of risks can be considered optimal in an operational portfolio? Is quality-at-entry a good predictor for project success and achievement of results? What factors beyond the control of specific interventions, institutional or governance-related in particular, can explain operational performance? Regarding the linkages between internal reforms and operational performance, we certainly do not fully understand the relationship between variables at play in CRFs. Does decentralization automatically support portfolio performance? At what cost? Is there an optimal pace for reaching gender parity in staffing structures? What is the appropriate allocation of resources between operations, operational support, and administration? How much flexibility in business processes can be achieved without jeopardizing due diligence and safeguards? What is the limit to unit costs containment? Such (difficult) questions can typically be answered, at least partly, only after the implementation of the said reforms (decentralization, modernization of business processes, skills alignment, etc.). Little attempt is made in practice by MDBs to learn from each other, from other institutions, or from their own past experiences. A more systematic look into available knowledge resources however would provide useful information to justify the assumed causality between levels of the frameworks.

QUALITY MATTERS

As we have seen, the mere reporting of volumes of physical outputs is not satisfactory from a development effectiveness perspective. The view that the quality of goods and services cannot be easily or reliably assessed – often used to reject the integration of qualitative dimensions in measurement frameworks – is simply flawed. We know how to gauge quality through a variety of techniques and methods: satisfaction surveys, beneficiary assessments, pricing of goods and services, compliance with quality standards, assessment of learning outcomes, etc. This can be undertaken flexibly at different levels (macro, sector, or micro), for different sets of clients (national and local administrations, beneficiary groups, other partners, etc.) and at relatively modest costs. A mix of qualitative and qualitative methods is thus necessary to better assess the actual impact of development interventions. This is feasible; it requires doing business "not exactly as usual" and changing well-established practices in aid agencies.

TOWARD A CULTURE OF RESULTS

Behind the corporate performance assessment aspect, the results agenda is fundamentally about instilling a culture of results and performance. MDBs are perceived as excessively bureaucratic, poorly responsive to changing conditions, and lacking transparency. CRFs created a habit of reporting and communicating performance based on clear performance indicators. Developing a culture of results in MDBs however, would require a whole new system of incentives that encourage quality project design, solid needs assessments, participatory processes, candid performance assessment, and evidence-based decision making. This corporate culture aspect was not explicitly considered in CRFs. It needs to be reintegrated, not just because it has value in itself but also because it is essential to strengthen the validity of the causality relationships of the CRF results chain. Setting operational quality standards and developing evidence-based rating systems are essential to both "bridging the gap" between levels 2 and 3 of the CRFs, but also to instill a culture of results and risks in MDBs. Developing incentives that can change staff attitudes toward risks, enhance learning and performance are equally important. These and other initiatives have to be explicitly and rigorously captured in CRFs.

PRIORITIES AND OWNERSHIP

We have seen that the voice of donor countries has been the dominant one in shaping CRFs and the overall results agenda. Value for money (the money of the aid providers, ultimately, the taxpayers) raises acute ownership questions. Are the results that donors want to see the same as those the beneficiaries in recipient countries are expecting? If not, how can beneficiaries voice their demands? Do they have the same political voice as taxpayers of rich countries? Even if there is some agreements on what those results should be, who better than beneficiaries can assess their real value?

In the case of domestic spending, beneficiaries and tax payers are broadly the same people and value for money can be assessed from their perspective. The paradox in the aid relationship model is that value for money is assessed by the provider of aid (i.e., the donors or funding agents accountable to their taxpayers) and not the customer (i.e., the beneficiaries of development interventions) of aid (Jackson, 2012). In such a relationship, key funding decisions are bound to remain supply driven with limited involvement from beneficiaries on the demand side.

Ownership is clearly at stake; the clients' perspectives to corporate assessment need to be integrated. The timing seems right with the reduced ability of traditional donors to shape the agendas of MDBs. The aid skepticism and budget constraints are one factor of their declining influence. The emergence of new donors from middle-income countries – not just China but also Turkey, Brazil, Korea, or Saudi Arabia to name a few – is another factor that radically modifies the aid industry. The voices of nongovernmental actors – civil society organizations, representatives of parliaments, media, local administration, businesses etc. – are also increasingly shaping the development agenda. Sooner or later, corporate performance will have to be revisited through the lenses of these new actors and reflect a new balance of power.

TOWARD JOINT INTEGRATED FRAMEWORKS

MDBs have developed their own frameworks to assess their own performances. Yet, through cofinancing, programmatic approaches, policy-based and budget support interventions, joint country strategies, etc. the reality of who finances what and delivers what can be complex. A legitimate question to ask is whether it is still possible – or actually whether it still makes sense – to attempt to isolate the impact of individual agencies? Current CRFs clearly do not provide incentives for joint work across development agencies. Capturing dimensions of the harmonization principle of effective aid would be a step forward. The simple single-agent model reflected in CRFs is slowly disappearing. Ultimately thus, joint results frameworks would be the way to go to better assess the developmental impact of the aid effort.

CONCLUSIONS

The results agenda has given rise to a number of concerns among development practitioners and academics alike, including claims that it may add to the bureaucratic overload in agencies, make aid less strategic, impose wrong priorities, or create perverse incentives (Barder, 2012b). CRFs developed by MDBs as part of their results agenda to report and demonstrate contributions to development results exemplify such concerns. CRFs, together with their by-products such as annual development effectiveness reports inherently reflect tensions between seemingly contradictory purposes and overambitious expectations. Are CRF measurement or management tools? Do they serve a communication or a learning purpose? Should they be accessible to a larger public or serve the needs of experts? Are they suitable for comparison across agencies?

The experience so far is that CRFs have proven successful measurement tools but with limited use for accountability and management purpose. CRFs have been powerful and relatively simple communication instruments that can speak to a broad spectrum of stakeholders (and in the first place, finance ministries in donor countries). Their application for learning however is questionable; as potential evaluation tools, they clearly lack robustness and conceptual underpinning. CRFs also played an important role in enhancing the operational focus of MDBs and advancing critical development agendas in response to political or politicized concerns; these concerns however, were not necessarily shared by all MDB shareholders. Corporate performance frameworks tended to encourage operations that can secure quick, tangible, and easily measurable results, probably at the expense of more innovative approaches and investments in policy and institutional reforms that are critical to sustain development gains. While CRFs rightly focused on operational results and organizational efficiency, there is no clear evidence that they contributed to develop a culture of results or to reduce the bureaucratic overload that characterize aid agencies.

Social complexity thinkers would argue that the entire results agenda – with its set of tools and concepts such as logical frameworks, results-based management, value for money, etc. – reflects a reductionist approach to problem solving that is not suitable to development work (Ramalingam, 2013). The results agenda however, is here to stay and pressures on aid agencies to demonstrate their effectiveness are unlikely to diminish. Isolating and fully assessing the overall impact of aid agencies may be an illusory goal but this paper argues that corporate performance reporting tools can become more relevant to the complex and rapidly changing realities of development.

REFERENCES

African Development Bank, 2010. The Bank Group Results Measurement Framework. African Development Bank, Tunis.

African Development Bank, 2013a. The One Bank Group Results Measurement Framework. African Development Bank, Tunis.

African Development Bank, 2013b. Annual Development Effectiveness Review 2013. African Development Bank, Tunis.

African Development Bank, 2014. Development effectiveness reviews. Available from: < http://www.afdb.org/en/topics-and-sectors/topics/quality-assurance-results/development-effectiveness-reviews/>.

Asian Development Bank, 2012. Review of the ADB Results Framework. Asian Development Bank, Manila.

Asian Development Bank, 2013a. Results Framework 2013-2016 Quick Guide. Asian Development Bank, Manila.

Asian Development Bank, 2013b. Guidelines for the Use of ADB's Results Framework Indicators for Core Sector Outputs and Outcomes. Asian Development Bank, Manila.

Asian Development Bank, 2013c. Development Effectiveness Review: 2012 Report. Asian Development Bank, Manila.

Asian Development Bank, 2014. Development effectiveness reviews. Available from: <http://www.adb.org/documents/series/development-effectiveness-review>.

Barder, O., 2012a. What are the results agenda. Owen Barder Blog. Available from: <http://www.owen.org/blog/5228>.

Barder, O., 2012b. Seven worries about focusing on results and how to manage them. Owen Barder Blog. Available from: <http://www.owen.org/blog/5483>.

Chauvet, L., Collier, P., 2005. Policy Turnaround in Failing States. Centre for the Study of African Economies, Oxford University, Oxford.

Cohen, M., 2007. Towards a Consolidated Results Framework at the ADB: Technical Note. Asian Development Bank, Manila.

International Development Association, 2002. Measuring Outputs and Outcomes in IDA Countries. World Bank, Washington, DC.

Jackson, P., 2012. Value for Money and International Development. OECD Development Co-operation Directorate, Paris.

Ramalingam, B., 2013. Aid on the Edge of Chaos: Rethinking International Cooperation in a Complex World. Oxford University Press, Oxford.

World Bank, 2011. World Bank Corporate Scorecard 2011. World Bank, Washington, DC.

World Bank, 2013. World Bank Corporate Scorecard: Integrated Results and Performance Framework. World Bank, Washington, DC.

ASSESSING THE IMPACT OF KNOWLEDGE ON DEVELOPMENT PARTNERS

William Loxley

Comparative Research Analyst, Philippines

CHAPTER OUTLINE

INTRODUCTION

Looking to the global economy over the next 20 years, ODA will continue to play an important role in promoting global progress among all nations. Therefore, every nation must seek to understand where transformative development is headed. It is widely reported that about 20% of all nations are well developed, accounting for 80% of economic effort (World Bank, 1999). To allow the remaining 80% of nations to achieve top 20% status in their chosen areas of comparative advantage, global development will need to be fair, effective, and continuous. Impact assessment (IA) is one way to ensure that ODA succeeds in strengthening global progress by sharing ideas. Likewise, nations cannot develop readily if policies to foster learning cannot improve comparative advantage in global trading. Generally, as social sectors become more complex, the comparative advantage of knowledge sharing increases the need for research in science, technology, and the social sciences to be participated in by society (Loxley, 2013). This is why information and knowledge transfer is so important to reduce knowledge gaps and increase understanding about how development improves capacity between physical and social infrastructure in aid projects. At the end of the day, IA findings do not have to claim unequivocal project success, but they do have to provide insight into reasons (pro and con) about how to design future interventions. As such, development will require deeper and more demanding forms of knowledge and information to enhance the collective wisdom of nations.

It turns out that knowledge transfer is what development is all about because too little information limits progress. Understanding how development works implies consensus building to change hearts and minds based on assessment and common sense. The need to know is enhanced by the number of networks among people who can communicate across cultures (e.g., language, methodology, philosophy, etc.) to find ways to reduce ignorance in the quest for a smarter world. It appears that social networking among people who know how to use knowledge is likely to change more minds and lead to national consensus. Increased understanding is precisely what ODA seeks through solving complex issues facing the social sectors. By tracing information flow, through these social networks, researchers see where new ideas originate, are implemented, and followed up in a process of openness and reflection. Following the information trail of who knows what, who learns most, and who employs findings wisely, is what IA is all about. Finding out what went wrong in the broader context of information sharing across the social, political, economic, and cultural spectrum allows ODA to be better coordinated; so that ownership, technical capacity, organization integrity, and flexibility in approach all come together in transparent ways given existing states of development.

Implementing change in any society is not easy because existing social pressures are highly intertwined and difficult to untangle given that change often leads to unintended consequences. In social science research there is no single best method because standards vary across the social, political, economic, and cultural landscape. So why evaluate? The answer lies in identifying those key questions needed by decision makers to employ the best methods of surveys, case studies, personal interviews, group reviews, meta-analyses, etc. In the end, IA credibility hinges on demonstrating the usefulness of programs in providing policy direction.

The ODA policymaking approach developed over the years is straightforward in linking tactics to goals. The evaluation approach asks what is the objective, what is the intervention, and what are the intended effects? The policymaking model runs the path from design to action to outcome, and back to problem redesign thereby allowing both *ex ante* and *ex post facto* analysis to be employed during each succeeding cycle that looks forward and backward. This iterative process leads from prediction to recommendation, evaluation to revision. The model provides a simple way of thinking through a problem and then designing appropriate projects that implement the goals so outcomes can be evaluated and the next stage redesigned. Over time, experience yields a wealth of strategies. Following this pattern, IA generally offers good advice to the ODA community as it provides realistic expectations, information on improvements, and effective rationales to defend continued assistance.

Within this policy framework, stakeholders come together. The ODA community consists of three basic groups: (i) multilateral and bilateral donors; (ii) recipient governments; and (iii) third-party vendors including universities, NGOs, consulting firms, corporations, community beneficiaries, and increasingly private enterprise. Donors fund ODA based on a collaborative effort choosing goals that can be justified to the wider public, are operationally feasible based on expert advice. ODA can deliver agreed upon solutions to existing social problems appropriate to the local setting. Donor organizations consist mainly of multilateral, bilateral, and charitable foundations. On the other hand, the recipient partners are generally national or local entities in areas with existing social problems found to inhibit progress.

These government agencies are accountable ultimately to their citizens. Accountability takes many forms but must ultimately revolve around maximizing benefit from goods and services acquired and provided. Often referred to as a value for money proposition, essentially, governments must balance efficiency in getting better results versus effectiveness in obtaining goals. This balance is important in the development process because outcomes for local constituents may be different from broader goals pursued by the government or donor community. Recipient nations must prioritize competing projects, justify them to local beneficiaries, and contribute time and effort to strengthening those institutions and human resources required to carry out agreed upon programs with donors. Finally, third-party stakeholders consist of a variety of groups that contribute indirectly to project success. Outside experts from universities and consulting firms are common while NGOs offer a plethora of insight into implementation prospects at the local level, and beneficiaries, themselves, need to fully contribute both by giving and receiving new ideas.

Newer models of collaborative thinking urge joint action based on complex insight where recipients think locally, donors think long-term, and stakeholders expand wider interests and connections. Figure 9.1 describes these development partners and their key attributes. Donors contribute project financing, planning, and coordination guidance to recipients; and provide mobility and accountability to stakeholders. Recipients contribute accountability and counterpart funding to donors, while providing stakeholders opportunities to participate in development. Third parties contribute the latest knowledge resources and recommendations to donors and recipients. In total, each partner aids the other when they do their best (Loxley, 2003). Projects and programs can begin, once the policymaking methods are in place with recognizable strategies and plans, and development partners are in agreement. Often starting as pilot programs, projects can be revised, and folded or mainstreamed after careful IA.

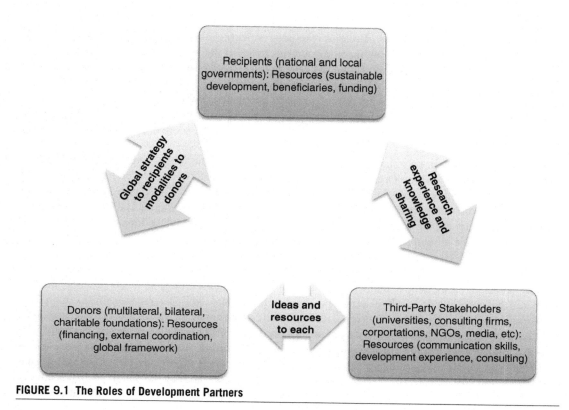

FIGURE 9.1 The Roles of Development Partners

DONOR INITIATED EVALUATION RESEARCH

This section focuses on those donors trying to understand the development process along several fronts when coordinating actions in the education sector. Given the wide variation in national settings, designing successful education projects is complicated when causality is not well understood. As a result, the World Bank was one of the first institutions to carry out research in-house focusing attention on specific issues facing the ODA community. This was especially true in the past, although today outsourcing research to third parties is a more common way for donors to disseminate the latest research technology, and to limit potential donor bias from creeping into findings. All major multilaterals including the regional development banks, OECD, UN agencies, and many bilateral donors and foundations conduct in-house evaluation, and provide findings to the public available on their websites. Advantages to in-house research provide multilaterals access to a wide range of national research settings for study at different stages of development that can be instrumental in setting ODA agendas, after debating theory and practice. The following in-depth research carried out by the World Bank illustrates how benefits from donor-driven modalities shed light on cross-national patterns of school impact.

To cite an example, in the 1970–1980s the reigning educational consensus claimed that schools did not make a difference in raising achievement scores. Based mostly on research from developed nations where school resources were already at a relatively high level, the idea that schools made little difference to learning offered few prospects to policy makers in the developing world seeking to invest in the social sector. Physical infrastructure trumped the social sectors. The World Bank (Heyneman and Loxley, 1983) looked at the effects of school resources on learning among many tens of thousands of 13–14 year-olds in 29 high- and low-income countries to see if the pattern of school effects found in advanced nations held. The research found students to have greater sensitivity to school resources in poor nations than in rich countries. These findings made intuitive sense because when resources are few to begin with, as found in poor nations (but plentiful in rich nations), wide exposure to small increases in quality are more likely to have greater impacts overall in poor environments (e.g., the "cultivating on virgin land" example in economics) even though gaps in output (i.e., scores) between the two groups remain large.

While controversial in part due to some methodological issues, the findings generated much debate and eventually helped lead the Organization for Economic Coordination and Development (OECD) in Paris, and the International Association for the Evaluation of Achievement in Amsterdam to implement repeated large-scale studies across academic disciplines by levels of schooling. OECD (2013) and International Association for the Evaluation of Achievement (2011) have introduced major surveys to track student performance around the world when looking to improve schooling and narrow learning differences. Today, there is a general recognition that nations need strong learning systems if they are to prosper in the global economy. It turns out schools do make a difference when they are fair, efficient, and sustainably operated – something less obvious when comparing nations with similar levels of school quality. It appears that early stages of school expansion emphasize quantity, while later stages stress quality.

Another brief example of donor-directed research also carried out by the World Bank (Psacharopoulos and Loxley, 1985) examined school assessments for secondary schools in Colombia and Tanzania. The authors compared students in various curriculum tracks on a series of school outcomes [(e.g., access to school type, cognitive learning (internal efficiency), labor market experience of graduates (external efficiency), and cost-effectiveness (economic efficiency)]. The researchers wanted to see if vocational education was a good investment to boost secondary school leavers' life chances. The debate in ODA circles centered on whether secondary vocational education was a good investment for developing nations in Africa and Latin America.

The research showed mixed results over a wide range of internal and external efficiency measures partly because of differences between stages of development found for the two national economies and educational systems. Apparently, social processes are never all good or bad when viewed in their wider contexts. Vocational education in relatively advanced Colombia and Latin America could sustain diversified education more easily than in a country like Tanzania with relatively underdeveloped institutions and economy at that time. With little enrollment capacity at secondary levels of academic education in Tanzania, the vocational education stream became a backdoor entry point into university that previously drew students mostly from the academic track. Students did not wish to pursue agricultural, industrial, or commercial education in preference to attending university. In Colombia, vocational knowledge taught to students can be useful when students apply that knowledge to specific disciplines. In the case of commercial education, it was found that graduates from commercial programs do better than noncommercial graduates working in commercial establishments when looking at earnings at 2 years of employment. Colombia had an economy that could absorb commercial student graduates while Tanzania did not.

Given the high cost of equipment required in vocational education, it appeared that expensive vocational education programs underway before the 1990s in many developing countries were not effective ways to get students to reorient academic careers into more technical fields. A major reason for this unintended outcome of expanding vocational education only to have graduates seek academic higher education was due to the initial low level of economic opportunity, which school graduates faced at the time. Often technical equipment was procured for vocational schools but never made operational due to inadequate infrastructure and poor staff assignment, for example power outages, few qualified teachers outside cities, and so on. The two-country study showed the need to be particularly sensitive to funding projects in nations where the existing institutional capacity and human resources and supply chains were poorly developed. It appeared that at lower stages of the development spectrum, vocational technical education was not an effective way to reduce unemployment and get school leavers to opt for work outside occupations reserved for graduates in the academic schools. In addition, technical vocational programs worked better in Colombia than in Tanzania where programs were more basic, suggesting school outcomes may depend on the level of economic development.

Debate raged between those who favored vocational education versus those who favored math and science academics. The study, which included both *ex ante surveys,* and *tracer* studies, found that curriculum diversification: (i) was relatively expensive; (ii) did not necessarily improve the fit between school and work; and, (iii) did not better prepare students for future study in their field of specialization (e.g., agriculture, industry, commerce, etc.). These findings along with others were debated within the Word Bank as well as at conferences and workshops within Tanzania, Colombia, and elsewhere in places where diversified education was widely practiced. By the 1990s as universal primary education gained dominance through the Millennium Development Goals (MDGs), the vocational school debate receded as focus turned attention to basic education.

Interestingly, a resurgence of technical education support recently has reoccurred in Asia as many nations in the region have secured universal basic and secondary education enrollments. As time has moved on and Asian nations have developed, new efforts are afoot to support technical education when it is closely tied to the private sector economy, and when public–private training partnerships can ensure the right skills are taught at the right level in the right amounts to avoid employment bottlenecks

(Asian Development Bank, 2004). Technical education in Singapore and South Korea is a good example of demand-based training to support sophisticated labor markets when institutional capacity is world class.

In a real sense, donor-driven research can disseminate information flow judged by the greater ODA community to be effective. However, such research must be totally transparent, open-ended, participatory, and collaborative among development partners. Over time and through sharing, consensus can be forged with full participation by stakeholders in IA. Information flow provides a global approach to finding answers to problems arising in the social sectors. Wherever research is carried out in good faith, IA keeps ODA on track so that capacity building continues to improve both institutional integrity and human resource capability among stakeholders. By following the knowledge trail, it is possible to diminish knowledge gaps among development partners. A clearer understanding of how knowledge increases alongside stage of development can improve designs that ensure project integrity from their inception. In a world of complex development, competent decisions require smart stakeholders. We now examine several case studies to see how IA links knowledge to progress within the development community.

CASE STUDY 1: ACCELERATING THE FLOW OF SCIENTIFIC KNOWLEDGE IN INDONESIA

Any nation seeking to improve its social infrastructure must put in place sets of institutions and management styles to accommodate competition (Lahl, 1999). Social infrastructure allows human competitiveness in science, technology, and skill formation. Otherwise, economies cannot support science until skills and technologies are upgraded to handle greater productivity including design, research, management, marketing, etc. So how does IA lead to improved information flow within institutions found among development partners?

A good example of information and technology transfer can be found in the World Bank funded Fellowship Project in Indonesia (World Bank, 1993) participated in by the author, which began in the late 1980s and continued for 10 years. Technological progress was coming to Indonesia. Development partners wanted to see an effectively run project that offered value for money, through overseas fellowships leading to scientific knowledge transfer across public and private institutions pursuing industrial development. The development questions posed by donors and recipients alike asked how best to improve intellectual capacity of professionals in government agencies serving as "scientific incubators?" How might policy on scientific research be used to comparative advantage in making Indonesia competitive in science and technology? The fellowship program carried out by Indonesia to boost scientific capability represents an interesting analysis of project impact to address these questions. The project allowed *ex-post evaluation of* long-run issues involving the capability of public and private sector science and technology found among professionals in national institutes of research in Indonesia.

Project assessment demonstrated what development specialists could learn from attempts to increase higher order knowledge and information flow within government research institutes needed to transform the science community. From the beginning, the Fellowship Project aimed to increase the level of intellectual competence among scientists in about a half-dozen nonministerial government research institutes in Jakarta covering areas such as atomic energy, aeronautics and space, survey mapping, statistics, social science research, and science and technology (S&T). Government funding for employee travel abroad to seek advanced degrees might be problematic if upon returning to their respective institutions, the quality of research and operations did not improve markedly. Some skeptics deemed the project risky if returning fellows left government employment after a 4-year grace period to pursue personal gain in the emerging private sector (only 3% did). Others counter-argued that Indonesians seldom opt to remain abroad, and besides private sector employment also contributes to national development. The concept of government borrowing for advancing a relatively small group of professionals also raised issues of equity for others. In any case, the overriding objective was about increasing scientific knowledge in support of national development.

The government firmly believed that increasing the intellectual capacity of the next generation of research scientists provided value for money so it strongly endorsed ownership and sought partnership with the World Bank and educational institutes around the world. Project preparation showed that government research institutes lacked sufficient graduate-level scientists to raise productivity in provision of government services, although later it was recognized that there was never an in-depth examination of the nature of supply and demand gaps in national scientific skills. Project institutes represented government science and research services often found to either promote competitive advantage in technology, or to provide essential services to monitor national priorities in transport, housing, social services, etc. The existing government institutes were often understaffed and poorly funded for world-class research. There was little public–private collaboration, and little mobility among scientists in the research community. For a country the size of Indonesia to invest in professional staff upgrading, thousands of overseas fellowships would be required. Once the project started, it was realized that the number of existing staff would be insufficient in number to meet the overseas fellowships required (too many staff going abroad simultaneously was impractical), so competition was opened to high school graduates provided they agreed to work for the government for a specified period after graduation.

About 25% of about 1,600 fellowships were set aside for advanced degrees. These fellowships were originally offered in developed European and Asian countries because tuition costs were waived (in Europe) or inconsequential in low-cost education systems (in Asia). Interestingly, the United States was originally considered too expensive given that tuition costs could not be waived in higher education. However, several years into the project a revised decision granted the 4,000 US colleges and universities eligibility to participate. Because the US college system tended to cater to undergraduate foreign students, the completion rate for overseas fellows improved. The result served as a reminder to higher education systems around the word that they must not neglect foreign students in their charge who often need special assistance when studying in a foreign culture. Another unexpected issue arose early on in project implementation when local universities feared that the top secondary school graduates were being siphoned off to foreign institutions under the project. However, this unintended outcome was viewed as only a temporary condition.

Overall, project efficiency was shown to meet most of its targets in the fellowship program, and the in-house implementation of the mammoth program was judged highly effective. Local capacity bolstered by international consultants helped to restructure the institutes to make them more compatible and less hierarchical among scientists facing more professional collegial contact. In addition, many associations were formed with local and overseas schools and research institutes allowing exchange programs; career paths for returning fellows were judged successful; and, as the private research sector developed as engagement with the public sector expanded.

So what was learned from IA? Opening up higher education to large numbers of foreign fellows taught donor participants the need for close cooperation to ensure fellows receive quality education and training. The cost borne by the Indonesian Government was seen by donors to offer value for money, especially over time as fellows returned and intellectual networks began to form within institutes and between institutes, universities, and private companies. Third-party foreign companies saw trade prospects in aircraft and rail industries, along with university participation in atomic energy, and social survey research. The World Bank was pleased that the recipient project implementation unit ran the complex project well. The Bank realized that building information capacity in the physical and social sciences was critical to overall development planning by government to create indigenous research in a host of public and private organizations. Allowing educated people to collaborate in the interest of national development is important while disseminating knowledge both from abroad and locally is vital to boosting scientific capability in Indonesia.

Likewise, assessment addressed by Indonesian officials focused on the realization that research budgets must increase, and organizational strategies for each institute must be put in place to ensure utilization of returning staff. The government also felt that increasing human resource levels, allowed greater intellectual collaboration within and between institutions in a culture not readily accustomed to independent thinking. By reformulating technology goals and plans, the nation might become independent in scientific research with strong links to the outside world of knowledge, research, and technological know-how.

A final review of monitoring and evaluation by the donor community indicated that there was no critical baseline on which to build indicators. There was no long-term monitoring follow up tracer study to track individuals, or guide institutions to increase resources to stay abreast of R&D developments. The Project met its targets but could not demonstrate national impact at the time of the project closing usually because it takes years and follow-up monitoring to judge long-term success. Follow-up through tracer studies of returned fellows for 10 years is required, and monitoring closely institutional collaboration to see how productive degree holders become over time. *Ex ante* analysis over the long run answers the question of whether long-term goals were achieved. Clearly, the added research capacity in science and technology has expanded cooperation between the public and private sectors, thereby creating a dynamic exchange of ideas in the scientific community.

The conclusion by the donor community at the time reiterated that there were no cheaper alternatives to radically increase the number of professional scientists than by overseas training. Today, the development community does not stress the need for large-scale science fellowship programs that send large numbers abroad all at once for degrees, and then integrate them into productive work upon return. Advanced fellowships will always be needed, but can be handled bilaterally through exchange programs, by universities and foundations on a selective basis. To monitor long-term knowledge sharing requires the government to continuously track careers of all returning fellows and to find ways to assess strategies and goals. Creating public sector research "incubators" is a task that must be carried out in partnership with the private sector under a clear national strategy.

CASE STUDY 2: INSTITUTIONAL CAPACITY BUILDING IN THE MALDIVES

If capacity means having adequate physical plants and equipment, then capability means having sufficient ability to use these inputs effectively. The Maldives story tells about the creation of the Maldives College of Higher Education (MCHE) in a small economically viable country based on social services, marine science, and tourism that wants its graduates to meet global standards (Asian Development Bank, 2009). In 2011, MCHE became the Maldives National University (MNU). This case study explores what happens when government commitment to higher education capacity building takes hold among nascent public research and training institutes run from a handful of ministries that unite under one umbrella organization to serve the needs of local scholars. These ministries included public health, technology training, hotel and tourism, business administration, distance education, teacher training, marine biology, and maritime studies.

In the Maldives, the entire system of research and diploma training is small so combining many small units under the MCHE would allow a critical mass to give strategic direction through a college and later a university. The overall project rationale was designed to save on foreign exchange since everyone previously seeking government employment had to travel abroad for postsecondary schooling including many diploma recipients paid by the government. Likewise, improving local capacity in implementing a national plan to employ graduates and create networks of professionals was central to increasing professional knowledge throughout the Maldives.

The project exemplified a major government initiative in calling for and managing a new institution considered indispensible, which required various ministries to surrender some research and training authority to this new government entity. The project called for establishing a multipurpose complex on government land in the center of the capital to serve as a focal point for students including classrooms, auditorium, student center, and registrar's office. Dormitory facilities were also provided for females coming from the outer atolls. Fellowships were provided for administrative staff, along with some equipment upgrade needed for training.

Overall, the project was deemed successful by both donors and government in meeting its targets mostly due to the small-scale nature of activities as well as the relatively advanced organizational capacity already found within existing institutes. Some of the assessment findings predicted that over time, the college would be a focal point for cross-national fellowship and university exchange programs including health, tourism, and marine biology, in which third-party foreign institutes were keen to participate. The project also strengthened distance education training programs within the atolls. Cost analysis showed that foreign exchange savings from the current government system of overseas fellowship training would pay for the project within 10 years thereby offering value for money. Knowledge networks developed within and across institutions would eventually improve the intellectual dialog among the nation's scientists, professors, and leaders. It turned out that in such a small country, the relatively homogenous nature of the social-political, economic, and cultural sectors worked in favor of supporting knowledge building as an intellectual enterprise.

In future, government needs to monitor MCHE progress by providing tracer studies of graduates, and web-based information on education plans and activities, which can be provided to donors who may then support programs of interest. Although institutional capacity building across the developing world will continue for decades, new projects will always be determined by existing organization and management capacity. In the case of the Maldives, MCHE helped to raise the quality and relevance of knowledge in development. The creation of MCHE demonstrates that as institutional complexity rises, it allows greater societal transformation. Educational institutions are good investments for ensuring nations keep ahead of the global knowledge curve. Without this added local institutional capability, trade for aid and value for money will have little effect on transformative development. Generally, past efforts determine the current state of development complexity so knowing the history of previous institutions greatly influences current practices.

CASE STUDY 3: CHOOSING FUNDING MODALITIES FOR PROJECT INTEGRITY IN PAKISTAN

IA is also useful in the context of monitoring large-scale projects in poor countries struggling to provide basic services. Providing basic services in under-served areas is something most donors wish to participate, especially when bottom-up approaches to transformative development can involve local beneficiaries. Development specialists know that knowledge distribution at this most basic level of the population strengthens the foundation of all future development. Consequently, project designs with stated interventions and expected outcomes play an important role in achieving basic social services. In turn, these outcomes support national competitiveness by an educated population, institutional capacity with local participation, and add value for money in reaching national strategies. By measuring these strengths and weaknesses of project/program design, IA plays a role in capturing how well integrated parts contribute to project integrity. IA becomes testament to success when projects run smoothly and findings offer insight into long-term impacts.

To illustrate how projects fit into national planning, a 12-year, two-stage project funded by the Asian Development Bank (2002) during the 1990s. The project was designed to improve the retention rate for girls through to primary school completion of grade-five throughout districts in all provinces of Pakistan. The project was a government designed and initiated project taken from a UNESCO prototype and cofinanced by ADB and the Islamic Development Bank (IDB), with counterpart funding from the government. The Norwegian government provided grant funds to be used for consumables for girls including pencils, paper, and school bags along with innovations including school swings. Incidentally, these swings proved very popular and teachers told stories of how children came to school early just to ride on the schoolyard swings.

Typically primary schools are two-room schools where first graders fill the first classroom, and grades 2-5 fill the second classroom. Obviously, this organizational setting does little to encourage school completion. In this system most children are forced out partly due to lack of desk space to continue, but also because poor children in rural areas are needed to work in the community at an early age. Alternatively, under the project, girls' schools (40 girls per each of five rooms - one for each grade) were designed with a total target of about 2,000 walled-in schools covering about half the districts in the country.

The main problem facing project implementation was a shortage of qualified female teachers willing to travel to rural districts to teach. There were few qualified female teachers residing in many rural areas, and government policy limited hiring locally trained females to gradually qualify over time. Fortunately, many of the 2,000 schools were built in semirural areas with access to main roads. Given typical coordination problems among the federal, provincial, and district levels, it took time to organize the various activities found in the project. These activities included building and equipping schools, staffing and training teachers in use of learning materials, etc. Technical assistance provided consultancies, along with project funds allocated for both international and local consultants. On balance, in spite of delays, the project met its targets and helped increase female primary school completion for as many as 400,000 girls over each 5-year school cycle. Still, these national and local government-led accomplishments represented only a fraction of the millions left unable to complete their schooling.

To speed up social sector achievements supporting the MDGs, it was decided that many individual donor funded projects throughout the social sectors in Pakistan were not aiding the country fast enough to meet the mammoth tasks of increasing enrollments in education, providing health, water, sanitation, etc., to the population. Consequently, to overcome social sector fragmentation in service delivery, the development partners jointly undertook the Social Action Program (SAP) to help meet MDG goals in several social sectors. Led by the World Bank, the massive SAP having one locally administered oversight unit began to coordinate the wide range of donor projects across multiple social sectors and reconcile them with national and provincial governments' own priorities and implementation schedules. Under the project, donors continued their funding support under one monitoring umbrella, while the government provided counterpart budget and expenditures necessary to increase spending annually on each sector. At the same time, the government devolved social sector implementation more fully while nongovernment organizations (NGOs) were encouraged to lend support to community mobilization. Overall, the hope was to meet the MDG goals set at the national level. Interestingly, the government agreed to temporarily expand social sector spending at the expense of other sectors to achieve these goals.

Under SAP, IA targeted individual project outcomes, government disbursements by sector, and the monitoring of selected national priorities to reach overall MDG goals by 2015 (e.g., hiring sufficient numbers of new teachers, encouraging community participation, etc.). These IAs required regular joint development partner meetings across all sectors and provinces. Monitoring eventually became unwieldy with too many participants and too frequent assessments. Nonsocial sectors resented resources not going to them, and eventually national and provincial governments along with donors began withdrawing political support to the SAP due to its unwieldy nature. Line ministries felt they spent too much time meeting with donors and struggling to meet the SAP timetables and disbursements. While noble in intent, SAP could not be sustained because it became impractical to monitor all social sectors together to make noticeable progress on the MDGs (Birdsall et al., 2005). The major IA lesson from SAP recommended donors not to micromanage national progress across all sectors together. IA claimed that SAP became bogged down by too many external socio-economic and political conditions that eventually broke the ability to manage the social sectors. A new approach was needed to meet MDG goals while simultaneously creating transparency on budgetary support in return for better organizing and managing the various social sectors independently.

By the early 2000s MDG targets lagged as growth without development occurred. It became apparent that another approach was needed to shape progress in the social sectors in Pakistan and in other large nations with low levels of progress on MDGs. A shift to a program loan structure was initiated in the social sectors where donors provide budgetary support in return for governments enacting policy decisions enabling progress on MDGs. This program modality works best individually by sector especially where chains of command function well. Under program interventions, both donors and governments provide substantial funds to the social sectors to ensure rapid disbursement to the districts. In return, a matrix of policy goals are set and disbursements are made according to how far along the implementation of policies have progressed. This approach works when all development partners agree on outcomes, collaborate in earnest to implement reforms, and stress sufficient institutional capacity to carry out complex policy making. Pakistan undertook this modality in the education sector starting around 2003. In Bangladesh, development partners implemented a similar modality with great success in raising enrollments and preventing dropout in a country with previous little success in achieving MDGs.

Employing program interventions, IA is kept relatively simple. Aside from assessing specific outcomes of consultancies, training, survey completions, etc., the main emphasis is placed on fulfilling requirements within the policy framework. As policies are enacted (partially and totally), tranches are released, and later the policies can be assessed to note their impact on achieving MDGs. In this way, IA becomes valuable in tracking progress to ensure fair, efficient, and sustainable adjustments to a sector, and can easily be extended to add new policies along with additional budgetary support. In addition, many subprojects can be added as needed, and program funds can be monitored as they are disbursed quickly to the local level. Under this modality, it is easy to assess sector management, administration, evaluation, training etc., and move resources to where bottlenecks arise.

Each of the above cases shows that any modality can be applied, but it is up to IA to determine the best approach given the needs of the sector: either at meeting national targets, or directly supporting specific requirements such as providing girls education in South Asia. Meeting the social sector needs of South Asia is challenging. Until capacity in the form of organization, equipment, and staff are readily available, institutional capability cannot be counted on. When examining institutional strengths, it is important to assess overall capacity of existing social, political, economic, and cultural forces in each society.

CASE STUDY 4: COMPUTER-ASSISTED INSTRUCTION IN SRI LANKAN SCHOOLS

Can placing computers in secondary schools increase the knowledge level of graduates? Curriculum and Instruction experts look to e-learning as a way to accelerate access to information among students with special emphasis on all sorts of simulation software exercises in laboratory science, math, and the humanities as well as improve school administration (Loxley and Julien, 2004). If students can be exposed to more learning opportunities, they should be able to score higher on national school leaving examinations. Based on this reasoning, the Sri Lankan government was keen to implement computers in education as a way to boost teacher instruction and student learning. However, they were unsure of the hidden costs for hardware and software upkeep throughout 4,000 secondary schools. Integrating curriculum with instruction was desired, but some asked whether schools and ancillary teacher education, curriculum, and training institutes were up to the implementation task.

Based on earlier pilot projects, desktop computers in computer labs were placed in 2,500 schools mostly in towns and cities on the stable electricity grid (Asian Development Bank, 2008). Under the project, the government began the mammoth task of procuring large numbers of computers and software at a time when vendors were not authorized to give discounts to educational institutes. Computer rooms had to be established, a system of teacher and high school lab assistants from the school computer club trained, supplementary software provided, and electronic curriculum materials designed to incorporate e-learning. At the time, the government was under pressure to increase pass rates on A-level exams in a system that prided itself in maintaining high standards. Educators believed that strengthening learning through e-learning, e-instruction, e-tutoring, etc., was a good way to increase classroom exposure for many who could not pay for private tutoring.

The idea that the younger generation must have access to computer knowledge drove the rationale. Started in 2000, the project lasted 7 years during which many of the targets were met to refurbish classrooms into computer labs, procure hardware and software, training, etc. School-based assessment was introduced alongside computer-assisted learning. A national computer school-net was established to handle software products, and digitalizing records. Without lowering academic standards on the national examination, the nation's pass rate actually increased by nearly 10% over the decade. Likewise, private sector capacity in the ICT industry grew dramatically thereby providing job opportunities for graduates with computer skills.

Was the project successful and did it offer an implementation strategy for other countries to follow? To fully answer this question, the time is ripe for an in-depth *ex post facto* assessment of project impact based on how well computer-assisted instruction has changed teaching methods, and increased online opportunities to apply learning to school subjects. Issues include whether afterschool activities such as math and chess clubs, library study, school administration, teacher training, and curriculum revision transformed the use of ICT for learning? A thorough assessment would indicate the probabilities of success required when introducing complex learning modalities into schools where capacity building is matched with the capability of employing new methods. Such IA findings can assist e-learning experts to design future projects during periods of rapid technological change where computer equipment can be rented or purchased economically.

The entire domain of ICT and e-learning (Asian Development Bank, 2004) has transformative potential to alter development with implications for commercially viable international trade, and collaborative global partnerships. It is up to IA specialists to design IAs that answer the many questions facing delivery of fair and effective interactive computer instruction on a national scale. Loxley and Julien (2004) offer criteria for evaluating computers in education to ensure (i) raising student computer skills; (ii) increasing student interest in computers; (iii) supplementing teacher instructional procedures with computers; (iv) expanding educational programs using computers; (v) expanding e-learning beyond the classroom walls; and (vi) providing efficient administration and cost savings through digitalization. Any assessment of computers in education must take account of student–teacher–classroom capability for independent study. Until teachers are trained in new ICT pedagogies, both teachers and students will find it difficult to adjust to new learning formats.

SUMMARY AND CONCLUSION

Clearly, there is no single panacea for assessing social sector projects given the complexity found among political, social, economic, and cultural perspectives within nations. The international community continuously must seek strategies that offer value for money through trade for aid and transformative development. The case studies provided in this chapter, suggest that impact evaluations are really about looking at the flow of knowledge and experience in social and economic transformation. Drawing on a policy-making framework, and understanding the role of key development partners, IA provides a context to follow knowledge transfer to see who learns the most and uses it wisely.

Knowledge transfer improves as the capacity and capability of organizations evolve throughout stages of development, and contributes to the collective wisdom of nations. This was seen in the case of the Indonesian science and technology community, the Maldives' university environment, the educational participation of girls in Pakistan, and the increase in computer skills among Sri Lankan secondary school students. These projects raise the collective wisdom of society needed to ensure development, while closing the gap between donor and recipient capacity to understand progress. Consequently, reassessing the capacity of institutions and individuals is essential prior to designing new programs. When institutional capacity allows knowledge and information to flow smoothly across different development stages, donor projects are more likely to yield project integrity needed to withstand the many implementation problems that invariably arise. Sharing information on findings from IA is essential if ODA is to remain effective in assisting global progress among the many nations and social sectors of the world. Evaluation conducted wisely is the best defense against ineffective projects and program failure.

REFERENCES

Asian Development Bank, 2009. Project Completion Report (Loan MLD 1643) Post Secondary Education Modernization Project. Manila, Philippines. Available from: <the ADB Website>.

Asian Development Bank, 2008. Project Completion Report (Loan No. SRI 1756) Secondary School Modernization Project. Manila, Philippines. Available from: <the ADB Website>.

Asian Development Bank, 2004. Improving Technical Education and Vocational Training: Strategies for Asia. ADB, Manila, Philippines.

Asian Development Bank, 2002. Project completion report (Loan PAK: 1454) Second Primary School Education Project (Sector). Manila, Philippines. Available from: <ADB Website>.

Birdsall, M., Malik, A., Vaishanav, M., 2005. Poverty and the Social Sectors: The World Bank in Pakistan 1990–2003. World Bank, Washington, DC.

Heyneman, S., Loxley, W., 1983. The effects of primary school quality on academic achievement across twenty-nine high and low income countries. Am. J. Sociol. 88 (6), 1162–1194.

International Association for the Evaluation of Achievement, 2011. International Results in Science. Amsterdam, The Netherlands.

Lahl, S., 1999. Competing with Labor: Skills and Competitiveness in Developing Nations. ILO, Geneva.

Loxley, W., 2013. Smart world dumb world: Developing knowledge rich economies. U.S. Library of Congress Registration No. TXu 1-835-878. Available on i-Books. Version 1.0.

Loxley, W., 2003. Donor support for educational research in Asia. In: Keeves, J., Watanabe, R. (Eds.), International Handbook of Educational Research in Asia and the Pacific. Kluwer, London.

Loxley, W., Julien, P., 2004. Information and Communication Technologies in Education and Training in Asia and the Pacific. ADB, Manila, Philippines.

Organization for Economic Cooperation Development, 2013. PISA 2012 Results in Focus. OECD, Paris.

Psacharopoulos, G., Loxley, W., 1985. Diversified Secondary Education and Development. World Bank Publication. Johns Hopkins Press, Baltimore, MD.

World Bank, 1999. World Development Report: 1998–99: Knowledge for Development. World Bank, Washington, DC.

World Bank, 1993. Project Completion Report. Indonesia Science and Technology Project. Washington, DC. Available from: <the World Bank Website (World Bank)>.

FROM EVIDENCE TO ACTION: STAKEHOLDER COORDINATION AS A DETERMINANT OF EVALUATION USE

10

Mateusz Pucilowski

Impact Evaluation, Social Impact, Inc., Arlington, Virginia, USA

CHAPTER OUTLINE

INTRODUCTION

Dissatisfied with the lack of progress in the continuing struggle against poverty, the global community has made strides toward tying investment decisions to evidence of programmatic impact. Documenting outcomes and providing policy makers with information regarding competing options about resource allocation have resulted in a growing market for development research. However, with more information at their disposal than any time before, managers continue to struggle with translating data into concrete decisions.

This chapter begins with a short overview of global trends toward increased accountability in foreign aid, before outlining challenges faced by policy makers in translating evidence into investment decisions. Four key determinants of evaluation usage are presented (rigor, timing, relevance, and communication) alongside guidance on how each can be enhanced. This section situates evaluation within the politicized context of foreign aid where managers have to consider a range of nonempirical factors in making decisions. In order to be effective agents of change, evaluators need to understand the organizational context within which they operate. However, there is a limit to what they can achieve in isolation. The following section frames evaluation as a complex system, outlining the roles and incentive structures of three primary evaluation stakeholders (client, implementer, and evaluator). The last section provides practical guidance for enhancing coordination between these parties through procurement, design, implementation, and dissemination phases.

BACKGROUND

On October 24, 1970 the UN passed a resolution stating that "economically advanced countries" will strive to provide 0.7% of gross national product to official development assistance (ODA) to developing nations. While compliance with the resolution has been minimal,[1] total outlays on foreign aid have increased and represent a significant source of economic activity. Over the last 5 years, the 29 member countries of the OECD-DAC have invested an average of USD132 billion in ODA per annum (OECD, 2015), a figure at par with the GDP of Hungary (World Bank, 2015). Inclusive of all other official assistance flows, the figure rises to USD 474 billion.[2] Adding to this total the substantial investments of non-DAC countries, particularly China, it is clear that development is big business.

In spite of this large-scale flow of money, it is estimated that over one billion people live in poverty (World Bank, 2015).[3] Dissatisfied with the lack of progress in the continuing struggle against poverty, the global community has made a series of commitments designed to increase the effectiveness of foreign assistance. Since the year 2000, the movement toward evidence-based decision making has been accelerating, with notable milestones including the establishment of the Millennium Development Goals, the ratification of the Paris Declaration on Aid Effectiveness, the publication of formal evaluation policies at many donor organizations, and the recognition by the UN General Assembly of 2015 as the International Year of Evaluation. The demand for a robust evidence base upon which to make policy decisions has led to increased investment across a wide range of analytical activities, including performance monitoring, program evaluation, impact assessment, and economic analysis. A product of these developments has been the proliferation of methodological and analytical approaches that are not always clearly systematized and mutually understood. In the case of impact assessment, the term is sometimes used to define *ex-ante* analyses that model "future consequences of a current or proposed action" (IAIA, 2009). However, application of this term to *ex-post* designs brings it in line with what has traditionally been defined as program evaluation. Using the definition proposed by Steele (1970), where "evaluation is the systematic process of judging the worth, desirability, effectiveness, or adequacy of something according to definite criteria and purposes," impact assessment can be thought of as a specialized extension of program evaluation. This chapter draws on the rich literature on program evaluation to derive lessons applicable to both *ex-ante* and *ex-post* designs, and refers to both approaches simply as program evaluation.

---

[1]Only five countries met or exceeded the target in 2014. In descending order, these were: Sweden (1.1%), Luxembourg (1.07%), Norway (0.99%), Denmark (0.85%), and the United Kingdom (0.71%) (OECD, 2015).

[2]Latest figure is for 2012, and includes "finance provided by public bodies at close to market terms and/or with a commercial motive, private finance at market terms, such as foreign direct investment, and private grants from philanthropic foundations and non-governmental organizations" (OECD, 2014).

[3]Most recent estimate is for 2012.

DETERMINANTS OF EVALUATION USE

Increases in both the demand for and supply of research have provided policy makers with more data than at any previous time in history. The availability of evidence alone, however, is not likely to affect aid effectiveness in a globally significant manner. In order for research to influence the development agenda, findings have to first be translated into managerial decisions of consequence. The likelihood that an evaluation report will influence management decisions is a product of a number of factors. Most concretely, there are four primary facets that can promote or inhibit utilization of evaluation products:

Rigor – Evaluation rigor relates to the strength (i.e., internal validity) of empirically derived conclusions. Evaluation products should have a sufficiently compelling empirical foundation to warrant influencing investment decisions. Reports driven by questionable sampling strategies, poorly designed instruments, anecdotal evidence, or ill-defined analytical approaches diminish the likelihood that decision makers will be persuaded to deviate from the *status quo*. Four factors stand out as key determinants of research rigor. First, the unbiased, independent status of the research team is a precondition for convincing the reader that findings are not driven by exogenous agendas. Secondly, research should be driven by the selection and correct application of the best methodological tools appropriate for a given context. Generally speaking, evaluation rigor is enhanced through mixed methods designs, where the incorporation of qualitative and quantitative data collection and analytical approaches allows researchers to leverage the strengths of both approaches, while triangulating findings and enriching analysis. Third, irrespective of the independence of the research team and the quality of the methodological approach, the appropriateness of the research team drives evaluation rigor. Dimensions of quality could be academic training, applied experience, knowledge of the local cultural–linguistic context, and team composition as it relates to sex, nationality, and academic discipline. Lastly, rigor is a product of the cumulative nature of the research design, or the extent to which it draws lessons from previous studies and other contexts.

Timing – Demand for evidence is time sensitive and the ability of research to influence policy is strongly dependent on whether results are received with sufficient lag time to inform pending decisions. It is not uncommon for evaluation products to be submitted after management decisions have been made, with the most common explanatory factors being delays in procurement, lack of foresight in planning, and factors beyond the control of evaluation stakeholders (e.g., weather, political instability, etc.). Incorporating considerations and concrete plans for evaluation at an early stage, however, could overcome the first two issues. The best strategies for ensuring the timely delivery of results are incorporation of evaluation into the design of programs, development of portfolio-level evaluation plans, realistic projections regarding elapsed time necessary to procure evaluation services, and proactive management on the part of the party responsible for managing the study.

Relevance – In order for research products to influence policy, they need to be aligned with the informational needs of decision makers and reflective of the realities of their operational context. Reports that do not directly answer research questions, or make recommendations that are impractical to implement, inhibit utility. Relevance of work products is enhanced when studies are structured around well-designed research questions, address informational needs of the most important potential users, evaluators understand the political context of the client organization, and dissemination activities are presented in a culturally appropriate manner.

Communication – Research results should be communicated with as wide a range of stakeholders as possible. Oftentimes findings have applicability beyond the narrow interest of the funding institution. While some sensitive topics (e.g., diplomacy) may warrant limitations on distribution of work products, many multilateral and bilateral aid organizations have formal policies on transparency of research findings. Free-access publication of reports (e.g., World Bank's Independent Evaluation Group website, USAID's Development Experience Clearinghouse, etc.) and publication of raw data (e.g., Millennium Challenge Corporation's Open Data Catalog) is becoming more widespread. Factors that inhibit effective communication include limitations on transparency and dissemination, overly technical language, inappropriate reporting formats (e.g., overly lengthy), a lack of understanding of interested parties, and cultural inhibitions against publishing negative results. In institutions without mandated transparency, unflattering findings may become grounds for censorship. Without a proactive communication strategy decision makers may wither not be aware of products or not sufficiently engaged by products.

Successful integration of all four factors greatly enhances the prospects that an evaluation product will influence policy. However, no matter how well-designed, expertly implemented, or appropriately reported a research effort is, there is no guarantee that findings will translate into decisions. Programmatic and resource allocation decisions are made in a complex operating environment influenced by a wide range of factors unrelated to programmatic performance. Examples include constraints across financial, political, administrative, technical, and time dimensions. It is a fact that, irrespective of the quality of research, the political context within which the evaluation operates exerts a strong influence over the likelihood of findings uptake (Weiss, 1988a, 1988b). In this light, it has been argued that empiricism "competes for credibility in decision-making contexts best characterized as non-rational and pluralistic" (Shulha and Cousins, 1997, p. 197). It is unavoidable that political and institutional considerations will continue to shape development policy. In fact, investment decisions should not be made exclusively on the basis of evidence of effectiveness. These other considerations provide important reality-checks and accountability mechanisms. However, policy should be made in a fully informed manner, with information regarding probable costs, benefits, and alternative approaches. It is the role of development evaluation to inform such decisions.

In order for evidence to exert influence over decisions, it needs to be presented in a manner consistent with the institutional culture. The provision of evaluation products is, due to the importance of impartiality, the purview of external researchers. Though these actors have limited influence over policy decisions, researchers should see it as a core responsibility to promote and cultivate use through an understanding of the political–institutional context within which they work (Patton, 1988). In fact, "evidence suggests that the more evaluators become schooled in the structure, culture, and politics of their program and policy communities, the better prepared they are to be strategic about the factors most likely to affect use" (Shulha and Cousins, 1997, p. 203) This chapter advocates for closer cooperation between evaluation stakeholders as a method for enhancing the prospects that evaluation results will translate into policy decisions. The following sections present a discussion of key evaluation stakeholders and their roles and responsibilities, and concrete recommendations for how increased coordination between stakeholders can lead to improved prospects for utilization.

EVALUATION STAKEHOLDERS

As the party responsible for drafting reports, it is common for researchers to be blamed if work products are perceived to have methodological defects or limited utility. However, researchers are neither the architects of study parameters, nor are they the ultimate end users. As such, the utility of work products is mediated by factors and actors well beyond their sphere of influence. Researchers do not have full control over any of the aforementioned determinants of evolution utility. They can design the most rigorous study, solicit stakeholder participation, and invest in dissemination activities, but only within parameters afforded by the research agreement. Responding to requests from clients, evaluators strive to answer research questions under the time, budgetary, and personnel requirements dictated by the client. When there are discrepancies between the complexity of research questions and the resources afforded to their answering, it is very likely that final work products will have deficiencies. Beyond resourcing, other factors that constrain production of rigorous, useful products are limitations on access to project and secondary documents, lack of baseline data, and obstructionist implementers.

Every evaluation involves varying degrees of participation from a multiplicity of organizations and individuals. The following section outlines the three key evaluation stakeholder groups, what interests they have in the evaluation process, and what their intended role should be in a high-quality research effort.[4]

Client - The party that sets a research agenda by initiating, funding, and giving structure to the evaluation. Motivated by informational needs, institutional requirements or some combination thereof, this stakeholder is defined as both the funding organization as well as the individual managing the research on its behalf. In the context of foreign aid, the most common funding agencies are multilateral/bilateral donor institutions, national governments, and NGOs. Irrespective of organizational structure, the client has a strong stake in the quality and utility of the research product. Clients use information to inform changes to the current project, modifications to similar projects, or to inform broader policy.

Implementer – The party responsible for implementing the intervention or policy being studied. Implementers have a key role in facilitating successful research. As the expert on the subject of the research, they provide information and documentation regarding design, implementation, and performance. Additionally, staff members of implementers regularly participate as key informants and facilitators of access to additional study subjects. Upon receipt of the final work product, it is the expectation that implementers will act upon research findings and modify their existing, and hopefully future, programming. Implementers of the intervention under review have a strong stake in the outcome of research.

Evaluator – The party designing, implementing, and communicating the results of the study. Evaluators have an interest in producing a product that is rigorous, well-received by the client, and useful to a broad constituency of potential policy makers. In addition to contributing to the improvement of development programming, evaluators have a stake in promoting their reputation for quality work as well as building relationships for future research.

External evaluations tend to be structured in a manner that ascribes each of the three key stakeholders well-defined roles with limited overlap. Donors establish the general parameters of the study by defining evaluation questions, timelines, evaluation team composition, and budgets. Evaluators leverage their methodological expertise to design, implement, analyze, and report answers to questions.

---

[4]The structure of research may be such that one or more functions are performed by a single institution.

Implementers provide documentation and answer evaluator inquiries as key informants. Separation of the functions is a product of the relative strengths of the three actors as well as the need for objectivity in research results. However, experience in the field suggests that high-quality, policy-relevant, useful research benefits from collaboration. Without a systematic integration of client, evaluator, and implementer into evaluation design and uptake of recommendations, investments in evaluation will not be realized to their full potential.

Given the interdependencies between the evaluation stakeholders, it is instructive to view the research process through the lens of systems theory. Most studies consist of nonlinear interactions between three primary nodes: client, implementer, and researcher. Each component represents varied, sometimes incentives, perspectives, and goals. Peripheral nodes (host country governments, beneficiaries, other donors, other implementers, other researchers) also exist, exerting pressure on one or more of the primary actors. Each research effort is characterized by a similar structure, but with varying degrees of collaboration. Much has been written about the benefits of cooperation between researchers and clients, and it is generally agreed that "engagement, interaction, and communication between evaluation clients and evaluators is key to maximizing the use of the evaluation in the long run" (Johnson et al., 2009). However, without incorporating implementers into the participatory process, researchers run the risk of producing work products with unrealized utility and rigor. In their review of the literature on evaluation use, Hofstetter and Alkin (2003) note: "The evaluator could enhance use by engaging and involving intended users early in the evaluation, ensuring communications between producers and users of evaluations, reporting evaluation findings effectively so users can understand and use them for their purposes, and maintaining credibility with the potential users."

The following section provides concrete recommendations regarding key points of coordination between the three groups throughout the research process. For the purposes of this chapter the stages are defined as procurement, design, and dissemination.

POINTS OF COORDINATION
PROCUREMENT AND EVALUATION PREDESIGN

The general parameters of research designs are often set by donors through the development and solicitation of Statements of Work (SOWs). The informational needs of the funding agency are expressed through one or more research questions alongside stipulations regarding timelines, budgets, and evaluation team composition. The SOW forms the foundation of a study, upon which evaluators propose concrete methodologies, sampling strategies, and analytical plans. It's not always the case, however, that the team drafting an evaluation SOW has a technical understanding of research designs or informational requirements necessary to answer complex research questions. Depending on the maturity of the funding organization, drafters may have access to guidance documents, previous examples, and/or technical support staff. However, even when these resources exist, they are sometimes underutilized due to time pressures or a lack of appreciation regarding the implications of certain research designs. As a result, SOWs distributed for procurement can have substantial weaknesses including feasibility, lack of clarity, and how likely the evidence generated from the research design will provide internally valid, conclusive answers to questions. While evaluators can strive to produce the strongest study, deficiencies in SOW oftentimes translate into low-quality and underutilized evaluation products.

The bureaucratic requirements of competitive procurement preclude open discussion of the evaluation SOW with professional evaluators. Given the centrality of this document in structuring the subsequent research, it is of critical importance that the SOW be precise, with a clearly stated purpose statement and research questions. Equally important, the resources budgeted for the study should be sufficient to adequately answer the questions. Beyond funding, this includes the period of performance, which should include enough time for researchers to draft a quality design, conduct fieldwork, perform analysis, and draft a report. If permissible for the funding agency, it is recommended that donors send draft RFPs for review by qualified evaluation service providers in advance of a formal procurement if there is any ambiguity about design or resources. The exchange, which comes at no cost to the client, can greatly strengthen the prospects for a strong and useful research product. Soliciting expert feedback on SOWs can be particularly helpful for technically complex issues such as sample size calculations, identification of counterfactuals, and plausibility of measuring and attributing higher-level outcomes.

Traditionally, evaluation agreements have been made between donor and researchers. As previously discussed, however, the potential benefit of robust research to implementers is significant. Most intimately involved in the day-to-day operations, implementers are likely to have unanswered questions about the performance of their intervention. Involving key representatives from this group in the design of the SOW will not only enhance the potential for utilization, but may also build buy-in on the part of the party under investigation. Implementers should be consulted in the development of evaluation questions and the timing of the study. Additionally, they are well-placed to provide background material to inform SOWs. The danger of involving additional parties into the drafting process is growth in the study scope (e.g., additional research questions) and a subsequent lack of focus. Prudent managers will find a compromise between the informational needs of the client and implementing organizations while maintaining a reasonable number of research questions.

Expanding participation in drafting evaluation SOWs creates benefits and costs. On the plus side, identifying and engaging primary intended users in the scope and purpose of the research has the potential to increase the informational benefits and eventual influence of the research product. It also tends to facilitate buy-in on the part of parties that may have acted in obstructionist ways. The primary costs are additional time required to draft SOWs, if informational interests are not closely aligned potentially increased research costs, and if informational needs of implementers are not met by the research potentially disappointment in results.

DESIGN

Oftentimes the information provided in an SOW is not sufficiently detailed to inform a comprehensive evaluation design. These contractual documents, oftentimes 10–30 pages in length, are not designed to convey all the necessary inputs. Upon award of a research contract, it has traditionally been the responsibility of evaluation teams to seek additional documentation from which to produce a methodological approach that best answers the research questions within constraints specified in the SOW. This process oftentimes plays out in a unidirectional manner, with researchers making informational requests of clients and implementers. There are a number of ways in which stakeholder coordination can inform and improve research designs. Before considering methodology, researchers should clarify the primary intended users of the work products, as well as their specific informational needs. Upon identification of users and potential uses, these stakeholders should be consulted with regard to design options in order to maximize the potential for recommendations uptake.

Given the heterogeneity of research questions and associated designs, this section will present some common design elements that could benefit from closer coordination between research stakeholders.

Value for money

Any economic analysis that quantifies costs and benefits relies on two distinct information streams. Benefits are derived through analysis of programmatic outcomes in accordance with the intervention theory of change. Estimation of benefits is the responsibility of the evaluation team. Costs are calculated from project budgets, requiring implementers to share sensitive information with evaluation teams.[5] Difficulties usually arise in the idiosyncrasies of financial record keeping. Interventions, particularly those operating through complex theories of change, oftentimes have multiple programmatic components. It is not common for these organizations to assign expenses separately to different financial accounts. Without this fiscal disaggregation, it becomes very difficult to determine what proportion of the total project budget was allocated to a given activity. Furthermore, if the evaluation team wishes to subtract out costs associated with home office support, so as to derive ratios of the activity in the field and the activity as a whole, the financial system would need to further account for the source of task-based expenses. Secondly, if the evaluation is tasked with computing a cost/benefit ratio for beneficiary units, a robust monitoring system is required to track the number and type of programmatic recipients.

While it is possible to derive estimates for these cost inputs, an *ex-post* economic analysis will never be as precise as a study that incorporated financial accounting into the design of the intervention. If we are to provide policy makers with sound economic analysis to inform investment decisions, we should strive to make the estimates as valid as possible. The best way to enhance the accuracy of the estimates is to involve both implementers and evaluators before either activity begins. Through a facilitated discussion of researchers' informational needs and limitations of implementing accounting systems, agreement can be reached regarding establishment, tracking, and sharing of expense accounts across the life of the project.

Counterfactual designs

Studies intended to quantify and rigorously attribute impacts to development interventions oftentimes necessitate a much more collaborative relationship between evaluators and implementers than traditional research. In order to control for contextual factors that may have simultaneously influenced outcomes of interest, these research designs use rigorously defined comparison groups to estimate what would have happened to the treatment group in the absence of the intervention (i.e., the counterfactual). Comparing longitudinal changes between treatment and comparison groups allows researchers to isolate the effect of the program as distinct from all other exogenous influences (e.g., economic growth). It is not always readily apparent how such a counterfactual might be identified, nor is it always possible that a plausible counterfactual exists (e.g., if all eligible units are participating, or being offered a chance to participate, in an intervention).

The aspect of these research designs that gives them the ability to explore causal inferences simultaneously necessitates intensive collaboration with implementing organizations. Most directly,

---

[5]This is generally operationalized through nondisclosure agreements.

implementers will have to agree not to provide programmatic benefits to units selected for inclusion in the comparison group. In the case of randomized control trials (RCTs), the ability of implementers to select beneficiaries is divested to a random assignment process. The inability of implementers to select recipients of their intervention is oftentimes a source of conflict, particularly in cases where randomized assignment leads to increased programmatic costs. In either event, the evaluation places demands on implementers that may be significant and may breed resentment. The best way to prevent friction is for the funding agency to write participation in the evaluation into the implementer's agreement, ideally with additional funding for contingency costs associated with participation in the study. This is why it is always advisable to integrate evaluation and implementation from the beginning. Having researchers provide inputs on the design of the activity could inform a mutually beneficial solution that would allow both the identification of a rigorous counterfactual and minimize disruptions to implementation. Building trust and mutual understanding between the three stakeholder groups is especially important in instances where research directly interferes with the implementation process. In these cases, it is imperative that implementers feel like they have a voice to advocate for the best interests of their project.

DISSEMINATION

Written recommendations that stem directly from evaluation conclusions are one of the most direct ways to promote evaluation utilization. These recommendations should be realistic, actionable, and assigned a responsible party. While evaluators are generally tasked with drafting recommendations, they are ill-placed to determine the practicality of proposed changes for other institutions to implement. The strength of recommendations is their specificity, and while evaluators can determine whether any item should be the responsibility of the donor or implementer, they are not well-suited to assign the correct office, unit, or individual. Both of these tasks require feedback from the affected stakeholder groups. Provision of a reality-check on recommendations is facilitated through consultation. Ideally, after the conclusion of fieldwork and analysis, evaluators would present findings and associated recommendations in an out-brief attended by the client and implementer. In that context, it would be the responsibility of all three parties to ensure that next steps are clear, realistic, and assigned a responsible party.

CONCLUSION

This chapter outlined a number of strategies for enhancing utilization of research findings. First, evaluators need to understand the organizational context within which their client operates. Only through a familiarity with the institutional environment will they be able to produce work products with a sufficiently high degree of relevance. There are, however, limits to what evaluators can achieve in isolation. Every evaluation is a political process that engages a multiplicity of stakeholders with oftentimes competing incentives. Engaging these actors early in the process and giving them space to inform the design, implementation, and utilization of the evaluation is one of the best, most cost-effective ways to enhance prospects for utilization. Successful coordination of these stakeholders begins with the manner in which the client frames the evaluation. If sufficient time or budget is not allocated for answering well-designed research questions, the likelihood for quality evaluation products is low. Equally important, is the involvement of primary intended users in the development of the evaluation scope. Once an evaluation begins, the responsibility for coordinating stakeholders shifts to the evaluators. At this time, researchers should engage primary intended users throughout the evaluation process. This framework of systematic integration of stakeholders throughout the evaluation process is the most cost-effective way to enhance returns on evaluation investment.

Development research is a tool for improving the effectiveness of policies and programs. Such efforts should have as an explicit aim the provision of rigorous, timely, relevant, and actionable information to inform management and/or investment decisions. In addition to enhancing the quality and utility of evaluations, deep engagement of parties traditionally on the periphery of evaluation fosters positive externalities. The literature presents two distinct and complementary concepts of evaluation utilization: findings use and process use (Alkin and Taut, 2003). The former is the application of research products to inform practical management and investment decisions. It has been the focus of this chapter, and is the primary intent of most evaluator activities. Process use is defined as "cognitive, attitudinal, and behavior changes in individuals, and program or organizational changes resulting, either directly or indirectly, from engagement in the evaluation process and learning to think evaluatively" (Patton, 2012, p. 143). Even in instances where the findings use has failed, increased collaboration of stakeholders in the evaluative process may yield lasting changes.

Evaluation should be viewed as an investment decision at par with that of development programming. Considerations of value for money should factor in whether research benefits warrant the costs. It could be argued that every report that is financed, produced, and relegated to a bookshelf, represents both a missed opportunity for improving development effectiveness and a misallocation of scarce resources. If returns on evaluation investment are not seen as positive, financial and political support for development research may diminish. If we want to continue making significant strides in alleviating poverty, it is imperative that we learn from our mistakes, and continually work to improve the effectiveness of limited development resources.

REFERENCES

Alkin, M.C., Taut, S.M., 2003. Unbundling evaluation use. Studies Educ. Eval. 29, 1–12, no. 1.

Hofstetter, C.H., Alkin, M.C., 2003. Evaluation use revisited. In: Kelleghan, T., Stufflebeam, D.L. (Eds.), International Handbook of Educational Evaluation. Kluwer Academic Publishers, Great Britain, pp. 197–222.

International Association for Impact Assessment, 2009. What is Impact Assessment? IAIA Publications, Fargo, ND.

Johnson, K., Greenseid, L.O., Toal, S.A., King, J.A., Lawrenz, F., Volkov, B., 2009. Research on evaluation use. A review of the empirical literature from 1986 to 2005. Am. J. Eval. 30, 377–410, no. 3.

OECD, 2014. Development co-operation report 2014 mobilising resources for sustainable development. OECD Publishing, Paris.

OECD, 2015. Query wizard for international development statistics. Available from: <http://stats.oecd.org/qwids/#?x=1&y=6&f=4:1,2:1,3:51,5:3,7:1&q=4:1,2,3,100+2:1+3:51+5:3+7:1+1:2+6:2009,2010,2011,2012,2013,2014> (accessed 30.05.2015).

Patton, M.Q., 1988. The evaluator's responsibility for utilization. Eval. Practice 9, 5–24, no. 2.

Patton, M.Q., 2012. Essentials of Utilization-Focused Evaluation. Sage.

Shulha, L.M., Cousins, J.B., 1997. Evaluation use: Theory, research, and practice since 1986. Eval. Practice 18, 195–208, no. 3.

Steele, S.M., 1970. Program evaluation – a broader definition. J. Exten. 8, 5–16, no. 2.

Weiss, C.H., 1988a. Evaluation for decisions: Is anybody there? Does anybody care? Eval. Practice 9, 5–19, no. 1.

Weiss, C.H., 1988b. If program decisions hinged only on information: A response to Patton. Eval. Practice 9, 15–28, no. 3.

World Bank, 2015. Poverty overview. Available from: <http://www.worldbank.org/en/topic/poverty/overview> accessed 06.06.2015).

INSIDE THE BLACK BOX: MODELING THE INNER WORKINGS OF SOCIAL DEVELOPMENT PROGRAMS

Sebastian Lemire* and Gordon Freer†

*University of California, Los Angeles, California, USA
†Department of International Relations, University of the Witwatersrand and Insight Strategies, South Africa

CHAPTER OUTLINE

INTRODUCTION

This chapter rests on three premises. Premise one is that the impact of development programs is increasingly evaluated across a broad range of settings, populations, and times. Simply consider the many social development programs that are implemented and then evaluated for impact, only to be reimplemented and re-evaluated again, with no apparent connection between the initial impact evaluation and the redesigned program. This seemingly endless evaluation cycle keeps spinning and spinning; around and around it goes, and around and around again. For the seasoned evaluator, the image of a hamster fervently spinning in its wheel may come to mind.

The second premise of the chapter is that the vast body of impact study reports resulting from premise one tends to be left scattered on bookshelves like a long list of ravished maidens – forever ignored, forgotten, and unfulfilled. Again, this is nothing new to many an evaluator – or at least the more seasoned (and cynical) ones. To be sure the last impact evaluation report to be shelved before informing future program decisions has yet to be produced. What continues to be produced are additions to a massive mountain of shelved, lonely, overlooked evaluation reports. The hamster might be dead, but the wheel keeps spinning.

The third premise of the chapter is that it is entirely possible to break this unfortunate cycle, to get the hamster out of the wheel, to make better use of the lost maidens on those lonely shelves. In fact, doing so simply requires our commitment to enlist and make better use of the body of knowledge produced and contained in the still growing mountain of impact studies. What we propose in this chapter is a feasible – yet systematic – approach for making better use of the growing body of knowledge contained in social development impact studies. The potential benefit of doing so would be better-informed future program design decisions, based on past experiences.

The case for making better use of findings and insight of existing impact studies is easily made. First and foremost, relying on multiple rather than individual impact studies provides for more comprehensive and robust assessments of impact. Integrating the findings of a diverse array of impact studies supersedes the idiosyncratic contextual conditions that may enhance or depress the performance of a particular program implementation in a particular setting. As such, synthesizing multiple impact studies allow us to distill the causal recipe that persistently generates desired outcomes across multiple conditions and settings.

Secondly, information about these causal recipes may serve as practical advice about how to design more effective programs for future implementation. From a cost-conscious perspective, accumulating past impact studies supports the development of best-practice programs, maximizing the positive impact of these. The persistent value-for-money perspective on social development programs only makes this potential all the more compelling. After all, we should place our development funds in programs that are – all things considered – most likely to be effective. Examining existing impact studies will help us identify those programs.

Third and finally, the integration of findings from past impact studies may complement individual impact studies of new program implementations. Accumulated findings from past impact studies may generate hypotheses and corroborate explanations about the ways in which a program works (or fails to work). More than that, findings from past impact studies may also support the generalization of findings from individual studies by connecting these with corroborating findings from a wider range of impact studies. In this way, synthesizing past findings holds a potential to both inform and strengthen the causal claims and explanations emerging from impact studies of individual program implementations.

With these observations as our backdrop, the purpose of the proposed synthesis approach is to capture and model how and why programs work, based on findings from existing impact studies. More specifically, we propose an approach that structures the synthesis of existing impact studies around the development of a meta-model. The approach is perhaps best viewed as a systematic and transparent method for summarizing how a program generates impact.

Four sections comprise the presentation of this approach. Part one sets the scene by briefly outlining the intellectual roots and grounding of the meta-modeling approach. The second part of the chapter outlines the operational steps of the approach. In part three, an application of meta-modeling is illustrated in the context of an impact study of Making markets work for the Poor (M4P) – a widely used approach to propoor market development. Finally, part four concludes by reflecting on the potential role of meta-modeling in the context of impact studies of social development programs more generally.

THE INTELLECTUAL ROOTS AND GROUNDING OF META-MODELING

The core idea of synthesizing existing impact studies is nothing new (Light and Pillemer, 1984). The most well-established and common approach is perhaps the generic literature review, often provided as a setting-the-scene segment in impact studies and evaluation reports (Cooper, 2010; Hunt, 1997). The classic literature reviews, while quick and efficient to produce, often suffer from being unsystematic in their selection and treatment of studies, resulting in a concern for bias in the conclusions drawn (Cooper, 2010; Hunt, 1997). To illustrate, one recent review of development practices stated, "Inevitably, a large volume of literature that is cited in [market development] areas comes from the World Bank Group and donors such as DFID that play a prominent role in market development" (Sinha et al., 2013). The potential for bias is real.

Lack of transparency is another oft-cited critique of these traditional reviews (Gough et al., 2012; Pope, Mays, and Popay, 2007). In our experience, the traditional literature reviews are often conducted in the early stages of impact studies, for example, in the development of scoping or inception reports, and typically left more or less ignored when assessing and explaining the impact of the program considered. In this way, traditional literature reviews have become ritualized with limited influence on and benefit to the impact study.

Another common approach for synthesizing past impact studies is that of systematic reviews, perhaps best defined as "… a review of research literature using systematic and explicit, accountable methods" (Gough et al., 2012). Systematic reviews emerged as part of the evidence-based policy movement with the promise of systematically and transparently bringing to order large bodies of variegated and scattered research (Cooper, 2010; Glass et al., 1981; Littell et al., 2008). By systematically combining the findings from multiple studies, systematic reviews provide robust information on what works across different settings, populations, and times (Bronson and Davies, 2012; Lipsey and Wilson, 2001). One oft-cited concern is that systematic review relies too narrowly on quantitative findings from experimental and quasi-experimental designs – the contested winners in the "hierarchy of evidence" (Bronson and Davies, 2012). Another oft-cited concern is the sheer amount of time and effort required by systematic reviews, making them practically obsolete in the context of many commissioned evaluations (Bronson and Davies, 2012; Pawson, 2006). For these reasons, systematic reviews are rare in the context of development programs.

These traditional synthesis approaches leave the impact-oriented evaluator of social development programs in a pickle. Whereas literature reviews score high on feasibility and broad application, they tend to score low on transparency and systematic procedures. Whereas systematic reviews score high on transparency and systematic procedures, they tend to score low on feasibility and broad application. What we need, then, in the context of impact studies of development programs, is an approach that falls between these two ends of the synthesis spectrum: We need a synthesis approach that is feasible and systematic, broadly applicable, and transparent. The meta-modeling approach we propose does just that.

Before advancing a more operational description of meta-modeling, a brief consideration of the conceptual and methodological roots of the approach is in place. Meta-modeling is methodologically anchored in the growing tradition of second generation literature reviews – more specifically the realist synthesis tradition (Pawson, 2006). However, the operational steps and procedures, including coding techniques and terminology, emerge from the growing body of literature on cross-case comparative techniques (Miles et al., 2014) and causal coding techniques. Briefly situating meta-modeling within these traditions will serve well to set the scene for the remainder of the chapter.

Meta-modeling emerges from what Pope, Mays, and Popay (2007) term "second generation" literature reviews. These reviews part with the traditional (first-generation) literature review by being more systematic, for example by "following formal and transparent review processes" and "using explicit approaches to the identification and selection of evidence" (Pope et al., 2007). More than that, second-generation reviews are also more analytically ambitious in their attempt to move beyond "a thin description of the evidence to produce higher order syntheses resulting in the production of new knowledge and/or theory" (Pope et al., 2007).

In the context of meta-modeling on the basis of impact studies, the analytical ambition is the development of a better understanding of how and why interventions work. In this way, the approach is in scope and focus inspired and informed by the realist synthesis approach developed by Ray Pawson (2006). In realist syntheses, the analytical strategy revolves around the development of Context, Mechanism, Outcome configurations (CMOs) corresponding to the underlying logic of the intervention. In broad strokes, the realist modus operandi is to develop an initial CMO on the basis of a subset of evidence, and then through iterative rounds of analysis of additional evidence (e.g., articles or other documents) to refine the initial CMO configurations of the program. The underlying idea is that the stepwise addition of evidence will serve to refute or confirm salient aspects of the CMO.

Following Pawson, meta-modeling aspires to the idea of understanding how and why interventions work; yet it adapts the procedure and scope for doing so. As we will go on to show, the meta-modeling approach relies on a more inductive process, in which causal chains are first located within primary studies, then summarized across studies, and finally reconstructed in "causal fragments." This inductive process is in our experience less iterative and more manageable than the process envisioned in the realist synthesis approach, in which a theory of change is revised through iterative cycles of data analysis and refinement (Pawson, 2006).

The meta-modeling approach also seeks to pave new way for synthesis researchers by offering more explicit, hands-on guidance on useful analytical techniques to be employed in synthesis. The inspiration stems from widely used qualitative data analytic methods developed by Miles et al. (2014), among others. These include specific techniques for coding, summarizing, modeling, and displaying data from primary studies. The reliance on more explicit analytical techniques does double-duty for meta-modeling: it enhances the explanatory strength of the approach and it supports procedural transparency. The latter is central to establishing the credibility of the conclusions drawn.

The meta-modeling approach also parts from other synthesis approaches in that it narrows the focus of the synthesis on developing "causal fragments" of individual program components, rather than more complete causal theories of entire programs (Miles et al., 2014). The focus on causal fragments is grounded on the observation that many social development programs (M4P included) primarily exists as varied configurations of specific program components. However, the specific configuration of these components often differs across implementation settings and times. As just one example, and as we will go to show in the case example below, M4P programs typically consist of varied constellations of facilitation of technical training, improved market linkages, or access to input services, among other things. However, the M4P program rarely exists as a "coherent whole," employing the same set of components, across the different implementation settings and times. Accordingly, the development of a causal theory depicting the M4P program as a whole would simply represent an illusion with little if any application in the real world.

Finally, meta-modeling also departs from other syntheses approaches by being conceptually grounded and acutely cognizant of the behavioral foundations of social development policies and programs. From this perspective, an intervention is best perceived as "a deliberate attempt by an agent to change the behavior of a group of individuals, a group that can range in size from a couple of people to an entire nation" (Miller and Prentice, 2013). This is admittedly a deceptively simple idea. This is also an idea that serves well to remind us that any type of intervention – at its core – revolves around generating a specific set of desired behavioral change. As such, understanding how and why interventions work demands attention to how and in what way interventions generate specific behavioral changes. Toward this aim, meta-modeling relies on the notion of motivational structures and mechanisms – both of which will be considered in more detail later in this chapter.

In summary, meta-modeling is motivated by the unmet need for a feasible and systematically transparent approach for synthesizing impact studies. The approach is in purpose inspired by realist synthesis, grounded on qualitative data analytic techniques in its analytical strategy, and conceptually anchored in core concepts from the behavioral foundations of public policy. The result is a hands-on, operational synthesis approach that is more systematic than the traditional literature review, yet less burdensome than the traditional research synthesis, carefully balancing feasibility and rigor, both of which are essential for successful application in commissioned impact studies.

THE FIVE STEPS OF META-MODELING

Let us then outline the meta-modeling approach. Table 11.1 provides an overview of the five steps. Step one is quite simply to specify the scope of the research question. This usually involves a specification of the population (e.g., poor rural farmers), the intervention (e.g., M4P market development program), the

---

Table 11.1 The Five Steps of Meta-Modeling

Step 1: Define the research question
- Define research question in terms of population, intervention, context, and outcome (PICO)

Step 2: Search and retrieve relevant studies using explicit search parameters
- Define search terms and inclusion/exclusion criteria
- Conduct search for empirical papers by using multiple avenues
- Maintain a log for all the identified studies

Step 3: Conduct a relevance appraisal of the studies
- Appraise each study abstract for its relevance to the research question
- Examine each study for information on causal chains

Step 4: Code the studies
- Identify key delivery mechanisms
- Identify causal chains

Step 5: Develop the meta-summary
- Develop a causal chain matrix
- Develop a meta model and causal story for each delivery mechanism

Note: Adapted from Greenhalgh et al. (2005).

context (e.g., northern Nigeria), and the desired outcome (e.g., farmers improve their crop yields). The parameters specified and their extent of specification depend on the context of the impact assessment. The degree of specification is often a balancing act between the informational needs of the impact study (what information we would like to have) and the available body of past impact studies to be reviewed (what information is possible to have). For instance, and in the context of the present review, an informational need of the impact evaluation revolved around the impact of M4P programs on female farmers, a subgroup of the poor rural farmers specified above. However, a precursory reading of existing impact evaluations of M4P programs revealed limited information on female farmers, indicating a level of specificity in our informational needs unlikely to be met in the body of impact evaluations to be sampled. Accordingly, the population scope of poor rural farmers, which was still consistent with the terms of reference for the commissioned impact evaluation, was considered more feasible.

The second step revolves around the search and retrieval of relevant primary studies. This generates the empirical grounding for the subsequent analyses. A central component of this step is the definition of search terms and inclusion criteria. The search terms and inclusion criteria usually emerge from the specification of the research question. In this way, the second step can be viewed as an operationalization of step one. Maintaining a log of the studies identified is essential for the purpose of transparency.

The third step involves carefully reading through the collected primary studies. The purpose is twofold: to confirm the relevance of the study in terms of the population, intervention, context, and outcomes specified in step one; and to confirm the presence of information on causal chains within each study. The latter refers to information on the inner workings of the intervention and is typically in the form of narrative explanations or even causal models of how the program worked (or failed to work). Primary studies outside of scope or without any causal chain information are not to be enlisted in the analysis.

Step four involves a more systematic coding of the retained studies. In our experience, the coding is best carried out in two successive rounds. The first round coding should primarily focus on the delivery mechanisms of the intervention(s): these are the core activities comprising the intervention. In the case of the M4P programs, delivery mechanisms might include "providing training," "facilitating meetings," "establishing networks," "coordinating events," and so forth. The aim of this first round of coding is to support the later identification of a typology of the core delivery mechanisms comprising the intervention.

The second round of coding focuses on the causally relevant information in the studies. Informed by Saldaña (2013) "causation coding," the coding scheme to be employed should at least consist of:

- *Attribute codes*. These are codes pertaining to the intervention characteristics, including sector (livestock) and subsector (artificial insemination services), characteristics of the target group, and so forth.
- *Causal chain codes*. These are codes capturing the causally relevant information in the primary studies, typically from sections of the report describing how and why the intervention works. Causal codes should cover:
  - *Motivational structures*. These are typically statements about attitudes, beliefs, and ideas among the target group(s) prior to the intervention. For example, eight evaluations in the present review stressed the farmers' lack of trust in buyers – a legacy from past experiences of being cheated by buyers using corrupted weights or nontransparent pricing schemes, among other things. Lack of trust, then, is central to understanding the behavioral uptake among these farmers.

- *Causal chains*. These are typically statements about how the core activities of the intervention generated a sequence of attitude and behavioral changes. For example, five studies described how facilitating meetings between farmer groups and a select set of buyers resulted in renewed trust among these, which in turn generated an incentive among farmers to improve their crops and invest in the coordination of their farming for the purpose of selling to these buyers, demonstrating a causal chain that speaks directly to the trust aspect of the motivational structure mentioned above.
  - *Influencing factors*. These are contextual factors that authors identify as enhancing or inhibiting the intervention's ability to generate behavioral changes (Lemire et al., 2012).
- *Magnitude codes*. These are evaluative terms or statements about the magnitude of impact generated by the interventions. For example, statement such as "significant changes," "slightly positive increases," "dramatic changes," or "no impact" are just some of the typical vague quantifications employed by researchers to express the direction and relative magnitude of the behavioral changes prompted by the intervention.

Collectively, these different types of codes allow for the subsequent development of causal models for each of the identified delivery mechanisms. More than that, the codes provide the building blocks for a deeper understanding of the underlying motivational mechanisms generating the desired behavioral changes. Illustrative application examples of the causation coding are provided in the M4P case below.

The fifth and final step is where the analytical modeling is carried out. A core component of this step is the development of a causal chain matrix, summarizing the causal chain(s) within each primary study (an example of an effects matrix is provided in the M4P case below). As described above, causal chains are statements about how the core activities of the intervention generated a sequence of attitude and behavioral changes. The causal chain matrix serves to provide an overview of the different causal chains contained within each of the interventions. As such, the matrix facilitates the identification of patterns in these causal chains.

Informed by the causal chain matrix, the next analytical step is the development of a meta-model for each of the delivery mechanisms in the intervention. The analytical strategy is to identify the most prevalent causal chains and to synthesize these in the meta-model. A meta-model is a visual depiction of the key causal chains generating the desired outcomes. A causal story, explicating the underlying motivational mechanism(s), supports the visual meta-model. Illustrative examples are provided in the M4P case below.

THE APPLICATION OF META-MODELING

The purpose of this section is to provide a step-by-step description of how meta-modeling is carried out in a real world context. Toward this aim, we would like to draw on a recent application of meta-modeling in a recent review of M4P programs, one of the most widely employed approaches to market development. Before advancing the application of meta-modeling a brief description of the making markets work for the poor model (M4P) is in place. Gibson et al. (2004) notes the need for systemic changes in market systems as if markets are inclusive in terms of offering what the poor need (jobs, opportunities, finance) then there are benefits. However, exclusive markets reduce the potential for poor people to participate, and benefit from the economic opportunities. As a developmental strategy, M4P has been implemented in many settings and across many markets, including factor markets such as labor, finance, product, and commodity markets as well as infrastructure and service markets.

Systemic change for M4P purposes can occur within any area of the market that is seen as excluding the participation and therefore not benefitting the poor, whether this is a change within the value chain or its informal, unwritten regulations, or changes within the service markets supporting the chain, or within the regulatory environment encompassing all of the market variables (for a discussion on the emergence of systemic change as an emergent trend in the development discussion see Taylor, 2013). The mechanisms to achieve these systemic changes vary greatly; from advocacy for policy changes, to provision of market price related information through farmer-appropriate channels.

As noted above, the impacts of many developmental or poverty alleviation programs have repeatedly been evaluated across multiple settings, populations, and times. Programs using the M4P model are no exception. Indeed, the prevalence of M4P programs in developing countries combined with the lack of any systematic reviews of the impact of M4P programs only makes the present meta-modeling-based review even more compelling. More than that, understanding how and in what way M4P programs bring about change is useful for program improvement decision-making, especially in an economic development context where bang-for-the-buck is front and center. In fact, the purpose of the Itad review of M4P programs commissioned by DFID was "to critically review the methods used to evaluate M4P programs and thereby help guide the design and implementation of future evaluations" (Ruffer and Wach, 2013).

The remainder of this section is structured according to the five steps of the meta-modeling approach. Experience-based guidance is provided for each step.

STEP 1: DEFINE THE RESEARCH QUESTION

The research question driving the meta-modeling of M4P programs was: What does the existing research tell us about the extent and manner in which M4P programs improve or fail to improve the conditions for poor market participants in developing countries. Two important features of the research question are worth noting. First, the question is fully exploratory in the sense that it involves no pre-specified set of hypotheses about whether or not M4P programs work or fail to work. Neither does the question imply specific hypotheses about how and in what way the M4P programs work or fail to work. In this way, the question is completely exploratory and open.

Secondly, the research question does specify the scope of the review by focusing on M4P programs (the intervention), targeting poor market participants (the population) in developing countries (the setting). However, these generic boundaries still leave the scope of the review very open, potentially including a broad range of studies, which corresponds well to the exploratory nature of the review. Notice, however, that the question could have been defined more tightly by specifying a specific set of outcomes (e.g., improved crop yields or incomes), a specific set of intervention features (e.g., use of demonstrations or cost-sharing), or even specified references for the purpose of comparison (e.g., is M4P more effective than traditional market development programs). All of these specifications would have served to focus the review.

For the present exploratory purpose, however, the open framing of the research question was deemed appropriate. That being said, the extent to which the research question should be open or narrow is entirely contingent on the specific context of the impact study.

STEP 2: SEARCH AND RETRIEVE STUDIES

The search process for M4P studies is visually depicted in Fig. 11.1. The studies identified for the present review were identified through two sources: a recent review of M4P evaluations conducted by ITAD and an online information hub on M4P programs. The first source was an existing review of M4P evaluations and approaches commissioned by DFID and conducted by ITAD in 2013. A total of 13 evaluation studies were identified through the review. The second source of studies for the present synthesis was an M4P website (www.m4phub.org) managed by Coffey International Development and The Springfield Center with the support of DFID, SIDA, and SDC. The site contains a repository of M4P case studies, among other resources. A total of 16 primary studies were retrieved from the M4P Hub.

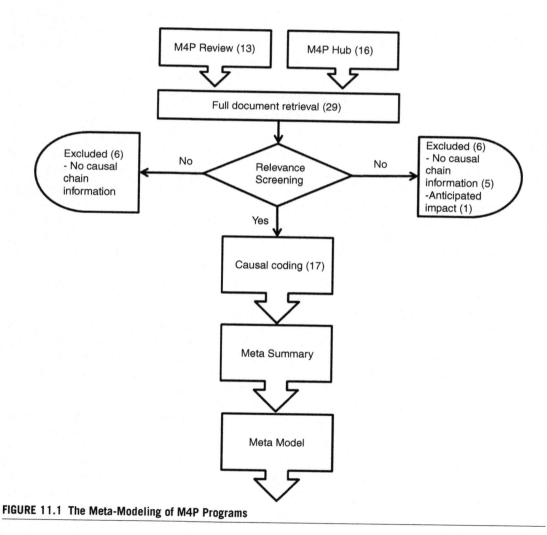

FIGURE 11.1 The Meta-Modeling of M4P Programs

A note of caution has to be raised about this purposive use of convenient sources. Because the primary purpose of this review is methodological – to test and illustrate meta-modeling as an synthesis approach for social development programs – the use of a predefined and manageable set of studies is acceptable, even preferred. However, for the purposes of most impact assessments a multipronged and more exhaustive search strategy with the aim of capturing a broader and more comprehensive set of relevant studies is advisable.

The advice to use multiple search strategies is made even more compelling by the challenge of identifying relevant evaluation studies. Impact evaluations are rarely published in scholarly journals and in effect are more difficult to identify using traditional search engines and databases. This often necessitates the reliance on multiple search strategies, such as internet searches using a broad range of key terms (e.g., Google search for "M4P"), manual browsing through funding agency websites (e.g., DFID or USAID), retrieving studies and cases from information repositories (e.g., the M4P hub web site), or contacting key professionals on the topic of interest (e.g., experts on M4P programs). Exemplary guidance on how to identify gray literature and primary studies more broadly is provided by Saini and Shlonsky (2012) and Sandelowski and Barrosso (2007).

In marked contrast with traditional systematic reviews, the aim of meta-modeling is not to identify all the available studies. This is not feasible in the context of commissioned impact assessment of social development programs. Instead, the would-be meta-modeler should seek to reach what might be termed a "point of saturation" – the point at which the introduction of additional studies does not result in changes to the main conclusions. The number of studies required to reach this point of saturation will vary from review to review. However, echoing Major and Savin-Baden (2010) "between 6 and 10 studies is optimal to provide sufficient yet manageable data" for the purpose of meta-modeling program components (cited in Saldaña, 2013, p. 182). We would further recommend that these guidelines are considered per delivery mechanism and remind ourselves and the reader that the adequate number of studies depends on the informational needs of the impact study, including the degree of specificity needed in the causal explanation, among other things. Accordingly, would-be meta-modelers should never fail to carefully and critically consider whether a point of saturation has been reached in the context of their impact study, rather than rigidly adhere to these guidelines.

STEP 3: RELEVANCE APPRAISAL

In the present review, the 29 primary studies were first read in their entirety for the purpose of relevance assessment. A total of 12 studies were "black box" studies, meaning that they failed to provide any insight into how and why the M4P program worked (or failed to work). In several instances these black box studies were monitoring reports containing limited analysis of the results tables provided. Two studies were midterm reviews without any empirical information on outcomes. Both types of studies were inadequate for this type of synthesis and in effect excluded from analysis.

A cautionary note should be raised about dismissing primary studies too easily. In the present review, several reports initially seemed out of scope, but eventually – upon closer reading – proved to provide information relevant to the review. For example, one study (AGLink Egypt program) dedicated the first and large part of the report on large commercial farmers, who are outside the scope of the present review. Accordingly, this section of the report was not included in the analysis. However, the remainder of the report, focusing on poor rural farmers, was retained for analysis. The general aim of the relevance assessment is to identify any information that might support the subsequent meta-modeling.

On a similar note, some reports provide uneven information on how the different M4P program components work. For example, the AGLink report, as just one example, only offered superficial descriptions of the processes comprising the Pilot Business Development Services Program component. As such, this program component could not be included in the subsequent analyses. The lack of information on the program components often stems from the component not being substantively realized by the time of the completion of the reports. This is from the perspective of the would-be meta-modeler an unfortunate situation, as there is no meaningful way of including these components in the analyses. Fortunately, other program components in the AGLink report were described in more detail, why these were included in the present review.

STEP 4: CODE STUDIES

The coding of the primary studies comprises a central step in the meta-modeling. One practical guideline is to resist the urge to code causal chains during the first read-through of the studies. Rather, it is advisable to read through all the sampled studies once before initiating the causation coding. In the first read through, simply make note of the types of delivery mechanisms and the general language and terminology used by the authors to define these core program components. In the present M4P review, we identified the following five delivery mechanisms:

1. *Technical assistance.* This delivery mechanism is typically some type of advisory service, for example in the form of a "model farmer" or a "demonstration farm" or some other type of farmer-to-farmer dissemination of advice on farming practices
2. *Market linkage formation (horizontal or vertical).* This delivery mechanism typically involves the formation of "farmers' organizations," seeking to strengthen linkages among farmers (horizontal). The delivery mechanism may also seek to establish "collection centers" or other types of coordination systems to sustain linkages between farmers and buyers or between agricultural input suppliers and farmers (vertical).
3. *Access to inputs and services.* This delivery mechanisms typically involve farmers trained to be input retailers, in effect improving or facilitating access to pesticides, improved seed varieties, fertilizer, veterinary services, agricultural mechanization (e.g., tilling machines), or livestock artificial insemination services.
4. *Finance schemes.* This delivery mechanism is often in the form of loan scheme programs, establishment of "funds" among farmers, or credit-based contract farming systems.
5. *Market governance reform.* This delivery mechanism is typically in the form of advocacy initiatives promoting a policy, regulatory and legal environment conducive to propoor farmers.

Each of these delivery mechanisms was identifiable across multiple primary studies and in effect well suited for meta-modeling.

Informed by the initial read-through of the primary studies, the second round of causation coding can begin. In the words of Saldaña (2013),

> Causation Coding is appropriate for discerning motives (by or toward something or someone), belief systems, worldviews, processes, recent histories, interrelationships, and the complexity of influences and affects ([author's] qualitative equivalent for the positivist "cause and effect" on human actions and phenomena (p. 165).

More specifically, the coding aims to map out causal chains (CODE1 > CODE2 > CODE3), corresponding to a delivery mechanism, an outcome, and a mediator linking the delivery mechanism and outcome (ibid). As Saldaña (2013) reminds us, these triplets are often made more complex by involving interactions between multiple delivery mechanisms, multiple mediators, and outcomes. As such, the causal chains may include subsets of codes (CODE1A + CODE1B > CODE2A + CODE2B > CODE3 > CODE4). Echoing Miles et al. (2014), we would recommend a maximum of five to seven descriptive codes per causal chain. In our experience, five to seven codes per causal chain balances the competing needs of reducing the causal complexity to an analytically manageable level while still retaining enough of the causal specificity to adequately explain how and why the causal mechanisms bring about the desired change. Perhaps needless to say, the number of codes per causal chain may vary from causal chain to causal chain, from study to study.

To illustrate, Table 11.2 provides an example of the causation coding of a text segment from the GMED effectiveness assessment of the India Project. The delivery mechanism in the project consists of "farmer demonstrations" and "facilitation of relations between farmers and buyers," among other things. The causal chain is comprised of a three-part process, in which "awareness of improved production practices" (mediator 1) in combination with "linkages to higher value markets" (mediator 2) leads to "economic incentives" (mediator 3) for the farmers to "upgrade production practices" (outcome).

There are several things to consider in relation to this type of causal coding. In our experience, it is important to award careful attention to the at times conflated distinction between empirically informed and hypothetically predicted causal chains. The latter express how the author(s) intended the intervention to work. In many evaluation studies, we suspect the eagerness to predict the success of the intervention often contributes to the inclusion of these hypothetical scenarios in results section, especially in midterm evaluations where empirical results might be scarce. Including these hypotheticals in the meta model, however, defeats the purpose of modeling how and why the intervention works. As such, attention should be awarded the empirically informed causal chains.

Echoing Saldaña (2013), another important point about causation coding is that it is highly interpretive. This is in part because the causal chains are rarely summarized in a three part sequence from cause(s) to mechanism(s) to outcome(s). In our experience, and as noted by Saldaña, the authors "may tell you the outcome first, followed by what came before or what led up to it, and sometimes explain the multiple causes and outcomes in a reverberative back-and-forth manner" (2013). As such, causation coding often involves a high degree of sensitivity to words such as "because," "in effect," "therefore," and "since" that might indicate an underlying causal logic (Saldaña, 2013).

Table 11.2 Causation Coding	
"Taken together, these results help to refine the general program model by clarifying the sequencing between farmer upgrading and the establishment of new vertical relations. The evidence indicates that linkages to higher value markets must be in place to provide farmers with enough economic incentives to upgrade their production practices. Awareness of improved production practices is a necessary precursor to upgrading, but it is not sufficient to elicit an upgrading response." (GMED, p. 32)	Awareness of improved production practices + linkage to higher value markets > economic incentive > upgrade production practices

To make matters more complicated, the information may be pieced together from causal information provided in different sections of the report. For example, in the present M4P review, the executive summary often contained a comprehensive summary of the main delivery mechanisms (causes) combined with information of the main outcomes of these. However, the mediating mechanisms were less often made explicit in these brief executive summaries. Information about these mechanisms was more often contained and extracted from the main body of the reports.

One useful tool to keep a record of the emerging causal chains is a causal chain matrix. An example of a causal chain matrix for one study is provided in Table 11.3. The matrix summarizes the causal chains identified in each study. The matrix specifies the "delivery mechanism," the "causal chain" for each delivery mechanism, a description of the "magnitude" of change generated, and "influencing factors" inhibiting or enhancing the delivery mechanism. A final column contains a verbatim description of how the mechanism functions, as described by the primary study author(s). This data display technique does double-duty: (1) It facilitates an overview of the causal chains to be synthesized in step 5 and (2) it provides a transparent chain-of-evidence that allows other researchers to examine the grounding for the final synthesis and conclusions drawn. This latter point is important for the purpose of methodological transparency.

In summarizing the causal chains in the matrix, it is important for the meta-modeler to stay close to the data. The name of the game for the meta-modeler is to lift relevant information from within each of the primary studies and organize it in the effect matrix in a descriptive fashion. One way of anchoring the causal chain matrix to the individual primary studies is by retaining the language and terminology from the individual studies. Another approach is to retain the causal explanation offered by the author(s) of the primary studies in a comments box (as illustrated in Table 11.3). The point to be made here is that the meta-modeler at this stage should retain interpretation as much as possible, allowing for the data to comprise the content of the matrix.

STEP 5: DEVELOP A META-SUMMARY

In step 4 the focus was entirely on coding the causal chains contained within each primary study and organizing these in a causal chain matrix. Informed by the overview provided by this matrix, the fifth step of the meta-modeling approach is (as the name implies) to synthesize these causal chains across the collective pool of individual primary studies. Three explanatory analytical strategies comprise the meta-modeling:

1. Synthesize the causal chains for each delivery mechanism in a meta-summary matrix.
2. Craft a causal story for each of the delivery mechanism.
3. Develop a visual meta model (causal fragment) for each delivery mechanism

The first analytical step is to develop a meta summary matrix, synthesizing across all the studies to tease out the most salient causal chains for each of the identified delivery mechanisms. Showcasing a complete analysis of each of the five delivery mechanisms is beyond the scope of this chapter. For the present purpose, which is primarily to illustrate meta modeling in a real world context, we will focus our attention on the technical assistance delivery mechanism – the most prevalent delivery mechanism in the present M4P review. However, the analytical techniques apply equally well to other delivery mechanisms.

In developing the meta summary matrix, we find that extracting and listing all the causal chains for each delivery mechanism is a simple and useful first step. Examining the resultant list allows us

Table 11.3 Causal Chain Matrix for The PROFIT Zambia Programme

Study	Delivery Mechanism	Causal Chain	Magnitude	Influencing Factor	Explanation
The PROFIT Zambia impact assessment (2010)	Recruit and establish agents from among farmers to build networks for agricultural inputs and services Facilitate training of input agents	Access to inputs and services + knowledge of how to use inputs + to a certain extent reduced transaction costs > incentives for farmers to upgrade crops (attitude change) > adopt upgrading (behavior change) > higher quality crops and higher yields > emerging commercial agriculture	Information level "changed dramatically" "positive increases in use of services and input"	Trust and relationship building Internal management capacity of input suppliers	"Farmers interviewed in the qualitative study expressed a positive view of the agent network model. Both men and women farmers said they have better access to inputs through the agents and benefit from reduced transport costs associated with accessing inputs They also benefit from advice on production techniques, planting and the correct selection and use of inputs" (p. 25)
	Encourage development of private vet services Herd health plans (fixed fee preventive care)	Training of vet subagents from among farmers + Formation of commercially viable relationships between vets and farmers > trust in agents + understanding of preventive care > change in farmer mindset about value of vet services > increase in use of vets > improvement in animal health > lower morbidity rates	"Very large increase in use of vets" "strong improvements in cattle morbidity and mortality"	Trust "The importance of cattle as a source of prestige and a vehicle for savings continues to outweigh herding as a regular source of income" – no increased commercial sales of cattle (p. 6)	"The research team found that the HHP promoted the formation of commercially viable relationships around preventive veterinary services in some communities ... Particularly important is the increased recognition of the value of preventive veterinary services" (p. 28)

to determine causal chains that are markedly similar across primary studies. The guiding analytical principle is that causal chains that hold significance across multiple studies may collate and generalize beyond the individual primary studies to say something more broadly about the delivery mechanism. For example, multiple causal chains for the technical assistance mechanism revolved around farmers becoming aware of improved farming techniques and attentive to crop quality, which combined with a more long-term view on their farming lead to farming practice upgrades. The adoption of improved techniques in turn generated improved crop quality and yield.

Another analytical task required by the meta summary matrix is that of identifying the motivational mechanism(s) underlying the causal chains. This is a higher order inference in the sense that primary studies rarely make the motivational aspects of their target group explicit. In identifying the motivational mechanism, we find it advantageous to first consider the motivational structure of the target group and then examine the primary studies for recurring motifs that speak directly to the motivational structure. In the case of technical assistance, the motivational structure was characterized by the farmers' lack of incentive to upgrade their farming for long-term gains. This lack of incentive for upgrading crops was grounded on the uncertainty surrounding the potential uptake of and economic compensation for higher quality crops. Farmers had experienced being cheated by aggregators and buyers in the past.

With this as our backdrop, further examination of the primary studies with a technical assistance component revealed a number of statements speaking directly to these barriers contained in the motivational structure, statements helping us develop a better understanding of how and why technical assistance may incentivize farmers to upgrade their crops. To illustrate, several studies referred to farmers emphasizing the bond of trust established with the advisor. These statements suggest that the use of local farmers is the change agent that allows farmers to trust the long-term perspective on their farming and in effect serves as a motivating force for their investment in upgrading their crops.

An illustrative example of a meta summary matrix is provided in Table 11.4. The matrix consists of a description of the most salient "motivational structure," the "delivery mechanism," the primary causal chain, the underlying motivational mechanism, the most common influencing factors, and the

Table 11.4 Meta-Summary Matrix of Technical Assistance

Motivational Structure (The "Status Quo")	Delivery Mechanism (The "What")	Causal Chain (The "How")	Motivational Mechanism (The "Why")	Influencing Factor (The "Context")	Magnitude (The Effect)
– Lack of trust in buyers and input retailers – Lack of long-term farming perspective	Farmer-to-farmer advisory.	Technical know-how + Quality sensitivity + long-term view on farming → Adoption of improved agricultural techniques + Improved use of inputs (e.g., fertilizer) → Improved crop quality and yield → Improved price → Improved income	The use of local farmers is the change agent that allows farmers to trust the long-term perspective on their farming upgrade	– Trustworthy and competent advisor (local) – Simple and low-cost recommendation with immediate gain – matchmaking with potential buyers	"Significant" "Noticeable"

magnitude. Collectively, these serve as a generic "story outline" of how and why the delivery mechanism works.

The opportunity to further examine the delivery mechanisms may be realized in the development of causal networks for these. As defined by Miles et al. (2014):

> A causal network builds a progressively integrated map of case phenomena and, for multiple cases, aligns their maps to make a cross-case map that contains more generalizable causal explanations, It neatly assembles and "anthologizes" into one thematic display all the stories of your individual cases. (p. 237)

In meta-modeling the aim is not to build a causal network encapsulating all the delivery mechanisms as a collective whole. As noted above, the modeling of entire programs often makes little sense given that programs are rarely implemented consistently across studies and settings and populations. As such, the aim in meta modeling is to build what Miles et al. (2014) refers to as "causal fragments," that is, causal networks for individual delivery mechanisms (e.g., technical assistance or linkage formation). An example of the causal fragment for the technical assistance delivery mechanism: (Fig. 11.2)

A couple of practical observations on developing causal fragments might be helpful. As cautioned by Miles et al. (2014): "Don't try to connect variables that don't go together empirically, even if on logical grounds they 'should'" (p. 239). The whole purpose of meta modeling is to build an empirically grounded model of what works. In effect, connections that are not empirically verified should not be included in the causal fragment. Second, and again echoing Miles et al., refrain from using bidirectional

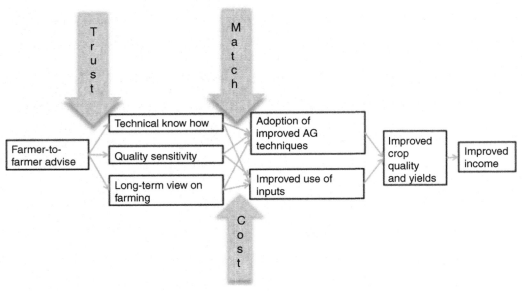

FIGURE 11.2 Causal Fragment for Technical Assistance

Table 11.5 Causal Story

To understand the technical assistance delivery mechanism, we must first consider the motivational structure within which it is often employed. The studies in the present review indicate that poor rural farmers often refrain from upgrading their crops because of their past experiences of failing to benefit from upgrading their crops. The lack of incentive among the farmers is for example rooted in profit being swallowed by volatile and nontransparent pricing schemes, buyers tampering with weighing scales, or upgrades failing to yield higher quality crops. As such, the farmers tend to seek immediate gain on their cash crops. The motivational structure then can be summarized as one of distrust with buyers and input providers combined with a lack of long-term perspective on farming.

The technical assistance delivery mechanism is often implemented as some type of advisory service, for example in the form of a "model farmer" or a "demonstration farm" or some other type of farmer-to-farmer dissemination of advice on farming practices. The advice might be provided one-on-one or in the form of group session. The primary aim is to upgrade farmers' skills and knowhow in relation to topics such as irrigation, pesticide use, and postharvest crop handling, among other things. All of these allow for farmers to increase their crop quality or yield, or both. A secondary aim is to promote a long(er)-term perspective on farming among the farmers.

The core component of the technical assistance, the component that is emphasized as essential across multiple studies, is the local farmer-to-farmer aspect of the delivery mechanism. The relationship building between the farmers and the advisor is central because it allows for the farmers to establish a bond of trust that speaks directly to the issues of mistrust identified in the motivational structure among the farmers. This suggests that the use of local farmers is the change agent that allows farmers to trust the long-term perspective on their farming and in effect what motivates their investment in upgrading their crops. This is the motivational mechanism that drives the technical assistance from behavior intent to changed behavior.

---

connectors in your causal fragments. Push yourself to flesh out the feedback loop for the purpose of enhancing the explanatory strength and accuracy of your causal fragment.

Perhaps needless to say, the above meta-summary matrix and causal fragment represent an oversimplification of the technical assistance delivery mechanism. The simplification is advantageous for the purpose of analysis. However, in many real-world situations, M4P programs entail a combination of the above-depicted strategies, sometimes even a complete integration of one or more of these. For example, a common approach to technical assistance is "embedded services" where technical guidance is provided as part of business transactions between input retailers and farmers (see SDC – Elola Case study for an example). For the present purpose, however, this blending of delivery mechanisms is not as much a problem as it is an analytical opportunity to examine how specific configurations of delivery mechanisms interact and correspond to variations in outcomes.

A complementary component of the causal fragment is a corresponding causal story for each delivery mechanism. The causal story allows for a more in-depth and coherent narrative of how and why the delivery mechanisms functions, including consideration of interactions with other delivery mechanisms. Table 11.5 provides an illustrative causal story for the technical assistance delivery mechanism. The causal story allows for the researcher to craft a more coherent and perhaps richer description of how the delivery mechanisms work.

FINAL THOUGHTS ON META-MODELING

The motivation for this chapter is that the impact of all too many social development programs are evaluated and reevaluated in a seemingly endless cycle, without sufficient consideration of past impact evaluations. Past impact studies often play no role in program design, redesign, and reevaluation. This is unfortunate. By not attending to past impact studies in a systematic fashion, we run the risk of making the same mistakes again and again, never learning from the mistakes we have made in the past, reproducing noneffective programs. To remedy this situation, we propose that meta-modeling offers a fruitful and operational approach for making better use of past impact studies.

Meta-modeling has several compelling features. First and foremost, the causal modeling approach not only allows for the identification of typical delivery mechanisms (other synthesis potentially do this also), but furthermore pushes the researcher to explicate the underlying motivational structures and mechanisms generating the desired outcomes. By explicating these motivational foundations of programs, meta-modeling allows us to enter the programmatic black box, to understand and explain how and why programs work. This type of information serves well to inform the design of future programs as well as their implementations, promoting in effect increasingly more effective programs.

Secondly, meta-modeling offers a more systematic and transparent treatment of impact studies than traditional literature reviews. In line with other synthesis approaches, meta-modeling follows a specified set of steps that serves to ensure a systematic treatment of the primary studies. The causal chain matrix and the meta summary matrix collectively provide a visible chain of evidence, allowing for verifiable and transparent findings. In this way, the meta-modeling approach speaks directly to concerns raised about the lack of transparency and systematic procedures characterizing traditional literature reviews.

Thirdly, and equally important, meta-modeling is both operational and pragmatic. The approach may include a broad range of impact studies, from experimental to observational, from quantitative to qualitative. The range of possible applications is potentially broad. The procedural steps are also made operational by way of concrete analytical strategies and data display techniques. The aim of these is to facilitate the operational steps as well as the transparency of the synthesis. Meta-modeling is an efficient approach for making use of impact studies already available.

The potential role of meta-modeling in impact evaluation is also broad. Meta-modeling may serve as an independent, stand-alone approach to assess how and why a program of interest works (or fails to work). The M4P review in the present chapter is an illustrative example. In this way, the approach may support further cross-fertilization of information from individual evaluation studies. While we cannot claim to have arrived at a comprehensive and determinate explanation of how and when M4P programs will be effective, the meta-modeling approach employed has provided important insights about how and why specific delivery mechanisms might work. The meta-models developed as part of the synthesis may serve as a common reference for evaluators to develop and build on in future individual impact evaluations. In this way, the meta-model may serve as the apex around which a burgeoning body of evidence develops.

Alternatively, meta-modeling can serve as an integrated, complimentary component of an impact study of a specific program implementation, perhaps taking the place of the more traditional literature review. Framed in this way, meta-modeling might serve as a stepping-stone toward developing empirically grounded hypotheses about how and why the program might work (i.e., bring about change) prior to the data collection and analysis. More than that, the findings from the meta-modeling may also support the generalizability of the findings from the impact study by connecting these with similar findings from other impact studies on similar programs. In both instances, meta-modeling will inform and strengthen the causal claims and explanations of the program.

In the end, our modest hope is that the meta-modeling approach will be tested and refined in other settings, at other times, and with other programs. One size never fits all. And we invite – even encourage – the further development and refinement of the analytical strategies presented. The overarching aim is to make better use of existing impact studies, to get that hamster out of the wheel.

STUDIES INCLUDED IN REVIEW

ACDI/VOCA, 2004. AgLink final report. Available from: <http://www.enterprise-development.org/page/download?id=1689>.

Anderson, G., Hitchins, R., 2007. Expanding the Poor's access to business information and voice through FM radio in Uganda. Available from: <http://www.bdsknowledge.org/dyn/bds/docs/614/M4P_case_study_Media_Uganda_april2007.pdf>.

Brown, S., 2010. Market alliances against poverty in the Samtskhe-Javakheti region of Georgia. Available from: <http://www.mercycorps.org/sites/default/files/sdc2009georgiamarketalliancessamtskesarcasestudy2010.pdf>.

DAI, 2010. Profit Zambia Impact Assessment – final report. Available from: <http://pdf.usaid.gov/pdf_docs/PDACR843.pdf>.

Department for International Development, 2011. Nigeria PrOpCom project completion report. Available from: <http://www.propcommaikarfi.org/propcom-resources/studies/nigeria-propcom-project-completion-report-october-2011/attachment/project-completion-report-october-2011>.

Department for International Development, (no date). Making tractor markets work for the poor in Nigeria – a PrOpCom case study. Available from: <http://www.setoolbelt.org/resources/1839>.

Dunn, E., Schiff, H., Creevey, L., 2011. Linking small-scale vegetable farmers to supermarkets: effectiveness assessment of the GMED India Project. Available from: <https://www.microlinks.org/sites/microlinks/files/resource/files/Effectiveness_Assessment_of_GMED_India.pdf>.

Gibson, A., 2006a. Bringing knowledge to vegetable farmers – improving embedded information in the distribution system. Available from: <http://businessinnovationfacility.org/forum/topics/katalyst-vegetable-farmers-improving-information-distribution>.

Gibson, A., 2006b. Enhancing the supply-side of the maize market. Available from: <http://m4phub.org/userfiles/resources/211201118202441-c9_Enhancing_the_Supply-side_of_the_Maize_Market.pdf>.

Gibson, A., 2006c. Developing financial services markets for the poor: FinMark in South Africa. Available from: <http://www.springfieldcentre.com/wp-content/uploads/2012/10/sp0604.pdf>.

Intercooperation and Swisscontact, 2011. Case interview – Rural Livelihood Development Programme. Available from: <http://www.m4phub.org/userfiles/resources/2452011174723863-M4P_Hub_Case_Interview_RLDC.pdf>.

Katalyst, no date. Access to quality seeds to small and marginal farmers through Mobile Seed Vendors (MSVs). Available from: <http://www.katalyst.com.bd/docs/ibriefs/Intervention%20Brief_Seed.pdf>.

Mercy Corps, 2011. Case interview – market alliances against poverty. Available from: <http://www.m4phub.org/userfiles/resources/822011162439365-Market_Alliances_Against_Poverty_CI_Stage_2.pdf>.

Sebstad, J., and Snodgrass, D., 2008. Impacts of the KBDS and KHDP projects in the tree fruit value chain of Kenya. Available from: <http://pdf.usaid.gov/pdf_docs/PDACN958.pdf>.

Swiss Agency for Development and Cooperation SDC, 2011. Bangladesh: Changing markets in favour of the poor. Available from: <http://www.m4phub.org/userfiles/resources/222012154953483-SDC_Asia_Brief_Dec_2011_-_Maize_in_Bangladesh.pdf>.

The Springfield Centre, 2008. Developing markets for dairy production through service development and public-private partnerships in rural Armenia. Available from: <http://www.bdsknowledge.org/dyn/bds/docs/725/DairyArmeniaDec08.pdf>.

The Springfield Centre, 2009. The enter-growth project Sri Lanka – applying a market development lens to an ILO local enterprise development project. Available from: <http://www.ilo.org/employment/Whatwedo/Publications/employment-reports/WCMS_152820/lang--en/index.htm>.

REFERENCES

Bronson, D.E., Davies, T.S., 2012. Finding and Evaluating Evidence – Systematic Reviews and Evidence-Based Practice. Oxford University Press, New York, NY.

Cooper, H., 2010. Research Synthesis and Meta-analysis – a Step-by-Step Approach, fourth edition Sage Publications, Thousand Oaks, CA.

Gibson, A., Scott, H., Ferrand, D., 2004. Making markets work for the poor – an objective and an approach for governments and development agencies Commark, South Africa.

Glass, G.V., McGaw, B., Smith, M.L., 1981. Meta-Analysis in Social Research. Sage Publications, Beverly Hills, CA.

Gough, D., Oliver, S., James, T., 2012. An Introduction to Systematic Reviews. Sage Publications, Thousand Oaks, CA.

Greenhalgh, T., Robert, G., Macfarlane, F., Bate, S.P., Kyriakidou, O., Peacock, R., 2005. Storylines of research in diffusion of innovation: A meta-narrative approach to systematic review. Social Sci. Med. 61 (2), 417–430.

Hunt, M., 1997. How Science Takes Stock – the Story of Meta-analysis. The Russell Sage Foundation, New York, NY.

Lemire, S., Bohni-Nielsen, S., Dybdal, L., 2012. Making contribution analysis work: A practical framework for handling influencing factors and alternative explanations. Evaluation 18 (3), 294–310.

Light, R.J., Pillemer, D.B., 1984. Summing Up – the Science of Reviewing Research. Harvard University Press, Cambridge, MA.

Lipsey, M.W., Wilson, D.B., 2001. Practical Meta-analysis. Applied Social Research Methods Seriesvol. 49Sage Publications, Thousand Oaks, CA.

Littell, J.H., Corcoran, J., Pillai, V., 2008. Systematic Reviews and Meta-analysis. Oxford University Press, New York, NY.

Major, C.H., Savin-Baden, M., 2010. An introduction to Qualitative Research Synthesis: Managing the Information Explosion in Social Science Research. Routledge, London.

Miles, B.M., Huberman, A.M., Saldaña, J., 2014. Qualitative Data Analysis – a Methods Sourcebook, Third ed. Sage Publications, Thousand Oaks, CA.

Miller, D.T., Prentice, D.A., 2013. Psychological levers of behavior change. In: Shafir, Eldar (Ed.), The Behavioral Foundations of Public Policy. Princeton University Press, Princeton, NJ.

Pawson, R., 2006. Evidence-Based Policy – a Realist Perspective. Sage Publications, Thousand Oaks, CA.

Pope, C., Mays, N., Popay, J., 2007. Synthesizing qualitative and quantitative health evidence – a guide to methods. Open University Press, Maidenhead.

Ruffer, T., Wach, E., 2013. Review of M4P evaluation methods and approaches. Available from: <http://www.itad.com/wp-content/uploads/2013/05/M4P-Evaluation-Review_ITAD_Final-Copy.pdf>.

Saini, M., Shlonsky, A., 2012. Systematic Synthesis of Qualitative Research. Oxford University Press, New York, NY.

Saldaña, J., 2013. The coding manual for qualitative researchers, Second ed. Sage Publications, Thousand Oaks, CA.

Sandelowski, M., Barrosso, J., 2007. Handbook for Synthesizing Qualitative Research. Springer Publishing Company, New York, NY.

Sinha, S., Holmberg, J., Thomas, M., 2013. What works for market development: A review of the evidence. UTV Working Paper, 1, SIDA.

Taylor, B., 2013. Evidence-based policy and systemic change: Conflicting trends? Springfield Working Paper Series, no. 1.

IMPACT ASSESSMENT AND OFFICIAL DEVELOPMENT ASSISTANCE: ETHNOGRAPHIC RESEARCH OF THE WORLD BANK'S COMMUNITY-BASED RURAL DEVELOPMENT PROJECTS IN GHANA

Kwadwo Adusei-Asante and Peter Hancock

School of Psychology and Social Science, Edith Cowan University, Western Australia, Australia

CHAPTER OUTLINE

INTRODUCTION

The purposes of this chapter are twofold: one, to explore the need for stronger links between and *ex post* and *ex ante* in Official Development Assistance (ODA) and; two to argue for an ethnographic approach to impact assessment (IA) methods which we argue, provides a more nuanced, and context-specific capacity to highlight potential issues, and impacts, both positive and negative of ODA. Questions about the efficacy of ODA raises questions on the rigor and validity of the methods and tools used in assessing them before, during, and after their implementation. This chapter provides insights on the usefulness of ethnography as a credible IA tool for understanding how ODA implementation impacts on the people and communities it is designed to help.

This chapter is based on a research that was conducted as part of a doctoral program, which focused on the outcomes of the World Bank's Community-Based Rural Development Projects (CBRDP), implemented in Ghana between 2005 and 2011. The study focused on a primary research question, which was: How were the outcomes of the Community-Based Rural Development Projects in selected Districts of Ghana influenced by contested decentralization theories and complex concepts such as "community" and "empowerment"?

The CBRDP was designed as a type of the World Bank's Community-Driven Development (CDD) program. The CBRDP sought to empower rural populations, and strengthen the country's decentralization system. The pilot project served as one of the principal vehicles for the implementation of Ghana's Poverty Reduction Strategy (GPRS) and to bridge the gap of uneven distribution across socioeconomic groups and geographical locations. It was funded with loan facilities from the World Bank's International Development Association and the Agençe Francaise Development (USD $80 million). The Government of Ghana implemented the project under the Ministry of Local Government and Rural Development (MLGRD) and the Regional Coordinating Units (RICUs) in conjunction with an independent CBRDP secretariat (CBRDP, 2006; Yaron, 2008; Binswanger et al., 2010).

Like most CDD programs, the principle underlying Ghana's CBRDP was to allow beneficiary communities to choose, implement, and maintain local development projects (Dongier et al., 2003; World Bank, 2000, 2004; Binswanger et al., 2010). Consequently, Area Councils, believed to be the closest local government body to people at the grassroots level in Ghana (Ahwoi, 2010), were taken through the rudiments of the CBRDP to facilitate the process. They were trained in financial, project tendering, and procurement management processes, after which they were required to prepare their respective Community Action Plans. This document contained the community's project "road map." Once endorsed by the CBRDP Headquarters, the beneficiary locality received seed money in three equal installments to implement the project. Both the preparation of the Community Action Plan and the disbursement of funds were supposed to be participatory and consultative between the local people, the Assembly and Unit Committee Members, and Traditional Chiefs.

Conceptualized as "community-based," the CBRDP implementation model was based on an assumption that residents in the beneficiary localities would contribute labor or offer hired services at a reduced market rate to complete and maintain the project. Further, as per the model, Ghana's local government structure was considered to be highly functional and could support the implementation of the CBRDP without any adjustment to the model (CBRDP, 2006; Yaron, 2008; Binswanger et al., 2010). However, as discussed below, through the application of ethnographic research, the deleterious state of most of the projects studied suggested that the grounded realities and contexts of the beneficiary localities were at odds with three pivotal concepts that were used in the design and implementation of the World Bank's CBRDP in Ghana.

Our research of the World Bank's CBRDP in Ghana underscores the critical role methodology plays in both *ex ante* and *ex post* assessment of ODA programs. Based on our ethnographic IA of the CBRDP we argue that top-down evaluation approaches that only set quantitative goals (that nations have to aspire to) seldom work. We argue further that quantitative methods commonly associated with IA, render IA exercises unnecessarily technocratic, ostracize those who are supposed to benefit from ODA, while empowering those with the skills to conduct and manipulate quantitative methods, rather than vulnerable people. It is our contention that quantitative dominance of IA is far removed from the social and environmental factors it was designed to investigate, and that an appropriate way of conceptualizing how an intervention impacts on people is to measure how it will or has brought changes to intended beneficiaries' way of life, culture, political systems, their environment, health and wellbeing, personal and property rights, as well as their fears and aspirations (Vanclay, 2003; Li, 2007). Below, we discuss the relevance of ethnographic IA to *ex post* and *ex ante* ODA evaluation processes. This will be followed with a summary of our findings on the CBRDP, as revealed by our ethnographic IA tools.

APPLIED ETHNOGRAPHY

"Ethnography" is derived from two Greek words: "ethnos" (tribe or people) and "graphia" (writing). Translated literally, it means writing about a people or describing a culture or group of people (Jones and Watts, 2010). Bronislaw Malinowski (1884–1942) is credited with establishing modern and systematic ethnography. He emphasized that ethnographers' "ultimate goal is to grasp the native's point of view, his relation to life, to realize his vision of the world" (Malinowski, 1922, p. 25 cited in Jones, 2010). Malinowski's fieldwork in New Guinea and other places followed seven key phases, which have become the template for contemporary ethnographic practice: (1) Living in the field, immersing yourself in this social world; (2) Learning to use the language of your field subjects; (3) Isolating yourself from "outside influences"; (4) Collection of as much data as possible on everything in the field setting, from folklore stories, to social rules and customs, descriptions, and observations; (5) Taking copious field notes; (6) Participating in field activities (participant-observation); and (7) Keeping a detailed field dairy to use as a safety valve to release emotional pressures (Young, 1979).

Since the 1980s, ethnography has grown out of being about "the other" into producing knowledge that informs development policies-applied ethnography. In the wake of repeated failures that plagued development programs at the time, Robert Chambers and Micheal M. Cernea and other influential scholars brought the attention of development stakeholders to the sociological incompetence of the programs. For example, in his *Rural Development: Putting the Last First,* Chambers (1983) argued that most development programs at the time emphasized top–down development paradigms, and advocated for the need to include local knowledge in development program designs. Similarly, Cernea (1985) found the programs as being guided by technocratic or econocratic models, a practice he argued, created social imbalances and ignored social and cultural variables. Cernea asserted further that socio-anthropological knowledge produced through ethnography is highly impactful and needed to be used as the "entrance point" to policy design. As a result of these criticisms, ethnographic knowledge was adopted in many projects and has informed the design and implementation of several international development interventions. For instance, in 2003, the United States General Office published a report, which examined the use of ethnography in the federal government and how 10 federal departments used the results of ethnographic studies to improve agency programs policies and procedures. Other evidence that supports ethnographic techniques can also be found in Mosse (2005), Mosse and Lewis (2005), Lee (2013), and Jones and Watts (2010).

Despite the evidence above, ethnography is not widely recognized in many fields, IA being a case in point; there is dearth of literature on applied ethnography and IA. Quantitative methods have dominated IA practice because of the perception that ethnographic methodological approaches are subjective, and produce "soft evidence" (see Lee, 2013; Brady et al., 2013). Naysayers have also argued that ethnography is expensive and time consuming and hence its inapplicability to IA, which normally requires quick turnover process. We disagree with these criticisms on the grounds that understanding experience is much more important than measuring outputs and that numbers and metrics rarely capture the complex individual transformation and collective social change at the heart of many humanitarian interventions (Jones and Watts, 2010; Lee, 2013). ODA and by default IA and development is about people, thus recognizing their centrality in project design, implementation, and evaluation cannot be taken for granted.

The need for ODA assessment methods to be beneficiaries experiences focused is crucial for two reasons. First, as most countries are facing economic challenges, citizens and stakeholders of donor nations and organizations are pushing for ODA cuts and/or tangible proofs that their taxes are positively impacting aid beneficiaries. Second, the lack of or poorly executed *ex ante* IA can lead to poor ODA program planning and design, and result in situations where the project fails to target those who needed it most, as our findings will show. The last issue relates to the idea that without a rigorous evaluation tool the effectiveness of an ODA program cannot be properly measured. The latter also raises ethical concerns about the independence and authenticity of evaluation reports that are either carried out by donors internally or outsourced to their "preferred evaluation consultants" (Howitt, 2005; Patton, 2008; McIvor, 2009; Volkov and Baron, 2011). Below, we describe how ethnography enabled us to fully explore the effectiveness of the World Bank's CBRDP in Ghana. At the same time, the chapter will show how a rigorous *ex ante* IA would have possibly led to the avoidance of some of the mishaps the CRBDP generated, many of which were based around the interplay between the project, culture, context, and other situational factors. We argue that statistically driven IA and evaluation models could not have uncovered these subtleties.

THE FOUR DIMENSIONAL ETHNOGRAPHIC IMPACT ASSESSMENT FRAMEWORK

Guided by Malinowski's ethnographic framework, modern ethnographers use terms such as participation, immersion, the 3Rs (reflection, reflexivity, and representation), thick description, active participative ethics, empowerment, and understanding (Jones, 2010). A four-dimensional ethnographic framework can be identified in Malinowski's ethnographic tools and modern ethnographic practice, and are relevant for both *ex ante* and *ex post* IA. These include (1) Planning; (2) Participative Presence; (3) Refelctive Flexibility; and (4) Ethical Representation.

PLANNING

Ethnographic IA work requires careful planning. The planning phase allows researchers or impact assessors to conceptualize the project, develop its objectives, establish key contacts in the field, develop working knowledge of the field, draw up implementation and contingency plans as well as methods of measuring outcomes. Our seven-month fieldwork in nine Districts of three Regions of Ghana occurred in 2010/2011, and was preceded by a two-phase 6 months planning period. The first phase involved the conception of the research, preliminary literature review, proposal writing and defense, and obtaining research ethics clearance. Most of the planning happened at phase two, where personal contacts with all relevant persons in all nine Districts researched were established. This was mostly done through emails and phones, using a snowball technique, although other contacts were secured in the field. This phase was crucial as it afforded the researchers the opportunity to secure and review the CBRDP documents. Reviewing the project's documents within the context of the general literature review was instrumental in framing research questions and choice of a research method.

PARTICIPATIVE PRESENCE

Participative presence is a key ethnographic technique relevant for both *ex ante* and *ex post* IA purposes. We refer to it as "being in the field," consciously participating in and observing the field. "The field" is used here to refer to a (1) specific project at stake; and the (2) way of life of the project's beneficiaries. Contemporary ethnographers have noted that every field setting varies and may not allow the researcher to participate fully and for a long time (Senah, 1997; Jones, 2010). Thus, participation has overtime become a commitment on the part of researchers in the social world of their research subjects on different levels: physical, social, mental, and emotional (see Senah, 1997; Jones and Watts, 2010). Malinowski's concept of being immersed in the field has also changed overtime. Being immersed in the field is a resolve on researchers part to gain as much knowledge as possible, and/or as Jones (2010 p. 8) puts it "seek to get up close and personal." The more a researcher is able to participate or be immersed in the field the better.

Despite the obvious reconceptualization of participation and immersion, participative presence remains a useful ethnographic technique and is relevant for understanding how a program will or has impacted on people. Participative presence set ethnographic IA apart from conventional community consultation processes. It is an immersive IA approach, which provides the means to understanding the impact of a program holistically, providing the impact assessor first-hand data and an opportunity to appreciate social, cultural, and political contexts of the project and how these could or have influenced program outcomes. It is a paradigm shift from an observation of several commentators that some development brokers who design projects sit in ivory towers and have never set foot in the countries and contexts in which they are applied (Lancaster, 1999; Easterly and Pfutze, 2008).

Relative to our research in Ghana, participative presence was applied in the *ex post* sense, as the project was completed at the time of the fieldwork. The technique enabled the researchers to participate in the social life of the CBRDP beneficiaries over a long period, leading to what Bryman (2008) states "high level of congruence between concepts and observation". As an *ex post* technique, participative presence led to the observation of IA subjects social systems, routines, spaces, events and cultural-norms and practices that underpinned the behavioral pattern and perceptions (Boudewinjse, 1994; Patton, 2002). For example, the CBRDP stipulated that beneficiary localities consultatively choose and implement projects that addressed their *most* important needs (CBRDP, 2006). Accordingly, in all localities assessed, such infrastructure elements as the state of roads, school buildings; and basic necessities such as water, electricity, public toilet facilities, and so on were observed. The aim was to gain first-hand and experiential knowledge of the "potential needs" of the localities and to what degree they matched the projects implemented.

As we discuss in the findings section below, participative presence exposed us to issues that were not revealed in interviews and focus group discussions. For example, it enhanced our understanding of the grounded meanings and realities of the theories and concepts such as "community" and "empowerment," which were pivotal in the implementation of the CBRDP. It also offered first-hand information, other than any prior conceptualization of the projects and the localities gathered through reading (Patton, 2002). The technique also allowed an appreciation of the forms of local knowledge and repetitive routines in the localities that must have escaped the project implementers or were taken for granted (Mosse, 2001; Tesoriero, 2010). Through this technique, issues such as people's political affiliations, which many respondents were unwilling to reveal in formal interviews, were discovered. To keep track of data observed in the localities researched, photographs and detailed fieldnotes were written to create a "holistic description of the field setting" for review and analysis (Light, 2010).

REFLECTIVE FLEXIBILITY

According to Jones (2010, p. 14), ethnography has never been a neutral term nor used as a neutral tool for collecting data. The methodology seeks to understand issues from the inside, with a particular focus on everyday lived experiences. Consequently, in ethnographic IA the researcher is not detached or an impartial scientist who seeks the truth; instead s/he acknowledges his/her subjectivity, adjusts accordingly, and strategizes to minimize biases (Light, 2010). We refer to this process as reflective flexibility. It is the responsibility of researchers to recognize their own position in relation to the field and IA subjects, the potentiality to impact on data collection, analyses, and writing up results.

The Principal Investigator (PI) on this project is Ghanaian who had to reflect and adjust to the insider and outsider realities of fieldwork (Sustein and Chiseri-Strater, 2012). Thus, while researching in Ghana allowed the PI much flexibility and independence, as no permit was required throughout the fieldwork, the PI was an "outsider." As a result, the PI consciously reduced all asymmetrical variables between him and the IA subjects. Being reflective enabled the PI to; (1) Collect rigorous data, which stemmed from the need to scrupulously observe familiar sociocultural patterns; and (2) Present findings as were found and experienced in the field. While some would consider this as a weakness, it is a strength in disguise in the sense that it afforded the opportunity to apply other tools for triangulation and validity of the findings. We demonstrated this in our innovative use of open-ended questionnaires (see below).

Conventionally, questionnaires are considered as a quantitative or survey technique (Robson, 2002). In recent times however, that narrow stance is giving way to a contextualized usage of the technique, which allows for qualitative analysis. Responses to open-ended questions, we discovered, can provide details about perceptions, opinions, personal experiences, and deeply held beliefs (Carpenter and Suto, 2008; Padgett, 2008). As Liamputtong (2009, p. 282) puts it, "qualitative researchers need to know that we sometimes count too." This implies that questionnaires could be used quantitatively or qualitatively, depending on their design. Questionnaires were used qualitatively to reach out to the residents of the CBRDP beneficiary localities who were not included in the individual interviews and focus group discussions, while obtaining some sense of quantity of the emergent themes for contextualization and triangulation (Carpenter and Suto, 2008; Padgett, 2008; Liamputtong, 2009). Accordingly, 225 questionnaires were distributed in all nine localities researched. They were administered randomly to residents who had intimate knowledge of the CBRDP implementation in the locality. Respondents were asked to explain their; (1) Commitments to the locality; (2) Participation in the identification and implementation processes of the CBRDPs; and (3) Opinions on the functions of their local government officials. Overall, the questionnaires enhanced triangulation of the data and increased the data sample size that would have otherwise been covered in the interviews and focus group discussions.

ETHICAL REPRESENTATION

The Ethics Committee of Edith Cowan University approved several ethics formalities before and after the data collection to protect the confidentiality of respondents' identity, while ethically representing their views. In the field, all respondents were briefed about the research purposes and gave their consent before the implementation procedures with the protocols of the interviews and questionnaires. Respondents were also assured of confidentiality and informed about their rights to withdraw, if they felt uncomfortable. The names of the respondents and the towns and districts, where the fieldwork was carried out were deidentified.

Interviews and focus group discussions formed a substantial part of our ethnographic study of Ghana's CBRDP. A total of 50 formal and in-depth individual interviews were conducted. Those included in the individual interviews were key informants, local government officials (Assembly Members, Area Council Executive, or Unit Committee Members), Traditional Chiefs, and CBRDPs' maintenance committee members. The questions, many of which were based on what was observed in the localities or taken from the project documents, were semistructured and open-ended to allow the respondents the flexibility of expressing themselves (Liamputtong, 2009; Travers, 2010). The interviews elicited information on the processes leading to the selection and implementation and the state of the CBRDPs. Key Informants were asked to identify issues that affected local organizing tendencies in their respective localities as well as the sustainability of the projects. To obtain a larger sample of respondents without having to interview them individually (Liamputtong, 2009), 10 focus group discussions were held, one in each locality, except for a town in the Greater Accra Region, whose circumstances warranted two.

The analysis of the primary data – field notes, interviews, focus group, and open-ended questionnaires – commenced with immersing in and organization of the data (Willis, 2010). This involved manually reviewing the field notes, verbatim transcriptions of all audio interviews, and the interpretation of the questionnaires on a district basis. Another round of organizational procedure involved thematic coding of the data. In writing up the findings, we were guided by Light's (2010) key principles for ethnographic writing. As a result, we used vigorous descriptions and extensive references from the original field data. In order to "give voice" to our research participants we also resisted tendencies to correct or improve on what people said about their experience with the CBRDP, although we endeavored to capture the depth and diversity of the data. We also employed "Member-checking" and audit trail mechanisms to review and enhance the credibility of the findings.

THE WORLD BANK'S CBRDP IN GHANA: SUMMARY OF ETHNOGRAPHIC RESEARCH FINDINGS

This section presents summaries of three key findings of our ethnographic IA of the World Bank's CBRDP in Ghana, namely; (A) "Highly functional" decentralization system and CDD programs; (B) When empowerment disempowers; and (C) Community-based programs in nonexistent communities. These are discussed in turn below.

"HIGHLY FUNCTIONAL" DECENTRALIZATION SYSTEM AND CDD PROGRAMS

One of the key principles of World Bank's CDD/CBRDP implementation is the theory that better outcomes are guaranteed if the implementing country's existing intergovernment institutions are effective, or have genuine commitment to decentralization (Dongier et al., 2003; Binswanger et al., 2010). The World Bank's indicators of a high-functioning intergovernment systems include contexts where there exist: (1) Local elections; (2) Decentralization laws that create local government structures with autonomy in resource management; (2) Fiscal decentralization; and (3) Devolution of service delivery. Accordingly, the World Bank had operational strategies appropriate for both the low- and high-functioning contexts: the Leading, the Conservative or Lagging, and the Matching strategies (Dongier et al., 2003; Binswanger et al., 2010). The "Matching strategy" was employed in Ghana, as it was believed to have a consolidating decentralized system (Serrano-Berthet et al., 2010; Binswanger et al., 2010).

However, our ethnographic research found that Ghana's intergovernmental system was not highly functional, and questioned the usefulness of some of the World Bank's indicators for measuring the functioning of decentralization systems. Our findings suggested that while the country's constitution and various Local Government Acts made provision for a decentralized local government system, the same statutes promote centralization, which hinders the autonomy of local authorities, and effective fiscal and administrative decentralization (see Adusei-Asante and Hancock, 2012). In addition, the atrophied state of the local government system was corroborated in almost all the CBRDP documents that the CBRDP was designed to strengthen the country's weak local government substructures (CBRDP, 2006, CBRDP Annual Reports 2005–2010, CBRDP Zone IV Annual Reports 2005–2010). A program of this nature should have been preceded by a rigorous *ex ante* IA to unearth the potential consequences and implication of the project on Ghana's local government. As it turned out, the CBRDPs were implemented on the country's highly politicized and weak local government substructure, an error that had debilitating impact on the maintenance of the projects (see Adusei-Asante and Hancock, 2012).

Relative to the indicators of a high functioning local government system, we found that "local government election" was not a robust indicator for measuring the level of decentralization (as indicated in World Bank definitions of high functioning), particularly when the percentage of patronage indicative of its success or otherwise was not provided. As a result we assumed that the World Bank measured local government election by higher voter turnout. While local government elections have been held in Ghana since 1978, the process has not been taken seriously at the central government and local levels. As illustrated in Fig. 12.1 below, Voter turnout to local government elections from

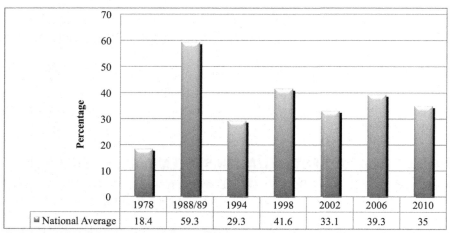

FIGURE 12.1 Percentage of National Average of Voter Turnouts in District Assembly Elections 1978–2010

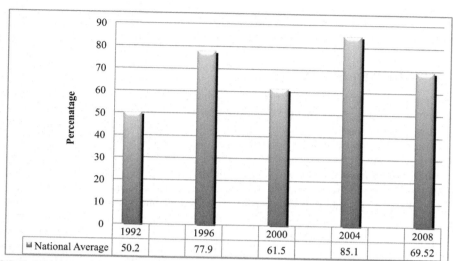

FIGURE 12.2 Percentages of Voter Turnouts to Presidential Elections 1992–2008

(Data source: Electoral Commission of Ghana 2010, 2000, & 2008 are averages of the first and second round voting.)

1994–2010 has averaged nearly 36%; significantly lower than the almost 70% patronage of presidential elections for the 1992–2008 period (see Fig. 12.2). Moreover, Ghana's local government elections are characterized by low involvement of women, although they constitute 51.2% of the population (Ghana Statistical Service, 2010). Although women's participation in parliamentary elections as candidates is also significantly lower, it is better than their involvement in District Assembly and Unit Committee elections. For example, in the 2010 District Assembly elections, only 7.3 % and 6.8% of women were elected as Assembly and Unit Committee Members, respectively; nearly 200 Unit Committee positions were uncontested nationally (Electoral Commission of Ghana, 2010). This proves that local government election is not accorded any significance in Ghana, making it an unreliable indicator for assessing the functioning of decentralization in the country.

Another factor that explains the rather low-functioning state of Ghana's government was the weakness of local government substructures, specifically, the functions of Assembly Members and Unit Committee Members. These are key facilitators of developments at the local level in Ghana and were supposed to be the champions of the CBRDP. They are elected for 4-year re-electable twice terms (12 years in all), and are not to be identified with any political party (ILGS and MLGRDE, 2006). Interviews with Assembly Members and Unit Committee Members revealed they were saddled with many challenges that impacted on their functions. These included: (1) Managing their personal lives and people's expectations in an unpaid job; (2) Working with political appointees, specifically District Chief Executives; and (3) Sharing power with Traditional Chiefs (see Adusei-Asante, 2012 for a detail analysis). Relative to the World Bank's CBRDP, we observed that these challenges accounted for the poor state of some the projects studied that constituted the CBRDP. For example, in two localities, a rift between the Traditional Chief and Assembly and Unit Committee Members had left a library project and a 16-seater public toilet facility unmaintained for several months, as these project stakeholders were responsible for galvanizing local support to maintain them. Further ethnographic data revealed that the rift was a direct consequence of the project designers' misconceptualization and application of the concept of "empowerment" and a failure regarding gender and empowerment.

WHEN EMPOWERMENT DISEMPOWERS

The term "empowerment" is complex and presents many theoretical difficulties. Aside from the tendency to be applied in a gender-biased manner (World Bank, 2000; Cornwall and Edwards, 2010), measuring empowerment presents many challenges (Lavarack and Wallenstein, 2001; Cornish, 2006). Scholars also disagree on whether the term is a process or an outcome or both (Mosedale, 2003; Yaron, 2008). The fact that "empowerment" is predicated on the concept of "power" makes it even more complicated. The reason for this dilemma is that "power" is not a neutral concept and cannot be shared; empowering one group may mean disempowering others by breaking certain traditional norms or monopolies. This may lead to conflicts, if outcomes are not properly monitored (Foucault, 1980, 1982; Cornish, 2006).

Despite these theoretical challenges we found that "empowerment" was loosely applied in the CBRDP as the project: (1) Had no working definition of the term; (2) Targeted women and vulnerable groups, although it was meant to empower the general population; and (3) Measured "empowerment" only in term of participation, ignoring the conditions that perpetuated the "powerlessness." As a result of the imprecise application of "empowerment" in the CBRDP, Ghana's Ministry of Local Government and Rural Development and the World Bank's Advisory Team, designers of the project, appeared to have overlooked the country's Traditional Chiefs and had no strategy in place to monitor unintended outcomes.

Other failures were revealed in our data. These were integral to the CBRDP and related to a Library Project implemented in Aboloo (Greater Accra Region) and a Public Toilet Facility in Ntoaso (Eastern Region). In their pursuit to strengthen Ghana's decentralization process through the CBRDP, the designers of the CBRDP appeared to have focused only on the local government substructures, and overlooked the country's influential traditional establishment. While the intent to empower Assembly and Unit Committee Members was important, the project's designers ignored the reality that the local government officials did not function in isolation, but were part of a very complex sociocultural system. Two case studies showed that the Traditional Chiefs felt sidelined, and were uninformed about the CBRDP's objective of empowering the country's local government substructures. Acting within their usual traditional "powers," the Traditional Chiefs clashed with the "newly empowered" local government officials, a situation that left the projects poorly maintained and in a state of dereliction. Specifically, the Aboloo Library Project was faced with many crucial administrative and resource challenges that impacted on its efficiency, while the Ntoaso Public Toilet Facility was almost always left in an untidy state. In the latter case, the Traditional Chief of the locality refused to collaborate with the Assembly Member to organize the residents to clean the toilet facility periodically. Hence the researchers found that the CBRDP's two major assets were not being fully utilized by the people for whom they were designed; instead they had become the center of a protracted legal battle (see Adusei-Aasante and Hancock, 2013).

COMMUNITY-BASED PROGRAM IN NONEXISTENT COMMUNITIES

The concept of "community" as applied in the CDD/CBRDP was also challenged in our data. Although a complex term, "community" tends to be often misused in development program designs, because of its appealing value. In the case of the CBRDP we found that the complexity of the term was ignored, as it was conceptualized in the spatial sense, although the concept transcends the notion of territoriality. A community, it was argued, must have: (1) Functions that drives the group; (2) Opportunity for interaction; (3) Membership who identifies with and contributes to it; and (4) Culture that makes it distinct from others (Kenny, 2010; Tesoriero, 2010). The ethnographic data showed that the dynamics, ground settlement, and mobility patterns of most of the CBRDP beneficiary localities did not support interaction to the levels required for a coherent "community" to exist. Several case studies clearly illustrated this "community-based project in non-existent communities" contradiction and the concomitant repercussions for the CRBDPs (see Adusei-Asante, 2015 for details). The failure of the Abaase Market Shed project is presented below.

Residents of Abaase in the Eastern Region of Ghana received a 40-shed market project. However, we observed and learned through interviews that most of the residents did not associate with the town as "members" and had no obligation to it because of its rurality and remoteness. The attitude of temporality toward the locality meant that organizing community-based projects there would be a challenge, an issue that an *ex ante* ethnographic IA could have identified and resolved before implementation. The sense of temporality toward the locality, coupled with mistrust of local leaders made it difficult for the local project's leaders to organize support for the project. As the CBRDP seed money was insufficient to complete the project, local leaders had to finds ways to raise additional monies to complete the market sheds. Because of the lack of "community" in Abaase it was difficult convincing the local people to contribute monetary sums to the project. As a result, they resorted to collecting monetary contributions from local traders whom they guaranteed spaces in the limited market sheds. The strategy worked, but caused many problems for the project, as the local leaders over-collected money from traders, who apparently outnumbered the sheds available; this occasioned disputes over who is allocated a shed and who is not. As a result we found and took photographic evidence of the ODA-funded market shed that had been abandoned and become home for squatters, while traders sold in tents and under umbrellas. At the time of completing the study, 18 months after leaving the fieldwork, the project the situation had not changed.

What was clear in all the case studies as exemplified above is that many of the projects that made up the CBRDP were unguided by *ex ante* principles and evidence. If this was properly carried out, it might have necessitated the need to develop the "communities" within which to base the project in the beneficiary localities. Although a complex term, a community could be nurtured around a function (Tesoriero, 2010; Kenny, 2010). For example, the CBRDP officials could have developed a strong Traders Community in Tease before implementing the Market Sheds project. This way, the traders would have taken ownership of and maintained the shed better than was apparent during the fieldwork. However, those who designed the project clearly ignored the need to develop a community in Tease before constructing the now abandoned market sheds.

DISCUSSION

This chapter has presented research findings from an ethnographic study of the World Bank's Community-Based Rural Development Projects in Ghana (CBRDP). It has juxtaposed the research findings against the failures of the project and ODA literature. In essence what we argue is that ethnography as a research tool revealed a large number of failures in the CBRDP and weaknesses in its implementation and conceptualization, these we argue would not have been captured in a typical IA. It has also been our experience researching in the area of International Development Studies for 20 years that aid agencies rarely have time for the *ex ante* stage of IA correctly and call in evaluators after the project has started, negating the rigor of *ex ante* research. We argue that ethnography IA techniques should be considered in future ODA assessment and used in conjunction with these methods. In depth research in Ghana allowed us to identify and explore many of the implementation failures in the CBRDP and to identify how the project should have been implemented with consideration for key concepts such as community, empowerment, and CDD theories.

The findings have several implications for development theory and practice. First, development projects cannot be sufficiently based on idealized, yet complex and contested terms such as "empowerment," "community" and inherently flawed decentralization theories. It is important that programs attempting to apply the concepts clearly are guided by evidence, define and conceptualize it within the confines of the grounded realities and social dynamics of beneficiary localities. In this way development projects may receive maximum local support, be more likely to be effectively maintained and improve the reputation of ODA-funded projects. Second, there is the need for international development agencies, donors, and other development brokers to: (1) Invest in IA that apply ethnographic research methods before, during, and after the design and implementation of ODA programs. Researching aid beneficiary settings is crucial, as it provides empirical grounds for designing and implementing programs in a contextually appropriate manner. Such an exercise may be cost effective, compared to the consequences of ignoring it; (2) Expose local project officials to the theoretical intricacies of key terms and concepts that underpin their development projects, and; (3) Channel aid funds into improving the political institutions of developing countries, as the outcomes of the CBRDP may have been different, if Ghana had an efficient decentralization system.

CONCLUSION

Official Development Assistance (ODA) is a contentious issue and this chapter has outlined some of the important debates surrounding its efficacy. Many scholars argue that it has failed and created dependency in Africa for example, where despite significant ODA over many decades, many countries on the continent remain in dire poverty, stricken by corruption, political instability, war and conflict, and health crises. On the other hand, many also argue that ODA has been successful and has helped to move many nations out of poverty and famine. This chapter focused on ethnographic IA as a form for measuring the efficiency and effectiveness of ODA, especially when and how to conduct *ex ante* and *ex post* assessments. Relying on our research conducted in Ghana on a group of World Bank projects (CDRBP) we argue that statistical evaluations fail to address the fundamental nature of human society and development aid. Instead we employed an ethnographic approach, in conjunction with surveys and interviews to explore the implementation and effectiveness of the World Bank's CBRDP. Using this method we found that the project and the conceptual premises on which it was based were ignored at the ground level or not understood by key stakeholders. As a result the project was found to be quite flawed, and while is it yet to be assessed by "expert consultants" employing typically prescribed IA methods, it is unlikely such an evaluation would uncover the failings we found in our research.

REFERENCES

Adusei-Asante, K., 2012. The state of Ghana's local government. The case of assembly members. Inkanyiso: J. Humanities Social Sci. 4 (2), 94–103.

Adusei-Asante, K., 2015. Community-based programs in non-existent communities. Afr. Studies Q. 15 (2), 69–83.

Adusei-Asante, K., Hancock, P., 2012. Theories in community-driven development operations. Eur. J. Business Social Sci. 1 (5), 83–98.

Adusei-Asante, K., Hancock, P., 2013. When empowerment disempowers: The case of Ghanaian Traditional Chiefs and Local Government Officials. Ghana J. Dev. Studies 9 (2), 43–62.

Ahwoi, K, 2010. Local government and decentralization in Ghana. Unimax Macmillan, Accra, Ghana.

Binswanger, M.H.P., de Regt, J.P., Spector, S., 2010. Local and Community Driven Development. The World Bank, Washington, DC.

Boudewinjse, B., 1994. Fieldwork at home. ETNOFOOR VII (1), 73–95.

Brady, M., McDavid, J.C., Huse, I., Hawthorn, L.R.L., 2013. Applying qualitative evaluation methods. In: McDavid, J.C., Huse, I., Hawthorn, L.R.L. (Eds.), Program Evaluation and Performance Measurement: An Introduction to Practice. Second ed. Sage publications, Thousand Oaks, CA.

Bryman, A, 2008. Social Research Methods, Third ed. Oxford University Press, Oxford.

Carpenter, C., Suto, M., 2008. Qualitative Research for Occupational and Physical Therapist: A Practical Guide. Blackwell Publishing, Oxford.

Cernea, M. (Ed.), 1985. Putting People First. Oxford University Press, New York, NY.

Chambers, R., 1983. Rural Development: Putting the Last First. Longman, London.

Community-Based Rural Development Project, 2006. Implementation Manual. CBRDP Secretariat, Accra.

Cornish, F., 2006. Empowerment to participate: a case study of participation by Indian sex workers in HIV prevention'. J. Commun. Appl. Soc. Psychol. 16, 301–315.

Cornwall, A., Edwards, J., 2010. Introduction: Negotiating empowerment. IDA Bull. 41 (2), 1–9.

Dongier, P., Van Domelen, P., Ostrom, E., Ryan, A., Wakeman, W., Bebbington, A., Alkire, S., Esmail, T., Polsky, M., 2003. Community-driven development'. In: Klugman, J. (Ed.), 2003, Poverty Reduction Strategy Paper Sourcebook (Chapter 9). The World Bank, Washington, DC.

Easterly, W., Pfutze, T, 2008. Where does the money go? Best and worst practices in foreign aid. J. Econ. Perspect.' 22 (2), 29–52.

Electoral commission of Ghana, Various years. District Assembly Election Results, EC, Accra, Ghana.

Foucault, M., 1980. Power/Knowledge: Selected Interviews and Other Writings 1972-1977. Harvester Press, Brighton, UK, Ed.

Foucault, M., 1982. Subject and power. Crit. Enquiry 8 (4), 777–795.

Ghana Statistical Service, 2010. Population and Housing Census. Summary of Final Results. Ghana Statistical Service, Accra.

Howitt, R., 2005. The Importance of process in social impact assessment: ethics, methods and process for cross-cultural engagement. Ethics Place Env. 8 (2), 209–221.

ILGS/ MLGRDE, 2006. A Handbook: The Role of Assembly Member in Ghana's Local Government System. ILGS/ MLGRDE, Accra, Ghana.

Jones, S.J., 2010. Origins and Ancestors: a brief history of ethnography. In: Jones, S.J., Watts, S. (Eds.), Ethnography in Social Science. Routledge, New York, NY, pp. 13–27.

Jones, S.J., Watts, S. (Eds.), 2010. Ethnography in Social Science. Routledge, New York, NY.

Kenny, S, 2010. Developing communities for the future, Fourth ed. Cengage Learning, Australia.

Lancaster, C., 1999. Aid effectiveness in Africa: Unfinished agenda. J. Afr. Economies 8 (4), 487–503.

Lavarack, G., Wallenstein, N., 2001. Measuring empowerment: A fresh look at organizational domains. Health Promotion Int. 16 (2), 179–185.

Lee, P., 2013. An ethnographic approach to impact evaluation: Stop measuring outputs and start understanding experiences. Available from: <http://reboot.org/2013/05/20/an-ethnographic-approach-to-impact-evaluation-stop-measuring-outputs-start-understanding-experiences> (accessed 20.03.2015).

Li, T.M., 2007. The will to improve. Governmentality, development and the practise of politics. Duke University Press, Durham, NC.

Liamputtong, P., 2009. Qualitative Research Methods, Third ed. Oxford University Press, Australia.

Light, D., 2010. The final stage? Writing up ethnographic research. In: Jones, S.J., Watts, S. (Eds.), Ethnography in Social Science. Routledge, New York, NY, pp. 173–186.

McIvor, R., 2009. How the transaction cost and resource-based theories of the firm inform outsourcing evaluation. J. Oper. Manage. 27 (1), 45–63.

Mosedale, S., 2003. Towards a framework for assessing empowerment, Working Paper Series, Paper # 3, Institute for Development Policy and Management, University of Manchester, Harold Hankins House, Precinct Centre, Oxford Road, Manchester.

Mosse, D., 2001. People's knowledge, participation and patronage: Operations and representations in rural development. In: Cooke, B., Kothari, U. (Eds.), Participation: The New Tyranny. Zed Books, New York, NY, pp. 16–35.

Mosse, D., 2005. Cultivating Development: An Ethnography of Aid Policy and Practice. Pluto Press, London.

Mosse, D., Lewis, D. (Eds.), 2005. The aid effect. Pluto Press, London.

Padgett, D.L., 2008. Qualitative methods in social work, Second ed. Sage Publications, Los Angeles, CA.

Patton, M., 2008. Utilization-Focused Evaluation. Sage Publications Inc, Thousand Oaks, CA.

Patton, M.Q., 2002. Qualitative Research and Evaluation Methods. Sage Publications Inc, Thousand Oaks, CA.

Robson, C., 2002. Real World Research, Second ed. Blackwell Publishing, Victoria, Australia.

Senah, K.A., 1997. Money be Man: The Popularity of Medicines in a Rural Ghanaian Community. Universiteit van Amsterdam, Amsterdam.

Serrano-Berthet, R., Helling, L., Van Domelen, J., Van Wicklin, W., Owen, D., Poli, M., Cherukupalli, R., 2010. Lessons from Africa. In: Binswanger et al.,(Ed.), Local and Community Driven Development. The World Bank, Washington, DC, pp. 121–150.

Sustein, B.S., Chiseri-Strater, E., 2012. FieldWorking: Reading and Writing Research, Fourth ed. Bedford/St. Martin's, Boston, MA.

Tesoriero, F., 2010. Community-Based Alternatives in an Age of Globalization, Fourth ed. Pearson Australia, Australia.

Travers, M., 2010. Qualitative interviewing methods. In: Walter, M. (Ed.), Social Research Methods. Second ed. Oxford University Press, Australia, pp. 287–322.

Vanclay, F., 2003. International principles for social impact assessment. Impact Assess. Project Appraisal 21 (1), 5–11.

Volkov, B.B., Baron, M.E., 2011. Issues in internal evaluation: Implications for practice, training, and research. Volkov, B.B., Baron, M.E. (Eds.), Internal Evaluation in the 21st Century. New Directions for Evaluation, vol. 132, pp. 101–111.

Willis, K., 2010. Analysing qualitative data. In: Walter, M. (Ed.), Social Research Methods Australia and New Zealand: Second ed. Oxford University Press, Oxford, pp. 407–436.

World Bank, 2000. The Community-Driven Development Approach in the Africa Region: A Vision of Poverty Reduction Through Empowerment. The World Bank, Washington, DC.

World Bank, 2004. Community–driven development in local government capacity building projects: Emerging Approaches in Africa', Urban services for the Poor, Number 86 /July 2004. The World Bank, Washington, DC.

Yaron, G., 2008. Measuring Empowerment: A Mixed-Method Diagnostic Tool for Measuring Empowerment in the Context of Decentralization in Ghana. The World Bank, Washington, DC.

Young, M.W. (Ed.), 1979. The Ethnography of Malinowski: The Trobriand Islands, 1915-1918. Routledge & Kegan Paul, London.

FINDING BALANCE: IMPROVING MONITORING TO IMPROVE IMPACT ASSESSMENTS OF DEVELOPMENT PROGRAMMES

Donna Loveridge

CHAPTER OUTLINE

INTRODUCTION

International development efforts up until the turn of the new century were characterized by a focus on inputs, activities and outputs. The intended benefits and the pathways between the things produced and the impacts were often not well-defined. Demands, whether coming from donors or the public, to assess performance in terms of program impacts were relatively low (Bamberger et al., 2009). Rather, the primary focus of performance management was on whether things had been produced as expected and in line with the budget. The emphasis was on accounting for the use of funds and this was the basis for obtaining further funding. Hence, key questions guiding performance management activities were "what was done?" and "how much did it cost?" Meeting donor-centered compliance requirements was the key focus. Monitoring data provided donors with confidence that things were on track but was largely seen by implementers as a bureaucratic box-ticking exercise that was for donor purposes and was not important for program management (Pritchett et al., 2012).

Expectations of development programs have been progressively changing. There are increasing demands from donors and the public to clarify the intended impacts of programs, how they will be achieved, and how it will be known if they have been achieved (Bamberger et al., 2009; Jones et al., 2009; Stern et al., 2012). The key question that programs are now expected to answer is "what works?" (Sanderson, 2010). However, this question is still driven more by donors' information needs than those of implementers (since postimplementation assessments of impact provide little value to implementers). In particular "impact assessments" have come to be seen by donors as the ultimate provider of rigorous information on "what works" and have been prioritized for providing evidence to support decisions regarding future policies and programs (Pritchett et al., 2012).

This chapter focuses on the contribution that impact assessment can make to development effectiveness. However, despite the potential for making an important contribution, this chapter will argue that monitoring practices need to be updated and improved. The increased attention given to impact assessment in international development has not been matched by a commensurate increase in attention to other important aspects of performance management. In particular, the attention given to monitoring has been limited compared to the recently increased attention to impact assessment, and this has contributed to a delinking of monitoring activities from assessment work (Perrin, 2012). This chapter argues that the trend of delinking the two activities is to the detriment of both impact assessment and monitoring. Performance management works best when monitoring and impact assessment are designed to be mutually supportive (Bamberger et al., 2009). This chapter also argues that, at the same time as this delinking process has been occurring, there is an emerging opportunity to rebalance the relationship between the two activities and develop a more useful, integrated approach to monitoring and impact assessment that better serves the aims of more effective development. This opportunity arises from the increasing recognition that many development processes are complex and involve a high degree of uncertainty, necessitating real-time monitoring that expands the narrow scope of conventional monitoring as conceived in the past.

In summary, this chapter proposes that more concerted efforts to modernize and improve monitoring practices are needed. Firstly, the focus needs to be on the information needs of program implementers managing complex development programs. Donors and the public should expect that program implementers have an important contribution to make in answering the question "what is working?" Effectiveness in the short- and medium-term and while the program is in implementation is necessary for the achievement of the intended impact in the longer term. Program implementers thus need to generate real-time data and analysis useful for management purposes. Secondly, focusing monitoring activities on producing such data and analysis for management purposes increases the relevance and quality of information for impact assessments. This should ultimately be in donor interests but it is important that donor interests are not seen to be driving the process or they will come to assume primary importance, which risks repeating the problems of the past and as outlined above.

Part 1 section of this chapter reviews some key definitions for impact, impact assessment, and monitoring and evaluation, highlighting how these terms are used in this chapter. This is an important scene-setting section of the chapter since the fields of international development and performance management use of key terms is inconsistent and a regular source of confusion. Part 2 section summarizes the rise of impact and in particular two key issues, methods and independence, which have driven key impact assessment debates over the last 10 years. Understanding these issues is important since they are likely to also feature in debates concerning updating and improving monitoring practices. Both of these sections draw on debates in Chapter 2. Part 3 highlights how monitoring as conventionally practiced has failed to be relevant to implementers and those undertaking impact assessment but also summarizes some areas of mutual benefit. Lastly, Part 4 section highlights a number of recent attempts to improve monitoring approaches to better support implementers of complex programs, and how these efforts can assist impact assessment.

PART 1 – KEY DEFINITIONS AND CONCEPTS

The development industry is rife with terms that are used by different organizations in a variety of ways. Performance management terminology is equally inconsistent and diverse. When terms from both fields are used together it is a recipe for confusion. In short, understandings of these terms cannot be taken for granted and it is important to be clear about what we take the terms to mean for the purposes of this chapter. For this reason, this section reviews definitions of impact, impact assessment, monitoring, evaluation, impact evaluation and provides a definition that will be used in this chapter. This section also summarizes the characteristics of complex programs and how these differ from other types of programs, along with some key arguments about why thinking and responding to complexity is important for international development programmes.

Generally, monitoring, evaluation, and impact assessment may be considered performance management activities, but ones that may have different foci, audiences, and purposes. There will likely even be readers who disagree with my use of "performance management" to encapsulate impact assessment. However, for simplicity this umbrella term is used when speaking about monitoring, evaluation, and impact assessment.

Impact assessment can be *ex-post*, or *ex-ante* impact assessment determining the impact of an intervention on the economic, social, and environment well-being. For instance, often approval for infrastructure projects require impact assessments before they are able to obtain government approval. *Ex-ante* assessments have important implications for *ex-post* assessments since the latter make a comparison between what happened and what was thought would happen.

Confusion arises between the terms assessment and evaluation. The OECD (2002, p. 21) definition of evaluation states:

> The systematic and objective assessment of an on-going or completed project, programme or policy, its design, implementation and results. The aim is to determine the relevance and fulfilment of objectives, development efficiency, effectiveness, impact and sustainability.

Therefore, an evaluation is an assessment and one of the criteria that an evaluation can assess is impact. White (2010) notes that any evaluation that refers to impact is an impact evaluation, noting that various forms of impact assessment, that he sees as largely using qualitative approaches, also falling under the impact evaluation banner. In contrast to White (2010), O'Flynn (2010) distinguishes between evaluation and impact assessment. She argues that evaluations are concerned with the immediate or intermediate changes or outcomes generated from a program's efforts while impact assessment relates to changes in peoples' lives that are connected to the program's efforts and outcomes.

As discussed in Chapter 2, impact is widely understood as the difference between an indicator of interest with and without an intervention, and therefore attribution is the distinguishing factor and attribution analysis is undertaken in completing an impact evaluation (cf. World Bank Poverty Net Website cited in Stern et al., 2012; White, 2010). The emphasis on attribution in the World Bank's definition implies that the focus is on direct impacts (Stern et al., 2012). O'Flynn (2010) views impact as the significant or lasting changes in people's lives, distinguishing this from outcomes that are the results of a program's efforts, thereby placing greater recognition on indirect linkages between a program and impact. O'Flynn (2010) argues it is often difficult to claim a direct link, or attribution, due to the distance between what a program does and the actual target beneficiaries and changes in their lives. Rather, contribution is frequently a more reasonable goal and attribution can only be claimed for direct causal links (O'Flynn, 2010). Others, such as the Donor Committee for Enterprise Development (2015) use the term attribution but with a definition that many may understand as the same as the term contribution. White (2010) basically does the same by further distinguishing between "attribution" and "sole attribution," noting that a good impact evaluation will also assess what percentage of change an intervention contributed to and therefore quantifying the impact is essential.

In this chapter, impact is defined as a program's direct, indirect, intended, and unintended contribution to the positive and negative, primary and secondary long-term effects on the well-being of individuals, households, communities, or firms. Impact is arguably, similar to an outcome, a change that a programme contributes to. However, impacts may take a long time to occur and they are changes that occur for the ultimate beneficiary. In this chapter, impact assessment is, therefore the systematic and objective assessment of an ongoing or completed project, programme, or policy and its impact.

For the purposes of this chapter, no distinction is made between impact assessment and impact evaluation since both are concerned with understanding the "how" and "why" of the causal link between a program and outcomes or effects (Stern et al., 2012). The focus of this chapter, as with much development programming is *ex-post*, which differs from forward-looking *ex-ante* assessments. To align with the title and focus of this book, the term impact assessment is used, except in situations where citations refer directly to impact evaluation. Similarly, the terms assessors and evaluators, or those who conduct assessments, are used interchangeably.

O'Flynn (2010) views monitoring as related to a program's implementation efforts, or activities and outputs. This is a more traditional definition in that monitoring is not concerned with outcomes. However, it also differs from the OECD definition of monitoring whereby monitoring could be seen to extend to outcomes. Monitoring is "A continuing function that uses systematic collection of data on specified indicators to provide management and the main stakeholders of an ongoing development intervention with indications of the extent of progress and achievement of objectives and progress in the use of allocated funds." (OECD, 2002, p. 27) The OECD's definition is aligned with the results-based management interpretation of monitoring. Results-based management was developed in the 1990s and took monitoring beyond inputs and outputs to increasing the emphasis on outcomes, using indicators to measure change, and on learning in addition to accountability (Stephenson, 2010; Kusek and Rist, 2004). Broadly, performance monitoring, performance measurement, managing for results, and results-based management can be categorized as forms of traditional monitoring although there are some distinctions between them. Monitoring is seen as distinct from evaluation and impact assessments. Patton (1997 p. 23) defines program evaluation as the "systematic collection of information about the activities, characteristics and outcomes of programs to make judgments about the program, improve program effectiveness, and/or inform decisions about future programming." Overall, monitoring is seen as having little to do with evaluation (Perrin, 2012), despite them being linked together as M&E (monitoring and evaluation, a term used in the field of international development). In terms of impact assessment, an additional distinction might be because monitoring does not seek to determine attribution. However, White (2010) also notes that outcome monitoring could be seen as a form of impact assessment because it is concerned with outcomes, but only if, as per White's (2010) earlier assertion, attribution analysis is part of the outcome monitoring.

The last part of this section summarizes the characteristics of complex problems and complex development programs. Complex problems have not suddenly appeared where once there were no complex problems. Rather, there is an increased recognition that many development problems, but not all, are complex and viewing all programs as simple, results in "irrelevant interventions that will have little impact" (Building State Capacity, 2014). Patton (2011, p. 1) further notes:

> A complex system is characterized by a large number of interacting and interdependent elements in which there is no central control. Patterns of change emerge from rapid, real time interactions that generate learning, evolution, and development – if one is paying attention and knows how to observe and capture the important and emergent patterns. Complex environments for social interventions and innovations are those in which what to do to solve problems is uncertain and key stakeholders are in conflict about how to proceed.

To highlight how complex programs differ from programs that seek to address simple problems with simple solutions, numerous authors (such as Glouberman and Zimmerman, 2002; Rogers, 2008; Pritchett et al., 2012; Ramalingham, 2013) have developed or built on earlier conceptual frameworks to try and better illustrate the different characteristics of different types of programs. One often-repeated analogy is the framework that articulates the differences between baking a cake, sending a rocket to the moon, and raising a child. Following a recipe is easy to understand, no particular expertise is necessary, and the outcome is predictable should the recipe be followed. At the other end of the analogy, the outcomes and impacts are rather more unpredictable. For instance, it is fairly safe to assume that few parents with children who are convicted of crimes purposefully seek to raise them to become criminals. Despite the numerous books on parenting, it is difficult to predict what direction that a child and then adult will take and what the outcome will be. Sending a rocket to the moon is the middle ground – not simple as it requires numerous highly skilled individuals to put together an intricate change process, but despite these challenges the outcome is fairly certain (Rogers, 2008).

This understanding of complex development processes and programmes differs in how problems and solutions were previously conceptualized and therefore how programs were designed. Programs dealing with complex problems are, therefore, fraught with uncertainties and solutions are often best guesses. Program outcomes and impacts, and their sustainability, are unpredictable. In contrast, previously programs were viewed as having levels of certainty and predictability and therefore performance management activities, from monitoring through to impact assessment were designed and implemented on this basis (Ramalingham, 2013).

PART 2 – THE RISE OF IMPACT ASSESSMENT

Impact assessment has risen in prominence with more assessments being undertaken to answer the "what works?" question. For some, such as White (2010) this increase addresses an "underinvestment in impact analysis." The rise in impact assessment is linked to the growth of evidence-based policy and programming that became popular in the 1990s as politicians sought to modernize policy making and programming ensuring that decisions were guided by evidence rather than politics. Evidence-based policy ideals are underpinned by classical economics and rational choice theories and assume that the context is knowable, actors are good, consistent, and stable and it is therefore possible to determine what actions are connected to outcomes (Sanderson, 2000). Little recognition was yet given to the complexities of many development problems.

Two key factors have driven the direction of impact assessments over the last 15 years, both of which are guided by a narrow interpretation of rigor (Befani et al., 2014). For some individuals and organizations, the "what works?" question can only be answered if specific methods are used, and only assessors, external to and independent of the program implementation team, are sufficiently trustworthy to answer the "what works?" question.

GOLD STANDARD METHODS

Organizations influential in international development (such as the World Bank, International Initiative for Impact Evaluation and Abdul Latif Jameel Poverty Action Lab) have led the use of particular methods, which are experimental, and quasi-experimental methods, for impact assessment. They emphasized using counterfactuals to examine causation rather than before and after assessments that assume there has been no change in the context had the program not been implemented. They labeled these methods as the "gold standard" for research and evaluation (Jones et al., 2009; Pritchett et al., 2012). The prevalence of experimental and quasi-experimental methods grew as proponents argued that too much performance management effort was placed on justifying funding decisions or conducting baselines (at the *ex-ante* stage) at the detriment of more *ex-post* studies that would help determine how effective programs had been (Jones et al., 2009; Pritchett et al., 2012). However, impact assessment was viewed as research, rather than a performance management activity. With this delinking with monitoring and evaluation, impact assessment was a specialist function for economists rather than evaluators or program staff (Mackay and Horton, 2003). White (2010) argues that attempts to assess impact that do not use experimental methods cannot be considered impact evaluations. Rather these studies are impact assessments that largely use qualitative methods. The choice of other methods is relegated to circumstances which are difficult, and therefore other methods, or the "silver standard," is acceptable.

Opponents to the focus on experimental methods have argued that the most appropriate method depends on what you want to monitor, evaluate, or assess, and this is the only gold standard (cf. Chapter 2). The American and European professional evaluation associations published statements, critical of those that advocated powerfully that Randomized Controlled Trials (RCTs) were the best or only way to rigorously assess a development program's impact. The American Evaluation Association (American Evaluation Association, 2003) and EES (2007) emphasized that RCTs are not the only type of study to examine causality; that they are not always the most appropriate method since RCTs examine a small number of factors that can be isolated that may not reflect live situations and that they are not sensitive to local contexts and unexpected causal factors. The ethical reasons such as denying control group subjects access to potential benefits were also highlighted. The EES in particular noted that experimental methods were rarely appropriate for complex situations with multiple factors contributing to changes, and where it is difficult if not impossible to control for other factors; limited in their ability to deal with emergent and/or unintended and unanticipated outcomes since many of the outcomes from development programs will be related rather than identical to those defined at the program design stage. Since programs are rarely implemented as planned, using methods that are inflexible and cannot adapt to the program that is actually implemented means that the assessment can become irrelevant (Bamberger et al., 2009).

If impact assessment uses a limited range of methods, is not adapted to the realities of complex programs, and is the remit of economists it seems that it will add little value to improving the effectiveness of development.

INDEPENDENCE

Apart from the focus on methods, the other key indicator of rigor has been independence which in turn is assumed to be unbiased (Befani et al., 2014). This position assumes that an unbiased assessment is only achieved by using assessors who are independent from the program being assessed, since internal assessors are more likely to give positive findings and conclusions. However, it is also not always very clear about what independence means (Mayne, 2011). Many factors may influence independence, from the selection of projects or issues to be assessed; the terms of references; methodologies used; findings, conclusions, or recommendations; and reporting; and the culture of the organization or program being assessed. Donors are also the most likely funders of impact assessments, and this may influence the external assessors' independence as some donors may also not have a strong evaluative culture, and prefer success over failure (Mayne, 2007, 2011). There is little recognition that internal assessors have a better understanding of the program and internal dynamics as well as a longer-term commitment to the program (Patton, 2011) or that rigorous thinking and use of a credible and strong argument could also be considered an example of objectivity (Bamberger and Rugh, 2008). While there may be cases where external assessors are an appropriate strategy, this may not always be the case. Greater involvement by internal implementation staff, not only as stakeholders, but also as assessors may increase the contribution of impact assessment to improved effectiveness in relation to complex programs. While rigor, or thoroughness, may be one aspect of quality others include robustness, ownership, ethics, transparency, and usefulness (Patton, 2012). The appropriateness of the particular methods being used and the nature of the program being assessed, and taking into account the available, time, logistical, political, budget, and ethical constraints, is another aspect of rigor (Bamberger et al., 2009). No one aspect is considered more important than another.

It needs to be acknowledged that over the last 5 years there has been some debate on the question of what constitutes rigor. For instance, there is a growing body of writing on the importance of nonexperimental methods; and the importance of mixed methods, that combine methods using qualitative and quantitative data and analysis, and drawing on a range of disciplinary perspectives (see Bamberger et al., 2009; Jones et al., 2009; Patton, 2011; Stern et al., 2012; and Befani et al., 2014). Approaches that have become more widely used such as theory of change and realist approaches seek to identify the triggers that explain the effects from programs (Stern et al., 2012). Other approaches include contribution analysis that seeks to develop a reasonable explanation of causation, one that is developed after looking at alternative explanations for results and examining contributing factors beyond the program (Mayne, 2011); and participatory rural appraisal, which try to find out beneficiaries perceptions of causation (Bamberger et al., 2009). These approaches are interested in processes of implementation, in addition to impact, as assessors seek to understand the process of implementation and how this effected outcomes and impact. Yet, the thinking behind such approaches is yet to be broadly adopted as standard practice in monitoring development initiatives. It is the status of current monitoring practices within development and the potential for strengthening it in the future that is the topic in the next section of this chapter.

PART 3 – THE STATUS OF MONITORING AND ITS FUTURE

The rise of interest in impact and impact assessment is not necessarily the core reason for a devaluing of monitoring. Its status in the eyes of donors, evaluators, or implementers is not always high. One result of this is far less development of monitoring theory and practice than has occurred in relation to evaluation and impact assessment (Pritchett et al., 2012; Guijt, 2008). Monitoring processes have remained donor-centered and focused on inputs and compliance to provide donors with a level of comfort that things are going okay. The program manager's job remains to, simply, track the inputs and completion of activities, ensure that the project continues to deliver what it was designed to do and on time, and provide assessors with information to answer their assessment questions, to verify facts and in some cases respond to the report findings and recommendations. There is a consistent and persistent challenge to influence program managers and teams that monitoring has purposes and uses related to development effectiveness, and beyond meeting donor compliance requirements. Processes that over-emphasize compliance and "authorization" limit program managers' ability to manage programs flexibility (Pritchett et al., 2012) and may decrease their motivation to try. Often the incentives to comply with donor requirements are greater than the incentives to be effective (Morton, 2010).

Monitoring, with its focus on developing indicators and regular and systematic collecting, collating, analyzing, and reporting of data, has often been considered "conceptually weak and simplistic," by evaluators or assessors (Nielsen and Hunter, 2013). Critics of monitoring have focused on a number of factors. This includes the use and misuse of monitoring information; the perverse incentives that monitoring may create; the limited use of rigorous research methods; ad-hoc measurement of indicators; and lastly the lack of independence of those undertaking the monitoring (Nielsen and Hunter, 2013; Hunter and Neilsen, 2013). There are also differing views about whether analysis is part of the monitoring process or should be restricted to assessments (Guijt, 2008). This lack of analysis of the data collected could be one reason for the low priority also given by implementers, who see it as another bureaucratic task to tick off along with cross-cutting issues like gender, sustainability, and anticorruption (Guijt, 2008; Pritchett et al., 2012; ALNAP, 2003). ALNAP (2003, p. 127) describes monitoring as failing to "build meaningful and continuous information exchanges between stakeholders" and as a result does not contribute to ongoing learning. However, similar criticisms have also been made in relation to other performance management activities. Several authors (such as Datta, 2006; Picciotto, 2008; and HummelBrunner and Jones, 2013) argue that performance management activities, including evaluation, have not yet adapted adequately to deal with complexity because development planning and management, more broadly, has not adapted sufficiently to deal with risk and uncertainty and there remains an underlying assumption of linear relationships.

The low value given to monitoring, and its limited relevance to program implementers, has implications for impact assessment. Firstly, in the context of complex development contexts the lack of attention given to the monitoring of change processes and their short- and medium-term effectiveness, beyond the conventional input and output focus, means that it is possible that impact will not materialize since adjustments to program implementation are not being made. Rather than plans based on extensive ex-ante analysis (as may be undertaken in the case of ex-ante impact assessments), plans are more likely to be based on an initial analysis and as more information becomes available or is generated and understanding of the context, change processes and opportunities then plans are adapted along the way (HummelBrunner and Jones, 2013). Implementing organizations, therefore, require a large amount of creativity to manage implementation issues and challenges and to do the best they can with their funding (Pritchett et al., 2012). The initial program design is often only the starting place. During implementation, understanding of problems, what strategies to use to address problems, and expected outcomes often change are important issues to be considered. Planning and management "should be sufficiently adaptive to incorporate new developments, challenges and opportunities" and hence the implementation team should "provide the necessary guidance and leadership, communicating a vision of change around which responses can emerge" (HummelBrunner and Jones, 2013, p. 4). The DDD group (2014) advocates that there should be a blurring of the lines between design and implementation by way of short feedback loops, action and reflection, and managing risks by placing "small bets"; that might be expanded or dropped depending on what happens. This way of working differs from approaches based on applying "international best practice" and "supplying solutions" which assume, often implicitly, that the answer is already known to one where implementers need to admit that the solution is not known in advance (Easterly, 2006). Conventional performance management activities may not support these ways of working. Rather, to manage risks and "small bets," development managers need real-time, or close to real-time, information that draws on multiple forms of evaluative knowledge rather than relying on single studies to support decision-making processes (Rist, 2011; Stame, 2011). The argument is that these adaptive practices give programs a better chance of achieving impacts than previously, and in doing so give the impact assessors something to assess.

Secondly, many assessments have been commissioned only to conclude it was impossible to determine their impact due to unclear objectives, performance indicators, and monitoring data (Ramalingam, 2013). Consequently, these are missed opportunities. If monitoring was improved then it could provide impact assessment with data and insights. This could be achieved in a variety of ways. For instance, if monitoring was viewed as forward looking, rather than only backward-looking and focused on accountability, it could be used to identify ways of improving the efficiency, effectiveness, and sustainability of programs using small feedback loops (Hunter and Nielsen, 2013; Saunders, 2012; and Perrin, 2012). Monitoring could be used to document and measure multiple pathways on complex programs. This, in turn, could assist to better clarify how outcomes may be assessed as they become clearer during implementation, and help redefine what good performance may look like (Rogers, 2008). Additionally, priorities for impact assessment could be identified and subsequently what monitoring data were needed to support impact assessments (Perrin, 2012).

While monitoring may benefit impact assessment, the reverse is also possible. There exists a mutually beneficial relationship, "a two-way street" where the practices of each inform the other (Nielsen and Hunter, 2013, p. 121). Monitoring may lead to the development of specific evaluation and impact assessment questions or evaluations and impact assessments may identify regular information needs that are not currently collected by monitoring systems. Monitoring, evaluation, and impact assessment may ask different questions or complete different analysis but draw on the same data sources. Organizations or programs may also share monitoring, evaluation, and impact assessment data with managers and staff to support continuous improvement through access to information (Rist, 2011). Additionally, if effective monitoring systems are in place then impact assessments could validate information collected and analyzed through monitoring processes thereby giving greater credibility to the overall performance management processes, and potentially decreasing the cost of assessments (Kessler and Tanburn, 2014).

Lastly, while impact assessments undertaken near or at the end of a program may be useful for donors to make policy decisions, they are often not timely for supporting decision making processes regarding existing programs. Therefore, better quality monitoring could also provide funders with more timely information.

Therefore, there seems a need to redefine the definition or scope for monitoring on complex programs, one that provides real-time or near real-time quantitative and qualitative data and analysis on implementation processes as well as the short- and medium-term outcomes, and the program's contribution to these changes. The primary purpose is to support program managers and implementers to use in short-feedback cycles linked to decision making, which may result in adapting program activities or implementation approaches. Forward and reverse linkages between monitoring processes and products to evaluation and impact assessment should be made explicit from the beginning of a program to ensure that the relevant systems and capacities are put in place to maximize the potential benefit of each. It is at this point, that donors and implementers should agree on what is good enough evidence for monitoring, evaluation, and impact assessment. A critical aspect of this is being realistic about such constraints as contexts, logistics, resources, ethics and time understanding that there can be a significant difference between the ideal and on-the-ground realities of development programs.

PART 4 – EMERGING APPROACHES TO IMPROVE MONITORING

The discussion below highlights three recent approaches to improve the real-time information and analysis practices on complex programs. These are:

1. Developmental Evaluation;
2. The Donor Committee for Enterprise Development Results Measurement Standard; and
3. MeE (Monitoring, experiential learning, Evaluation).

None of the approaches call themselves monitoring approaches, but they have been selected because each blurs the lines between what is considered conventional monitoring, evaluation and impact assessment so that program implementers are actively engaged in regular reflection and analysis of results, not just administrative and quantitative data collection and reporting. Each demonstrates a clear recognition of complex development contexts and processes and the need for program managers and implementers to be using information for learning and adapting implementation in an ongoing effort to be more effective. Therefore, they fit the redefined scope of monitoring proposed above. Each approach has different origins. Two of the approaches, developmental evaluation and the results measurement standard, have been developed based on the expressed needs of implementers. Developmental evaluation was developed by an evaluator, Michael Quinn Patton, working with a North American organization. The results measurement standard was developed by the Donor Committee for Enterprise Development with substantial input from development consultants working on private sector development programs. The MeE, adding an additional learning process sitting between monitoring and evaluation, was developed by a group of academics.

The first approach examined is *developmental evaluation*, not to be confused with the evaluation of international development or development evaluation. Developmental evaluation seeks to support real-time, or near to real-time, feedback to program implementers to create a continuous development cycle of implement–learn–adapt–implement (Patton, 2011). The approach is not fixed, it is not based on specific methods, and measures and monitoring processes develop as a program goals emerge and the actual needs become more apparent (Dozois et al., 2010). The evaluator is not independent, but is part of the implementation team, either as an internal staff or an external consultant, and asks evaluative questions of team members, bringing thinking and data to reflections, discussions, and ongoing implementation. The approach obviously differs from conventional monitoring and evaluation as the evaluator has a key role in decision making and the direction of the program as well as increasing the team members' evaluative thinking, sense of ownership, and use of the data and analysis (Dozois et al., 2010). Patton (2011) developed the approach after program managers he was working with said that they did not see their program design as fixed and did not see the value in standard approaches to program evaluation. He is clear that the approach is not for every program, or for every phase of a program, but is suited to programs that are complex, involve innovations, and where it is difficult to plan.

The *Donor Committee for Enterprise Development Results Measurement Standard* (referred to here as the Standard) was developed in 2008 by a small group of private sector development practitioners and consultants, who believed that the performance management of private sector development programs needed improvement and good management is critical for good management (Kessler, 2014; Kessler and Tanburn, 2014). The Standard was not instigated by evaluators or M&E consultants. Since its conception there has been a growing number of programs using the Standard, with strong support by some donors. The Standard outlines criteria for designing and implementing a results measurement system (a term that is used by the developers to distinguish it from monitoring), from the development of results chains, or theories of change, through to assessing a program's contribution to changes. As such, it clouds distinctions between conventional monitoring and impact assessment by incorporating aspects from both, such as using indicators that may be more closely associated with monitoring, assessing outcomes, and sustainability that is often associated with evaluation and examining impact that is at the core of impact assessment. However, these activities are undertaken by the implementation team for the benefit of program managers who are managing complex programs.

The DCED Results Measurement Standard includes the option of having its implementation audited to increase its credibility. While the audit is normally paid for by the implementing program, donors could also pay for it directly if they were concerned about the independence of the auditors (Kessler and Tanburn, 2014). The audit differs from developmental evaluation's strategy to increase credibility, which focuses, principally, on applied good research practices to minimize potential biases and suggests that parallel information systems may need to be established. This aspect of the Standard may be attractive to those conducting impact assessments, since it provides some assurance about the quality of the system and its management. While the audit does not audit the data, this could be a role for assessors if it was felt to be necessary. If a program implements the Standard, the role of an external evaluator may differ to one that may include validation of baseline data, reviewing the quality of data used and reported, and providing an independent review of findings (Kessler and Tanburn, 2014).

The third approach was developed by academics in response to the growth in impact assessments using experimental methods. Pritchett et al. (2012) added a third component, an "e" or structured experiential learning activities, to the M&E that is used extensively in international development. This produces a "*MeE*" for complex programs or pilots. "(M)onitoring and impact (E)valuation is not conducive to learning" therefore "we introduce (e)xperiential learning, which is the process of disaggregating and analyzing existing data to draw intermediate lessons that can then be fed back into project design, over the course of the project cycle" (Pritchett et al., 2012, p. 1). The MeE approach aims to provide implementing organizations with sufficient monitoring information that will enable them to have real-time performance information to feed into the management decision making process regarding different project designs. Experiential learning is defined as "the process of disaggregating and analyzing data on inputs, activities, and outputs chosen to be collected by the project to draw intermediate lessons that can then be fed back into project design during the course of the project cycle" (p. 24). Pritchett et al. (2012) propose a more formal approach to the data collection and analysis based on the principles of experimentation, whereby a number of projects are established with different design variables that allow them to be tested and decisions made about whether individual projects should continue, be modified, or stopped. If designs change then the information collected on outputs and outcomes need to change accordingly. The authors propose that this approach allows for midimplementation adjustments rather than being constrained to a program, and performance management activities, designed according to a static model of implementation. Pritchett et al. (2012) are pragmatic, acknowledging that there are trade-offs between the integrity of the experiment and flexibility as donors may want reassurance that adaption for adaption sake is not occurring.

The above approaches are critical for development effectiveness, because each supports program managers and implementers to be actively engaged in regularly examining whether programs or individual interventions are on the path to outcomes and impact. This, therefore, potentially creates a situation where complex programs will achieve more than what they might otherwise do. These programs may be more likely to give those conducting impact assessment impacts to assess. If more robust analytical monitoring practices are embedded in program implementation, impact assessors may find more common ground and mutual understanding with program teams than might otherwise be. Such a situation could improve the development and implementation of better integrated and supporting performance management frameworks, or provide more opportunities for impact assessments to contribute to the development of monitoring systems and practices for existing programs, depending on the timing of the impact assessment or for future programs. Use of the approaches outlined above may also give impact assessors and donors increased confidence in program managers and implementers as implementation of each approach requires a higher commitment to rigorous thinking (as well as resources) and hence could decrease concerns about internal biases. To further build confidence with donors and external assessors, it would be worthwhile to ensure that changes to monitoring systems and processes are documented and justified.

Each approach generates more information and analysis than conventional monitoring and evaluation processes, and as such also provide opportunities for impact assessors to use this data to assess impact as well as to analyze how and why impacts occurred, or not, and therefore extends the usefulness of the impact assessment for future policy and programming decisions. If impact assessors were concerned about the quality of the data or biases arising from the internal nature of the data collection and analysis they could review the quality of the data collection and analysis systems, as included in the Results Measurement Standard, or check the reliability of the data and analysis.

CONCLUSION

The rise of impact assessment within international development has been associated with a narrow interpretation of impact assessment rigor, focusing on particular (experimental) methods and independence. It was argued that this limited interpretation has limited the effectiveness and value of impact assessment in assessing complex international development programs. Improving monitoring on complex programs is necessary if impact assessment is to make a more useful contribution to development effectiveness. Conventional monitoring, with its focus on inputs and activities and complying with donor information needs, and assessment practices (largely grounded in single *ex-ante* and *ex-post* studies) are not meeting the real information needs of program implementers managing complex programs. The increased focus and value given to impact assessment by donors has further devalued monitoring reinforcing that its primary role is to provide donors with some confidence that implementation is going okay and produce the expected things within established budget parameters. If monitoring is redefined to include more real time analysis and reflection and designed to inform program management and adaption, then the usefulness of monitoring for impact assessment increases as does the contribution that impact assessment may be able to make to stronger monitoring practices.

This chapter explored three new approaches to monitoring complex programs in a more iterative, reflective, and adaptive way. Each approach emphasizes the need for shorter feedback cycles, feeding information and analysis into program implementation. Reflection and analysis is a vital part of monitoring to enable program managers to make judgments about the worth of the activities and strategies they are pursuing and whether they are worthwhile or need to be changed. These questions need to be asked during implementation and not just in relation to an entire program at its end as tends to happen with impact assessments as currently applied in international development. Better impact assessment requires better data on processes and short- and medium-term changes that more robust, real-time monitoring, reflection, and analysis at the program level can provide.

The recent trend of increasing interest, from donors and the public, in whether development programs are effective and achieving positive impacts is welcomed. The increase in the numbers of impact assessments has partly addressed the impact analysis gap, as discussed in "Part 2 – the rise of impact assessment" section, yet the practice of research-based impact assessments based on a narrow range of methods limits the potential for impact assessments to contribute significantly to effective development. This chapter has argued that especially in light of the increasingly recognized complex nature of many development processes, more investment in monitoring in balance with that for impact assessment would make a far-reaching contribution to effective development.

Opportunities to improve the usefulness of impact assessment are apparent in the more recent discussions centering on using a broader set of methods, better understanding implementation processes, and subsequently a program's contribution to impact, and a more expansive understanding of rigor. However, the development and use of these approaches are in their infancy and this presents a challenge to improving impact assessment. In this space, strong proponents of a narrow definition of impact assessments may continue to have an undue influence in how impact assessment practice develops in international development. However, in this space there is also an option of ensuring that good practice monitoring is considered alongside efforts to improve impact assessments, that the link between the two is reconnected. Another challenge is pushing forward to get practice happening on the ground, and not to remain at an academic or theoretical level. In my experience, the examples outlined in "Part 4 – emerging approaches to improve monitoring" section do not illustrate the norm for monitoring, which largely remains donor-centered and compliance focused. Designing, implementing, monitoring, and evaluating complex programs using nonstandard approaches is hard work and a significant challenge to the way development has been done in the past. It requires funding and program management knowledge, skills, and attitudes that have tended not to be valued in development assistance and may present challenges for large well-established donor bureaucracies or the way that parts of the development industry are arranged, such as milestone payments to consultancy contracting companies. Above all it requires both donors and impact assessors to relinquish some of the control they may traditionally exercise in their roles. This requires a certain a level of trust between implementers and funders. To build this trust implementers can provide a greater degree of transparency with funding agencies.

REFERENCES

ALNAP, 2003. Annual Review 2003. Humanitarian action: Improving monitoring to enhance accountability and learning. London: ODI. Available from: <http://www.alnap.org/resource/5201>.

American Evaluation Association, 2003. Scientifically based evaluation methods – American Evaluation Association response to U.S. Department of Education. Available from: <http://www.eval.org/p/cm/ld/fid=83>.

Bamberger, M., Rugh, J., 2008. A framework for assessing the quality, conclusions validity and utility of evaluations. Paper presented at AEA conference, Baltimore 2007. Cited in Stern, E., Stame, N., Mayne, J., Forss, K., Davies, R., & Befani, B. (2012).

Bamberger, M., Rao, V., Woolcock, M., 2009. Using mixed methods in monitoring and evaluation: Experiences from international development. Brooks World Poverty Institute Working Paper 107. University of Manchester, Manchester.

Befani, B., Barnett, C., Stern, E., 2014. Introduction – Rethinking impact evaluation for development. In: IDS Bulletin, Vol. 45, No. 6 November 2014. Institute of Development Studies, University of Sussex.

Building State Capacity, 2014. The doing development differently manifesto. Available from: <http://buildingstatecapability.com/the-ddd-manifesto/>.

Datta, L.e, 2006. The practice of evaluation: Challenges and new directions. In: Shaw, Ian F., Greene, Jennifer C., Mark, Melvin M. (Eds.), The Sage Handbook of Evaluation. Sage Publications, London.

Dozois, E., Langlois, M., Blanchet-Cohen, N., 2010. A Practitioner's Guide to Developmental Evaluation. The J.W. McConnell Family Foundation, Quebec.

Easterly, W., 2006. The White Man's Burden: Why the West's efforts to aid the rest have done so much ill and so little good. Oxford University Press, Oxford.

European Evaluation Society (EES), 2007. EES Statement: The importance of a methodologically diverse approach to impact evaluation – specifically with respect to development aid and development interventions. EES Secretariat, Nijnerk.

Glouberman, S., Zimmerman, B., 2002. Complicated and complex systems: What would successful reform of medicare look like? Discussion Paper N. 8, Commission for the Future of Health Care in Canada, Ottawa.

Guijt, I., 2008. Seeking surprise: Rethinking monitoring for collective learning in rural resource management. Communication Studies. Wageningen, Wageningen University. PhD.

HummelBrunner, R., Jones, H., 2013. A guide for planning and strategy development in the face of complexity, ODI Briefing Note, March 2013, Overseas Development Institute, UK. Available from: <http://www.odi.org/sites/odi.org.uk/files/odi-assets/publications-opinion-files/8287.pdf>.

Hunter, D.E.K., Nielsen, S.B., 2013. Performance management and evaluation: Exploring complementarities. Nielsen, S.B., Hunter, D.E.K. (Eds.), Performance management and evaluation. New directions for evaluation, 137, pp. 7–17.

Jones, N., Jones, H., Steer, L., Datta, A., 2009. Improving impact evaluation production and use. Working Paper 300, Overseas Development Institute, London.

Kessler, A. (Ed.), 2014. The 2014 reader on results measurement: Current thinking on the DCED Standard. Cambridge: The Donor Committee for Enterprise Development. Available from: <http://www.enterprise-development.org/page/download?id=2367>.

Kessler, A., Tanburn, J., 2014. Why Evaluations Fail: The Importance of Good Monitoring. The Donor Committee for Enterprise Development, Cambridge.

Kusek, J., Rist, R., 2004. Ten steps to a results-based monitoring and evaluation system. A handbook for practitioners. World Bank, Washington, DC.

Mackay, R., Horton, D., 2003. Expanding the use of impact assessment and evaluation in agricultural research and development. Agric. Syst. 78, 143–165.

Mayne, J., 2007. Challenges to implementing results-based management. Evaluation 13 (1), 87–109.

Mayne, J., 2011. Independence in evaluation and the role of culture. Inteval Evaluation Notes, Evaluation Notes 2011-1 - 1 -. Available from: <http://www.inteval-group.org/IMG/ckfinder/files/Inteval%20Notes%202011-1.PDF>.

Morton, J., 2010. Why we will never learn: A political economy of aid effectiveness. Available from: <http://www.jfmorton.co.uk/pdfs/Why%20We%20Will%20Never%20Learn.pdf>.

Nielsen, S.B., Hunter, D.E.K., 2013. Challenges to and forms of complementarity between performance management and evaluation. Nielsen, S.B., Hunter, D.E.K. (Eds.), Performance management and evaluation. New directions for evaluation, 137, pp. 115–123.

OECD, 2002. Glossary of Key Terms in Evaluation and Results Based Management. The OECD Development Assistance Committee (DAC) Working Party on Aid Evaluation, Paris.

O'Flynn, M., 2010. Impact assessment: Understanding and assessing our contributions to change. M&E Paper 7. Oxford: INTRAC. Available from: <http://www.intrac.org/data/fi les/resources/695/Impact-Assessment-Understanding-and-Assessing-our-Contributions-to-Change.pdf.>.

Patton, M.Q., 1997. Utilization Focused Evaluation. The new century text. Sage Publication Saint Paul, MN.

Patton, M.Q., 2011. Developmental Evaluation: Applying Complexity Concepts to Enhance Innovation and Use. The Guildford Press, New York, NY.

Patton, M.Q., 2012. Hot issues on the M&E agenda. Report from an Expert Seminar. Centre of Development Innovation, 23 March 2012.

Perrin, B., 2012. Linking monitoring and evaluation to impact evaluation. Impact Evaluation Notes, No. 2, April 2012. InterAction and Rockefeller Foundation. Available from: <www. Interaction.org/impact-evaluation-notes>.

Picciotto, R., 2008. The new challenges of development evaluation. Evaluating the complex – A NORAD Evaluation Conference. Oslo, 29–30 May 2008.

Pritchett, L., Samji, S., Hammer, 2012. It's all about MeE: Using structured experiential learning ('e') to crawl the design space. Working Paper No. 2012/104. UNU-WIDER, Helsinki.

Ramalingam, B., 2013. Aid on the Edge of Chaos: Rethinking International Cooperation in a Complex World, first ed. Oxford University Press, Oxford.

Rist, R., 2011. The "E" in monitoring and evaluation – Using evaluative knowledge to support a results based management system. In: Rist, R., Stame, N. (Eds.), From Studies to Streams: Managing Evaluative Systems. Comparative Policy Evaluation: Volume XII. Transaction Publishers, New Jersey, NJ.

Rogers, P., 2008. Using programme theory to evaluate complicated and complex aspects of interventions. Evaluation 14 (1), 29–48.

Sanderson, I., 2000. Evaluation in complex policy settings. Evaluation 6 (4), 433–454.

Sanderson, I., 2010. Is it 'What Works' that Matters? Evaluation and Evidence-Based Policy-making. Research Papers in Education 18 (4), 331–345.

Saunders, M., 2012. The use and usability of evaluation outputs: A social practice approach. Evaluation 18, 421.

Stame, N., 2011. Introduction Streams of Evaluative Knowledge. In: Rist, R., Stame, N. (Eds.), From Studies to Streams: Managing Evaluative Systems. Comparative Policy Evaluation: Volume XII. Transaction Publishers, New Jersey, NJ.

Stephenson, K., 2010. Results-based management. In: Anderson, G. (Ed.), Shaping International Evaluation A 30-Year Journey. Universalia Management Group, Montreal and Ottawa.

Stern, E., Stame, N., Mayne, J., Forss, K., Davies, R., Befani, B., 2012. Broadening the range of designs and methods of impact evaluations. Working Paper 38. Department for International Development, London.

White, H., 2010. A contribution to current debates in impact evaluation. Evaluation 16 (2), 153–164.

IMPACT ASSESSMENT IN PRACTICE: CASE STUDIES FROM SAVE THE CHILDREN PROGRAMS IN LAO PDR AND AFGHANISTAN

14

Veronica Bell and Yasamin Alttahir

Save the Children Australia, Australia

CHAPTER OUTLINE

INTRODUCTION

This chapter discusses Save the Children's organizational approach to measuring and demonstrating the results we are achieving to save and improve children's lives. This will be illustrated through two particular case studies that have been purposefully selected to demonstrate our experiences in two highly contrasting contexts and over two very different implementation periods. The case studies explore the particular strategies Save the Children has adopted to collect, analyze, and utilize evidence to inform program delivery and measure program results; reflect on how successful these have been; and analyze the factors that have enabled and constrained assessment of program progress and ultimate impact. While the case studies focus on the specific program operating contexts, the findings have broader relevance for Save the Children's overall programming.

SAVE THE CHILDREN AUSTRALIA

Save the Children Australia is one of 30 members of Save the Children International, the world's leading independent organization for children. Globally, Save the Children supports children in 124 countries around the world. The principles, rights, and obligations set out in the United Nations Convention on the Rights of the Child (United Nations Convention on the Rights of the Child, 1989) provide a fundamental framework for the work that Save the Children carries out globally. Our vision, mission, values, and organizational theory of change all reinforce this. We are committed to developing and supporting effective implementation of programs and policies that deliver positive outcomes and the fulfillment of all children's rights, and leveraging our knowledge to catalyze sustainable impact at scale. Sustainable impact at scale is about working with and inspiring others to change how pivotal institutions set policies, allocate resources, and deliver quality services that make long-term measurable improvements in the lives of children, including the most deprived. To achieve this, it is vital that we can clearly articulate, demonstrate, and document the results we are achieving to save and improve children's lives.

SAVE THE CHILDREN'S GLOBAL THEORY OF CHANGE

The members of Save the Children International work together to share expertise, coordinate activities, and pool resources, which means we can extend our reach and impact for children. A set of global initiatives underpins and drives our work to ensure that we are delivering the best outcomes for children's education, health, and child protection and to assist children in emergencies.

Save the Children has developed a global Theory of Change as a framework to reflect on how we can have the greatest impact on children's lives (Fig. 14.1). The Theory of Change was introduced as part of our 2010–2015 global strategy (Save the Children, 2009) and is applied to all our programs. It offers the organization guidance when examining options for interventions and program development, and it helps in conversations with partners and donors to consistently explain our approach.

Save the Children's Theory of Change is designed to help country programs reflect on their strategic priorities and determine what innovative solutions that creatively meet the needs of children are being implemented in that program. It asks how programs are investigating and documenting their results to construct a base of solid evidence to generate lessons learned and good practices to contribute toward

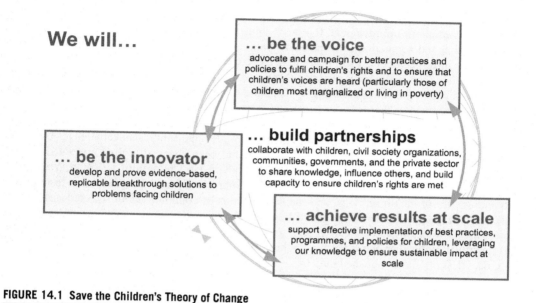

FIGURE 14.1 Save the Children's Theory of Change

the improvement of program implementation and the achievement of results at scale. Not everything we do has to be innovative. Impact at scale is often achieved by promoting well-established, tried, and tested approaches. But we need to document our results to know what is and what is not working and act upon that information. The Theory of Change also asks programs to reflect on the extent to which advocacy objectives are included in their interventions, and how programs are tracking these and contributing evidence to relevant policy dialog. Robust evidence is critical to influencing government policy makers and civil society organizations who have the ability to meet the needs of children or advocate on their behalf. Central to Save the Children's Theory of Change is building partnerships. We need to continuously ask ourselves if we are working with the right partners to achieve results at scale. Which partners can deliver at scale?; who can help us build our evidence base?; who can enhance our credibility for advocacy? We also need to consider what support do our partners need to help us achieve results at scale together and examine if we are working effectively with them to realize this.

MEASURING OUR RESULTS

Save the Children's Monitoring, Evaluation, Accountability and Learning (MEAL) approach is designed to help us measure and demonstrate our strategic impact; be accountable to ourselves, children, donors, and partners; and ensure and increase the quality of our work. MEAL is a key part of realizing our Theory of Change. It aims to define a consistent level of quality for programs through the development of quality benchmarks; enhance accountability to children and their communities by creating a platform to give feedback on our performance; and instill a culture of learning across the organization to support our ambition to become a recognized knowledge hub for what works for children and how to take those interventions to scale.

The MEAL approach emphasizes the collection and use of data to support decision-making, accountability, and continuous improvement. It is an ongoing process throughout the life of a project with a focus on reflection and adaptation in response to findings. If applied well, MEAL enables country programs to make informed decisions in order to achieve the greatest impact for children, their families, and communities. The challenge is ensuring that project teams are collecting the most relevant data to assess change, and that they have the capacity – and the necessary systems and support – to analyze, reflect on, and utilize the data that is being generated.

The following case studies demonstrate Save the Children's approach to measuring our results in two highly contrasting contexts. The case studies present unique opportunities and challenges but there are also shared lessons across the two. Save the Children has been engaged in the Lao PDR Primary Healthcare Program for more than 20 years whilst the Afghanistan Children of Uruzgan Program is a 4-year program that commenced in 2011. The Laos Primary Healthcare Program aims to improve access to and quality of health services, and the health status of communities in selected districts in northern Laos. The purpose of the Children of Uruzgan Program is to improve access to, quality of and demand for basic health and education services in the seven districts of Uruzgan Province. Both programs have well-defined frameworks for tracking and documenting their results, tailored to their specific project designs and established targets.

PRIMARY HEALTH CARE PROGRAM, SAYABOURY AND LUANG PRABANG PROVINCES, LAO PDR
BACKGROUND

Save the Children in partnership with the Lao PDR Ministry of Health began implementing a comprehensive primary health care program in two districts of Sayaboury Province in 1992. Over a period of 12 years, the program expanded into a province-wide program, reaching all 11 districts in the province. In 2007, Save the Children was invited by the Ministry of Health to expand the program into the neighboring Luang Prabang Province where it is currently being implemented in five districts.

The Save the Children primary health care model promotes a health systems approach, supporting provincial and district level government health services to deliver a package of comprehensive primary health care, placing priority on maternal and child health, with the objective of increasing access to health services and improving the overall quality of care.

The program model comprises four phases through which target districts are intended to transition:

- *Intensive Phase*: Collection of baseline data and completion of detailed needs assessments to understand the health situation in target districts. There is significant investment in infrastructure construction at district and subdistrict levels and formation of provincial and district health management teams during this phase. Technical training starts immediately and integrated outreach mobile clinics to reach remote villages commence.
- *Strengthening Phase*: Focus on ensuring provincial and district health management teams are functioning well and building competency in data collection, analysis, interpretation, and utilization for health program planning. Advanced technical and management training is provided for relevant health staff, focusing on increasing understanding of the local health situation and developing the capacity of health staff to improve the quality and coverage of services to meet the

needs of communities. Integrated outreach mobile clinics and community health promotion days are conducted on a regular basis to all villages in the district to increase immunization, antenatal care, and other key health indicators.

- *Consolidation Phase*: Focus on quality improvement, utilizing data to inform health service delivery planning and decision-making. Refresher training for frontline health staff and deepening health planning and management skills.
- *Recurrent Funding Phase*: Focus on monitoring results and key indicators, continued strengthening of quality of service provision, and management strengthening. This phase also envisages a transition from recurrent external funding from Save the Children to the allocation of recurrent local (government) funding to sustain service delivery. (Note: this latter phase has not yet been fully achieved in any of the districts.)

A study commissioned by Save the Children in 2014 found that the timeframe for transitioning through the multiphase model to reach the recurrent funding phase is approximately 8 years (Save the Children, 2014). All activities in the Save the Children primary healthcare program are delivered by government staff at either provincial, district, or village levels. In remote areas, community volunteers work as health volunteers and traditional birth attendants. The Save the Children staff provides training, advice, and mentoring for senior health managers, and oversee quality aspects such as construction and provision of equipment.

UNDERSTANDING AND WORKING WITHIN LOCAL SYSTEMS

The program has developed an intensive monitoring and evaluation (M&E) framework to guide the management, monitoring, and evaluation of the program. The M&E framework, developed in collaboration between District and Provincial Health Managers and Save the Children, is designed to strengthen the capacity of Ministry of Health staff at district and provincial levels to collect, analyze, and utilize data to inform primary health care decision making, as well as for reporting on the results of the program over time. The M&E approach includes checklists for monitoring quality of care, tools for monitoring health systems functions, investigation reports, and periodic household cluster surveys. Importantly, aligned with the focus on health systems strengthening, routine reports from the government Health Information System (HIS) form part of the core M&E process. This ensures the program is supporting the improvement of government data-collection systems so they function as an effective management tool for local health managers, rather than simply creating parallel systems designed to meet external donor reporting needs. The program level M&E framework was designed before Save the Children adopted the MEAL approach. Nevertheless, the framework is consistent with MEAL. Key performance indicators related to health outcomes, health services, and health management have been established and progress against these is examined in detail at quarterly program management meetings. Findings are discussed between the Provincial and District Health Managers and Save the Children staff and lessons used to inform the next quarter work plan. Results are also reported on a six-monthly basis by the Provincial Health Departments. This reinforces a cycle of continuous analysis, reflection, and improvement.

A CONTEXTUALLY RELEVANT APPROACH TO MEASURING RESULTS

Save the Children has worked to systematically strength the ability of the provincial and district health services to monitor themselves. There is a concerted focus on ensuring that data is not simply collected for upward accountability purposes; its primary purpose is to improve all aspects of health service planning, delivery, and oversight. The quality of care checklists has been designed to enable health staff to improve quality of care at all health facilities, as well as improving the routine monitoring of the health service. In a context where many staff have had limited formal training, the checklists also support supervisors to provide appropriate clinical supervision.

A standard tool has been developed for periodic surveys designed to provide impact level data. Save the Children worked with the Centre for International Health at the Burnet Institute, Melbourne to adapt and test the World Health Organization (WHO) standard household cluster survey tool. Since 1999, the survey has been used as the baseline when the program expands into new districts and is repeated at 3–4 year intervals, giving a consistent and reliable set of data for tracking impact progress. The methodology is a two-stage, cluster sample of 600 households in 30 clusters. Members of the District Health Department are trained as enumerators, and the report findings form the basis of district level primary health care planning. The surveys are a supplement to the annual government HIS data and useful to both Save the Children and the Provincial and District Health Managers to regularly assess longer term progress.

In the four northern districts of Sayaboury Province, the survey has been utilized to track results over a 10-year period, commencing with a baseline survey in 1999, follow-up surveys in 2001 and 2004 to assess program progress, and a fourth survey in 2009 intended to inform a scaled-down package of support as part of the phase-out strategy for the program. The results from these surveys have enabled Save the Children and the partner Provincial and District Health Departments to refine the primary health care model into the clearly defined multiphase intervention strategy outlined above. Whilst the model will always require some level of contextualization to each district, the overall framework is grounded in clear evidence drawn from the impact level data generated from these surveys.

BUILDING THE EVIDENCE BASE – MAKING THE CASE FOR SCALE-UP

In 2014, with funding from the Australian Department of Foreign Affairs and Trade, Save the Children undertook a study to look not only at the impact of the primary health care model but also the costs associated with its delivery (Save the Children, 2014). The purpose of the study was to examine if the Save the Children model is of reasonable cost for its impact and to apply the related evidence for further discussion to strengthen primary health care in the context of the Lao PDR Health Sector Reform to 2025. The Health Sector Reform aims to introduce a systematic approach to address public health issues and to achieve a health sector common goal: affordable, reliable, and accessible health services to all. Save the Children set out to examine the value for the investment of its primary healthcare model. Whilst there had been many programmatic evaluations conducted and the effectiveness of the model was well-documented in terms of health impacts, examining the cost of the model was a new level of assessment. The primary audience for this study was the Lao PDR Ministry of Health at national, provincial and district levels, and other key health development partners in Laos.

The study found that the total estimated cost of the Save the Children primary health care model for a district of 30,000 people is USD $1,557,900 over an 8-year period. This amounts to USD $6.49 per capita per year over the course of the entire multiphase Save the Children primary health care intervention. The study found that Save the Children costs are in line with basic packages of health services in various countries and relative to proposed primary health care spending estimates in the health economics literature (Blaakman et al., 2013a; Blaakman et al., 2013b; Bowie and Mwase, 2011;

Indicator	Sayaboury Ranking Among Lao PDR Provinces	Actual Indicator	Source
Fertility Rate	2nd Lowest	2.2%	LSIS/2012
Use of Contraception	Highest	69.8%	LSIS/2012
Antenatal Care Received	2nd Highest	78.6%	LSIS/2012
Antenatal Care 4+ visits	2nd Highest	62.5%	LSIS/2012
Assisted Delivery	5th Highest	44.0%	LSIS/2012
Percent of Children Vaccinated	Highest	79.0%	LSIC/2012
Percent of Children Sleeping Under Mosquito Nets	2nd Highest	94.70%	LSIS/2012
Nutritional Status of Children <2SD (Weight for Age)	6th Lowest	23.2%	LSIS/2012
Child Mortality (<5)	3rd Lowest	65/1000	LSIS/2012

FIGURE 14.2 Sayaboury Ranking Among Lao PDR Provinces,
Laos Social Indicator Survey, 2012

Drummond and Mills, 1987). Health monitoring data from the two program provinces, including HIS data and findings from the periodic household surveys mentioned above, confirm that the program is addressing identified needs and is clearly relevant. In a national survey conducted in 2012 (Laos Social Indicator Survey, 2012), Sayaboury Province ranked impressively for key primary health care indicators (Fig. 14.2). Given the level of investment in the target areas in the two provinces as reflected in the proportion of Save the Children primary health care spending to overall district primary health care spending, the study found it is a reasonable conclusion that Save the Children has made a significant contribution to the gains in maternal and child health in the target provinces – and to the achievement of Millennium Development Goals (MDG) 4 and 5 in Sayaboury Province.

Aligned with Save the Children's Theory of Change, the program has built a solid evidence base that it now needs to leverage to influence broader policy change. Strong and effective partnerships have been established at provincial and district levels but if the program is to catalyze impact at scale, it needs to be adopted at the national level. Within the context of the Health Sector Reform to 2025, the volume of evidence generated from this program provides the Government of Lao PDR, Save the Children and the provincial management teams of Sayaboury and Luang Prabang Provincial Health Departments with an opportunity to identify ways to integrate these findings into broader health sector reform and development in the country.

THE IMPORTANCE OF TIME

A continuous 22-year engagement in an individual program is relatively uncommon in the international development sector. One of the major benefits of this ongoing engagement is that Save the Children has been able to continuously refine the intervention model so that health gains are being realized in a shorter timeframe in the newer districts we are partnering with. We have been able to develop, trial, and refine standard tools to assess the impact of the model, and the strong program management mechanisms that have been put in place at provincial and district levels have ensured that these tools are embedded in the overall approach. Because of the duration of the program, and the comprehensive implementation approach it has adopted, Save the Children has also been able to draw from relevant and accessible national survey data to assess the impact the program is achieving.

The longevity of Save the Children's engagement in this program, and the systematic approach to routine monitoring and periodic evaluation of results which is embedded in the model, have enabled us to take a different approach to assessing impact than is possible in the more common 3–5 year project cycle period – namely contribution to the achievement of international MDG targets. In addition, the costing study conducted in 2014 has provided valuable economic data to back up the programmatic results. This program has enabled Save the Children to demonstrate the correlation between sustained investment and the realization of sustainable change.

CHILDREN OF URUZGAN PROGRAM, URUZGAN PROVINCE, AFGHANISTAN
BACKGROUND

The Children of Uruzgan (CoU) Program is Save the Children Australia's flagship program in Afghanistan. Funded by the Australian Department of Foreign Affairs and Trade (DFAT) (budget: AUD $35.7 m), CoU is one of the most ambitious development programs ever undertaken by an Australian NGO. The program aims to reach an estimated 300,000 beneficiaries over the 4-year implementation period, with a particular focus on women and girls, ethnic minorities, and those in remote and under-serviced communities.

In addition to the focus on health and education outcomes for communities in the region, the program also aims to instigate policy change at the national level through research and pilot studies conducted to demonstrate good practice and effective methodology. CoU commenced in December 2011 and programming activities concluded in September 2015.

Uruzgan is one of the poorest and most insecure provinces in Afghanistan. Every year an estimated 300 mothers and more than 3,000 children under the age of five die. Eight out of 10 children do not go to school. Only 8% of all men and 0.3% of women can read and write. It is estimated that nine out of 10 women in Uruzgan deliver at home without skilled assistance (Mayhew et al., 2008). Children are more prone to illness due to the high rate of malnutrition that leaves them stunted and weakened, and the lack of knowledge about good hygiene practices and healthy nutrition exacerbates this (Levitt, 2011). Less than half of all children are immunized against common preventable diseases such as measles, diphtheria, and whooping cough (Ikram et al., 2014).

Relative to other provinces, Uruzgan has historically been remote, poor, rural, minimally educated, conservative, and violent, even by Afghan standards. It is located in the center of the country, bordering Day Kundi to the north, Kandahar to the south, Helmand to the west, and Zabul and Ghazni to the east. The province is one of the most geographically dispersed in the country, placing much of the population in areas of extreme remoteness and poverty with little access to essential services such as basic infrastructure, running water, and power. The geography of the province is mountainous, with poorly established roads. The political and military situation in the province is highly insecure.

Politically and tribally, Uruzgan is part of "greater Kandahar" and the origin of many of the Taliban's original leaders (Fishstein, 2012). Uruzgan presents an enormously challenging operating environment for delivering and monitoring development work. Insecurity restricts organizational mobility and creates an imbalance of program coverage across the province. Development activities have mostly preferenced the provincial capital of Tirin Kot and neighboring districts considered relatively safe and accessible (Save the Children, 2012). Conflict sensitivity is vital in such a dynamic context to ensure that program interventions do not exacerbate an already volatile situation.

UNDERSTANDING AND WORKING WITHIN LOCAL SYSTEMS

CoU operates in all seven districts of the province and is supporting service delivery in both government and nongovernment controlled areas. Save the Children has managed to successfully operate in this challenging environment through a pragmatic approach grounded in forging a diverse set of relationships with different government ministries, key local figureheads including the Provincial Governor and other influential local leaders, other international nongovernment organizations (INGOs), local nongovernment organizations (NGOs), local communities, Shuras (community meetings), and religious leaders. Save the Children conducts in-depth consultation with local elders, community leaders, and relevant government departments before any program intervention is undertaken. This approach has been vital to building trust between Save the Children and the communities where the program is being implemented. Community mobilization is undertaken at an appropriate pace in each location to ensure adequate support is gained among all key stakeholders before any activities commence. Community mobilizers are drawn from their respective communities, ensuring they have a good understanding of the local context and dynamics and they are accepted by the community. Community mobilization teams comprising two members, one female and one male, have been established in target districts to facilitate consultation beyond just the male leaders of the community and to start to engage female community members in community decision-making processes.

The national health-focused NGOs CoU partners with: Afghan Health and Development Services (AHDS), Afghan Centre for Training and Development (ACTD), and the Humanitarian Assistance, and Development Association for Afghanistan (HADAAF) have a long presence in Uruzgan province and their relationships with communities have enabled Save the Children and CoU to access more remote and insecure regions. In 2014, Save the Children established a partnership with the Welfare Association for the Development of Afghanistan (WADAN) to take over delivery of CoU education programming as part of the program transition strategy.

A CONTEXTUALLY RELEVANT APPROACH TO MEASURING RESULTS

All CoU program activities are undertaken in coordination and consultation with the Ministry of Education and Ministry of Public Health at both the national and provincial level, as well as local NGO partners. Similar to the Laos primary health care program, and in line with Save the Children's MEAL approach and the setting of quality benchmarks, CoU has developed a program-specific comprehensive Performance Monitoring and Evaluation Plan (PMEP) that provides a framework for routine monitoring and periodic evaluation of program interventions. The PMEP is designed to document the program's progress toward achieving its established targets; allow for continuous feedback between Save the Children, program partners and beneficiaries; and promote reflection on lessons learned to inform forward planning, resource allocation, and progress assessment.

To continually improve the quality and effectiveness of CoU program interventions – and to enhance the potential for scale up – Save the Children has involved program staff, partners, representatives from government ministries, religious and community leaders, and community members in program monitoring and evaluation activities. This has been vitally important to build a level of trust and support for the program, to foster local ownership, and to ensure that definitions of success, and strategies for achieving it, are locally relevant.

Monitoring represents one of the biggest challenges for Save the Children in Uruzgan, both in relation to the ability to obtain important management information but also to validate that data. This has made it particularly challenging to look beyond outputs and to assess changes. The program has had to adopt a pragmatic approach to monitoring in response to the limited access to many of the locations where activities are being implemented, with much of the monitoring needing to be done through remote systems. There is a significant reliance on staff who are located within community, selected because they are able to reside and work in a community because they are from that area. Information is conveyed by these program staff to Save the Children's provincial office in Tirin Kot via mobile phone or brought there periodically when staff or partners are able to travel. It is then compiled into the central data management system. There is also a heavy reliance on community leaders and Shuras to gather information on program activities and achievements.

There are undoubtedly challenges associated with remote monitoring systems. They place a heavy reliance on particular individuals and in challenging social contexts such as Uruzgan, the voices of women and other minority groups can be largely excluded from the process. There are also issues with ensuring accuracy of information, even of simple checklists, due to the often limited capacity and understanding of the community members collecting the data. CoU has tried to address these challenges through various approaches including the use of pictorial tools to facilitate monitoring in areas where there is low literacy and understanding of complex information. Simple monitoring checklists have also been developed and the program has prioritized the provision of adequate training for staff and volunteers who are involved in the program. Emphasis has been placed on the local recruitment of dedicated monitoring and evaluation staff wherever possible. The engagement of female community members in the community mobilization teams has been a deliberate strategy to try and engage female community members, give them a greater voice in the program, and ensure they also enjoy program benefits.

In order to assess program effectiveness, there have been a series of assessments and case studies conducted throughout the life of the program to measure whether the program outputs are resulting in any demonstrable changes for the communities and individuals involved. As noted above, it is not feasible to have large teams of external actors operating in Uruzgan Province. Assessments have therefore been designed utilizing where possible existing tools developed for low-resource environments and that can be conducted by local staff as long as they are provided appropriate training.

BUILDING THE EVIDENCE BASE – MAKING THE CASE FOR SCALE-UP

The assessments and case studies conducted have enabled a more in-depth examination of key aspects of the program and the findings have been used to inform program planning, make adjustments where necessary, and most importantly to promote what is working to provincial and national level stakeholders in order to influence broader social and policy change. One example of this is a reading assessment conducted in 2014 in CoU-supported community-based education (CBE) classes. Baseline and endline assessments of the reading skills of CBE students were conducted in June and November 2014, respectively using a tool modeled on the Annual Status of Education Report (ASER) methodology developed by the Indian NGO Pratham and with text based on Grade 2 and Grade 3 Pashto textbooks. The results showed a clear improvement in the reading ability of the students over the 5 months with 91% of Grade

3 students demonstrating established literacy skills in the endline survey. It is a reasonable conclusion that this improvement is attributable to the quality of the learning environment and enhanced skills of the teachers who have been trained and supported through CoU.

Save the Children needs robust evidence to support the efficacy of program interventions if we want to engage meaningfully in broader policy discussions. This pertains to all of our global programming. In this specific case, the ultimate impacts of the improved literacy of these CoU-supported students are yet to be seen but it is well accepted that education is critical to reducing poverty and inequality. For girls in particular, who in 2014 made up approximately 25% of all CoU-supported CBE students, it has been shown that with even a few years of primary education, women have better economic prospects, have fewer and healthier children, and are more likely to ensure that their own children go to school (OECD, 2010). In a program with a limited timeframe, assumptions often have to be made on the potential for ultimate impact. There is a wealth of literature we can draw from to support our investment in CBE, and the immediate outcomes of the CoU CBE intervention provide a solid evidence-base for Save the Children to engage with relevant government and civil society stakeholders on the importance of education for all children, and to leverage their support in order to achieve our goal of sustainable impact at scale.

Another key area of assessment for CoU has been to closely track education and health service utilization in the program districts. Utilization can be a proxy indicator for quality of services. In Uruzgan it is also an important indication of acceptance of services, a critical factor for the sustainability of program benefits beyond the life of CoU. Health service provision has been less controversial in Uruzgan than education, where the program has had to deal with entrenched beliefs about girls and education.

Program data demonstrates that CoU has increased access to health services by expanding services to underserved areas through the establishment of health sub-centers and mobile health teams, through training increasing numbers of health workers including establishing a school for midwifery in Tirin Kot, and by training community health workers. In addition, the program supports private clinics, predominantly situated in remote or insecure areas. In the education sector, CoU supports early childhood development (ECD) and CBE classes, improved educational infrastructure and governance, and enhanced teaching capacity including increasing the number of female teachers in the education workforce.

The PMEP has closely tracked trends in utilization, paying particular attention to sex disaggregation of data in order to assess the extent to which women and girls are benefiting. Assessment data found that women and girls benefited from 62% of the health services provided by CoU during 2014 but there continues to be a bias in favor of boys in education programming, with boys making up 76% of CBE students. In addition to trying to increase access to health and education services by training more women for professional roles, the program has also worked with religious leaders to encourage demand. Tracking of utilization data is backed up with qualitative analysis from the trainees themselves and the religious leaders regarding their experiences, and with program beneficiaries to assess their satisfaction with the program and motivation for engaging with it. All of this enables CoU to make improvements in the design and delivery of services and enhances community participation in and demand for them. At a higher level, and aligned with Save the Children's commitment to ensuring long-term sustainability of program benefits and large-scale impact, this evidence enables Save the Children to advocate to health and education policy and decision-makers to influence national government-led policies and strategies.

THE IMPORTANCE OF TIME

Ultimately, aligned with our organizational ambition to achieve sustainable impact at scale, the PMEP is intended to generate relevant and necessary evidence that the program is improving the health and education outcomes and opportunities for the children of Uruzgan in order to influence its broader adoption by key national stakeholders, including both government and nongovernment actors. A 4-year timeframe provides us with a very different evidence base than what we have been able to gather over more than 20 years in Laos, but in terms of national policy influence, the CoU program has achieved impressive results in a short period of time.

A formal preschool teacher training package developed through the program is expected to be accredited and a national curriculum adopted and implemented nationally by the Ministry of Education. The teacher training package for CBE teachers developed by the program has been approved and adopted by the Ministry of Education's CBE Unit in an effort to assist all children to become literate and to increase children's access to education, especially in remote areas. The Ministry of Education is encouraging development partners to participate in the roll out of this strategy and will gradually incorporate CBE and outreach classes in the official education system. The Ministries of Education and Public Health are collaborating, with technical support from Save the Children, to incorporate the CoU school health and nutrition (SHN) model into their respective strategies and to roll it out nationwide. This would see community health workers (CHWs) located at all schools as part of the Basic Package of Health Services under the Ministry of Public Health and the promotion of these CHWs and their services through a revised curriculum and training for school teachers undertaken by the Ministry of Education.

Regarding increased opportunities for women and girls, the Ministry of Education is undertaking a series of efforts and initiatives to increase the number of female students and teachers in the system. The Girls Learning to Teach Afghanistan (GLiTTA) program developed by CoU aims to motivate girls studying Grade 11 and 12 to become a community-based teacher in their village, enroll in Teacher Training Colleges or apply to be a contract teacher with the Ministry of Education in their district. Save the Children is piloting GLiTTA beyond Uruzgan and is currently tracking participating girls and teachers in three provinces. The findings from this pilot study will enable Save the Children and the Ministry of Education to assess the potential for broader application of the program nationally. The Community Midwife Education School in Tirin Kot underwent its final and binding accreditation assessment by the Ministry of Public Health in July 2014. The government has formally accredited all 24 students who have graduated from the school. At the end of 2014, 12 were already working as midwifes in Uruzgan and nine were waiting for positions in their home districts.

The signs are optimistic that CoU has delivered results that have the potential to influence broader policy change. As already mentioned, robust evidence is vital to support behavior and practice change and policy influence. CoU has done a tremendous job in gathering a significant body of evidence and using that information to underpin its ambitious change agenda. The fact this has been achieved in such a challenging context is testament to the efforts of the staff and partners on the ground. CoU concludes in September 2015. As part of its close-out strategy, Save the Children will undertake a comprehensive final evaluation exercise to document achievements over the life of the program and assess the potential for ongoing impact as a result of the program investments. In line with Save the Children's organizational commitment to leveraging our knowledge to enable sustainable impact at scale, the final evaluation will analyze changes that have occurred in the target communities since the inception of CoU and assess if and/or how the program has contributed to these. Women and girls are a key constituency for CoU and the evaluation will place particular emphasis on the extent to which the program has considered and addressed gender issues, and the resulting effects, throughout its lifecycle. In addition, the evaluation will assess the extent to which CoU has delivered benefits for, and influenced any change in the lives of, other marginalized groups including ethnic and linguistic minority groups, people with a disability, and the most remote communities in the locations where the program has been delivered. As mentioned repeatedly in this case study, Uruzgan is a complex and insecure operating context and the final evaluation will critically examine the approaches Save the Children has adopted to deliver – and to assess the results of – the program and how efficient and effective these have been in order to share lessons internally and with other implementers and donors working in similar contexts.

CHALLENGES ASSOCIATED WITH IMPACT ASSESSMENT

In its purest form, impact assessment aims to assess the long-term effects that can be attributed to a particular intervention. It aims to determine whether the highest level goal was achieved. Save the Children has adopted the Organization for Economic Cooperation and Development's Development Assistance Committee (OECD-DAC) definition of impact which is the "positive and negative, primary and secondary long-term effects produced by a development intervention, directly or indirectly, intended or unintended" (OECD/DAC, 2002). Save the Children is committed to assessing the results we are delivering for children and their potential for sustainable impact at scale. In practice however, most development projects, including those of Save the Children, typically track effects at the immediate or intermediate outcome levels, and sometimes only track outputs. There are a range of factors that limit our ability to assess higher level changes or impacts.

TIMEFRAMES

The timeframe for engagement of most development projects constrains assessment of the desired impact level results and our specific contribution to these. Long-term change will not be delivered in a 3–5 year project lifecycle, a typical timeframe for many development projects. Interventions over such a period can lay the foundations for longer term change but assessing whether those ultimate impacts were actually realized will only be feasible further down the track, often after a period of many years. The two case studies presented here clearly demonstrate the different opportunities for assessment that are feasible with different project timeframes. In the Laos example, Save the Children has been able to build a systematic evidence base and demonstrate results at the ultimate impact level. There is clear evidence to demonstrate that Save the Children has made a significant contribution to the gains in maternal and child health in the target provinces (and to the achievement of Millennium Development Goals (MDG) 4 and 5 in Sayaboury Province). In the case of the CoU program in Afghanistan, the ultimate impacts of Save the Children's investments are yet to be seen but the program has established a solid evidence base of initial improvements in health and education outcomes and assumptions can be made, based on international literature, about the prospects for sustained impact.

COST-EFFECTIVENESS

The evaluation process itself must be cost effective. Development partners, including both donors and implementers, need to consider the level of effort required to extract meaningful information, the demands that process places on different stakeholder groups including time-poor community members, and the need to make pragmatic choices about how they use their limited resources. Impact assessments can be very costly exercises and results may take years to emerge. In the case of the Laos Primary Healthcare program and CoU in Afghanistan, there has been solid investment in assessment that has enabled both programs to build a strong evidence base and document their results for broader use. This is not always the case.

EX-POST EVALUATIONS

There is limited opportunity for international development agencies to participate in *ex-post* evaluations when impacts tend to emerge. In Save the Children's experience, donors do not prioritize this type of evaluation. It can also be challenging to engage communities in such an exercise after a development partner is no longer directly engaged in the community and the benefits for the community are unclear.

CONCLUSION

As noted at the start of this chapter, to achieve sustainable impact at scale, Save the Children needs to mobilize partners, evidence, political will, public attitude, and demand to deliver measurable improvements in the lives of children, including the most deprived. Catalyzing impact at scale is about working with others to shift the needle on national level indicators for children. The effect of sustainable impact at scale should be reflected in changes in national or subnational indicators for children.

As Save the Children moves into a new 2016–2018 strategy phase, the organization is reflecting on the challenges of delivering quality programs that have the potential to catalyze impact at scale. The global development model is evolving rapidly. Technology and improved education mean that a more informed population will have increasingly higher expectations of program quality and hold international organizations such as Save the Children and our partners and governments accountable for results. Children, their families, and governments will expect longer term outcomes at a national level, and corporate and institutional donor expectations of results at scale as a return on investment will rise – with this being seen as a key measure of our value addition. To respond to these trends and achieve our goals, Save the Children must consistently catalyze high-quality impact for children at scale through our Theory of Change and ensure excellence in our programming for children (Save the Children, 2015).

For Save the Children, the Child Rights framework drives the legitimacy of our programming. Our Theory of Change provides the roadmap for strengthening program quality and galvanizing ourselves and others toward breakthroughs for children at national or global scale. Our focus on Monitoring, Evaluation, Accountability and Learning sets the standard for assessing program quality, learning and using and sharing our knowledge.

We recognize that we need to allocate appropriate resources (people, money, time) to measure quality and impact at scale. This includes allocating resources for continuous program assessment, periodic evaluation, and longer-term impact studies beyond program funding timeframes.

REFERENCES

Blaakman, A., Kioko, U., Korir, J., 2013a. Results from the Dynamic Costing Model in Kenya (2012/2013). International Health Economics Association Conference, Sydney, Australia July 7–10, 2013.

Blaakman, A., Salehi, A.S., Boitard, R., 2013b. A cost-efficiency analysis of two alternative models for implementing the BPHS in Afghanistan. Global Public Health. Available Sept 5, 2013 from: <http://dx.doi.org/10.1080/17441692.2013.829862>.

Bowie, C., Mwase, T, 2011. Assessing the use of an essential health package in a sector wide approach in Malawi. Health Res. Policy Syst. 9, 4–13, 2011.

Drummond, M.F., Mills, A., 1987. Cost Effectiveness of Primary Health Care: A Review of Evidence. Commonwealth Secretariat, London.

Fishstein, P., 2012. Winning Hearts and Minds in Uruzgan Province. Feinstein International Centre, Tufts University Medford, MA..

Ikram Mohammad, S., et al., 2014. Communicable disease control in Afghanistan. Global Public Health 9 (Supp. 1), S43–S57.

Laos Social Indicator Survey, 2012.

Levitt, E., 2011. Malnutrition in Afghanistan: Scale, Scope, Causes, and Potential Response. World Bank Publications Washington, DC..

Mayhew, M., et al., 2008. Determinants of skilled birth attendant utilization in Afghanistan: A cross-sectional study. Am. J. Public Health 98.10, 1849–1856, PMC.

OECD/DAC, 2002. Glossary of key terms in evaluation and results-based management. Available from: <http://www.oecd.org/development/peer-reviews/2754804.pdf> (accessed 30.06.2015).

OECD, 2010. Investing in women and girls: the breakthrough strategy for achieving all the MDGs. Available from: <http://www.oecd.org/dac/gender-development/45704694.pdf>.

Save the Children, 2009. Save the Children Global Strategy 2010-2015. Save the Children, Australia.

Save the Children. 2012. 'Access Restricted: A review of remote monitoring practices in Uruzgan Province'.

Save the Children, 2014. Costs and Effects of the Save the Children Primary Health Care Model in the Context of the Evolving Health System in Lao PDR. Save the Children, Australia.

Save the Children, 2015. Ambition for Children 2030. Save the Children, Australia.

United Nations Convention on the Rights of the Child, New York, 1989. United Nations treaty collection. Available from: <http://www.ohchr.org/EN/ProfessionalInterest/Pages/CRC.aspx> (accessed 30.06.2015).

THE NONGOVERNMENTAL DEVELOPMENT SECTOR AND IMPACT ASSESSMENT

15

Jonathan J. Makuwira

School of Economics, Development and Tourism, Nelson Mandela Metropolitan University, Port Elizabeth, South Africa

CHAPTER OUTLINE

INTRODUCTION

Gone are times when charity seemed a normal thing and no questions were asked. The current state of affairs in nongovernmental development organizations (NGDOs) has drastically changed. People and institutions that support them are no longer concerned about where the money goes. Rather the fundamental question that many well-wishers are asking and, especially popular in the current development landscape, is what impact does the money make in the lives of the so-called beneficiaries of development interventions? The historical metamorphosis of charity has a significant bearing on the way charitable organizations have evolved over time to entities in the development field. This shift represents a pendulum swing in the way benevolence is viewed and has far-reaching implications on the current nonprofit or nongovernmental organizations in general.

Since the 1960s, nongovernmental organizations (NGOs) have benefitted from continued donor support due to their perceived comparative advantage over states and, also, the belief that the sector is closer to where key development challenges are – the community itself (Fowler, 1997;

Tendler, 1982). The status which the NGO sector has enjoyed so far has, over the years, allowed then to leverage various actors and stakeholders, particularly governments and grassroots organizations, to engage in the provision of basic social services in the form of projects which, in some instances, range from small- to large-scale operations. Most NGDOs in development countries, especially those that are fairly established, and other international NGDOs such as Care, World Vision international, and Oxfam have now combined advocacy and social service provision. It is the social service provision aspect that has had its own critics, especially when it comes to attributing impact solely as a result of such one-off projects (Bond, 2001b). At the center of this debate is the question of "evidence" versus "measurable impact."

Earlier studies by the Overseas Development Institute ODI (1996), The Danish NGO Impact Assessment (IA) (Oakley et al., 1998), and the AusAID NGO Effectiveness Review (AusAID, 1999), shed a little light on the many claims the NGO sector makes on the kind of impact they make in their development activities. Over the past decade, the NGDO impact debate has since intensified (see Cameron, 2006; Hershey, 2014; Holmen, 2009; Kelly et al., 2004; Makuwira, 2014). While the intensity of the debate is symptomatic of increased frustration between and among the NGDO sector itself and the beneficiaries, it seems clear that to date, there is no proper agreement among development practitioners, researchers, and donors as to whether development projects do make significant impact on the lives of peoples affected by such interventions when there is such lack of evidence to attribute success to projects. A new dimension to the current development discourse has also emerged – that of value for money. Not only are donors and development supporters interested in the "impact" but there is also a growing desire to know whether there is "added value" for the money they spend.

The purpose of this chapter is to contribute to the ongoing debate about the role of the NGO sector in advance long-term change that is not only transformative but sustainable. It is mainly about *Ex-Post* IA. The chapter is divided into four sections. The section "Introduction" explores the current but, at the same time competing perspectives and views about IA. The section "Contemporary debates in impact assessment" analyses how NGOs go about assessing the impact they make to their intended beneficiaries through development projects. In doing so the section further highlights the major tools and methodologies used in assessing their impact, and the motivation in doing so. The section "Impact assessment methods and tools" aims to review the current practices through case studies that highlight the strengths, weaknesses, threats, and opportunities in NGO IA. The chapter concludes by identifying critical issues for improving NGO IA and the implications for sustainable development.

CONTEMPORARY DEBATES IN IMPACT ASSESSMENT

The theory and practice of IA has, over the past two decades, expanded and is now becoming a professionalized field of development practice (Harlock, 2013; Pope et al., 2013). At the same time the field has also witnessed the growth of a distinct and specialized form of practice which until now, is part of a continued global conversation. Furthermore, the question of measurement (qualitative, quantitative, or a combination of methods) has also heightened amid conflicting debate about what should be measured or assessed (cf. Chapter 2). What is comforting though is the fact that IA is now recognized with an international body like The International Association for Impact Assessment (IAIA) whose core values are to advance sound decision-making processes through assessment of environmental, social, economic, cultural, and health issues globally (Vanclay, 2003). For example, the establishment of the Third Sector Research Centre (University of Birmingham), International Society for Third Sector Research (ISTR) in the United States, and many other global networks in the field of NGOs and civil society at large, attest to the importance of the sector in their contribution to society. While such bodies provide a platform for contemporary debates around the role of the sector and its overall contribution to development, the conversation around IA remains polarized and problematic.

The word "impact" resonates well in the current global development discourse where, despite billions of dollars spent in the name of foreign development assistance (FDA), poverty continues to be a major challenge. Even when donors, governments, and stakeholders in the development field agreed in 2005 to come up with ways of measuring aid effectiveness, which was the main issue in understanding impact. But, in theory, what do we mean by impact? And, in what ways can it be measured?

There are events and occurrences in life that we acknowledge to have had direct impact on our lives. These can also be people. Such impacts can be of a positive or negative nature depending on the situation and circumstances. At best, what is central to the concept of impact is "change" – intended or unintended. Building from the discussion on various debates on impact in Chapter 1 (this volume), it is essential to note that in the context of development NGOs, the importance of IA cannot be overemphasized. Given the claims and counterclaims in development work by most of the NGOs, people are interested to know not only what has changed but also how significant was the change/impact. More importantly, to claim that an intervention has made an impact, is to claim totality in the contribution of that particular project and/or program in the lives of people. However, one of the major challenges to IA is the difficulty of attributing impact or change as a result of often short time-bound projects for which the NGO sector is known for. In any case, IAs, are conducted for a number of reasons. Some of them include but are not limited to the following (Roche, 1999; INTRAC, 2001; Cameron, 2006).

- Facilitating better-informed decision-making processes in the planning, design, implementation, monitoring, and evaluation of development programming;
- Demonstrating the level of success and/or failure;
- Enhancing understanding of how a development intervention impacts on intended beneficiaries;
- As a demonstration of accountability to various stakeholders including intended beneficiaries of development;
- Helping to understand how change occurs and thereby allowing organizations to frame and/or reframe their approach to development programming;
- Maintaining coherence in some of the assessment and/or evaluation approaches; and
- Helping better design of development policies

While the aims of IA sound rosy and somehow easy, the manner in which they are operationalized in practice is not as straightforward. For the NGDO sector that continues to suffer issues of legitimacy, accountability, and transparency (Bendell, 2006; Edwards and Hulme, 1992; Makuwira, 2014), proving their worth by ticking all the boxes often demanded by the funders of such projects and, answering the question "so what"?, is by no means easy. As earlier argued, while most of the NGDO sector's approach to IA is in the form of evaluation studies, at the center of this debate is whether the evidence to judge the impact of their work is credible and reliable. As observed by Hughes and Hutchings (2011), impact evaluation, as is the case with other IA, is a research process which, like any good research, will often demand an investment in terms of both material as well as expert human resources in order to systematically collect credible data.

IMPACT ASSESSMENT METHODS AND TOOLS

There are different ways NGDOs go about assessing the impact of their work using various methods and tools. The INTRAC NGO Policy Briefing No. 3 of March 2001 (INTRAC, 2001) has comprehensively looked at various kinds of methods and tools used in IA. However, over the past decade and half, there have been significant shifts in some of these which will be highlighted later. But, this section is concerned with Program Logic and Theory of Change Approaches; Most Significant Change (MSC) Approach; Participatory Rural Appraisal (PRA)/Participatory Learning Action (PLA); and Tiny Tools. While there are many other tools and methods, this list is not exhaustive.

THE LOGIC MODEL

Donor-funded projects or publicly funded projects with short- to medium-term timeframe are often designed with a project design document in a logical framework format. This means strict adherence to planned activities and routine monitoring and evaluation practices that are rushed through in order to meet donor demands and, quite often, with minimal or no engagement of project beneficiaries. The greater part of the current contemporary debate is perhaps less about how successful NGOs are in contributing to broader development. Rather the fundamental issues is how NGOs move from claiming success in "Outcomes" to actual "Impact" when, crucially, impact is about changes beyond immediate, intermediate, or long-term effects of a development intervention.

To decipher the popularity and use of the logic model in IA by NGOs, we use here an example of a situation where an NGO is implementing a project whose ultimate goal is improved community–local government relationships. To use the program logic as a framework, we need inputs that will give us the outputs we need which, in turn, will lead to expected outcomes – be it short-term, medium-term, or long-term. When these are achieved, it is hoped that the project can realize an improved community–local government relationships. The *inputs* may be in form of *staff, money, partners,* and *research.* One of the *outputs* could be, for example, *50 community-based awareness meetings organized* and *attended by community members.* The expected *short-term outcome* could be that *community members have increased awareness of good relationship.* In the *medium-term outcome,* it may be expected that the *community is able to identify appropriate courses of action* to strengthen relations between themselves and local government authorities. In the *long-term outcomes,* we envisage *reduced tension between local communities and local government.* The *impact* of all these outcomes is, at best, *strong community–local government relationships.*

The example above highlights first, the linearity of the process and, second, the potential and often inherent confusion that exists when impact is used as a measure of immediate and intermediary or outcomes of a development intervention. The challenge in contemporary NGDO development work is establishing benchmarks of each of the stages of the outcome to assess the ultimate impact. Hughes and Hutchings (2011) attest to this when they observe that one of the key challenges NGDOs face as they work in various contexts is how to authenticate effectiveness of their work when, in the first place, research is not their core business. Here, reference is made to the importance of research because it is an activity that may provide ample evidence of where communities are in terms of their development needs. Linked to that is also what Pope et al. (2013) cite as a growing threat to the field (IA) due to the fact that IA is an expensive undertaking, time-consuming, and goes with lots of regulatory hurdles.

As pointed out earlier, one of the major questions that lingers over NGO work is attribution as opposed to contribution. The European Science Foundation (n.d.) aptly states that

> ...related to the question of attribution is the challenge of defining an appropriate counterfactual position. To determine an impact of an intervention, one must also estimate what would have happened if the intervention had not taken place, as it may be possible that the outcomes we are tracing might have occurred anyway. (p. 9)

It is one thing to claim that some of the observable changes are solely due to one development intervention yet, proving that indeed it is due to the said intervention is practically impossible (White, 2009b). Part of this problem, in the first instance, lies in the lack of baseline data. Not only that, any development intervention is also likely to be influenced by external factors of which the project or the NGDO may have no control over. With poor risk assessment during the design of the project, it is, as stated already, very difficult to attribute change to one project. In some cases, there are instances where different projects run concurrently but implemented by different organizations thereby making it questionable to attribute change in people's lives as a result of one NGO work. These practicalities confirm the difficulty in designing not only the IA tools but also where to draw a line and claim credit to contribution.

PROGRAM LOGIC AND THEORY OF CHANGE

So far I have argued that there is a link between assessing impact and program logic. But program logic in itself does not tell us much unless we also acknowledge that such a logic is part of a wider understanding of how change occurs. It is therefore important that we also note that there is a link between program logic and theory of change. Theory of change, according to Funnell and Rogers (2011) and Valters (2014) simply means a process through which change occurs in individuals, groups, and communities. Weiss (1995) describes theory of change as a process of analyzing how and why an initiative works. In its broader theorizing, we can extrapolate that when an intervention engages good strategies, the likelihood of witnessing a positive change is high. However, life is not as linear as it sounds to be, especially when impact or change is read from a theoretical model developed from a different context but applied blindly in a foreign context untested and challenged. The change (Results) may not necessarily be due to the strategies (Resources, Activities, and Outputs). Rather such a change must also be attributed to other factors such as conditions under which the project was able to succeed and contribute to that level. This could be enablers of availability of resources, factors that enabled processes to allow maximization of the use of resources, people's capacity, and levels of community participation in the project as well as sustenance of such factors over a period of time when the project was implemented.

The idea of cause and effect is a central theme to the logical framework model. According to Taylor-Powell and Henert (2008), the logic model is simply a depiction of program's assumed causal connections yet, in the real world of development, such assumption of cause–effect relationships are highly problematic for a number of reasons. First, development projects, as is the case with any other community development programs, have only a partial influence over results because the eternal factors are often beyond the program's control and, likewise, be able to influence the flow of events. This is particularly the case when it comes to longer-term outcomes. Second, there are a number of factors that affect the implementation of development initiatives to the extent that teasing out the cause and effect connection is rather impossible. This is especially so when we consider the diversity of intended beneficiaries, issues of social capital, culture, economic status, and local power dynamics. The project itself can affect the external environment while at the same time the external environment may also affect the project.

Project managers in the NGDOs and all those involved in the implementation of projects need to pay attention not only to such factors but also how these unfold during the entire project cycle. Third, seldom is there "one" cause. There are more likely multiple cause–effect chains that interact. Fourth, because most development projects have a very short time span, it is hard to document the assumed causal connections. Fifth, Bell and Aggleton (2012) concede that measuring cause and effect relationships while at the same time controlling contextual factors through experimental or quasi-experimental designs (see also White, 2009a), is not only expensive but often not feasible. Since IA data is sourced using different methods both qualitative and quantitative, results may be different and often contradictory. This makes it rather difficult to prove that a particular outcome is the result of a particular intervention. The emphasis on the "if"….and … "then" in the logic model is rather misleading as it seems to suggest the linearity of causation yet, based on practice, there are multiple and interacting relationships that affect change, often functioning as feedback loops with the possibility of delays. Part of this problem is also the unidimensionality of project cycles which, when looked at from a critical angle, are not only reductionist in nature but also limited in their conception of everyday life.

THE MOST SIGNIFICANT CHANGE

The MSC (most significant change) approach (Davies, 1996) has lately become one of the popular instruments for measuring impact. Predominantly qualitative, MSC is concerned about the question if what change has occurred is significant as a result of an intervention. This approach is now widely used by NGOs in Africa, Asia, Latin America, and some parts of the Australasian region (Davies and Dart, 2005). The major contrast between MSC and other traditional IA methods is that while the conventional wisdom has it that in order to attribute impact to a project or a development intervention, randomized control trials or more generally scientific methods should be applied (see White, 2009a). MSC, broadly speaking, is about hearing people's stories of change. Obviously there are merits and demerits in this approach. Stories are stories and how to authenticate them may not be easy. The validity of the information against which to establish attribution is perhaps one of the major pitfalls of this approach. Hence, it is not surprising that there is now a shift from focusing on attribution to rather acknowledging the contribution projects make.

On its own, MSC provides an appreciation of how the intended beneficiaries view and feel about the intervention and the changes brought about by the project. Rather than relying on outside expertise, the views from an insider are crucial as a feedback loop to project implementers. Depending on how the IA process is designed, the changes observed may not necessarily be those from primary beneficiaries. The data can also be triangulated using views solicited from frontline staff. However, the use of this approach by many NGOs has demonstrated that rather than using it as a tool to unearth lessons from where to learn, there is also an increasing suppression of information by the frontline staff as any "bad news" may be construed as failure, hence hindering them further support from donors.

PARTICIPATORY RURAL APPRAISAL/PARTICIPATORY LEARNING ACTION

The current practices in monitoring and evaluation of development projects have become associated with participatory processes and learning. For many NGOs, conducting an impact evaluation without the participation of the intended beneficiaries is a weakness. PRA and PLA (Chambers, 1997) have become widely used methods to monitor and evaluate projects and generate lessons that can be fed into the design of projects. The wide usage of tools that comes with these methods demonstrate not only the popularity but also the user-friendliness. Causemann et al. (2011) call these "tiny tools," although they distinguish them significantly from their own methods. While most of the PRA tools have been widely used in the planning and design of projects, many of them have also been used by NGOs in impact evaluation. Tools such as wealth ranking, Venn diagrams, resource cards, income and expenditure matrix are among the many tools used by NGDOs in formative, summative and, ultimately, impact evaluation.

TINY TOOLS

As mentioned in the previous section, "Tiny Tools" as a subset of evaluation tools used by NGOs, is not quite as popular as the ones discussed so far, yet they provide down-to-earth opportunity to understand impact of development interventions on the lives of people. Causemann et al. (2011) acknowledge that there is a link between "Tiny Tools" and the PRA family of tools and often complementary in nature and application. Some of the examples of the "Tiny Tools" tools are life/quality of life curve; trend analysis; influence matrix; gender disaggregation; MSC light; tree of change; and causal diagrams (p. 3). While the tools help in visualizing change, they are useful when used in reflecting on practice and the reasons why a change occurred. What is perhaps important is the fact that these tools can be used by local community members and frontline staff.

Other IA methods that are out there but not widely used include but are not limited to:

- Participatory Impact Analysis and Reflection (PIAR)
- Contributions Analysis (CI)
- Participatory Wellbeing Ranking
- Livelihood Asset Status Tracking (LAST)
- Social Accounting
- Rolling Baseline
- BDS Performance Measurement Framework
- Simplified Cost Benefit Analysis
- Sustainability Self-Assessment (Bond, n.d.)
- Social Returns on Investment (SROI) (Kumar, 2014).

NGO practices in impact evaluation

Most NGOs may use one or a combination of these methods depending on the nature of IA undertaken. As previously argued, different IA questions, level and depth of program and/project; the availability of resources and expertise, may dictate the scale of IA. In some cases, some of these IAs are done with a particular purpose and utilization such that the design, operationalization, and reporting will have a particular audience in mind.

Case Study 1: PACT and assessment of capacity building

PACT is an international NGO specializing in various development activities one of which is capacity building of other organizations. For years it has been facilitating organizational capacity assessment

(OCA) using tools they have developed out of their field experience globally. One of the tools they use is "Discussion-Oriented Organizational Self-Assessment" (DOSA). The major usage of OCA lies in its focus on identification of organizational strengths, weaknesses, and future trajectory of organizational growth and their ability to ascertain organizational change. More important is the focus on participation, customization, user-ownership, communication, and continuous reflection for learning purposes (PACT, 2012).

Case Study 2: Oxfam Community Aid Abroad (Oxfam CAA)

Oxfam Community Aid Abroad has been very radical in its approach to development and, more importantly in nonrandomized and nonexperimental IA (Roche 1999; Hughes and Hutchings, 2011). In one of their IAs in India and Sri Lanka (see Kelly et al., 2004), Oxfam CAA was interested in measuring the extent to which women exercised choices resulting from a project on women's empowerment and, further, assesses how they acted upon those choices as an expression of empowerment. The study used open-ended questions to document women's experiences of empowerment. Of particular importance was the extent to which Oxfam CAA partners contributed to those changes in women's lives. The study concluded that IA cannot be confined to the use of a singular tool. The process of "trial and error" seemed to emerge as a way of learning on how measuring impact can effectively be done.

In Tanzania, Oxfam CAA works with local partners who in turn provide support to 4,000 smallholder farmers in Shinyanga region (Hughes and Hutchings, 2011). Part of the project is to promote social capital and, hence, participants are encouraged to work collaboratively. Oxfam piloted to global performance indicators to measure change on their living standards and decision-making among women. The process of IA comprised an external consultant working with local members to administer household surveys and questionnaires. The use of both quantitative and qualitative data collection instruments was to triangulate the findings in order to unearth both quality and quantitative gains in the project.

Case Study 3: Nepalese Participatory Learning and Advisory Project (NPLAP)

Nepalese Participatory Learning and Advisory Project was a community-based NGO that was founded in 1998 to support community-based organizations and other local NGOs in Nepal and funded by DfID (see Cameron, 2006). NGOs with the potential to contribute to change were identified. In addition, there was also a focus on enhancing organizational effectiveness through capacity development. In measuring the impact of their activities, it engaged two local but independent Nepalese consultants to carry out the IA of a sample of intermediary organizations (IOs). The consultants engaged in participatory assessments with members of IOs and members of community. The consultants also collected quantitative data which, as we have noted in this paper, is very technical in analyzing it. The critical aspects of the IA findings may be attributed to changes in the DfID-funded project going beyond the popular technical issues in IA.

Case Study 4: The Consulting Sector

The complex landscape of development, especially with regard to understanding the impact it makes to the broader society, has resulted in a growing call for experts to try and help make sense of issues. One such case is the consultancy firms. The professionalization of consulting firms is growing. The so-called "experts" are everywhere offering expert advice in such activities as IA.

Lessons from case studies

The case studies highlighted above were not meant to provide conclusions to the assessments but rather help us identify various approaches NGOs use to measure impact. From the few cases above, it is clear that the nature of development intervention will dictate the approach to IA and the tools used. In any case it seems clear from the lessons in case studies that there is less use of technical and highly complex randomized control trials and experimental assessment. Perhaps we can only guess that in most NGOs the staff are not highly qualified to undertake such complex and labor-intensive measures. There is a dominance in the use of traditional participatory approaches which, at best, indicates the importance of qualitative measures.

We also have seen that most of the IAs are usually done by consultants – local or international. This is especially the case where the projects are funded by external donors. The idea of "independent" consultants is important in understanding the global interest in measurement and authentication of results. This is about credibility and accountability. This is aptly highlighted by Hughes and Hutchings (2011) who note that "accessing credible intervention effectiveness feedback is no easy task, and most of our organizations are not set up as 'development labs' (p. 12)".

CHALLENGES OF IMPACT ASSESSMENT AND THE WAY FORWARD

Right from the outset we have established that there is tension in the definition of impact and impact assessment. The fact that the world in which NGOs operate is diverse and, also, that this environment is clustered with a diversity of stakeholders, IA becomes problematic. This is mainly because different stakeholders may have different ways of measuring impact based on the nature and scale of their projects and/programs. In addition, the disagreement in methodological approaches, especially on the choice of indicators, creates a situation where IA results are called into question on grounds of validity and trustworthiness of data. This is particularly true when on the one hand we have proponents of quantitative measures by using randomized control trials while, on the other hand, we have proponents of qualitative story-telling approaches who are interested in qualitative measures of how change is perceived and lived by the beneficiaries of development interventions. In whatever methodological orientation, credibility and trustworthiness of data are critical to any assessment of development impact.

There exists an enormous opportunity for the NGDO sector to contribute to change by using evidence and developing a culture where every action is based on right decision informed by empirical evidence. This is research. However, the practices witnessed in some of the case studies in this chapter call for a wider reaction to how NGDO can make a difference (Bebbington et al., 2008). One of the ways in which NGOs can improve on the use of research is, first and foremost, building their capacity in evaluation research methodologies and information management. It is from here that the essence of information will trigger the need to use data for measuring results and their impact. As other commentators have noted (see Kareithi and Lund, 2012; Bell and Aggleton, 2012; Mueller-Hirth, 2012), unless NGO work is documented it will be very hard to appreciate the contribution of the sector. Furthermore, the fear to learn from mistakes is hampering progress. While the few case studies have highlighted their desire to learn from their work, most of the NGDOs are slow in reflecting on their work and readjusting their approaches to IA.

For a while the NGO sector has operated in isolation from academic institutions and, similarly, academic institutions have not made strong inroads in appreciating what the NGO sector offers in terms of lessons that can contribute to theory. It is therefore recommended that part of increasing professionalism in IA by NGOs is building NGO–University linkages. In Australia, this is now gathering momentum by formation of University–ACFID linkages where the annual conferences provide a forum for exchange of ideas and strengthening research and collaboration.

The heart of the matter in IA starts with the planning and design of development interventions themselves. No tangible success can be achieved in isolation of the primary stakeholders. The people we purport to support know their situations very well and only if they understand what is going on well around them can they state the truth of whether there is an impact or not. Progressive changes in the process of a development intervention obviously need to be documented. However, the common practice is the primary beneficiaries of such interventions become zones of extraction of information more than anything else. The "consultants" often operating in the business mind frame, have very little time to consider the benefits of engagement of primary stakeholders. This falsifies the impact story. So there has to be a shift in our approaches.

The question of "indicators of success" is a major issue in IA. Unless we understand what "success" means at the grassroots level of, at least from the beneficiaries, our measure of success are often misplaced. This is especially true when projects are conceived far away and rubber-stamped in the destinations of projects, success becomes meaningless at least from the impact level of the intervention logic. This then calls for a rethinking of the approach to localize the meaning of success and its measurements as conceived by the recipients of a development intervention.

There is no question that IA needs to be enhanced by using a cocktail of methods. If the NGO sector truly believes that the beneficiaries of development are the ones who can tell the real success story, then the proponents of randomized control trials need to reconsider how the technical aspects of such methodologies can be brought down to earth.

REFERENCES

AusAID, 1999. A Review of the Effectiveness of AusAID Support to NGO Programs. AusAID, Canberra.

Bebbington, A., Hickey, S., Mitlin, D. (Eds.), 2008. Can NGOs Make a difference? The Challenge of Development Alternatives. Zed Books, London.

Bell, S.A., Aggleton, P., 2012. Integrating ethnographic principles in NGO monitoring and impact evaluation. J. Int. Dev. 24 (6), 795–807.

Bendell, J., 2006. Debating NGO accountability, Geneva: UN-NGLS Development Dossier Available from: <http://www.un-ngls.org/orf/pdf/NGO_Accountability.pdf> (accessed 20.02.15).

Bond, R., 2001b. Common methods used in impact assessment. Available from: <http://www.enterpriseimpact.org.uk/word-files/CommonMethodsinIA.doc> (accessed 28.02.15).

Cameron, J., 2006. A participatory approach to evaluating the impact of NGOs on development in Nepal. Dev. Practice 16 (1), 91–96.

Causemann, B., Gohl, E., Brenner, V. 2011. "Tiny tools" – Measuring change in community groups: An overview. Available from: <http://www.dochas.ie/sites/default/files/NGO_Ideas_Tiny_tools-Handout%5B1%5D_0.pdf> (accessed 15.02.15).

Chambers, R., 1997. Whose Reality Counts? Putting the First Last. Intermediate Technology Publications, London.

Davies, R., Dart, J., 2005. The 'most significant change' (MSC) technique: A guide to its use, Available from: <http://www.mande.co.uk/docs/MSCGuide.pdf> (accessed 27.02.15).

Davies, R.J., 1996. An evolutionary approach to facilitating organisational learning: An experiment by the Christian Commission For Development In Bangladesh. Available from: <http://www.mande.co.uk/docs/ccdb.htm> (accessed 26.02.15).

Edwards, M., Hulme, D., 1992. 'Scaling up NGO impact on development: Learning from experience'. Dev. Practice 2 (2), 77–91.

European Science Foundation, n.d. The challenges of impact evaluation. Available from: <http://www.dfg.de/download/pdf/dfg_im_profil/evaluation_statistik/programm_evaluation/impact_assessment_wg2.pdf>.

Fowler, A., 1997. Striking a Balance: A Guide to Enhancing the Effectiveness of Non-Governmental Organizations in the International Development. Earthscan Publication, London.

Funnell, S.C., Rogers, P.J., 2011. Purposeful Program Theory: Effective Use of Theories of Change and Logic Models. Jossey-Bass, San Francisco, CA.

Harlock, J., 2013. Impact measurement practice in the UK Third Sector: A review of emerging evidence. Third Sector Research Centre Working Paper No. 106. Available from: <http://www.birmingham.ac.uk/generic/tsrc/documents/tsrc/working-papers/working-paper-106.pdf> (accessed 01.03.15).

Hershey, M., 2014. 'Measuring the success of HIV/AIDS NGOs among Nairobi's youth'. Dev. Practice 24 (1), 51–62.

Holmen, H., 2009. Snakes in Paradise: NGOs and the Aid Industry in Africa. Kumarian Press, Sterling, VA.

Hughes, K., Hutchings, C., 2011. Can we obtain the required rigour without randomization? Oxfam GB's non-experimental global performance framework. Available from: <http://www.ipdet.org/files/PublicationCan_we_obtain_the_required_rigour_without_randomization.pdf> (accessed 28.02.15).

INTRAC, 2001. NGOs and Impact Assessment. NGO Briefing Paper No. 3. INTRAC, Oxford.

Kareithi, R.N.M., Lund, C., 2012. Review of NGO performance research published in Academic Journals between 1999 and 2008. South Afr. J. Sci. 108 (11/12), 1–8.

Kelly, L., Kilby, P., Kasynathan, N., 2004. Impact measurement for NGOs: Experiences from India and Sri Lanka. Dev. Practice 14 (5), 696–701.

Kumar, S., 2014. Social return on investment (SROI) analysis: An innovative framework for measuring the impact of One Health. GGRF Davos Planet@Risk 2 (3), 150–154.

Makuwira, J.J., 2014. Non-Governmental Development Organisations and the Poverty Reduction Agenda: The Moral Crusaders. Routledge, London.

Mueller-Hirth, N., 2012. If you don't count, you can't count: Monitoring and evaluation in South African NGOs. Dev. Change 43 (3), 649–670.

Oakley, P., Pratt, B., Clayton, A., 1998. Outcomes and impact: Evaluating change in social development, NGO Management and Policy Series No. 6. INTRAC, Oxford Available from: <http://www.intrac.org/resources.php?action=resource&id=358> (accessed 02.03.15).

Overseas Development Institute (ODI), 1996. The impact of NGO development projects. ODI, London. Available from: <http://www.odi.org/sites/odi.org.uk/files/odi-assets/publications-opinion-files/2636.pdf> (accessed 26.02.15).

PACT, 2012. Pact Organizational Capacity Assessment (OCA) Handbook. Available from: <http://pactworld.org/sites/default/files/OCA%20Handbook_ext.pdf> (accessed 27.02.15).

Pope, J., Bond, A., Morrison-Saunders, A., Retief, F., 2013. Advancing the theory and practice of impact assessment: Setting the research agenda. Env. Impact Assess. Rev. 41, 1–9.

Roche, C., 1999. Impact Assessment for Development Agencies. Oxfam, Oxford.

Taylor-Powell, E., Henert, E., 2008. Developing a logic model: Teaching and training guide, University of Wisconsin-Extension, Cooperative Extension, Program Development and Evaluation: Madison, Wisconsin. Available from: <http://www.uwex.edu/ces/pdande/evaluation/pdf/lmguidecomplete.pdf> (accessed 28.02.15).

Tendler, J., 1982. Turning Private Voluntary Organisations into Development Agencies: Questions for Evaluation Programme Evaluation, Discussion Paper No. 12, USAID, Washington D.C. Available from: <http://pdf.usaid.gov/pdf_docs/PNAAJ612.pdf> (accessed 02.03.15).

Valters, C., 2014. Theories of change in international development: communication, learning, or accountability? JSRP Paper 17. Available from: <http://www.lse.ac.uk/internationalDevelopment/research/JSRP/downloads/JSRP17.Valters.pdf> (accessed 04.03.15).

Vanclay, F., 2003. International principles for social impact assessment. Impact Assessment Project Appraisal 21 (1), 5–12.

Weiss, C.H., 1995. 'Nothing as practical as good theory: Exploring theory-based evaluation for comprehensive community initiatives for children and families'. In: Connell, J., Kubisch, A., Schorr, L., Weiss, C. (Eds.), New Approaches to Evaluating Community Initiatives: Concepts, Methods and Contexts. Aspen Institute, New York, NY, pp. 65–92.

White, H., 2009a. Some reflections on current debates in impact evaluation, international initiative for impact evaluation. Available from: <http://www.3ieimpact.org/media/filer_public/2012/05/07/Working_Paper_1.pdf> (accessed 27.02.15).

White, H., 2009b. Theory-based impact evaluation: Principles and practices. J. Dev. Effectiveness 1 (3), 271–284.

IMPACT ASSESSMENT: FROM THEORY TO PRACTICE

Viktor Jakupec* and Max Kelly†

*School of Education, Faculty of Arts and Education, Deakin University, Warrnambool, Australia
†School of Humanities and Social Sciences, Faculty of Arts and Education, Deakin University, Warrnambool, Australia

CHAPTER OUTLINE

INTRODUCTION

Foreign aid is intended to be a major contributor to poverty reduction. However, significant questions arise as to the capacity for development funding to contribute to human development, through service provision, through advocacy, through actions and interventions that change power relations, change the social and institutional arrangements that reinforce inequality, threaten or reproduce well-being, and prevent the fulfillment of human rights. In conjunction with questions about what aid "does," there is equal focus on how it does it. Questions of efficiency, effectiveness, transparency, accountability, social license to operate, relevance, and many others are all embedded in contemporary aid discourse and practice. The aim of this volume was to contribute to a critical understanding of Impact Assessment (IA) clearly informed by contemporary development theory and practice. There is a significantly increasing push for impact assessment, across the whole aid architecture. This is exacerbated by a much stronger focus on value for money, and accountability – to taxpayers specifically in the context of public funds, and donors in an increasingly competitive NGO environment. As was noted by many authors, since the GFC, a significant number of donor governments have reduced or are considering funding reduction for bilateral aid agencies and their contributions to multilateral aid agencies. At the same time they imposed a more stringent and rigorous requirement focusing on "aid-for-trade" and "value-for-money" strategies. There is a drive to ensure the positive impacts of the grant or loan in a sustainable manner.

As noted by many of the contributors in this book, there is a significant literature on methods and techniques for assessing the impact of foreign aid. However, there is less critical engagement with the theoretical link between development theory and discourse, global economic paradigms, and results/impact agendas in foreign aid. Given the move away from a quantity focus in foreign aid (as personified by the 0.7% target of GDP), and a shift to a focus on quality and performance management, not only the public but also the political decision-makers are questioning the validity of ODA. Within the relevant literature, emerging policies in donor countries and the public media a range of questions have been posed, relating to the amount of funding allocated to ODA, the advantages of ODA spending to the donor country, and the positive verifiable impact of ODA in relation to the tax dollar. A further question of enormous relevance to countries in which ODA is in the form of concessional loans is the cost benefit of engaging in the program, accountability goes a lot further than the donor.

So we have an increasing demand for an assessment of the impact of foreign aid, in its many forms, for example even within social sector development there are issues such as service delivery, advocacy, aid conditionality. However, even a cursory review of the IA reports, case studies, and discussions in this field attests to a significantly varying degree of understanding, methodologies and methods, quality, scope, complexity, and limitations. Some commentators have described the existing IA of foreign aid as suffering from "methodological anarchy" (OECD, 1999, p. 2). Others have pointed out that many development aid agencies have failed to address or take IA seriously and often it is undertaken haphazardly. In many instances, IA has been regarded as irrelevant at policy and the day-to-day practical levels. Some recipient governments see impact assessment as an unnecessarily time consuming and a financial burden. Whereas donor governments see it often as a precarious tool in hands of consulting firms and consultants, unfamiliar with the professional practices and theoretical frameworks governing IA in foreign aid leading to pejorative outcomes. It is also fair to argue that impact assessment may not be required in every case. The use and perhaps misuse of impact assessment needs unpacking.

One of the key strengths of the contributions to this volume is the breadth of experience and contexts from which impact assessment is discussed. From the multilaterals, bilateral donors, private sector, Non-Government Development Sector, and private consultancy the combined experience of the authors in this field, and across the above context provides for excellent cross-fertilization. Many of the core issues raised were common, such as the lack of clarity of what impact is, the substantial costs of conducting impact assessment, a tendency to equate IA with *ex-post* IA, the complexities of the methodological debate, and many more. Yet, at the heart of this volume is a genuine commitment to better development outcomes for the people with whom development actors are working – the beneficiaries. There were aspirations for more effective development architecture, the requirement for accountability, but needing to be to the right people, and the acknowledgment of the complexity inherent in much development, particularly with transformational development as intent. This is balanced by an appreciation of the realities of having to be accountable to tax payers, and donors, to be efficient as well as effective, and to provide justification for decisions made and actions taken.

This chapter cannot adequately cover all issues raised, and most issues are very well addressed and situated by the many contributors to this volume. This chapter will attempt more pragmatically to highlight the most pressing conceptual and practical issues, in situating IA in foreign aid. This chapter addresses the global economic context for aid, and the political drivers of aid flows, followed by an analysis of the key features of IA in this context, ending with a reflection on lessons learned, and recommendations resulting from the many viewpoints of the contributors.

In order for us to draw some conclusions based on the preceding chapters, we will first address development theory, and global economic paradigms, followed by a quick review of politics and foreign policy, as well as complexity thinking in foreign aid.

DEVELOPMENT THEORY AND GLOBAL ECONOMIC PARADIGMS

While many of the chapters implicitly or explicitly recognize the political and economic environment in which aid operates, McKay (this volume) really unpacks the evolution of a global paradigm, based on neoliberal economic principles that drives the existing aid and development industry, from donors, to organizations and institutions that drive development. However, there are substantial challenges to economic growth paradigm underpinning ODA. Firstly, the jury is out on whether investments in development interventions for economic growth reduce poverty. The link between economic growth and inequality is a substantial challenge, in particular for the developing world. Secondly, the emergence of new political and economic allegiances may provide the impetus for substantial changes in development theory. Potential new directions for aid policy are highlighted by McKay (this volume) in particular but the impetus to engage with goals (and impact) of development that go beyond "economic rationalism" is a thread that ties together much of this book. The implications and the potential for a much better, nuanced, and contextualized understanding of the impact of foreign aid, must underpin any changes, whether minor or major, to ODA.

A confounding factor in the whole aid architecture and development environment is the emergence of new (BRICS) donors and new institutions, such as the AIIB and the BRICS bank. The impact of these is yet to be felt. However, there is likely to be at least some impact on the way aid is perceived and allocated. Calls for partnerships between existing development institutions and the new institutions may require new and innovative mechanisms for engagement, and potentially more requirement to demonstrate impact. This must also be understood in light of the dwarfing of the international aid budget with foreign direct investment and remittances, as well as Other Official Flows.

Contemporary discourse in aid and development, in conjunction with global economic forces has shone an intense spotlight on the role of the private sector, and associated issues of aid for trade. However, Loxley (this volume) highlights some important and relevant findings in assessing the impact of education on long-term employability, where a resurgence of technical education is a result of parts of Asia having achieved near universal primary education, and if there is a clear link between technical education and private sector skills then there is now demand for this sector. He highlights how changes in one sector can have significant and long-term impacts in another not clearly related sector. Does this strengthen the argument for IA as broader policy tool, linking context with policy and impact (of previous and current programming decisions).

Impact Assessment can be a technical and statistical exercise, or it can be a much more substantive process contributing to real change, and the question here is whether they are mutually exclusive. The following sections demonstrate why we would argue that it depends on the context, but that there is significant potential for IA to be the substantive process that it can be.

THE ELEPHANT IN THE ROOM...POLITICS AND FOREIGN POLICY

The political context of aid is mostly beyond the scope of this volume, yet the foreign policy and trade objectives of bilateral donors in particular are of direct relevance. Milligan et al. raise the specter of assessing the impact of aid on foreign policy and trade objectives. It is unlikely that there would be political will for such a process. Yet, given the evolution of foreign aid in many countries into a trade-related construct, it seems that not acknowledging this aspect, and somehow still framing aid as a reflection of the values and moral disposition of the tax payers is problematic. Australian aid has frequently been open about its multiple mandates, with humanitarian interests competing against strategic and commercial interests. Notions of attributability seem relevant here. To which of these mandates should the impact of aid be attributed. What may be a success under one mandate may be an abject failure in another. A blatant example of the potential contradiction is the issue of economic growth being associated with rising inequality, yet the "aid for trade" focus on the aid program is promoting economic growth at the expense of addressing inequality and poverty. So how should impact be framed?

A second, and equally big question, may indeed be whether or not should donors be held accountable for meeting high-level targets in other countries as result of interventions funded by them? Milligan et al. (this volume) state that this is not possible. However, it raises all sorts of moral and ethical questions with respect to sovereignty and so on that are way beyond the scope of this volume. However, the focus on aid money for trading and private enterprise development really does focus attention on this area.

COMPLEXITY

Debates around complexity and the emergence of complexity discourse in development gave rise to many comments, Loveridge (this volume) argues that complexity or complex programming requires a much more adaptive focus – with short time frames and local relevance. This is a challenge to the notion of international best practice and scaling up of interventions and so on, arguing for active adaptive management. The whole top-down approach, in terms of "supplying solutions" is strongly challenged in this volume. However, this is hardly surprising as so much debate has occurred in the realm of alternatives to top-down development over the past 20 or more years. The challenge raised here is the capacity of IA to explicitly acknowledge complex diverse impacts that are beyond normal quantitative measures. This is a gauntlet well thrown down as it provides a potential avenue to move beyond the divisive and polarized debates of RCTs versus qualitative, *ex-ante* versus *ex-post* IA, impact assessment versus impact evaluation, and seeks to find a series of ways of approaching IA that may work with the appropriate tools and theories, from any or all of the camps. Programs and projects need adaptive and flexible approaches to deal with real world context. However, this needs to be based on a clear Theory of Change, although the trajectory of change is far from certain and hence the requirement for adaptability and flexibility.

A point well made by Cohen (this volume) is that the results agenda is here to stay with all of the associated contradictions that brings, and although this kind of linear results-based thinking runs contrary to complexity thinking. However, rather than being an insurmountable obstacle, we would argue that IA, if conceptualized as a process, and therefore less of an end product as per linear results chain thinking then there is strong potential to incorporate context appropriate IA that promotes adaptation to complex and diverse environments, where this is required. The potential for *ex-ante* IA to engage with complex context in trying to identify potential impacts, and therefore adapt becomes worthy of attention, from donors, managers, evaluators, and of course key stakeholders, the beneficiaries. It is worth making explicit here that this is not necessarily a negative risk mitigation strategy. In a complex social development programming environment, the identification of potential impacts, both positive and negative, intended and unintended, allows for much more nuanced, and effective program design. Some examples of this were raised by Adusei-Asante and Hancock (this volume) as well as Bell and Altahir (this volume). Complexity thinking is firmly embedded in development discourse, and there is untapped potential to contribute to complexity thinking in program/project design, or policy through the use of impact assessment. We would strongly endorse the use of IA as a process in any kind of development programming that incorporates uncertain, diverse, risk prone, or otherwise complex contexts.

Instead of asking whether development works perhaps we should be asking what works best, where, why, and when, whether and how we can we scale this up (or not). All of the authors in this volume are engaged in aid and development interventions in one form or another. Therefore, it is unsurprising that the underlying message is not whether aid works, but what works best, where and why. There is an underlying sense of wanting do what produces "good change." In many instances a core question relates to the scalability of programs or projects (cf. Bell and Altahir; Milligan et al. (this volume)). However, this has not precluded robust discussion on the capacity of aid and development to contribute to real, systemic, or transformative change (cf. Milligan et al.; Jakupec and Kelly; Ravuvu and Thornton; Makuwire; this volume).

Underpinning the potential for real, structural, or systemic change is of course both the political and economic driver as discussed above at a higher level, but also evidence for evidence-based decision-making.

IMPACT...
CONCEPTUAL UNDERSTANDINGS

As discussed by most contributors the high-level understanding of impact on face value appears clear. However, if one looks at how to operationalize the concept there are significant differences. There emerge two main schools of thought, impact evaluation and impact assessment. Within this there are a number of polarizations, *ex-post* versus *ex-ante* impact assessment, quantitative versus qualitative, impact assessment versus impact evaluation, impact as a subset of evaluation versus evaluation as a subset of impact, and so on. Those that relegate IA to an *ex-post* product are focused pretty much purely on the long(er) term impact, with no scope for learning, feedback mechanisms, or any kind of adaptive management. Thus *ex-ante* IA has the potential to provide a great tool for designing and implementing a development process with a view to the impact, rather than just the short-term results. Rather than argue it seems both logical and highly beneficial to conceptualize impact assessment as a process rather than a product (whether *ex-ante* or *ex-post*). This kind of thinking has permeated the Social Impact Assessment philosophy, at least in theory.

It is also important to consider the scale of the IA, and therefore the relationship with the underlying theory of change, and associated development theory and practice. IA can occur at macro, meso, and micro levels, as well as short-, medium-, and long-term. Impact assessment of institutional behavior and capacity, as analyzed in terms of corporate results frameworks by Cohen (This volume), has great potential to contribute to a much better overall understanding of impact and effectiveness. However, there are reasonable limitations in terms of what can reasonably be achieved, with institutional learning perhaps the greatest loser.

Although polarization of debate is often problematic there is quite a division between the impact evaluation camp (ADB, 2006; Bamberger, 2012; White, 2009) and the IA camp (Bond and Pope, 2012;

Howitt, 2012; Vanclay et al., 2015). If the current "civil war" is to pass then we need to look at the best fit for various contexts, rather than best practice. Qualitative, quantitative, and mixed methods all have a place. *Ex-post* impact evaluation provides a final part of a linear results framework, which can be of benefit to future programming. However, it has limitations for complex contexts and design and management improvements. Throughout this volume we have used the term impact assessment (IA) as the central focus. However, it can be seen that many of the contributions would be much more aligned with impact evaluation. The focus on impact assessment allowed discussion of an assessment of impact for accountability, transparency, learning, and management purposes. Impact evaluation can meet some of these objectives some of the time. However, there is limited evidence of quality IA that meet many or all of these and other mandates.

METHODOLOGY AND METHOD

The discussions of impact assessment as a quantitative exercise were never intended to be the focus of this volume, and the "civil war" of the "randomistas" versus the qualitative set is acknowledged but not engaged with at any in-depth level. However, the relevance of context to the design of development interventions is paramount, with the related issues of addressing particular challenges in measuring results through appropriate and context-specific assessment design, data collection, and analysis running through many contributions (Bell and Altahir; Loveridge; Adusei-Asante and Hancock; Loxley; and Pucilowski; this volume). The issue of alternative and mixed methods was repeatedly raised, with focus on both the effectiveness and efficiency of IA (see in particular Adusei-Asante and Hancock, this volume). The efficacy of qualitative methods was argued by Adusei-Asante and Hancock in their analysis of the opportunities provided by ethnographic methods, that may otherwise not be realized. However, Lemire and Freer (this volume) highlight an often-overlooked aspect of impact assessment, and that is the case of existing information and studies. 3ie (The International Initiative for Impact Evaluation) have a strong focus on systematic reviews, and the benefits of synthesis of all high-quality research evidence are an excellent source of knowledge. However, there are capacity and cost-related issues with full in-depth systematic reviews. Initiatives like the systematic review database are one way of trying to maximize the benefits of systematic reviews as a "public good." Lemire and Freer (this volume) highlight an alternative and potentially less resource-intensive option of metamodeling. Loxley's (this volume) strong arguments that development is really the flow of knowledge and experience would strongly support the use of existing knowledge as well as the generation of new knowledge.

In terms of knowledge generation, issues of rigor are rife in IA discourse. Rigor as Pucilowski (this volume) identifies is both methodological rigor, as well as independence and the quality and training of the research team. However, others (Loveridge, this volume) raise the issue of the familiarity of the internal staff in the context and program/project as a potentially significant contributor to impact assessment quality. Can rigor be guaranteed with internal assessors?

Evidence is embedded in the IA discourse. However, Milligan et al. (this volume) note that the role of evidence in decision-making should not be overstated. Funding decisions are rarely made on technical decisions alone. The link between evidence and rigor is clear but there are also issues of independence of the whole process and some of the imitations of this as well as the more frequent debates about why assessments need to be conducted by independent evaluators.

There is frequent comment from the contributors that there is a need for a better "toolkit" whether for impact assessment, or for overall program quality purposes that can be integrated (cf. Loveridge, this volume). Although a range of tools were touched on (cf. Makuwire, Loveridge, this volume). Bamberger (2012) notes that there is "rarely a single evaluation methodology that cab fully capture all of the complexities of how programs operate in the real world" (p. 3) as part of a rationale for the use of mixed methods.

IMPACT ASSESSMENT IN THE REAL WORLD – *EX-ANTE, EX-POST,* OR SOMEWHERE IN BETWEEN?

The question was framed in the introduction as to whether impact assessment was a product, as per the *ex-ante* or *ex-post* document, or a process. We have argued that impact assessment as a process has much to offer development programming. If IA sits somewhat outside the intervention, as in an *ex-post* evaluation (as framed strongly by the impact evaluation theorization) then this has little to offer learning in a complex real-world context requiring adaptive management. If however it moves toward a more systematic process embedded in program or project cycle, then there are questions to be asked of the interrelationship with monitoring and evaluation and given the move toward Monitoring, Evaluation, Accountability, and Learning (cf. Bell and Altahir, Loveridge, this volume) this is not completely impossible. Loveridge (this volume) focuses on these interrelationships and argues that better monitoring is likely to contribute to better IA outcomes, although this discourse is framed from an *ex-post* perspective! The question is whether too much attention is being paid to IA at the expense of monitoring, and potentially evaluation. Much of the discussion in this volume is focused on a far more positive view of IA, whether *ex-post* impact evaluation, or more process-oriented IA, or product-oriented *ex-ante* assessment (of which as a stand-alone concept there has been little discussion).

Adusei.Asante and Hancock (this volume) identified a range of factors related to the social, cultural, and political context in their case study that contradicted directly assumptions in project design. Similar questions are raised by Bell and Altahir (this volume). Appropriate and context-sensitive *ex-ante* IA would have identified these risks, or potential impacts. Context sensitivity is also argued by Milligan et al. They explored IA in the context of program and project cycle that provides a much more focused exploration of the potential of IA, although primarily in the context of *ex-post* IA.

The issue, of course, with context-sensitive development is that scalability and context sensitivity are not always entirely compatible aims. Context sensitivity also can require a rejection of linear or mechanistic views of aid and development. Much of the above discussion does indicate a requirement for IA to be responsive to the context (context-sensitive development). Does this argue to IA as a process rather than as a product? If IA is retrospective (*ex-post*) then the process of adaptation must remain linked entirely to monitoring and evaluation conducted within the program timeframe, which requires a clear understanding of the result chain, and a look to impact as well as output and outcome? The cost of not completing an *ex-ante* IA may be far greater than the opportunity cost of not doing it, moving beyond risk identification and mitigation. This is an argument Vanclay and colleagues at IAIA have been making strongly for the last few years (Vanclay et al., 2015; Vanclay and Esteves, 2012).

There were a number of different issues raised in terms of determinants of utilization of IA, or impediments to its use. Some of these briefly are rigor, timing, relevance, and communication (Pucilowski, this volume), timeframes, cost effectiveness, and problematics of conducting *ex-post* evaluations, including no funding, lack of will, lack of relevance to current programming (Bell and Altahir, this volume). Stakeholder communication was an additional yet seemingly critical component of effective evaluations (Pucilowski, this volume).

Loxley (this volume) argues there is a need to reduce knowledge gaps and increase understanding about how development improves capacity between physical and social infrastructure in aid projects. There need to be more demanding forms of knowledge to enhance the collective wisdom. This of course comes back to the underpinning notion that IA, and indeed most forms of evaluation in development have a public good aspect. The underlying argument in Loxleys (this volume) work seems to be that we require newer models of collaborative thinking to promote joint action that promotes development in complex contexts. IA is about the flow of information and knowledge, and experience. IA provides a context to follow knowledge transfer and see who learns the most and uses it wisely! The capacity and capability of nations is essential.

There is general agreement among practitioners about some of the issues and shortcomings of IA. However, there seems little movement at an institutional level then impact must be understood as being necessary at much broader range of levels – what is the impact of the political environment, and the institutional context for development programming. If DFAT assesses the impact both in terms of self-interest and poverty reduction there may be a much greater sense of what we are trying to do – transparently. Ravuvu and Thornton (this volume) note the issue of donor recipient bureaucratic relationship, contained within the aid effectiveness agenda, that often wears the blame for aid failures. They argue that the potential of neostructural reforms to promote the emergence of participatory and decentralized aid modalities is inhibited by neoliberal reforms that refuse to go away. However, the question remains, whether IA is politicized – and capable of providing answers to what the impact of aid interventions are for addressing poverty, inequality, human rights violations, structural impediments to reducing inequality. Can development aid address the structural causes of these issues, or is it addressing the symptoms. The framing of success must be contextualized by a realistic and in-depth appraisal of the objectives of the development program, and what the long-term impact is. Framing, or reframing success underpins any attempt to make IA a more useful process in striving to achieve "good change."

CONCLUSION

The bottom line appears to be: What is success, how is it framed, and how is it measured. It is interesting to look at the utility of IA in light of the constraints raised, the many issues encountered over a wide range of assessments, and how these were addressed for better development outcomes. IA is methodologically challenging but the rewards of well-designed IA on development policy and programming are immense. One of the key rewards of effective impact assessment is Accountability. Accountability has to be more than project managers otherwise there are perverse incentives for reporting success only. Accountability should be to the beneficiaries as well as to the donors. This is a vexatious question that has been embedded in aid evaluation for decades!

Most of the this volume does argue strongly for investment in high-quality measurement and performance management systems and tools that provide both information on program performance, but also its broader context.

One of the themes at the political economic level is the strong critique of the neoliberal agenda, which dominates a number of chapters. The arguments, which were put forward, focus on the ideology as being too dogmatic and donor-centered rather than looking at the social political and economic relevance of the recipient countries.

At the policy level there is a tendency to look rather simplistically at the counterfactual. Particularly in social development programming, with the range of complex and confounding factors, this is unlikely to give us a better understanding of the social, economic, cultural, or environmental benefits of sustainable development.

Other issues include that although every OECD country and the EU itself is committed to *ex-ante* Regulatory Impact assessment (RIA), the same is not necessarily true as far as the donor organizations are concerned. Thus, it follows that there is no appreciation of the proposed or demanded regulatory impositions or requirements from the donor. Conditionality is taken for granted with a strong emphasis on one size fits all.

At the administrative level there is a sense that donor agencies regard IA is too onerous, fiscally and with regard to human resource. At the administrative level there is very little evidence provided of what is to be expected *ex ante* at macro, meso, or micro levels. Therefore, any *ex-post* IA may be rendered of dubious benefit. However speculative, it has been argued that there is reluctance by donor agencies to publish IA findings. The negative consequences of failure being reported, to the aid community, political decisions makers and the public is maybe perceived as outweighing the positive benefits of shared experience and lessons learned.

At the operational level there is a distinct lack of clarity or definition between outcome and impact (cf. ADB, 2007). In the reviewed literature especially from multilateral development agencies, and in particular the World Bank, there is continuous confusion between outcome and impact. Unless there is a better understanding by such agencies about the differences, the whole enterprise of IA can be rendered ineffective as it is practiced by them.

A further and related point is that we must differentiate between effectiveness and efficiency. By effectiveness we can refer to qualitative indicators, but efficiency is much more focused on the qualitative. However, if we are not mistaken, there is a very strong, dogmatic, and ideological tendency toward the quantitative measures, highlighting a deficit in alternatives, either qualitative (or mixed methods). A reliance on quantitative IA is insufficient to provide adequately for social development impacts. Although quantitative has a place in IA, when accounting for social change, it may contribute, but on its own is insufficient. In perhaps a slightly controversial stance, we would also argue that qualitative methods equally can contribute significantly but may be equally insufficient. *Ipso facto*, mixed methods have a lot to offer, and within the social sector it seems likely that impact will be best understood using mixed methods. In order to achieve that, a lot of unpacking needs to be done by donor agencies. At the political level there needs to be a change in donor approaches that are dogmatic, ideologically driven inflexible, and discredited.

REFERENCES

ADB, 2006. Impact evaluation; methodological and operational issues. Manila: Economic Analysis and Operations Support Division Economics and Research Department, Asian Development Bank. Available from: <http://www.adb.org/sites/default/files/institutional-document/33014/files/impact-analysis-handbook.pdf>.

ADB, 2007. Project Performance Management System: Guidelines for Preparing a Design and Monitoring Framework. ADB, Manila.

Bamberger, M., 2012. Introduction to mixed methods in impact evaluation. Impact Evaluation Notes No. 3, August. Available from: <http://www.interaction.org/sites/default/files/Mixed%20Methods%20in%20Impact%20Evaluation%20%28English%29.pdf>.

Bond, A., Pope, J., 2012. The state of the art of impact assessment in 2012. Impact Assess. Project Appraisal 30 (1), 1–4. http://doi.org/10.1080/14615517.2012.669140.

Howitt, R., 2012. Theoretical foundations. In: Vanclay, F., Esteves, A.M. (Eds.), New Directions in Social Impact Assessment: Conceptual and Methodological Advances. Edward Elgar Publishing, Northampton, MA.

OECD, 1999. Guidance For Evaluating Humanitarian Assistance In Complex Emergencies, Development Assistance Committee of the OECD, Paris. Available from: <http://www.oecd.org/dac/evaluation/2667294.pdf> (Accessed 30.06.15).

Vanclay, F., Esteves, A.M., 2012. Current issues and trends in social impact assessment. In: Vanclay, F., Esteves, A.M. (Eds.), New Directions in Social Impact Assessment: Conceptual and Methodological Advances. Edward Elgar Publishing Ltd., Northampton, MA.

Vanclay, F., Esteves, A.M., Aucamp, I., Franks, D., 2015. Social impact assessment: guidance for assessing and managing the social impacts of projects. International Association of Impact Assessment. Available from: <http://www.iaia.org/pdf/IAIA%202015%20Social%20Impact%20Assessment%20guidance%20document.pdf>.

White, H., 2009. Theory-based impact evaluation: Principles and practice. J. Dev. Effectiveness 1 (3), 271–284.

Index